LINDO
An Optimization Modeling System

FOURTH EDITION

LINDO
An Optimization Modeling System

FOURTH EDITION

by
Linus Schrage
Graduate School of Business
University of Chicago

▲ *The Scientific Press*
651 Gateway Boulevard • Suite 1100 • South San Francisco, CA 94080-7014

LINDO: An Optimization Modeling System, Fourth Edition
(Formerly titled *Linear, Integer and Quadratic Programming with LINDO*)
by Linus Schrage

Copyright © 1981, 1984, 1986, 1991 by The Scientific Press

All rights reserved. No part of this book may be reproduced, stored in a retrieval system, or transcribed in any form or by any means without the prior written permission of the publisher, The Scientific Press.

Printed in the United States of America

10 9 8 7 6 5 4 3

ISBN 0-89426-149-5 (with 5¼" MS/DOS disk)
ISBN 0-89426-150-9 (with 3.5" MS/DOS disk)
ISBN 0-89426-191-7 (with Macintosh disk)

Publisher: The Scientific Press
Text design & production editor: Gene Smith
Cover design by Rogondino & Associates

To my parents

William and Alma Schrage

CONTENTS

Preface xiii

Chapter 1 What Is Linear Programming? 1

Introduction 1
A Simple Product Mix Problem 1
Linearity 4
Analysis of LP Solutions 6
Sensitivity Analysis, Reduced Costs, and Dual Prices 8
Unbounded Formulations 9
Infeasible Formulations 9
Multiple Optimal Solutions and Degeneracy 11
Problems 16

Chapter 2 Solving LPs on the Computer: The LINDO Program . . 19

Introduction 19
Getting Started on Small Problems 19
Altering and Editing a Model 21
Saving, Retrieving and Printing Your Work 23
Integer Programming with LINDO 27
More Sophisticated Use of LINDO 30

Chapter 3 Sensitivity Analysis of LP Solutions 35

Economic Analysis of Solution Reports 35
Economic Relationship Between Dual Prices and Reduced Costs . . 35
Range of Validity of Reduced Costs and Dual Prices 37
Sensitivity Analysis of the Constraint Coefficients 42
The Dual LP Problem, or the Landlord and the Renter 43
Problems 46

Chapter 4 The Model Formulation Process 51

The Overall Process 51
Approaches to Model Formulation 52
Constructive Approach to Model Formulation 52
The Template Approach 54
Common Errors in Formulating Models 56
The Nonsimultaneity Error 59
Problems 60

Chapter 5 Product Mix Problems 63

Introduction 63
Process Selection Product Mix Problems 66
Problems 70

Chapter 6 Covering, Staffing, & Cutting Stock Models 73

Introduction 73
Staff Covering Problems 74
Cutting Stock and Pattern Selection 76
Crew Scheduling Problems 81
Problems 85

Chapter 7 Networks, Distribution, & PERT/CPM 91

What's Special About Network Models 91
Variations of the Network Problem 94
PERT/CPM Networks and LP 95
Activity-on-Arc vs. Activity-on-Node Network Diagrams 99
Crashing of Project Networks 100
Path Formulations 105
Multicommodity Network Flows 106
Undirected Networks 107
Problems 110

Chapter 8 Multiperiod Planning Problems 115

Introduction 115
A Dynamic Production Problem 116
Multiperiod Financial Models 119
Financial Planning Models with Tax Considerations 122
Accounting for Income Taxes 126
Summary Discussion of Multiperiod Models 129
Problems 130

Chapter 9 Blending of Input Materials — 133

Introduction . . . 133
The Structure of Blending Problems . . . 134
A Blending Problem Within a Product Mix Problem . . . 138
Proper Choice of Alternate Interpretations of Quality Requirements . . . 140
Interpretation of Dual Prices for Blending Constraints . . . 142
Fractional or Hyperbolic Programming . . . 143
Problems . . . 144

Chapter 10 Decisionmaking Under Uncertainty & Stochastic LP — 151

Introduction . . . 151
The Scenario Approach . . . 152
A More Complicated Two-Period Planning Problem . . . 154
Expected Value of Perfect Information (EVPI) . . . 160
Risk Aversion . . . 160
Decisions Under Uncertainty with More than Two Periods . . . 164
Chance Constrained Programs . . . 165
Problems . . . 165

Chapter 11 Economic Equilibria as LPs — 167

What Is an Equilibrium . . . 167
Representing Supply and Demand Curves in LPs . . . 167
Auctions as Economic Equilibria . . . 171
Transportation Equilibria . . . 174
Problems . . . 180

Chapter 12 Game Theory — 183

Introduction . . . 183
Two Person Games . . . 183
Nonconstant-Sum Games Involving Two or More Players . . . 186
Problems . . . 188

Chapter 13 Quadratic Programming — 191

Introduction . . . 191
The Markowitz Portfolio Model . . . 191
Important Variations of the Portfolio Model . . . 196
Measures of Risk other than Variance . . . 200
Quadratic Programming Applied to Simultaneous Price/Production Decisions . . . 202
Least Squares Regression . . . 203
Two Person Nonconstant-Sum Games . . . 206
Problems . . . 210

Chapter 14 Formulation of Integer Programs **215**

Introduction 215
Computational Difficulty of Integer Programs 215
Exploiting of the IP Capability, Standard Applications 216
Outline of Integer Programming Methods 224
Problems with Naturally Integer Solutions and the Prayer Algorithm 227
The Assignment Problem and Related Sequencing and Routing Problems . . 231
Problems of Grouping: Matching, Covering, Partitioning and Packing . . . 240
Linearizing Products of Variables 243
Problems 248

Chapter 15 Application to Statistical Estimation **255**

Introduction 255
Least Absolute Deviations (LAD) Estimation 256
Least Maximum (LMAX) Deviation Regression 258
Exploiting the Dual to Obtain a More Compact Formulation 260
Ordinal Regression 264
Problems 270

Chapter 16 Design & Implementation of Optimization Based Decision Support Systems **271**

General Structure of the Modeling Process 271
Appropriate Level of Detail, Verification and Validation 272
Separation of Data and System Structure 273
Marketing the Model 273
Reducing Model Size 277
Matrix Generators 284
On-the-Fly Column Generation 285

Chapter 17 Multiple Criteria & Goal Programming **291**

Introduction 291
Approaches to Multicriteria Problems 292
Goal Programming and Soft Constraints 296
Minimizing the Maximum Hurt, or Unordered Lexico Minimization 298
Comparing Performance with Data Envelope Analysis 303
Problems 304

Chapter 18 Parametric Analysis **305**

Motivation of Parametric Analysis 305
Types of Parametric Analysis 305

Graphical Derivation of Parametric Profit Curve (Right-hand Side) 308
Graphical Derivation of Parametric Profit Curve (Objective Coefficient) . . . 310
Changing Several Coefficients Simultaneously 311
Supply and Demand Curves Derived via Parametric Analysis 312
Parametric Programming and Tracing Out
    the Efficient Frontier in Multi-Objective Problems 313
Problems 315

Chapter 19 Methods for Solving Linear Programs 317

Methods 317
The Simplex Method 317
The Revised Simplex Method and Coefficient Sparsity 326
Revised Simplex Method with Product Form of Inverse 330
Interior Path Methods for Solving LPs 339
Problems 344

Appendix: Summary of LINDO Help Commands 345

Bibliography 359

Index 363

Loading & Printing Instructions—MacLINDO 369

Loading & Printing Instructions—LINDO/PC 370

PREFACE

It has been ten years since the appearance of the first edition of this text. It would be nice to claim that we were clairvoyant in 1980 and the original text needed no updating to reflect changes in the real world since then. The most notable change has been in the accessibility of computing power. When this text was first assembled in the late 1970s, time-shared computing was the standard mode of computing. Some of the smaller examples that are still in this text were first developed on a single time-shared HP-2000F computer that served a community of approximately 1000 students and faculty. That machine initially had 25 megabytes of disk storage and about 32,000 bytes of main memory. Now a typical business person or student would probably be embarrassed if his or her personal computer had capabilities as limited as the HP-2000F. Thus one of the subtle changes in this edition is that many of the examples can be and are larger and more realistic.

The emphasis in the text continues to be on teaching how to apply linear programming (LP) and related planning methods to problems of business and industry. The teaching style that is used might be characterized as a "template" style. That is, we give example models of how LP is applied to close to a dozen standard classes of industrial problems. This approach can be contrasted with a "teach the basic principles" approach. The advantages of the template approach are: (a) if the reader has a potential application close to one considered in the text, then the leap from the text to actual application is a small one, and (b) for many readers, the leap from a number of practical examples to a single important underlying, unifying concept may be an easier one than the leap from the single important concept to new applications of the concept. In the long run, learning the important concept is the important achievement; however, if the value and generality of the concept is not appreciated, the motivation to learn it will not be there.

At a more specific level, we have learned a bit about which existing topics in the text need more explanation, and which topics not previously in should be included. So for example, the introductory chapters have been supplemented with considerably more graphical illustrations. The chapter on integer programming has been restructured and expanded.

New chapters have been added on goal programming and multi-criteria, and implementation of decision support systems. An introduction to interior point algorithms has been added in the chapter on solution methods.

We continue to benefit from the helpful comments of readers and colleagues. Local colleagues Kipp Martin, Gary Eppen, Bob Graves and Ananth Iyer deserve special thanks. Kevin Cunningham has continued to provide superb help on the software front. We are also grateful to our publisher, Paul Kelly at The Scientific Press, for his practical understanding of the concept of soft constraints, especially as applied to such things as deadlines.

1
What Is Linear Programming?

Introduction

Linear Programming (LP) is a mathematical procedure for determining optimal allocation of scarce resources. LP is a procedure which has found practical application in almost all facets of business, from advertising to production planning. Transportation, distribution and aggregate production planning problems are the most typical objects of LP analysis. The petroleum industry seems to be the most intensive user of LP. A data processing manager at a large oil company recently estimated that from 5 percent to 10 percent of the firm's computer time was devoted to the processing of LP and LP-like models.

It is important for the reader to appreciate at the outset that the "programming" in Linear Programming is of a different flavor than the "programming" in Computer Programming. In the former case it means to plan and organize as in "Get with the program!," while in the latter case it means to write instructions for performing calculations. Training in the one kind of programming has very little direct relevance to the other.

For most LP problems one can think of there being *two important classes of objects*: first, limited *resources* such as land, plant capacity and sales force size, and secondly, *activities* such as "produce low carbon steel," "produce stainless steel," and "produce high carbon steel." *Each activity consumes* or possibly *contributes* additional amounts of the *resources*. The problem is to determine the best combination of activity levels which does not use more resources than are actually available. We can best gain the flavor of LP by considering a simple example.

A Simple Product Mix Problem

The Enginola Television Company produces two types of TV sets, the "Astro" and the "Cosmo." There are two production lines, one for each set. The capacity of the Astro production line is 60 sets per day, while the capacity of the Cosmo line is 50 sets per day. The Astro set requires 1 manhour of labor, while the Cosmo set requires 2 manhours. Presently there is a maximum of 120 manhours of labor per day which can be assigned to production of the two types of sets. If the profit contributions are $20 and $30 respectively for each Astro and Cosmo set, what should be the daily production?

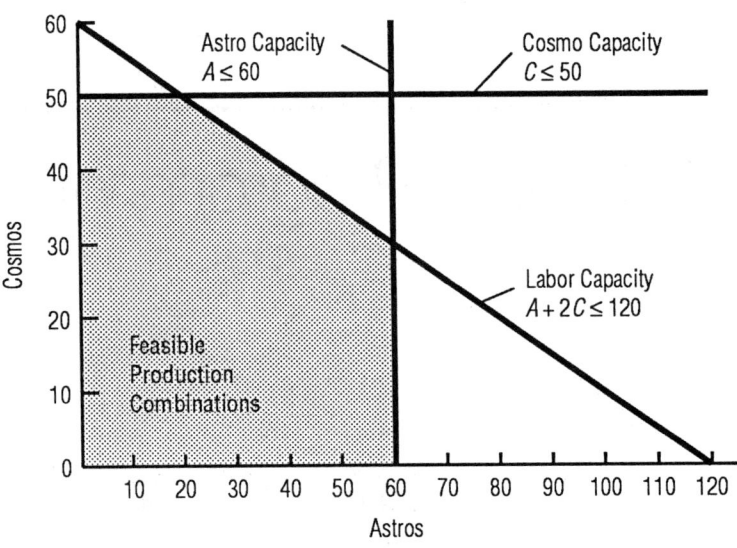

Figure 1.1
Feasible Region for Enginola

A structured but still verbal description of what we want to do is:

    Maximize   Profit contribution

    subject to   Astro production less than or equal to Astro capacity,
                  Cosmo production less than or equal to Cosmo capacity,
                  Labor used less than or equal to labor availability.

Until there is a significant improvement in artificial intelligence/expert system software, we will need to be more precise if we wish to get some help in solving our problem. We can be more precise if we define:

    A = units of Astros to be produced per day,
    C = units of Cosmos to be produced per day.

Further, we decide to measure:

    Profit contribution in dollars,
    Astro usage in units of Astro's produced,
    Cosmo usage in units of Cosmo's produced and,
    Labor in hours.

Then a precise statement of our problem is:

$$\begin{array}{lrcll}
\text{Maximize} & 20A + 30C & & & \text{(Dollars)} \\
\text{subject to} & A & \leq & 60 & \text{(Astro Capacity)} \\
& C & \leq & 50 & \text{(Cosmo Capacity)} \\
& A + 2C & \leq & 120 & \text{(Labor in hours)}
\end{array}$$

Figure 1.2

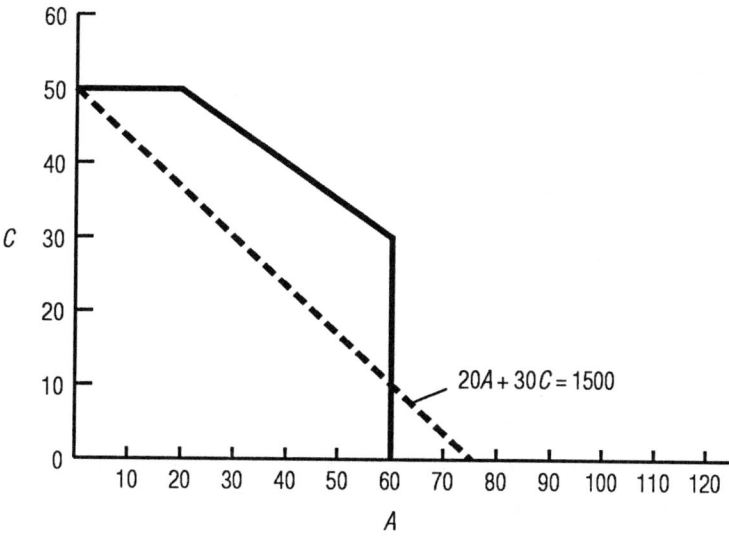

Enginola Problem with "Profit = 1500" Line

The first line: "Maximize 20A + 30C" is known as the *objective function* while the remaining three lines are known as *constraints*. Most LP computer programs assume that all variables are constrained to be nonnegative, so the constraints $A \geq 0$, $C \geq 0$ are unnecessary.

Using the terminology of resources and activities, there are three resources: Astro capacity, Cosmo capacity and labor capacity. The activities are Astro and Cosmo production. It is generally true that with each constraint in an LP one can associate some resource while for each decision variable there is a corresponding activity.

Graphical Analysis

The Enginola problem is represented graphically in Figure 1.1 The feasible production combinations are the points in the lower left enclosed by the five solid lines. We want to find the point in the feasible region which gives the highest profit.

To gain some idea of where the maximum profit point lies, let's consider some possibilities. The point $A = C = 0$ is feasible but it does not help us out much with respect to profits. If we spoke with the manager of the Cosmo line the response might be: "The Cosmo is our more profitable product, therefore we should make as many of it as possible, namely 50 and be satisfied with the profit contribution of $30 \times 50 = \$1500$. You, the thoughtful reader, might observe that there are many combinations of A and C, other than just $A = 0$ and $C = 50$, that achieve $1500 of profit. Indeed, if you plot the line $20A + 30C = 1500$ and add it to the graph you get Figure 1.2. Any point on the dotted line segment achieves a profit of $1500.

If we next talk with the manager of the Astro line, the response might be: "If you produce 50 Cosmo's, you still have enough labor to produce 20 Astro's. This would give

Figure 1.3

Enginola Problem with "Profit = 1900" Line

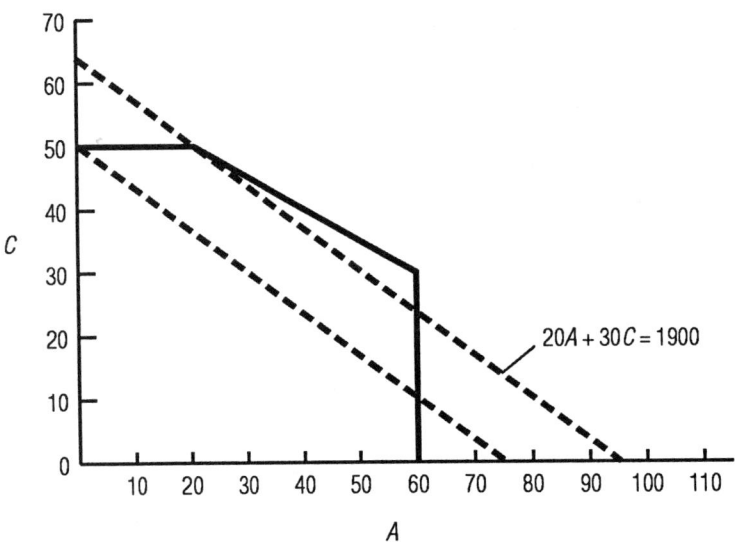

a profit of 30 × 50 + 20 × 20 = $1900. That is certainly a respectable profit, why don't we call it a day and go home."

Our ever alert reader might again observe that there are many ways of making $1900 of profit. If you plot the line $20A + 30C = 1900$ and add it to the graph, you get Figure 1.3. Any point on the higher rightmost dotted line segment achieves a profit of $1900.

Now our ever perceptive reader makes a leap of insight: As we increase our profit aspirations, the dotted line representing all points that achieve a given profit simply shifts in a parallel fashion. Why not shift it as far as possible as long as the line contains a feasible point? This last and best feasible point is $A = 60$, $C = 30$. It lies on the line $20A + 30C = 2100$. This is illustrated in Figure 1.4. Notice that even though the profit contribution per unit is higher for Cosmo, we did not make as many (30) as we feasibly could have made (50). Intuitively, this is an optimal solution, and in fact it is. This graphical analysis of this small problem will help us understand what is going on when we analyze larger problems.

Linearity

We have now seen one example. We will return to it regularly. The possible formulations to which LP is applicable are substantially more general than that suggested by the example. The objective function may be minimized rather than maximized; the direction of the constraints may $\geq$ rather than $\leq$, or even $=$; any or all of the parameters, e.g., the 20, 30, 60, 50, 120, 2, 1, etc., may be negative instead of positive. The principal restriction on the class of problems which can be analyzed results from the linearity restriction.

Figure 1.4

Enginola Problem with "Profit = 2100" Line

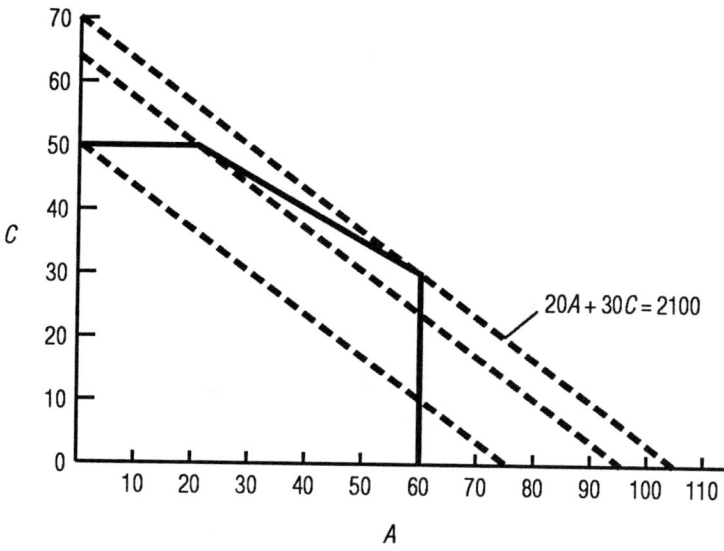

Linear programming applies *directly* only to situations in which the effects of the different activities in which we can engage are linear. For practical purposes we can think of the linearity requirement as consisting of three features:

1. The effects of a single variable or activity by itself are proportional; e.g., doubling the amount of steel purchased will double the dollar cost of steel purchased.
2. The interactions among variables must be additive; e.g., the dollar amount of sales is the sum of the steel dollar sales, the aluminum dollar sales, etc., while the amount of electricity used is the sum of that used to produce steel, aluminum, etc.
3. The variables must be continuous; i.e., fractional values for the decision variables, such as 6.38, must be allowed.

A model which included the two decision variables "price per unit sold" and "quantity of units sold" is probably not linear. The proportionality requirement is satisfied; however, the interaction between the two decision variables is multiplicative rather than additive; i.e., dollar sales = price × quantity, not price + quantity.

If a supplier gives you quantity discounts on your purchases then the cost of purchases will not satisfy the proportionality requirement, e.g., the total cost of the stainless steel purchased may be less than proportional to the amount purchased.

A model which includes the decision variable "number of floors to build" might satisfy the proportionality and additivity requirements but violate the continuity conditions. The recommendation to build 6.38 floors might be difficult to implement unless one had a designer who was ingenious with split level designs; nevertheless, the solution of an LP might recommend such fractional answers.

Figure 1.5
Nonlinear Relations

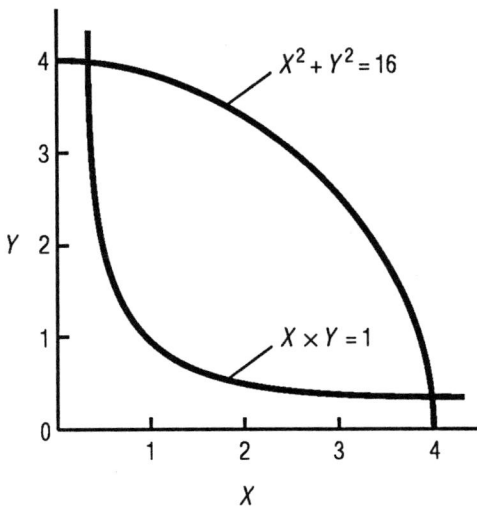

Fortunately, we will see later, in the chapters on integer programming and quadratic programming, that there are other ways of accommodating these violations of linearity.

Figure 1.5 illustrates some nonlinear functions. For example, the expression $X \times Y$ satisfies the proportionality requirement but the effects of X and Y are not additive. In the expression $X^2 + Y^2$, the effects of X and Y are additive but the effects of each individual variable are not proportional.

Analysis of LP Solutions

When you direct the computer to solve an LP, the possible outcomes are indicated in Figure 1.6.

For a properly formulated LP the leftmost path will be taken. The solution procedure will first attempt to find a feasible solution; i.e., a solution which simultaneously satisfies all constraints but does not necessarily maximize the objective function. The rightmost, "No Feasible Solution," path will be taken if the formulator has been too demanding; that is, two or more constraints are specified that cannot be simultaneously satisfied. A simple example is the pair of constraints $x \leq 2$ and $x \geq 3$. The nonexistence of a feasible solution does not depend upon the objective function. It depends solely upon the constraints. In practice, the "No Feasible Solution" outcome might occur in a large complicated problem in which an upper limit was specified on the number of productive hours available and an unrealistically high demand was placed on the number of units to be produced. An alternative message to "No Feasible Solution" is "You Can't Have Your Cake and Eat it Too."

If a feasible solution has been found then the procedure attempts to find an optimal solution. If the "Unbounded Solution" termination occurs then it implies that the formu-

Figure 1.6
Solution Outcomes

```
                    Solve the LP
                   /            \
              Feasible      No Feasible Solution
             /        \
       Optimal      Unbounded
       Solution      Solution
```

lation admits the unrealistic result that an infinite amount of profit can be made. A more realistic conclusion is that an important constraint has been omitted or the formulation contains a critical typographical error.

When the Enginola problem is solved with the LINDO computer program, the following solution report is produced:

```
        OBJECTIVE FUNCTION VALUE

   1)         2100.000

    VARIABLE        VALUE           REDUCED COST
       A          60.000000           0.000000
       C          30.000000           0.000000

    ROW            SLACK             DUAL PRICES
     2)          0.000000             5.000000
     3)         20.000000             0.000000
     4)          0.000000            15.000000

  NO. ITERATIONS=    3
```

The output has two sections, a "variables" section and a "rows" section. The first two columns in each section are straightforward. The maximum profit solution is to produce 60 Astros and 30 Cosmos for a profit contribution of 2100. This solution will leave zero slack in row 2 (the constraint $A \leq 60$), a slack of 20 in row 3 (the constraint $C \leq 50$), and no slack in row 4 (the constraint $A + 2C \leq 120$). Note that $60 + 2 \times 30 = 120$.

Useful by-products of the computations are a number of opportunity or marginal cost figures which appear in the third column. The interpretation of these "reduced costs" and "dual prices" is discussed in the next section.

Sensitivity Analysis, Reduced Costs, and Dual Prices

Realistic LPs require large amounts of data. Accurate data are expensive to collect and so we will generally be forced to use data in which we have less than complete confidence. A time honored adage in data processing circles is "garbage in, garbage out." A user of a model should be concerned with how the recommendations of the model are altered by changes in the input data. Sensitivity analysis is the term applied to the process of answering this question. Fortunately, an LP solution report provides supplemental information which is useful in sensitivity analysis. This information falls under two headings, reduced costs and dual prices.

Sensitivity analysis can reveal which pieces of information should be estimated most carefully. For example, if it is blatantly obvious that a certain product is unprofitable, then little effort need be expended in accurately estimating its costs. The first law of modeling is don't waste time accurately estimating a parameter if a modest error in the parameter has little effect on the recommended decision.

Reduced Costs

Associated with each variable in any solution is a quantity known as the *reduced cost*. If the units of the objective function are dollars and the units of the variable are gallons, then the units of the reduced cost are dollars per gallon. The reduced cost of a variable is the amount by which the profit contribution of the variable must be improved before the variable in question would have a positive value in an optimal solution. Obviously a variable which already appears in the optimal solution will have a zero reduced cost.

It follows that a second, correct interpretation of the reduced cost is that it is the rate at which the objective function value will deteriorate if a variable currently at zero is arbitrarily forced to increase a small amount. Suppose the reduced cost of x is \$2/gallon. This means that if the profitability of x were increased by \$2/gallon, then 1 unit of x (if 1 unit is a "small change") could be brought into the solution with no effect on profits. If, however, 1 unit of x were forced into the solution without first improving x's profitability, then clearly the solution value must be harmed by the amount of \$2.

Dual Prices

Associated with each constraint is a quantity known as the *dual price*. If the units of the objective function are cruzeiros and the units of the constraint in question are kilograms, then the units of the dual price are cruzeiros per kilogram. The dual price of a constraint is the rate at which the objective function value will improve as the right-hand-side or constant term of the constraint is increased a small amount.

Different LP packages may use different sign conventions with regard to the dual prices. LINDO uses the convention that a positive dual price means that increasing the right-hand side in question will improve the objective function value, while a negative dual price means increasing the right-hand side will cause the objective function value to deteriorate. A zero dual price means that changing the right-hand side a small amount will have no effect on the solution value.

It follows that under this convention, $\leq$ constraints will have nonnegative dual prices, $\geq$ constraints will have nonpositive dual prices and $=$ constraints can have dual prices of any sign. Why?

Understanding Dual Prices. It is instructive to analyze the dual prices in the solution to the Enginola problem. The dual price on the constraint A ≤ 60 is $5/unit. At first one might suspect that this quantity should be $20/unit because if one more Astro is produced the simple profit contribution of this unit is $20. An additional Astro unit will require sacrifices elsewhere, however. Because all of the labor supply is being used, producing more Astros would require the production of Cosmos to be reduced in order to free up labor. The labor tradeoff rate for Astros and Cosmos is 1/2; that is, producing one more Astro implies reducing Cosmo production by 1/2 of a unit. Because Cosmos have a profit contribution of $30/unit, the net increase in profits is $20 − $\frac{1}{2}$ × $30 = $5.

Now consider the dual price of $15/hour on the labor constraint. If we have 1 more hour of labor it will be used solely to produce more Cosmos. One Cosmo has a profit contribution of $30/unit. Because 1 hour of labor is only sufficient for one half of a Cosmo, the value of the additional hour of labor is $15.

Unbounded Formulations

If we forget to include the labor constraint and the constraint on the production of Cosmos, then an unlimited amount of profit is possible by producing a large number of Cosmos. This is illustrated here:

```
LOOK ALL
MAX      20 A + 30 C
SUBJECT TO
   2)       A ≤   60
END
:GO

    UNBOUNDED SOLUTION
    UNBOUNDED VARIABLES ARE:
        C
```

There is nothing to prevent C from being infinitely large. The feasible region is illustrated in Figure 1.7. In larger problems there are typically several variables which are unbounded and it is not as easy to identify the manner in which the unboundedness arises.

Infeasible Formulations

An example of an infeasible formulation is obtained if the right-hand side of the labor constraint is made 190 and its direction is, inadvertently, say, reversed. In this case the most labor that can be used is to produce 60 Astros and 50 Cosmos for a total labor consumption of 60 + 2 × 50 = 160 hours. The formulation and attempted solution are:

```
MAX      20 A + 30 C
SUBJECT TO
   2)       A ≤   60
   3)       C ≤   50
   4)       A + 2 C ≥  190
END
```

10 Infeasible Formulations

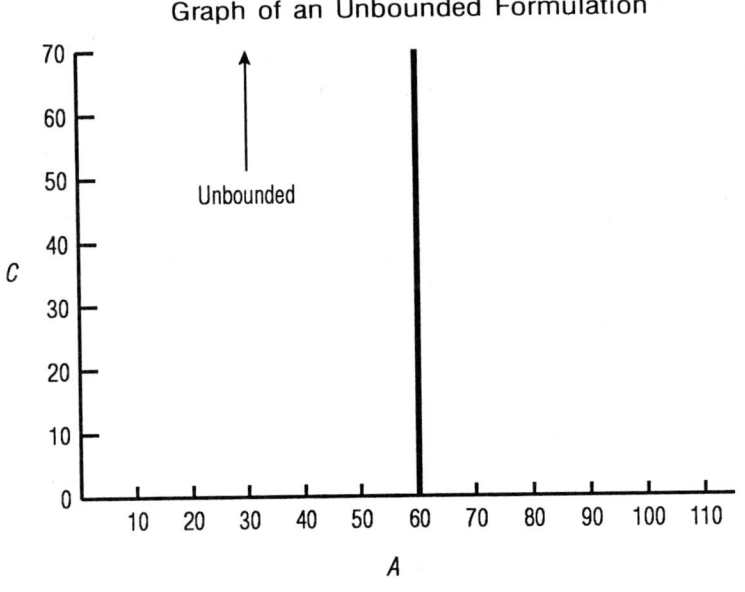

Figure 1.7

Graph of an Unbounded Formulation

```
:GO
            NO FEASIBLE SOLUTION.

    VIOLATED ROWS HAVE NEGATIVE SLACK.
    OR (EQUALITY ROWS) NONZERO SLACKS.
    ROWS CONTRIBUTING TO INFEASIBILITY HAVE
    NONZERO DUAL PRICE.

             OBJECTIVE FUNCTION VALUE

        1)           3300.000

    VARIABLE         VALUE              REDUCED COST
      A            90.000000              0.000000
      C            50.000000              0.000000

    ROW              SLACK              DUAL PRICES
     2)           -30.000000              1.000000
     3)             0.000000              2.000000
     4)             0.000000             -1.000000
```

The dual prices in this case give information helpful in determining how the infeasibility arose. For example, the +1 associated with row 2 indicates that increasing its right-hand side by one will decrease the infeasibility by 1. The +2 with row 3 means that if we allowed 1 more unit of Cosmo production, the infeasibility would be decreased by 2 units because each Cosmo uses 2 hours of labor. The −1 associated with row 4 means that if the right-hand side of the labor constraint was decreased by 1, then the infeasibility would be reduced by 1.

Figure 1.8 illustrates the constraints for this formulation.

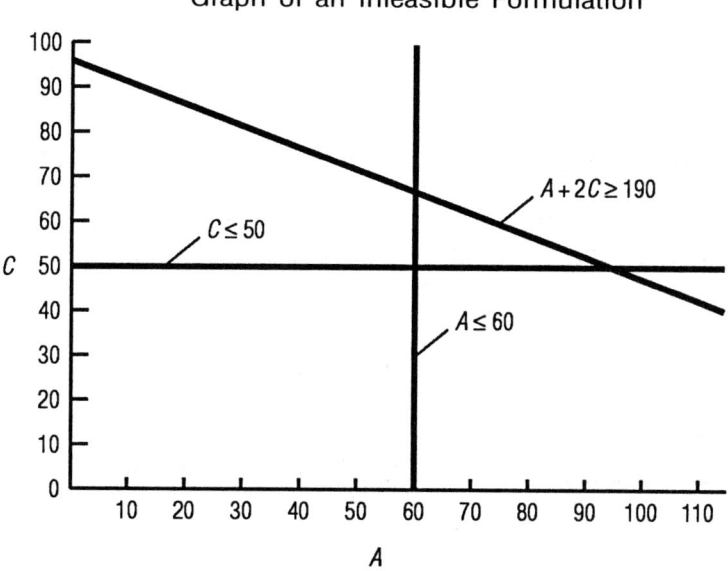

Figure 1.8

Graph of an Infeasible Formulation

Multiple Optimal Solutions and Degeneracy

For a given LP formulation having a bounded optimal solution there will be a unique optimum objective function value. You may, however, encounter different solution reports which have this same value. For example, suppose that in the Enginola problem the profit contribution of A happened to be $15 rather than $20. The problem and a solution is:

```
MAX     15 A + 30 C
SUBJECT TO
    2)      A ≤     60
    3)      C ≤     50
    4)      A + 2 C ≤ 120
END
:GO
```

```
              OBJECTIVE FUNCTION VALUE

        1)            1800.000

    VARIABLE          VALUE            REDUCED COST
        A            60.000000           0.000000
        C            30.000000           0.000000

    ROW              SLACK             DUAL PRICES
        2)            0.000000           0.000000
        3)           20.000000           0.000000
        4)            0.000000          15.000000
```

The feasible region as well as a "profit = 1500" line are shown in Figure 1.9. Notice that the lines $A + 2C = 120$ and $15A + 30C = 1500$ are parallel. It should be apparent that any feasible point on the line $A + 2C = 120$ is optimal.

Multiple Optimal Solutions and Degeneracy

Figure 1.9

Model with Alternate Optima

The particularly observant may have noted in the solution report that the constraint, $A \leq 60$, i.e., row 2 has both zero slack and a zero dual price. This suggests that the production of Astros could be decreased a small amount without any effect on total profits. Of course there would have to be a compensatory increase in the production of Cosmos. We conclude that there must be an alternate optimum solution which produces fewer Astros but more Cosmos. We can discover this solution by increasing the profitability of Cosmos ever so slightly. Observe:

```
MAX      15 A + 30.0001 C
SUBJECT TO
   2)   A ≤    60
   3)   C ≤    50
   4)   A + 2 C ≤ 120
END
:GO
      LP OPTIMUM FOUND   AT STEP    1
           OBJECTIVE FUNCTION VALUE

    1)        1800.001

  VARIABLE        VALUE          REDUCED COST
     A          20.000000          0.000000
     C          50.000000          0.000000

    ROW          SLACK           DUAL PRICES
    2)         40.000000          0.000000
    3)          0.000000          0.000010
    4)          0.000000         15.000000
```

As predicted, the profit is still $1800; however, the production of Cosmos has been increased to 50 from 30 while the production of Astros has been decreased to 20 from 60.

The "Snake Eyes" Condition

In general, alternate optima may exist only if some row in the solution report has zeroes in both the second and third columns of the report, a configuration that some applied statisticians call "snake eyes." That is, alternate optima may exist only if some variable has both zero value and zero reduced cost or some constraint has both zero slack and zero dual price. Mathematicians, with no intent of moral judgment, refer to such solutions as degenerate.

If there are alternate optima, you may find that your computer gives a different solution from that in the text. You should, however, always get the same objective function value.

There are in fact two ways in which multiple optimal solutions can occur. For the example in Figure 1.9 the two optimal solutions reports differ only in the values of the so-called primal variables, i.e., our original decision variables A, C, and the slack variables in the constraint. There can also be situations where there are multiple optimal solutions where only the dual variables differ. Consider this variation of the Enginola problem wherein the capacity of the Cosmo line has been reduced to 30. The formulation is:

```
MAX      20 A + 30 C
SUBJECT TO
   2)    A         ≤   60
   3)         C    ≤   30
   4)    A + 2 C   ≤  120
END
```

The corresponding graph of this problem appears in Figure 1.10. An optimal solution is:

```
         OBJECTIVE FUNCTION VALUE
   1)          2100.0000

   VARIABLE        VALUE           REDUCED COST
      A          60.000000             0.000000
      C          30.000000             0.000000

   ROW       SLACK OR SURPLUS      DUAL PRICES
   2)            0.000000             5.000000
   3)            0.000000             0.000000
   4)            0.000000            15.000000
```

Again notice the "snake eyes" in the solution, i.e., the pair of zeroes in a row of the solution report. This suggests that the capacity of the Cosmo line (the RHS of row 3) could be changed without changing the objective value. Figure 1.10 illustrates the situation. Three constraints pass through the point $A = 60$, $C = 30$. Any two of the constraints determine the point. In fact, the constraint $A + 2C \leq 120$ is mathematically redundant, i.e., it could be dropped without changing the feasible region.

If you decrease the RHS of row 3 very slightly you will get essentially the following solution.

Figure 1.10
Alternate Solutions in the Dual Variables

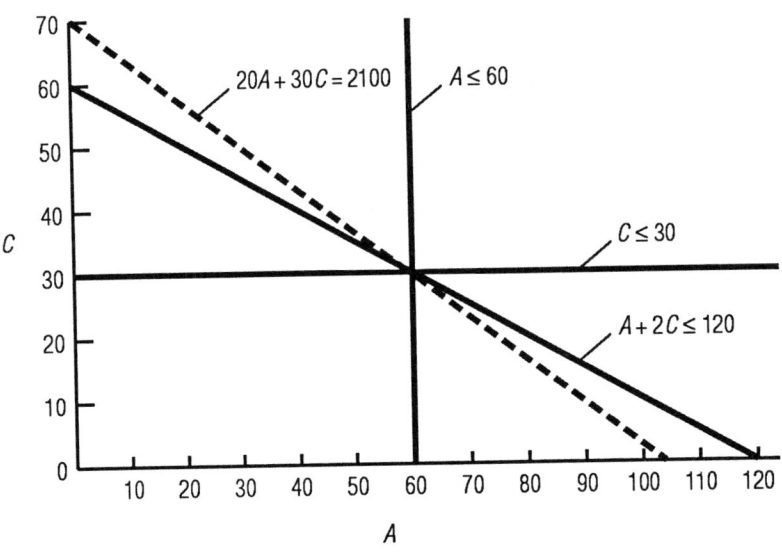

```
            OBJECTIVE FUNCTION VALUE

       1)         2100.0000

    VARIABLE        VALUE           REDUCED COST
       A          60.000000           0.000000
       C          30.000000           0.000000

    ROW       SLACK OR SURPLUS       DUAL PRICES
     2)           0.000000            20.000000
     3)           0.000000            30.000000
     4)           0.000000             0.000000
```

Notice that this solution differs from the previous one only in the dual values.

We can now state the following rule: If a solution report has the "snake eyes" feature, i.e., a pair of zeroes in any row of the report, then there is another alternate optimal solution that differs either or both in the primal variables or the dual variables.

If a solution report exhibits the "snake eyes" configuration a natural question to ask is: can we determine from the solution report alone, whether the alternate optima are in the primal variables or the dual variables? The answer is "no," as the following two related problems illustrate.

Problem D

```
MAX    X + Y
SUBJECT TO
   2)   X +    Y + Z ≤ 1
   3)   X + 2 Y     ≤ 1
END
```

Problem P

```
MAX    X + Y
SUBJECT TO
   2)   X + Y +   Z ≤ 1
   3)   X     + 2 Z ≤ 1
END
```

Both problems possess multiple optimal solutions. The ones that can be identified by the standard simplex solution methods are:

Solution 1

Problem D   Problem P

	Problem D			Problem P	
OBJECTIVE FUNCTION VALUE			OBJECTIVE FUNCTION VALUE		
1)	1.00000000		1)	1.00000000	
VARIABLE	VALUE	REDUCED COST	VARIABLE	VALUE	REDUCED COST
X	1.000000	0.000000	X	1.000000	0.000000
Y	0.000000	0.000000	Y	0.000000	0.000000
Z	0.000000	1.000000	Z	0.000000	1.000000
ROW	SLACK OR SURPLUS	DUAL PRICES	ROW	SLACK OR SURPLUS	DUAL PRICES
2)	0.000000	1.000000	2)	0.000000	1.000000
3)	0.000000	0.000000	3)	0.000000	0.000000

Solution 2

Problem D   Problem P

	Problem D			Problem P	
OBJECTIVE FUNCTION VALUE			OBJECTIVE FUNCTION VALUE		
1)	1.00000000		1)	1.00000000	
VARIABLE	VALUE	REDUCED COST	VARIABLE	VALUE	REDUCED COST
X	1.000000	0.000000	X	0.000000	0.000000
Y	0.000000	1.000000	Y	1.000000	0.000000
Z	0.000000	0.000000	Z	0.000000	1.000000
ROW	SLACK OR SURPLUS	DUAL PRICES	ROW	SLACK OR SURPLUS	DUAL PRICES
2)	0.000000	0.000000	2)	0.000000	1.000000
3)	0.000000	1.000000	3)	1.000000	0.000000

Notice that:

- *Solution 1* is exactly the same for both problems.
- *Problem D* has multiple optimal solutions in the dual variables (only), while
- *Problem P* has multiple optimal solutions in the primal variables (only).

Thus, one cannot determine from the solution report alone the kind of alternate optima that might exist. You can generate Solution 1 by setting the RHS of row 3 and the coefficient of X in the objective to slightly larger than 1, e.g., 1.001, and Solution 2 by setting the RHS of row 3 to the coefficient of X in the objective to slightly less than 1, e.g., 0.9999.

Some authors refer to a problem that has multiple solutions to the primal variables as *dual degenerate* and a problem with multiple solutions in the dual variables as *primal degenerate*. Other authors say a problem has multiple optima only if there are multiple optimal solutions for the primal variables.

Degeneracy and Redundant Constraints

Looking at two dimensional examples usually gives good insight into the behavior of larger problems, however, sometimes these "insights" are wrong. In two dimensions the following is true:

Figure 1.11
Degeneracy but No Redundant Constraints

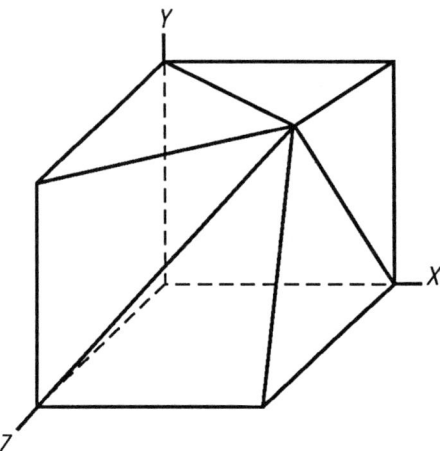

In two dimensions, if n inequality constraints, $n > 2$, all pass through a single point, then at least $n - 2$ of them are redundant.

The "obvious generalization" to three dimensions does not hold. In fact:

In three dimensions, if n inequality constraints, $n > 3$, all pass through a single point, all of them may be nonredundant.

Thus, in large problems, degeneracy does not imply that there are redundant constraints. The constraint set below and the corresponding Figure 1.11 illustrate.

$$2x - y \leq 1 \qquad 2y - x \leq 1 \qquad 2z - x \leq 1$$
$$2x - z \leq 1 \qquad 2y - z \leq 1 \qquad 2z - y \leq 1$$

These constraints define a cone with apex or point at $x = y = z = 1$, having six sides. The point $x = y = z = 1$ is degenerate because it has more than three constraints passing through it. Nevertheless, none of the constraints are redundant. Notice the point $x = 0.6$, $y = 0$, $z = 0.5$ violates the first constraint but satisfies all the others. Therefore the first constraint is nonredundant. By trying all six permutations of 0.6, 0, 0.5, you can verify that each of the six constraints is nonredundant.

Problems

1. Your firm produces two products, Thyristors (T) and Lozenges (L) which compete for the scarce resources of your distribution system. For the next planning period your distribution system has available 6,000 person hours. Proper distribution of each T requires 3 hours and each L requires 2 hours. The profit contributions per unit are 40 and 30 for Ts and Ls. Product line considerations dictate that at least 1 T be sold for each 2 Ls.

(a) Draw the feasible region and draw the profit line which passes through the optimum point.

(b) By simple commonsense arguments, what is the optimal solution?

2. Graph the following LP problem:

$$\text{Minimize} \quad 4X + 6Y$$
$$\text{subject to} \quad 5X + 2Y \geq 12$$
$$3X + 7Y \geq 13$$

In addition, plot the line $4X + 6Y = 18$. Show an iso-cost line and indicate the optimum point.

3. The Volkswagen Company produces two products, the Bug and the SuperBug, which share production facilities. Raw materials cost are $600 per car for the Bug and $750 per car for the SuperBug. The Bug requires 4 hours in the foundry/forge area per car, while the SuperBug, because it uses newer, more advanced dies, requires only 2 hours in the foundry/forge. The Bug requires 2 hours per car in the assembly plant, while the SuperBug, because it is a more complicated car, requires 3 hours per car in the assembly plant. The available daily capacities in the two areas are 160 hours in the foundry/forge and 180 hours in the assembly plant. The selling price of the Bug at the factory door is $4800 while for the SuperBug it is $5250. It is safe to assume that whatever number of cars are produced by this factory can be sold.

(a) Write the linear program formulation of this problem.

(b) The above description implies that the capacities of the two departments, foundry/forge and assembly are sunk costs. Reformulate the LP under the conditions that each hour of foundry/forge time costs $90 while each hour of assembly time costs $60. The capacities remain as before. Unused capacity has no charge.

4. The Keyesport Quarry has two different pits from which it obtains rock. The rock is run through a crusher to produce two products: concrete grade stone and road surface chat. Each ton of rock from the South pit converts into 0.75 tons of stone and 0.25 tons of chat when crushed. Rock from the North pit is of different quality. When it is crushed it produces a "50–50" split of stone and chat. The Quarry has contracts for 60 tons of stone and 40 tons of chat this planning period. The cost per ton of extracting and crushing rock for the South pit is 1.6 times as costly as from the North pit.

(a) What are the decision variables in the problem?

(b) There are two constraints for this problem. State them in words.

(c) Graph the feasible region for this problem.

(d) Draw an appropriate objective function line on the graph and indicate graphically and numerically the optimal solution.

(e) Suppose all the information given in the problem description is accurate. What additional information might you nevertheless wish to know before having confidence in this model?

5. A problem faced by railroads is that of assembling engine sets for particular trains. There are three important characteristics associated with each engine type, namely,

operating cost per hour, horsepower, and tractive power. Associated with each train, e.g., the Super Chief run from Chicago to Los Angeles, is a required horsepower and a required tractive power. The horsepower required depends largely upon the speed required by the run while the tractive power required depends largely upon the weight of the train and the steepness of the grades encountered on the run. For a particular train, the problem is to find that combination of engines which satisfies the horsepower and tractive power requirements at lowest cost.

In particular, consider the train, the Cimarron Special which runs from Omaha to Santa Fe. This train requires 12,000 horsepower and 50,000 tractive power units. Two engine types, the GM–I and the GM–II, are available for pulling this train. The GM–I has 2,000 horsepower, 10,000 tractive power units and its variable operating costs are $150 per hour. The GM–II has 3,000 horsepower, 10,000 tractive power units and its variable operating costs are $180 per hour. The engine set may be mixed, e.g., use two GM–Is and three GM–IIs.

(a) Write the linear program formulation of this problem.

6. Graph the constraint lines and the objective function line passing through the optimum point and indicate the feasible region for the Enginola problem when:

   (a) All parameters are as given except that the labor supply is 70 rather than 120.

   (b) All parameters are as given originally except that the variable profit contribution of a Cosmo is $40 instead of $30.

7. Consider the problem

$$\begin{aligned} \text{Minimize} \quad & 4x_1 + 3x_2 \\ \text{Subject to} \quad & 2x_1 + x_2 \geq 10 \\ & -3x_1 + 2x_2 \leq 6 \\ & x_1 + x_2 \geq 6 \qquad x_1 \geq 0, x_2 \geq 0 \end{aligned}$$

Solve the problem graphically.

2
Solving LPs on the Computer: The LINDO Program

Introduction

The process of solving an LP requires a large number of calculations and is therefore best performed by a computer program. The computer program we will use is called LINDO. The acronym stands for Linear, INteractive, Discrete Optimizer. The main purpose of LINDO is to allow a user to quickly input an LP formulation; solve it; assess the correctness or appropriateness of the formulation based on the solution and then quickly make minor modifications to the formulation and repeat the process.

LINDO is an interactive program; that is, essential instructions for the use of LINDO are contained in LINDO. Depending upon the situation, LINDO will either ask the user what is to be done next or it will wait for the user to type a command.

LINDO is command oriented rather than menu oriented. That is, it does not lead you through a fixed sequence of steps, allowing small options along the way. Rather, there is a wide range of commands, any of which may be invoked at any time. LINDO checks whether a particular command makes sense in a particular context.

Getting Started on Small Problems

The commands useful for the novice are:

Command	Use
MAX	Start input of a maximization problem.
MIN	Start input of a minimization problem.
END	End problem input and return to command level.
GO	Solve the current problem and print solution.
LOOK	Print selected portions of current formulation.
ALTER	Alter an element of the current problem.
EDIT	Move about screen and scroll to make changes.

For example, the following input is valid for describing a small problem:

```
MAX   2X + 3Y
ST
4X + 3Y < 10
3X + 5Y < 12
END
```

Typing GO will cause this problem to be solved.

If LOOK is typed, then LINDO asks for a row specification. Typical responses might be 3, or 1, 2, or ALL, causing, respectively, row 3, or rows 1 through 2 or all the rows to be printed.

If ALTER is typed, then LINDO will ask for a row, a variable, and a new coefficient. Responding 2, X, and 6 respectively to these queries would change the 4X in the above formulation to 6X. At this point GO could again be typed to solve the new problem.

After solving a problem, LINDO will ask if you wish to do sensitivity or range analysis. Unless you are already familiar with these concepts you should answer no to this question.

The following is an example session illustrating how the above commands might be used in analyzing the Enginola problem. User input appears in lower case.

```
:! Some comments:
:! Notice that comments can be inserted by prefacing with a "!".
:! When LINDO is awaiting a command, it prompts with a ":".
:! When it is expecting input other than a command it prompts with a "?".
:max 20A +   ! Notice that you can (and should) split long rows
?30C         ! over several input lines by typing a carriage return
?            ! or 'enter' at a convenient split point.
?st
?A < 60
?C < 50
?A + 2 C < 120
?end

:look
ROW:
?all
MAX      20 A + 30 C
SUBJECT TO
    2)     A ≤    60
    3)     C ≤    50
    4)     A + 2 C ≤   120
END
```

Notice how LINDO interprets the strict inequalities, "<", that we typed in as loose inequalities, "≤".

```
:go
LP OPTIMUM FOUND AT STEP      3
        OBJECTIVE FUNCTION VALUE
    1)        2100.00000
```

```
VARIABLE        VALUE           REDUCED COST
   A          60.000000             .000000
   C          30.000000             .000000

  ROW     SLACK OR SURPLUS      DUAL PRICES
   2)          .000000            5.000000
   3)        20.000000             .000000
   4)          .000000           15.000000

NO. ITERATIONS=     3
DO RANGE (SENSITIVITY) ANALYSIS?
?no
```

Altering and Editing a Model

Depending upon which version of LINDO you have, there are two ways of modifying or editing a model: (a) use the ALTER command, (b) use the EDIT command. All versions of LINDO have the ALTER command. Recent PC versions of LINDO have the EDIT command.

Using the ALTER Command

This section illustrates the use of the ALTER command to do simple editing. The ALTER command is available in all versions of LINDO. Continuing where we left off, we might use the ALTER command as follows.

```
:alter
ROW:
1
VAR:
a
NEW COEFFICIENT:
?15

:look 1

MAX     15 A + 30 C

:go
   LP OPTIMUM FOUND AT STEP     2
      OBJECTIVE FUNCTION VALUE
   1)       1800.00000

VARIABLE        VALUE           REDUCED COST
   A          20.000000             .000000
   C          50.000000             .000000

  ROW     SLACK OR SURPLUS      DUAL PRICES
   2)        40.000000             .000000
   3)          .000000             .000000
   4)          .000000           15.000000

NO. ITERATIONS=     2
```

Here is how you change a right hand side value:

```
:alter 3 rhs
NEW COEFFICIENT:
?30
```

```
:look 3
   3)   C ≤   30
:go
   LP OPTIMUM FOUND AT STEP     0
         OBJECTIVE FUNCTION VALUE
    1)          1800.00000
  VARIABLE        VALUE          REDUCED COST
     A          60.000000             .000000
     C          30.000000             .000000
  ROW        SLACK OR SURPLUS      DUAL PRICES
    2)            .000000           5.000000
    3)            .000000            .000000
    4)            .000000          15.000000
  NO. ITERATIONS=         0
  DO RANGE (SENSITIVITY) ANALYSIS?
  ?n
```

Using the EDIT Command

A full screen editor is available on the student PC version of LINDO. The major advantage of a full screen editor is that it allows you to use the "arrow" keys to move the cursor about the screen. For most other keys, pressing that key will cause the character associated with that key to be inserted at the cursor position.

You access the editor by typing the command: EDIT. The screen will then look something like the following:

```
LINDO/PC 5.0                                    © 1990 LINDO SYSTEMS INC.
    1   MAX    20A + 30C
    2   SUBJECT TO
    3         2)    A  <  60
    4         3)    C  <  50
    5         4)    A + 2C < 120
    6   END
    7
    8
    9
   10
   11
   12
   13
   14
   15
   16
   17
   18
   19
   20
   21
   22
   23
         <Esc> - Exit with compile    <Cntrl-Break> - Exit without compile
```

The line numbers (as opposed to the constraint numbers) along the extreme left are supplied by the editor. The effects of other, special keys are summarized in the table below.

Key with Label	Effect
[→]	Moves cursor right one character
[←]	Moves cursor left one character
[↑]	Moves cursor up one line
[↓]	Moves cursor down one character
[Home]	Moves cursor to beginning
[End]	Moves cursor to end
[PageUp]	Moves cursor up one screen
[PageDown]	Moves cursor down one screen
[Ctrl][S]	Moves cursor to start of current line
[Ctrl][E]	Moves cursor to end of current line
[Ctrl][→]	Moves cursor to end of current word
[Ctrl][←]	Moves cursor to beginning of current word
[Del]	Deletes character at current cursor position
[Enter]	Inserts a carriage return at current cursor position
[Ins]	Inserts a carriage return at current cursor position
[Backspace]	Deletes character to the left of cursor
[Esc]	Exit the editor and try to interpret the edited model
[Ctrl][Break]	Exit the editor without interpreting the edited model

Saving, Retrieving and Printing Your Work

As you become more sophisticated you may wish to save your work for future reference or you may wish to print some of your results. The commands useful in this regard are:

Command	Use
SAVE	Save a problem onto disk (long term) storage
RETR	Retrieve a SAVE(d) problem
DIVERT	Divert output to disk or printer

We discuss these commands further in the following sections.

SAVE and RETRIEVE Commands

When we left off in our example session things looked as follows:

```
:look all
MAX      15 A + 30 C
SUBJECT TO
   2)     A ≤   60
   3)     C ≤   30
   4)     A + 2 C ≤   120
END
```

Suppose we are interested in saving this version of the problem. First, let's look at the HELP SAVE command:

```
:help save
```

SAVE COMMAND:

SAVES THE CURRENT MODEL IN A FILE IN CONDENSED LINDO FORMAT.
THE MODEL MAY BE RETRIEVED USING "RETR".

So lets try it . . .

```
:save
FILE NAME:
engins.lpk
```

We arbitrarily use the suffix ".lpk" to identify files containing LINDO problems. Let's alter the RHS back to the original version:

```
:alter 3 rhs
NEW COEFFICIENT:
?50
```

Now to check what we have done:

```
:look all
MAX      15 A + 30 C
SUBJECT TO
    2)   A ≤    60
    3)   C ≤    50
    4)   A + 2 C ≤    120
END
```

Suppose we change our mind again and wish to retrieve the previous version. First, let's look at the HELP RETR command:

```
:help retr
```

RETRIEVE COMMAND:

FETCHES A MODEL FROM DISK. LINDO WILL PROMPT YOU FOR A
SPECIFIC FILE NAME OR UNIT NUMBER. THE MODEL BEING
RETRIEVED MUST HAVE BEEN PREVIOUSLY SAVED VIA THE "SAVE"
COMMAND.

IF YOU HAVE A PC DOS VERSION OF LINDO YOU MAY INCLUDE THE
DOS WILDCARD CHARACTERS '*' AND '?' IN THE FILENAME TO BE
PRESENTED WITH A MENU OF FILES MATCHING THE SPECIFICATION.

If we type:

```
:retr *.lpk
```

We see the screen at the top of the next page. If we highlight ENGINS.LPK with the cursor and press [ENTER], that's the file we get. To check . . .

```
:look all
MAX      15 A + 30 C
SUBJECT TO
    2)   A ≤    60
    3)   C ≤    30
    4)   A + 2 C ≤    120
END
```

```
┌─────────────────────────────────────────────────────┐
│  ▐DUQUESN.LPK▌   ENGINS.LPK                         │
│                                                     │
│                                                     │
│                                                     │
│         Use the direction keys to highlight a file and ... │
│             <ESC>    return to command level        │
│             <PgDn>   display additional files       │
│             <Enter>  select highlighted file        │
│                                                     │
│                                                     │
└─────────────────────────────────────────────────────┘
```

Diverting Output to a File or Printer

The DIVERT command allows us to send output to a file or printer. If we continue our example session:

```
:help divert

DIVERT COMMAND:

YOU WILL BE ASKED FOR A FILE.  ALL SUBSEQUENT HIVOLUME
OUTPUT, E.G.  SOLUTION REPORTS, WILL BE DIVERTED TO THIS
FILE UNTIL A RVRT (REVERT) COMMAND IS GIVEN.

    :dive
    FILE NAME:
    engins.lot
```

We arbitrarily use the suffix ".lot" to identify LINDO output files. Now, notice that the solution report seems to have disappeared!

```
        :go
           LP OPTIMUM FOUND AT STEP      2
              OBJECTIVE FUNCTION VALUE
        1)         1800.00000
    DO RANGE (SENSITIVITY) ANALYSIS?
    ?n
```

It was not displayed! Where did it go? It was sent to the file ENGINS.LOT. The RVRT (revert) command returns subsequent output to the screen.

```
:help rvrt

RVRT COMMAND:

CAUSES ALL SUBSEQUENT OUTPUT TO REVERT TO THE TERMINAL. IT
UNDOES THE EFFECT OF THE "DIVERT" COMMAND.

    :rvrt
```

Alternatively on PC-DOS machines, output can be sent directly to the printer by using a file name of PRN.

```
    :dive
    FILE NAME:
    prn
    :look all
    :GO
       LP OPTIMUM FOUND AT STEP        2
             OBJECTIVE FUNCTION VALUE
      1)         1800.00000
    DO RANGE (SENSITIVITY) ANALYSIS?
    ?n
    :rvrt
```

Notice that neither the model formulation nor the solution appeared on the screen. Guess where they went. The following, however, would have appeared on the printer (do not try the above if you have no printer).

```
     MAX      15 A + 30 C
     SUBJECT TO
        2)     A  ≤   60
        3)     C  ≤   30
        4)     A + 2 C ≤    120
     END
         LP OPTIMUM FOUND AT STEP        2
               OBJECTIVE FUNCTION VALUE
        1)         1800.00000
           VARIABLE       VALUE          REDUCED COST
              A         60.000000           .000000
              C         30.000000           .000000
           ROW      SLACK OR SURPLUS      DUAL PRICES
            2)           .000000           5.000000
            3)           .000000            .000000
            4)           .000000          15.000000
           NO. ITERATIONS=         2
```

Once out of LINDO you could discover that the file ENGINS.LOT contains the following.

```
          LP OPTIMUM FOUND AT STEP      2
                OBJECTIVE FUNCTION VALUE
        1)           1800.00000
     VARIABLE         VALUE           REDUCED COST
        A            60.000000           .000000
        C            30.000000           .000000
      ROW        SLACK OR SURPLUS      DUAL PRICES
       2)              .000000          5.000000
       3)              .000000           .000000
       4)              .000000         15.000000
     NO. ITERATIONS=         2
```

On PC-DOS machines you could display this file on the screen by typing:

    type engins.lot

You could print the file by typing:

    print engins.lot

Alternatively, on most computers you could incorporate the file contents into a document you are preparing with your favorite word processor. LINDO Divert files are in standard text format that can be imported into most word processors with commands such as "TEXT IN."

Integer Programming with LINDO

Fairly shortly after you start looking at problems for which LP might be applicable, you discover the need to restrict certain variables to integer values, i.e., 0, 1, 2, etc. Even though this violates the linearity requirement, LINDO allows you to identify such variables. We give an introductory treatment here. It is discussed more thoroughly in Chapter 14.

Integer variables in LINDO can be either 0/1 or general. Variables which are restricted to the values 0 or 1 are identified with the INTEGER command. It is used in one of two forms, examples of which are:

    INTEGER x   or   INTEGER 8.

The first (and recommended) form identifies variable x as being 0/1. The second form identifies the first 8 variables in the current formulation as being 0/1. The order of the variables is determined by their order encountered in the input. This order can be verified by observing the order of variables in the solution report.

The second form is more powerful, but it requires the user to be aware of the exact order of the variables. This may be confusing if not all variables appear in the objective.

The following example session illustrates the INT command:

```
:max 4 tom + 3 dick + 2 harry
?st
?2.5 tom + 3.1 harry < 5
?.2 tom + .7 dick + .4 harry < 1
?end
```

```
:int tom
:int dick
:int harry

:go
    LP OPTIMUM FOUND AT STEP   4
            OBJECTIVE FUNCTION VALUE

    1)            7.65898620
SET HARRY TO  ≤  0 AT  1 BND=   7.0000000    TWIN= 7.4285715
NEW INTEGER SOLUTION AT BRANCH      1 PIVOT       6
            OBJECTIVE FUNCTION VALUE

    1)            7.00000000
BEST REMAINING SOLUTION NO BETTER THAN   7.428571
DELETE HARRY AT LEVEL     1
      ENUMERATION COMPLETE.  BRANCHES=  1  PIVOTS=      6
LAST INTEGER SOLUTION IS THE BEST FOUND

:solution
            OBJECTIVE FUNCTION VALUE

    1)            7.000000
    VARIABLE        VALUE           REDUCED COST
      TOM          1.00000             −4.00000
      DICK         1.00000             −3.00000
      HARRY        0.00000             −2.00000
    ROW        SLACK OR SURPLUS      DUAL PRICE
     2)            2.500000            0.00000
     3)            0.100000            0.00000

:quit
STOP
```

General integers, which can be 0, 1, 2, etc., are identified in analogous fashion by using GIN instead of INT, for example:

GIN TONIC   *or*   GIN 8.

The first restricts variable TONIC to 0, 1, 2, 3, . . . The second restricts the first eight variables to 0, 1, 2, 3, . . .

The solution method used is branch and bound. It is an intelligent enumeration process that will find a sequence of better and better solutions. As each one is found, a short message will be displayed, giving the objective value and a bound on how good a solution might still remain. After the enumeration is complete, the SOLUTION (or the NONZEROES, CPRI or RPRI) command can be used to reveal information about the best solution found.

Let's look at a slightly modified version of the original Enginola problem and see how the GIN command might help.

```
:look all
MAX      20 A + 30 C
SUBJECT TO
   2)   A ≤    60
   3)   C ≤    50
   4)   A + 2 C ≤    115
END
```

Notice the capacity of 115 on the labor constraint (Row 4).

```
:go
    LP OPTIMUM FOUND AT STEP    3
         OBJECTIVE FUNCTION VALUE
   1)         2025.00000

VARIABLE      VALUE           REDUCED COST
   A         60.000000            .000000
   C         27.500000            .000000

   ROW    SLACK OR SURPLUS     DUAL PRICES
   2)          .000000           5.000000
   3)        22.500000            .000000
   4)          .000000          15.000000

NO. ITERATIONS=    3

DO RANGE(SENSITIVITY) ANALYSIS?
?n
```

Note that a fractional quantity is recommended for C. If fractional quantities are undesirable, declare A and C as general integer variables:

```
:gin a
:gin c
:look all
MAX      20 A + 30 C
SUBJECT TO
   2)   A ≤    60
   3)   C ≤    50
   4)   A + 2 C ≤    115
END
GIN      2
```

The GIN 2 means the first two variables, A and C, are to be integer.

```
:GO
LP OPTIMUM FOUND AT STEP    0
OBJECTIVE VALUE =   2025.00000
SET       C TO ≥   28 AT   1, BND= 2020.   TWIN= 2010.       3
NEW INTEGER SOLUTION OF   2020.00000    AT BRANCH   1   PIVOT   3
         OBJECTIVE FUNCTION VALUE
   1)         2020.00000
```

```
VARIABLE         VALUE              REDUCED COST
   A            59.000000              .000000
   C            28.000000            10.000000

ROW       SLACK OR SURPLUS         DUAL PRICES
 2)           1.000000                .000000
 3)          22.000000                .000000
 4)            .000000              20.000000

NO. ITERATIONS=       3
BRANCHES=    1  DETERM.=  1.000E      0
BOUND ON OPTIMUM:  2020.000
DELETE         C AT LEVEL         1
ENUMERATION COMPLETE.  BRANCHES=       1  PIVOTS=       3
LAST INTEGER SOLUTION IS THE BEST FOUND
RE-INSTALLING BEST SOLUTION . . .
```

The SOLUTION command can be used whenever we need to see the current solution.

```
:help solution

SOLUTION COMMAND:

PRINTS STANDARD SOLUTION REPORT.  TO SEND IT TO DISK, SEE
THE "DIVERT" COMMAND.  TO GET AN ABBREVIATED REPORT SEE THE
"NONZ", "CPRI" AND "RPRI" COMMANDS.

:solution
          OBJECTIVE FUNCTION VALUE
   1)        2020.00000

VARIABLE         VALUE              REDUCED COST
   A            59.000000            20.000000
   C            28.000000            30.000000

ROW       SLACK OR SURPLUS         DUAL PRICES
 2)           1.000000                .000000
 3)          22.000000                .000000
 4)            .000000                .000000

NO. ITERATIONS=       4

BRANCHES=    1  DETERM.=  1.000E      0
```

Although the integer programming (IP) capability is very powerful, it requires skill to use effectively. It is very easy to prepare a bad formulation for an essentially easy problem. A bad formulation may require intolerable amounts of computer time to solve. Therefore you should have access to someone who is experienced in IP formulations if you plan to make use of the IP capability. LINDO, however, will cut short the IP solution process if it appears to be taking too long. Thus, the novice is protected somewhat against the cost of solving a poor formulation. Good formulations of integer programs are discussed further in Chapter 14.

More Sophisticated Use of LINDO

There are three commands for helping the user get more information on LINDO: HELP, CATEGORIES (or CAT for short), and COMMANDS (or COM). COM will simply list all the commands available, grouped into categories according to use, e.g., input, output, etc. HELP followed by a command name will describe the specified command. HELP by itself gives general information. CAT will list only the categories and then allow one to list the commands in a specific category. The following illustrates:

```
:cat

LINDO  COMMANDS BY CATEGORY.  FOR INFORMATION
ON A SPECIFIC COMMAND, TYPE:  HELP  FOLLOWED BY
THE COMMAND NAME.
   1) INFORMATION
   2) INPUT
   3) DISPLAY
   4) FILE OUTPUT
   5) SOLUTION
   6) PROBLEM EDITING
   7) QUIT
   8) INTEGER, QUADRATIC, AND PARAMETRIC PROGRAMS
   9) CONVERSATIONAL PARAMETERS
  10) USER SUPPLIED ROUTINES
  11) MISCELLANEOUS

WHICH CATEGORY IS OF INTEREST (1 TO 11)?
?5

THE COMMANDS IN THIS CATEGORY ARE:
      GO     PIV

WHICH CATEGORY IS OF INTEREST (1 TO 11)?
?0

:help go

GO COMMAND

USE:  SOLVES THE CURRENT MODEL.  THE MODEL REMAINS INTACT
THROUGH THE SOLUTION PROCESS.  A POSITIVE INTEGER TYPED AFTER
GO IS INTERPRETED AS AN UPPER LIMIT ON THE NUMBER OF PIVOTS.
```

For reference, the commands as of 1991 as listed by the command "COMMAND" are listed below.

1. *Information*

CAT	Lists categories of commands
COM	Lists commands by category
HELP	Gives help in various situations
LOCAL	Gives info specific to your local installation
TIME	Display compute time used

2. *Input*

LEAVE	Undo the previous TAKE
MAX	Start natural input
MIN	Start natural input
RDBC	Retrieve old solution

RETR	Retrieve old problem from file
RMPS	Retrieve an MPS format file
TAKE	Take terminal input from a file

3. *Display*

BPICTURE	Print logical PICTURE of basis
CPRI	Print column information
LOOK	Print (part of) problem in natural format
NONZEROES	Print nonzero variables solution report
PICTURE	Print logical PICTURE of matrix
RANGE	Print RANGE analysis report
RPRI	Print row information
SHOCOLUMN	Display a column of the problem
SOLUTION	Print standard solution report
TABLEAU	Print current tableau
TITLE	Display or change problem title

4. *File output*

DIVERT	Divert output to file
RVRT	Revert output to terminal
SAVE	Save current problem to file
SDBC	Save solution in database format
SMPS	Save current problem in MPS format

5. *Solution*

GO	Go solve the problem
PIVOT	Do the next simplex pivot

6. *Problem editing*

ALTER	Alter an element of current problem with prompts from LINDO
APPC	Append a new column to the formulation
DEL	Delete a specified constraint
EDIT	Full screen editor with cursor keys controlling the cursor
EXT	Extend problem by adding constraints
FREE	Declare a variable unconstrained in sign
SLB	Enter a simple lower bound for a variable
SUB	Enter a simple upper bound for a variable

7. *Integer, quadratic, and parametric programs*

BIP	Set IP bound on optimal solution
GIN	Identify general integer variables
INT	Identify integer variables
IPTOL	Set IP tolerance on optimal solution
PARA	Parametric programming
POSD	Check positive definiteness
QCP	Quadratic programming
TITAN	Tighten an IP

8. *Conversational parameters*

BATCH	Tell LINDO that this is a batch run
PAGE	Set page/screen size
PAUSE	Pause for keyboard action
TERSE	Set conversational style to terse
VERBOSE	Set conversational style to verbose (default)
WIDTH	Set terminal width

9. *User supplied subroutines*

USER	Call user written subroutine

10. *Miscellaneous*

BUG	What to do if you find a bug
DEBUG	Help debug an infeasible model
INVERT	Invert current basis to get more accurate answers
SET	Set solution parameters
STAT	Print matrix summary statistics
TITL	Specify or display title of current model

11. *Quit*

QUIT	Quit

Scaling and Other Numerical Considerations

You should avoid using extremely small or extremely large numbers in a formulation, e.g., you should not measure weight in ounces one place and volume in cubic miles someplace else in the same problem. A rule of thumb is that there should be no nonzero coefficient whose absolute value is greater than 100,000 or less than 0.0001. If LINDO feels that the matrix is poorly scaled, it will print a warning.

3

Sensitivity Analysis of LP Solutions

Economic Analysis of Solution Reports

A substantial amount of interesting economic information can be gleaned from the solution report of a model. In addition, optional reports such as range analysis can provide further information. The usual use of this information is to do quick "what if" analysis. The typical kinds of what if questions are

(a) What would be the affect of increasing a capacity or demand?

(b) What if a new opportunity becomes available, is it a worthwhile opportunity?

Economic Relationship Between Dual Prices and Reduced Costs

The reader hungering for unity in systems may convince him or herself that a reduced cost is really a dual price born under the wrong sign. Under our convention the reduced cost of a variable x is really the dual price with the sign reversed on the constraint $x \geqq 0$. Recall that the reduced cost of the variable x measures the rate at which the solution value deteriorates as x is increased from zero. The dual price on $x \geqq 0$ measures the rate at which the solution value improves as the right-hand side (and thus x) is increased from zero.

Our knowledge about reduced costs and dual prices can be restated as follows:

Reduced cost of an (unused) activity: amount by which profits will decrease if one unit of this activity is forced into the solution.

Dual price of a constraint: amount by which profits will decrease if the availability of the resource associated with this constraint is reduced by one unit.

We shall argue and illustrate that the reduced cost of an activity is really its net opportunity cost if we "cost out" the activity using the dual prices as charges for resource usage. This sounds like good economic sense. If one unit of an activity is forced into the solution, it effectively reduces the availability of the resources it uses. These resources have an imputed value by way of the dual prices; therefore the activity should be charged for the value used. Let's look at an example and check if the argument works.

The Costing Out Operation, An Illustration

Suppose that Enginola is considering adding a video recorder to its product line. Market Research and Engineering estimate the direct profit contribution of a video recorder as $47 per unit. It would be manufactured on the Astro line and would require 3 hours of labor. If it is produced, it will force the reduction of both Astro production (because it competes for a production line) and Cosmo production (because it competes for labor). Is this tradeoff worthwhile? It looks promising. It makes more dollars per hour of labor than a Cosmo and it makes more efficient use of Astro capacity than Astros. Recall that the dual prices on the Astro capacity and the labor capacity in the original solution were $5 and $15. If we add this variable to the model it would have a +47 in the objective function, a +1 in row 2 (the Astro capacity constraint) and a +3 in row 4 (the labor capacity constraint). We can "cost out" an activity or decision variable by charging it for the use of scarce resources. What prices should be charged? The obvious prices to use are the dual prices. The +47 profit contribution can be thought of as a negative cost. The costing out calculations can be arrayed as in the little table below:

Row	Coefficient	Dual Price	Charge
1	47	−1	−47
2	1	5	+5
3	0	0	0
4	3	15	+45

Total opportunity cost = +3

Thus, a video recorder has an opportunity cost of $3. A −1 is applied to the 47 profit contribution because a profit contribution is effectively a negative cost. The video recorder's net cost is positive, so it is apparently not worth producing.

The analysis could be stopped at this point, but out of curiosity we'll formulate the relevant LP and solve it. If V = number of video recorders to produce, then we wish to solve:

```
MAX     20 A + 30 C + 47 V
SUBJECT TO
  2)    A +           V  ≤   60
  3)          C          ≤   50
  4)    A + 2 C + 3 V    ≤  120
```

The solution is:

```
        OBJECTIVE FUNCTION VALUE
  1)         2100.000

  VARIABLE       VALUE          REDUCED COST
     A         60.000000          0.000000
     C         30.000000          0.000000
     V          0.000000          3.000000
```

```
ROW            SLACK              DUAL PRICES
 2)            0.000000           5.000000
 3)           20.000000           0.000000
 4)            0.000000          15.000000
```

Video recorders are not produced and notice that the reduced cost of V is $3, the value we computed when we "costed out" V. This is an illustration of the following relationship:

> The reduced cost of an activity equals the weighted sum of its resource usage rates minus its profit contribution rate, where the weights applied are the dual prices. A "min" objective is treated as having a dual price of +1, a "max" objective is treated as having a dual price of −1 in the costing out process.

Range of Validity of Reduced Costs and Dual Prices

In describing reduced costs and dual prices we have been careful to limit the changes to "small" changes; e.g., if the dual price of a constraint is $3/hour, then increasing the number of hours available will improve profits by $3 for each of the first few hours (possibly less than one) added. This improvement rate will, in general, however, not hold forever. We might expect that as we make more hours of capacity available, the value (i.e., the dual price) of these hours would not increase and might decrease. This might not be true for all situations but for LP's it is true that increasing the right-hand side of a constraint cannot cause the constraint's dual price to increase. The dual price can only stay the same or decrease.

As we change the right-hand side of an LP the optimal values of the decision variables may change; however, the dual prices and reduced costs will not change as long as the "character" of the optimal solution does not change. We will say that the character changes (mathematicians say the basis changes) when either the set of variables which are nonzero or the set of constraints which are binding changes. In summary, as we alter the right-hand side, the same dual prices apply as long as the "character" or "basis" does not change.

Most LP programs will optionally supplement the solution report with a range or sensitivity analysis report which indicates the amounts by which individual right-hand side or objective function coefficients can be changed unilaterally without affecting the character or "basis" of the optimal solution. Recall the previous model:

```
MAX     20 A + 30 C + 47 V
SUBJECT TO
        A +         V ≤  60
                C     ≤  50
        A + 2C + 3V ≤ 120
END
```

The sensitivity report for this problem appears below:

```
DO RANGE (SENSITIVITY) ANALYSIS?
>y
```

RANGES IN WHICH THE BASIS IS UNCHANGED

OBJ COEFFICIENT RANGES

VARIABLE	CURRENT COEF	ALLOWABLE INCREASE	ALLOWABLE DECREASE
A	20.00000	INFINITY	5.000000
C	30.00000	10.000000	30.000000
V	47.00000	3.000000	INFINITY

RIGHTHAND SIDE RANGES

ROW	CURRENT RHS	ALLOWABLE INCREASE	ALLOWABLE DECREASE
2	60.00000	60.000000	40.00000
3	50.00000	INFINITY	20.00000
4	120.00000	40.000000	60.00000

Again, we find two sections, one for variables and the second for rows or constraints. The 5 in the A row of the report means that the profit contribution of A could be decreased by up to $5/unit without affecting the optimal amount of A and C to produce. This is plausible because, currently Astros make more efficient use of labor, $20 per one hour vs., $30 per two hours for Cosmos. If the profit contribution of an Astro was reduced by $5 to $15 per unit then the two would make equally efficient use of labor and one would be willing to increase Cosmo production at the expense of Astros until the slack of row 3 (the constraint $C \geq 50$) went to zero (or "departed"). The INFINITY in the same section of the report means that increasing the profitability of A by any positive amount would have no effect on the optimal amount of A and C to produce. This is intuitive because we are already producing As to their upper limit.

The "allowable decrease" of 30 for variable C means that the profitability of C could be reduced by $30/unit (i.e., to zero) without changing the optimal solution. This makes sense because at the moment Cosmo production is made simply to make profitable use of any labor left over from Astro production. The 10 in the C's row means that the profitability of C would have to be increased by at least $10/unit (thus to $40/unit) before we would consider changing the values of A and C. Notice that at $40/unit for Cs, the profit per hour of labor is the same for both A and C.

In general, *if the objective function coefficient* of a single variable *is changed within the range* specified in the first section of the range report, *then the optimal values of the decision variables*, A, C and V in this case, *will not change*. The dual prices, reduced cost and profitability of the solution, however, may change.

In a complementary sense, *if the right-hand side* of a single constraint *is changed within the range* specified in the second section of the range report, *then the optimal values of the dual prices and reduced costs will not change*. The values of the decision variables and the profitability of the solution, however, may change.

For example, the second section tells us that if the right-hand side of row 3 (the constraint $C \geq 50$), is decreased by more than 20, then the dual prices and reduced costs will change. The constraint will then be $C \geq 30$ and the character of the solution changes in that the labor constraint will no longer be binding. The right-hand side of this constraint ($C \geq 50$) could be increased, according to the range report, an infinite amount without affecting the optimal dual prices and reduced costs. This makes sense because there already is excess capacity on the Cosmo line, so adding more capacity should have no effect.

Let us illustrate some of these concepts by resolving our three variable problem with the amount of labor reduced by 61 hours down to 59 hours. The formulation and solution are:

```
MAX     20 A + 30 C + 47 V
SUBJECT TO
   2)     A     +     V  ≤  60
   3)           C         ≤  50
   4)     A + 2 C + 3 V   ≤  59
END
:GO
    LP OPTIMUM FOUND AT STEP    1
        OBJECTIVE FUNCTION VALUE

   1)        1180.000

   VARIABLE        VALUE           REDUCED COST
      A         59.000000             0.000000
      C          0.000000            10.000000
      V          0.000000            13.000000

   ROW           SLACK             DUAL PRICES
    2)         1.000000              0.000000
    3)        50.000000              0.000000
    4)         0.000000             20.000000

           RANGES IN WHICH THE BASIS IS UNCHANGED
                       OBJ COEFFICIENT RANGES
   VARIABLE     CURRENT         ALLOWABLE        ALLOWABLE
                 COEF           INCREASE         DECREASE
      A        20.00000         INFINITY          5.000000
      C        30.00000        10.000000         INFINITY
      V        47.00000        13.000000         INFINITY
                         RIGHTHAND SIDE RANGES
    ROW         CURRENT         ALLOWABLE        ALLOWABLE
                 RHS            INCREASE         DECREASE
     2         60.00000         INFINITY          1.00000
     3         50.00000         INFINITY         50.00000
     4         59.00000         1.000000         59.00000
```

First of all note that with the reduced labor supply we no longer produce any Cosmos. Their reduced cost is now $10/unit, which means that if their profitability were increased by $10 to $40/unit then we would start considering their production again. At $40/unit for Cosmos both products make equally efficient use of labor.

Also notice that because the right-hand side of the labor constraint has been reduced by more than 60, most of the dual prices and reduced costs have changed. In particular, the dual price or marginal value of labor is now $20 per hour. This is because an additional hour of labor would be used to produce one more $20 Astro. You should be able to convince yourself that the marginal value of labor behaves as follows:

Labor Available	Dual Price	Reason
0 to 60 hours	$20/hour	Each additional hour will be used to produce one $20 Astro.
60 to 160 hours	$15/hour	Each additional hour will be used to produce half a $30 Cosmo.
160 to 280 hours	$13.5/hour	Give up half an Astro and add half of a V for profit of $0.5(-20 + 47)$.
More than 280 hours	$0	No use for additional labor.

In general the dual price on any constraint will behave in the above stepwise decreasing fashion.

Figures 3.1 and 3.2 give a global view of how total profit is affected by changing either a single objective coefficient or a single right-hand side. The artists in the audience may wish to note that for a maximization problem:

(a) Optimal total profit as a function of a single objective coefficient always has a bowl shape. Mathematicians say it is a convex function.

(b) Optimal total profit as a function of a single right-hand side value always has an inverted bowl shape. Mathematicians say it is a concave function.

For some problems, as in Figures 3.1 and 3.2 we only see half of the bowl. For minimization problems, the orientation of the bowl in (a) and (b) is simply reversed.

When we solve a problem for a particular objective coefficient or right-hand-side value we obtain a single point on one of these curves. A range report gives us the endpoints of the line segment on which this one point lies.

Figure 3.1

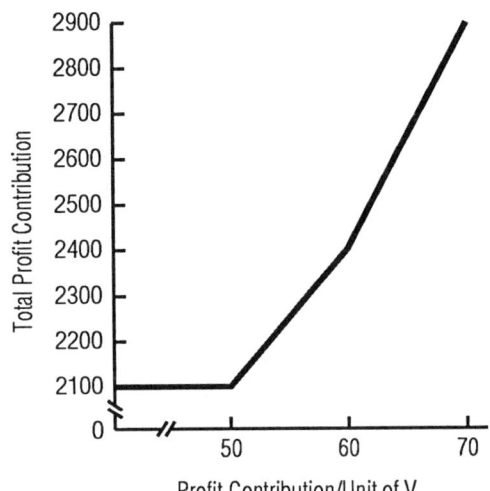

Total Profit vs. Profit Contribution per Unit of Activity V

Figure 3.2

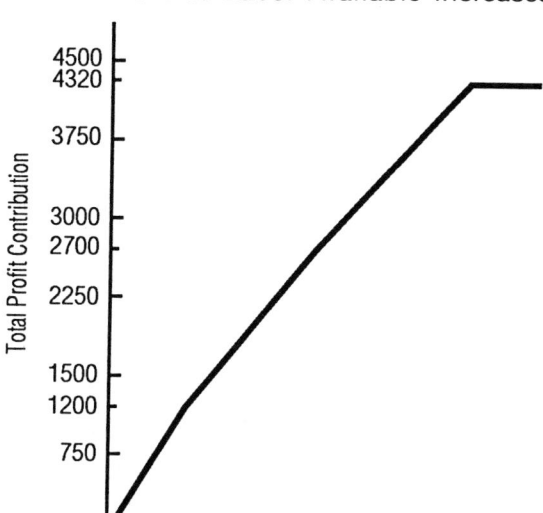

Profit as Labor Available Increases

Predicting the Effect of Simultaneous Changes in Parameters—The 100% Rule

The information in the range analysis report tells us the effect of changing a single cost or resource parameter. The range report for the Enginola problem is presented as an example:

RANGES IN WHICH THE BASIS IS UNCHANGED

VARIABLE	CURRENT COEF	OBJ COEFFICIENT RANGES ALLOWABLE INCREASE	ALLOWABLE DECREASE
A	20.00000	INFINITY	5.000000
C	30.00000	60.000000	30.000000

ROW	CURRENT RHS	RIGHTHAND SIDE RANGES ALLOWABLE INCREASE	ALLOWABLE DECREASE
2	60.00000	60.000000	40.000000
3	50.00000	INFINITY	20.000000
4	120.00000	40.000000	60.000000

The report indicates that the profit contribution of an Astro could be decreased by as much as $5/unit without changing the basis. In this case, this means that the optimal solution would still recommend producing 60 Astros and 30 Cosmos.

Now suppose that in order to meet competition, we're considering lowering the price of an Astro by $3/unit and the price of a Cosmo by $10/unit. Will it still be profitable to produce the same mix? Individually, each of these changes would not change the solution because $3 \geqq 5$ and $10 \geqq 30$.

But it is not clear that these two changes can be made simultaneously. What does your intuition suggest as a rule describing the simultaneous changes which don't change the basis (mix)?

The 100% Rule. You can think of the allowable ranges as slack which may be used up in changing parameters. It is a fact that any combination of changes will not change the basis if the sum of percentages of slack used sums to less than 100%. For the simultaneous changes we are contemplating, we have:

$$\left(\frac{3}{5}\right) \times 100 + \left(\frac{10}{30}\right) \times 100 = 60\% + 33.3\% = 93.3\% < 100\%$$

This satisfies the condition, so the changes can be made without changing the basis. Bradley, Hax, and Magnanti (1977) have dubbed this rule the 100% rule. Because the value of A and C do not change, we can calculate the effect on profits of this changes as $-3 \times 60 - 10 \times 30 = -480$. So the new profit will be $2100 - 480 = 1620$.

The altered formulation and its solution are:

```
MAX      17 A + 20 C
SUBJECT TO
    2)      A        ≤   60
    3)          C    ≤   50
    4)      A + 2 C  ≤  120
END
```

```
            OBJECTIVE FUNCTION VALUE

    1)           1620.000

    VARIABLE     VALUE              REDUCED COST
    A            60.000000          0.000000
    C            30.000000          0.000000

    ROW          SLACK              DUAL PRICES
    2)           0.000000           7.000000
    3)          20.000000           0.000000
    4)           0.000000          10.000000
```

Sensitivity Analysis of the Constraint Coefficients

Sensitivity analysis of the right hand side and objective function coefficients is somewhat easy to understand because the objective function value changes linearly with modest changes in these coefficients. Unfortunately the objective function value may change nonlinearly with changes in constraint coefficients. There is, however, a very simple formula for approximating the effect of small changes in constraint coefficients. Suppose we wish to examine the effect of decreasing by a small amount e the coefficient of variable j in row i of the LP. The formula is:

(improvement in objective value) $\approx$ (value of variable j) $\times$ (dual price of row i) $\times e$

Example: Consider the problem

```
MAX      20 A + 30 C
SUBJECT TO
    2)    A         ≤  65
    3)          C   ≤  50
    4)    A + 2 C   ≤ 115
END
```

With solution:

```
    LP OPTIMUM FOUND

        OBJECTIVE FUNCTION VALUE
   1)         2050.000

   VARIABLE      VALUE          REDUCED COST
   A          65.000000            0.000000
   C          25.000000            0.000000

   ROW          SLACK           DUAL PRICES
   2)         0.000000            5.000000
   3)        25.000000            0.000000
   4)         0.000000           15.000000
```

Now suppose that it is discovered that the coefficient of C in row 4 should have been 2.01 rather than 2. The formula implies that the objective value should be decreased by approximately $25 \times 15 \times .01 = 3.75$.

The actual objective value when this altered problem is solved is 2046.269, so the actual decrease in objective value is 3.731.

The formula for the effect of a small change in constraint coefficient makes sense. If the change in coefficient is small then the values of all the variables and dual prices should remain essentially unchanged. So the net effect of changing the 2 to a 2.01 in our problem is to effectively try to use $25 \times .01$ additional hours of labor. So there is effectively $25 \times .01$ fewer hours available. But we've seen that labor is worth \$15 per hour so the change in profits should be about $25 \times .01 \times 15$, which is in agreement with the original formula.

This type of sensitivity analysis gives some guidance in identifying which coefficient should be accurately estimated. If the product of variable j's value and row i's dual price is relatively large, then the coefficient in row i for variable j should be accurately estimated if an accurate estimate of total profit is desired.

The Dual LP Problem, or the Landlord and the Renter

You will probably discover as you formulate models for various problems that there are several rather different looking formulations for the same problem. Each formulation may be correct and may be based on taking a different perspective on the problem. An interesting mathematical fact is that for LP problems there are always two formulations (more accurately, a multiple of two) to a problem. One formulation is arbitrarily called the primal and the other is referred to as the dual. The two different formulations arise from two different perspectives that one can take towards a problem. One can think of these two perspectives as the landlord's and the renter's perspectives. We shall illustrate with the Enginola Company.

The Enginola Company has indicated that it is willing to entertain offers to rent time at an hourly rate on any of its three resources: (a) Astro production line capacity, (b) Cosmo production line capacity, and (c) labor. The Cooldot Company would like to rent all three of the resources to capacity. Denote by X, Y, Z the price per unit that Cooldot will offer for each of the three resources. Obviously, Cooldot wishes to

$$\text{Minimize} \quad 60X + 50Y + 120Z$$

Cooldot realizes that if either of Enginola's two products cost out attractively when costed out using rates $X, Y,$ and Z, then Enginola will prefer to produce the product rather than rent its resources. Thus, Cooldot must set its price offer sufficiently high so that each of Enginola's products is not profitable; i.e.,

(2) $\quad X \quad\;\; + Z \geq 20 \quad$ (Astro breakeven)
(3) $\quad\quad\quad Y + 2Z \geq 30 \quad$ (Cosmo breakeven)

The left hand side of the second constraint, for example, "costs out" a Cosmo. A Cosmo uses one unit of Cosmo line capacity, which has an opportunity cost of Y, and its uses two hours of labor, which has an opportunity cost of Z dollars per hour. Cooldot wants to set its offered prices high enough so that the opportunity cost of a Cosmo, $Y + 2Z$, is greater than or equal to a Cosmo's profit contribution, 30. We have just formulated the "Dual" LP of the Enginola problem.

We are now ready to introduce the idea of the dual problem. For any LP with m constraints and n variables, there is a closely related LP with n constraints and m variables. We have the choice of solving either one. The coefficients in a row of one appear in a column or variable of the other. Both effectively provide the same answer. For example, for the Enginola problem the two problems are:

The Primal Problem or First Problem

```
MAX     20 A + 30 C
SUBJECT TO
   2)     A          ≤    60
   3)          C     ≤    50
   4)     A +  2 C   ≤   120
END

        LP OPTIMUM FOUND AT STEP    3
              OBJECTIVE FUNCTION VALUE
        1)         2100.000

        VARIABLE       VALUE          REDUCED COST
           A         60.000000           0.000000
           C         30.000000           0.000000

        ROW          SLACK             DUAL PRICES
         2)         0.000000            5.000000
         3)        20.000000            0.000000
         4)         0.000000           15.000000
```

The Dual Problem or Second Problem

```
MIN     60 X + 50 Y + 120 Z
SUBJECT TO
   2)       X       +      Z  ≥   20
   3)              Y +    2 Z  ≥   30
END

     LP OPTIMUM FOUND AT STEP    2
         OBJECTIVE FUNCTION VALUE
   1)          2100.000

  VARIABLE        VALUE          REDUCED COST
     X          5.000000           0.000000
     Y          0.000000          20.000000
     Z         15.000000           0.000000

   ROW          SLACK            DUAL PRICES
   2)          0.000000          -60.000000
   3)          0.000000          -30.000000
```

Notice that the objective function values are the same for both Enginola and Cooldot. Except possibly for signs, the dual price values for one problem are the decision variable values for the other and the slack values for one are the reduced costs for the other. Why might the dual be of interest?

The computational difficulty of an LP is approximately proportional to $m^2 n$, where m = number of rows, n = number of columns. Thus, for the Enginola problem the difficulties are:

Primal   *Dual*
$3^2 \times 2 = 18$ vs. $2^2 \times 3 = 12$.

Note that the dual was solved in two iterations while the primal took three iterations.

Additionally, certain constraints, such as simple upper bounds, e.g., $x \leq 1$, are computationally less expensive than arbitrary constraints. If the dual contains only a small number of arbitrary constraints, then it may be easier to solve the dual even though it may have a large number of simple constraints.

The term "dual price" arose because the marginal price information to which this term is applied is a decision variable value in the dual problem.

We can summarize the idea of dual problems as follows. If the original or primal problem has a Maximize objective with $\leq$ constraints, then its dual has a Minimize objective with $\geq$ constraints. The dual has one variable for each constraint in the primal and one constraint for each variable in the primal. The objective coefficient of the kth variable of the dual is the right-hand side of the kth constraint in the primal. The right-hand side of constraint k in the dual is equal to the objective coefficient of variable k in the primal. Similarly, the coefficient in row i of variable j in the dual is equal to the coefficient in row j of variable i in the primal.

In order to convert all constraints in a problem to the same type so that one can apply the above, note the following two transformations:

1. the constraint $2x + 3y = 5$ is equivalent to the two constraints $2x + 3y \geq 5$ and $2x + 3y \leq 5$;
2. the constraint $2x + 3y \geq 5$ is equivalent to $-2x - 3y \leq -5$.

Example: Write the dual of the following problem:

$$\begin{aligned} \text{Maximize} \quad & 4x - 2y \\ \text{subject to} \quad & 2x + 6y \leq 12 \\ & 3x - 2y = 1 \\ & 4x + 2y \geq 5 \end{aligned}$$

Using transformations (1) and (2) above we can rewrite this as

$$\begin{aligned} \text{Maximize} \quad & 4x - 2y \\ \text{subject to} \quad & 2x + 6y \leq 12 \\ & 3x - 2y \leq 1 \\ & -3x + 2y \leq -1 \\ & -4x - 2y \leq -5 \end{aligned}$$

Introducing the dual variables r, s, t, and u corresponding to the four constraints, we can write the dual as

$$\begin{aligned} \text{Minimize} \quad & 12r + s - t - 5u \\ \text{subject to} \quad & 2r + 3s - 3t - 4u \geq 4 \\ & 6r - 2s + 2t - 2u \geq -2 \end{aligned}$$

Problems

1. The Enginola Company is considering introducing a new TV set, the Quasi. The expected profit contribution is $25 per unit. This unit is produced on the Astro line. Production of one Quasi requires 1.6 hours of labor. Using only the original solution below, determine whether it is worthwhile to produce any Quasis, assuming no change in labor and Astro line capacity.

   The original Enginola problem with solution is below.

   ```
   MAX      20 A + 30 C
   SUBJECT TO
       2)        A           ≤   60
       3)              C     ≤   50
       4)        A + 2 C     ≤  120
   END

   :go
        LP OPTIMUM FOUND AT STEP      3
              OBJECTIVE FUNCTION VALUE

       1)          2100.000

       VARIABLE        VALUE          REDUCED COST
         A           60.000000          0.000000
         C           30.000000          0.000000
   ```

ROW	SLACK	DUAL PRICES
2)	0.000000	5.000000
3)	20.000000	0.000000
4)	0.000000	15.000000

2. The Judson Corporation has acquired 100 lots on which it is about to build homes. Two styles of homes are to be built, the "Cape Cod" and the "Ranch Home." Judson wishes to build these 100 homes over the next nine months. During this time, Judson will have available 13,000 manhours of bricklayer labor and 12,000 hours of carpenter labor. Each Cape Cod house requires 200 manhours of carpentry labor and 50 manhours of bricklayer labor. Each Ranch Home requires 120 hours of bricklayer labor and 100 manhours of carpentry. The profit contribution of a Cape Cod is projected to be $5,100 while that of a Ranch Home is projected at $5,000. The problem when formulated as an LP and solved is as follows:

```
MAX      5100 C + 5000 R
SUBJECT TO
   2)       C +      R ≤    100
   3)   200 C +  100 R ≤  12000
   4)    50 C +  120 R ≤  13000
END
```

LP OPTIMUM FOUND

OBJECTIVE FUNCTION VALUE

1)   502000.000

VARIABLE	VALUE	REDUCED COST
C	20.000000	0.000000
R	80.000000	0.000000

ROW	SLACK	DUAL PRICES
2)	0.000000	4900.000000
3)	0.000000	1.000000
4)	2400.000000	0.000000

RANGES IN WHICH THE BASIS IS UNCHANGED

OBJ COEFFICIENT RANGES

VARIABLE	CURRENT COEF	ALLOWABLE INCREASE	ALLOWABLE DECREASE
C	5100.00000	4900.000000	100.000000
R	5000.00000	100.000000	2450.000000

RIGHTHAND SIDE RANGES

ROW	CURRENT RHS	ALLOWABLE INCREASE	ALLOWABLE DECREASE
2	100.00000	12.631579	40.000000
3	12000.00000	8000.00000	2000.000000
4	13000.00000	INFINITY	2400.000000

(a) A gentleman who owns 15 vacant lots adjacent to Judson's 100 lots needs some money quickly and offers to sell his 15 lots for $60,000. Should Judson buy? What assumptions are you making?

(b) One of Judson's salesmen who is a native of Massachusetts feels certain that he could sell the Cape Cods for $2,000 more each than Judson is currently projecting. Should Judson change its planned mix of homes? What assumptions are inherent in your recommendation?

3. Jack Mazzola, an industrial engineer with the Enginola Company, has discovered a way of reducing the amount of labor used in the manufacture of a Cosmo TV set from 2 hours per set to 1.92 hours per set by replacing one of the assembled portions of the set by an integrated circuit chip. It is not clear at the moment what this chip will cost. Based solely on the solution report below (i.e., do not solve another LP), answer the following questions:

   (a) Assuming that labor supply is fixed in the shortrun, what is the approximate value of one of these chips in the shortrun.

   (b) Give an estimate of the approximate increase in profit contribution per day of this change, exclusive of chip cost.

```
MAX       20 A + 30 C
SUBJECT TO
   2)     A            ≤   60
   3)           C      ≤   50
   4)     A + 2 C      ≤  120
```

OBJECTIVE FUNCTION VALUE

1)   2100.000000

VARIABLE	VALUE	REDUCED COST
A	60.000000	0.000000
C	30.000000	0.000000

ROW	SLACK	DUAL PRICES
2)	0.000000	5.000000
3)	20.000000	0.000000
4)	0.000000	15.000000

RIGHTHAND SIDE RANGES

ROW	CURRENT RHS	ALLOWABLE INCREASE	ALLOWABLE DECREASE
2	60.00000	60.000000	40.00000
3	50.00000	INFINITY	20.00000
4	120.00000	40.000000	60.00000

4. The Bug product has a profit contribution of $4100 per unit, requires 4 hours in the foundry department and 2 hours in the assembly department. The Superbug has a profit contribution of $5900 per unit, requires 2 hours in the foundry and 3 hours in assembly. The availabilities in foundry and assembly are 160 hours and 180 hours respectively. Each hour used in each of foundry and assembly costs $90 and $60 respectively. The following is an LP formulation for maximizing profit contribution in this situation.

```
MAX      4100 B + 5900 S - 90 F - 60 A
SUBJECT TO
   2)    4 B + 2 S - F        =    0
   3)    2 B + 3 S      - A   =    0
   4)                F        ≤  160
   5)                    A    ≤  180
END
```

On the next page is the solution report printed on a typewriter which skipped some sections of the report.

OBJECTIVE FUNCTION VALUE

332400.000

VARIABLE	VALUE	REDUCED COST
B	0.000000	
S	60.000000	0.000000
F	120.000000	
A	180.000000	0.000000

ROW	SLACK	DUAL PRICES
2)	0.000000	90.000000
3)	0.000000	1906.666700
4)	40.000000	
5)	0.000000	1846.666700

Fill in the missing parts, using just the available information, i.e., without resolving the LP.

5. Suppose the capacities in the Enginola problem were: Astro line capacity = 45; Labor capacity = 100.

   (a) Allow the labor capacity to vary from 0 to 200 and plot:
   - Dual price of labor as a function of labor capacity.
   - Total profit as a function of labor capacity.

   (b) Allow the profit contribution/unit of Astros to vary from 0 to 50 and plot:
   - Number of Astros to produce as a funciton of profit/unit.
   - Total profit as a function of profit/unit.

6. Write the dual problem of the following problem:

   Minimize $12q + 5r + 3s$

   subject to $q + 2r + 4s \geq 6$

   $5q + 6r - 7s \leq 5$

   $8q - 9r + 11s = 10$

4

The Model Formulation Process

The Overall Process

In using any kind of analytical or modeling approach for attacking a problem there are five major steps:

1. Understanding the real problem;
2. Formulating a model of the problem;
3. Gathering and generating the input data for the model, e.g., per unit costs to be used, etc.;
4. Solving or running the model;
5. Implementing the solution.

In general there is a certain amount of iteration over the five, e.g., one does not develop the most appropriate model the first time around. Of the above, the easiest is the solving of the model on the computer. This is not because it is intrinsically easiest but rather because it is the most susceptible to mathematical analysis. Steps 1, 3 and 5 are, if not the most difficult, at least the most time consuming. Success with these steps depends to a large extent upon being very familiar with the organization involved, e.g, knowing who knows what the real production rate is on the punch press machine. Step 2 requires the most skill.

Formulating good LP models is an art bordering on a science. It is an art because it always involves approximation of the real world. The artistic ability is to develop simple models which are nevertheless good approximations to reality. We shall see that there are a number of classes of problems which are well approximated by LP models.

With all of the above comments in mind we will devote most of the discussion to the formulation of LP models; stating what universal truths seem to apply for steps (3) and (5); and giving an introduction to the mechanics of step (4).

Approaches to Model Formulation

We take two approaches to formulating models:

1. Constructive approach,
2. Template approach.

The constructive approach is the more fundamental and general, however, students with less analytic skill may prefer the template approach. The latter is essentially a "model in a can" approach. In this approach, examples of standard applications are illustrated in substantial detail. If you have a problem that closely resembles one of these "template" models you may be able to make modest changes to the template model to adjust it to your situation. The advantage of this approach is that the user may not need much technical background if there is a template model that closely fits the real situation.

Constructive Approach to Model Formulation

The constructive approach is a set of guidelines for constructing a model from the ground up. This approach requires somewhat more analytical skill but the rules apply to any situation you are trying to model. The odds are low that you will find a template model that exactly matches your real situation. In practice, it is combination of these two approaches that get used.

In order to illustrate these ideas, consider the following situation.

Example

Deglo Toys have been manufacturing a line of precision building blocks for children for a number of years. Deglo is about to introduce a new line of glow-in-the-dark building blocks and thus would like to deplete its old-technology inventories before introducing the new line. The old inventories consist of 19,900 4-dimple blocks and 29,700 8-dimple blocks. These inventories can be sold off in the form of two different kits: The Master Builder, and the Empire Builder. The objective is to maximize the revenue from the sale of these two kits. The Master kit sells for $16.95 while the Empire kit sells for $24.95. The Master kit is composed of thirty 4-dimple blocks plus forty 8-dimple blocks. The Empire kit is composed of forty 4-dimple blocks plus eighty-five 8-dimple blocks. What is an appropriate model of this problem?

We suggest the following three step approach in constructing a model:

1. Identify and define the decision variables. Defining a decision variable includes specifying the units in which it is measured, e.g., tons, hours, etc.
2. Specify and define the objective function, including the units in which it is measured.
3. Specify the constraints, including the units in which each is measured.

It is useful to do each of the above in words first.

Defining Decision Variables

The following questions are often helpful in identifying the decision variables (the answers are even more helpful):

(a) What should be the format of a report which gives a solution to this problem? (For example, the numbers that constitute an answer are: the amount to produce of each product; and the amount to use of each ingredient.) The cells in this report are the decision variables.

(b) What is the *objective*? Among useable solutions, how would I measure preference/goodness, e.g., profit?

(c) What are the *constraints*? A way to think about constraints is as follows: given a purported solution to a problem, what numeric checks would you perform to check the validity of the solution.

The majority of the constraints in most problems can be thought of as *sources-equals-uses* constraints. Another common kind of constraint is the *definitional* or *accounting* constraint. Sometimes the distinction between the two is arbitrary. Consider a production setting where we: (a) start with some beginning inventory of some commodity, (b) produce some of that commodity, (c) sell some of the commodity, and (d) some commodity is left in ending inventory. From the sources-equals-uses perspective we might write:

beginning inventory + production = sales + ending inventory.

From the definitional perspective if we are thinking of how ending inventory is defined, we would write:

ending inventory = (beginning inventory + production) − sales.

The two perspectives are in fact mathematically equivalent.

Formulating Our Example Problem

This process for our example problem would be as follows:

(a) The essential decision variables are:

M = number of master builder kits to assemble and
E = number of empire builder kits to assemble.

(b) The objective function is to maximize sales revenue, i.e.,

Maximize $16.95M + 24.95E$

(c) If someone gave as a proposed solution, i.e., values for M and E, we would check its feasibility by checking that

(i) number of 4-dimple blocks used $\leq$ 19,900, and
(ii) number of 8-dimple blocks used $\leq$ 29,700.

Symbolically, this is:

$30M + 40E \leq 19{,}900$
$40M + 85E \leq 29{,}700$

In LINDO form the formulation is:

```
MAX     16.95 M + 24.95 E
SUBJECT TO
   2)    30 M + 40 E ≤    19900
   3)    40 M + 85 E ≤    29700
END
```

with solution

```
              OBJECTIVE FUNCTION VALUE

        1)         11478.5000

     VARIABLE        VALUE           REDUCED COST
        M          530.000000           0.000000
        E          100.000000           0.000000

      ROW      SLACK OR SURPLUS      DUAL PRICES
       2)            .000000           0.466053
       3)            .000000           0.074210
```

Thus, we should produce 530 Master Builders and 100 Empire Builders.

The Template Approach

You may feel more comfortable and confident in your ability to structure problems if you have a classification of "template" problems to which you can relate new problems which you encounter. For LP problems we will present a classification of about a half dozen different categories of problems. In practice a large real problem that you encounter will not fit exactly a single template model but might require a combination of two or more of the categories. The classification is not exhaustive, so you may encounter or develop LP models which seem to fit none of these templates.

Product Mix Problems

These are the problem types typically encountered in introductory LP texts. There are a collection of products which can be sold and a finite set of resources from which these products are made. Associated with each product is a profit contribution rate and a set of resource usage rates. The objective is to find that mix of products (amount of each product) which maximizes profit, subject to not using more resources than are available.

These problems are always of the form "Maximize profit subject to less than or equal to constraints."

Covering, Staffing, and Cutting Stock Problems

These problems are complementary (in the jargon they're called dual) to product mix problems in that their form is "Minimize cost subject to greater than or equal to constraints." The variables in this case might correspond to the number of people hired for various shifts during the day. The constraints arise from the fact that the mix of variables chosen must "cover" the requirements during each hour of the day.

Blending Problems

Problems of this type arise in the food, feed, metals and oil refining industries. The problem is to mix or blend a collection of raw materials, e.g., different types of meats, cereal grains, crude oils, etc., into a finished product, e.g., sausage, dog food, or gasoline, so that the cost per unit of the finished product is minimized, subject to satisfying certain quality constraints, e.g., percent protein $\geqq$ 15 percent.

Multiperiod Planning Problems

This is perhaps the most important class of models. These models take into account the fact that the decisions made in this period partially determine which decision are allowable in future periods. The submodel which is used each period may be a product mix problem, a blending problem, or some other type. These submodels are usually tied together by means of inventory variables, e.g., the inventory of raw materials, finished goods, cash, loans outstanding, etc., which are carried from one period to the next.

Network, Distribution, and PERT/CPM Models

Network LP models warrant specific attention for two reasons, (a) they have a particularly simple form which makes them easy to describe as a graph or network, and (b) specialized and efficient solution procedures exist for solving them. They therefore tend to be easier to explain and comprehend. Network LP's frequently arise from problems of product distribution. Any enterprise producing a product at several locations and distributing it to many customers may find a network LP relevant. Large problems of this type may be solved rapidly by the specialized procedures.

One of the simplest network problems is that of finding the shortest route from one point in a network to another. A slight variation on this problem, that of finding the longest route, happens to be an important component of the project management tools PERT (Program Evaluation and Review Technique) and CPM (Critical Path Method).

Close cousins of network models are input/output and vertically integrated models. General Motors, for example, makes engines in certain plants; these engines might be sold directly to customers such as industrial equipment manufacturers or the engines may be used in GM's own cars and trucks. Such a company is said to be vertically integrated. In a vertically integrated model there is usually one constraint for each type of intermediate product; the constraint mathematically enforces the basic law of physics that the amount used of an intermediate product by various processes cannot exceed the amount of this product produced by other processes. There is usually one decision variable for each type of process available.

If one expands one's perspective to the entire economy, then the models considered tend to be similar to the input/output model popularized by Wassily Leontief (1951). Each industry is described by the input products required and the output products produced. These outputs may in turn be inputs to other industries. The problem is to determine appropriate levels at which each industry should be operated in order to satisfy specific consumption requirements.

Multiperiod Planning Problems with Random Elements

One of the fundamental assumptions of LP is that all input data are known with certainty. There are situations, however, where certain key data are highly random. For example, when an oil company makes its fuel oil production decisions for the coming winter, the demand for that fuel oil is very much a random variable. If, however, the distribution probabilities for all the random variables are known, then there is a modeling technique for converting a problem which is an LP except for the random elements into an equivalent, although possibly larger, deterministic LP.

Game Theory Models

Game Theory is concerned with the analysis of competitive situations. In its simplest form a game consists of two players, each of whom has available to him a set of possible decisions. Each player must choose a strategy for making a decision in ignorance of the other player's choice. Some time after a decision is made each player receives a payoff which depends on which combination of decisions was made. The problem of determining each player's optimal strategy can be formulated as a linear program.

Applications in Statistical Estimation

Much of statistical theory is concerned with making a prediction based on a set of data. Usually the prediction is chosen so that the prediction in some sense minimizes the squared forecast error. Very roughly speaking, a datum which is twice as far from the mean gets four times the weight in constructing the prediction. If one wishes to use other measures of goodness, such as mean absolute error or maximum absolute error instead of squared error in determining the prediction, then LP provides a powerful tool.

Not all problems you encounter will fit into one of the above categories. Many problems will be combinations of the above types. For example, in a multiperiod planning problem the single period subproblems may be product mix or blending problems.

Common Errors in Formulating Models

When you develop a first formulation of some real problem, the formulation may contain errors or bugs. These errors will fall into the following categories:

1. Simple typographical errors;
2. Fundamental errors of formulation;
3. Errors of approximation.

The first two types of errors are easy to correct once they are identified. In principle, Type 1 errors are easy to identify because they are clerical in nature. In a large model, however, tracking them down may be a difficult search problem. Type 2 errors are more fundamental because they involve a misunderstanding of either the real problem or of the nature of LP models. Type 3 errors are more subtle. Generally an LP model of a real situation involves some approximation; e.g., many products are aggregated together into a single macro-product, or the days of a week are lumped together, or costs which are not quite proportional to volume are nevertheless treated as linear. Avoiding Type 3 errors require a skill of identifying which approximations can be tolerated.

Let us first discuss Type 1 errors. The major problem is detecting them. Many LP codes contain facilities for aiding detection of such gross errors. One of these facilities is the PICTURE command. It prints out an abbreviated picture of the coefficients in the formulation in table form. To illustrate its use, study the following formulation. It contains a typographical error which can be identified without understanding the formulation.

```
MIN    5 A0 + 6 A1 + 2 A2 + 4 B0 + 3 B1 + 7 B2
     + 2 C0 + 9 C1 + 8 C2
SUBJECT TO    2)     A0 + A1 + A2 ≤      8
       3)      B0 + B1 + B2 ≤     9
       4)      C0 + C1 + C2 ≤     6
       5)      A0 + B0 + C0 =     6
       6)      A1 + B1 + C1 =     5
       7)      A2 + B2 + C2 =     9
END
```

The PICTURE of the problem looks as follows: (The variable names are printed vertically across the top.)

```
     A A A B B B C C C
     0 1 2 0 1 2 0 1 2 0

1:   5 6 2 4 3 7 2 9 8     MIN
2:   1 1 1                 ≤ 8
3:         1 1 1           ≤ 9
4:               1 1 1     ≤ 6
5:   1     1         1   = 6
6:     1     1         1 = 5
7:       1     1         1 = 9
```

Just from observing the pattern of 1s in the constraints one can detect an aberration. The 1 appearing in the last column seems out of place. It should be in the fourth from last column. What seems to have happened is that the variable name C0 (zero) was misspelled as CO (letter O) in row 5. The computer is very literal and considers these as two separate variables. When the error is corrected, the picture looks as follows:

```
     A A A B B B C C C
     0 1 2 0 1 2 0 1 2

1:   5 6 2 4 3 7 2 9 8     MIN
2:   1 1 1                 ≤ 8
3:         1 1 1           ≤ 9
4:               1 1 1     ≤ 6
5:   1     1     1       = 6
6:     1     1     1     = 5
7:       1     1     1   = 9
```

Additionally, if the user is fortunate, Type 1 errors will manifest themselves by causing solutions which are obviously incorrect.

Errors of formulation are more difficult to discuss because they are of many forms. The kinds of errors made by a novice can frequently be exposed by doing what we call dimensional analysis. Anyone who has taken a physics or chemistry course would know it as "checking your units." Let us illustrate by considering an example.

A distributor of toys is analyzing his strategy for assembling Tinkertoy sets for the upcoming holiday season. He assembles two kinds of sets. The "Big" set is composed of 60 sticks and 30 connectors, while the "Tot" set is composed of 30 sticks and 20 connectors. An important factor is that for this season he has a supply of only 60,000 connectors and 93,000 sticks. He will be able to sell all that he assembles of either set.

The profit contributions are $5.5 and $3.5 per set, respectively, for Big and Tot. How much should he sell of each set to maximize profit?

He developed the following formulation. Define:

B = number of Big sets to assemble;

T = number of Tot sets to assemble;

S = number of sticks actually used;

C = number of connectors actually used.

```
MAX     5.5 B + 3.5 T
SUBJECT TO
        B - 30C - 60S = 0
        T - 20C - 30S = 0
        C          ≤ 60,000
        S          ≤ 93,000
```

Notice that the first two constraints are equivalent to:

$B = 30C + 60S$

$T = 20C + 30S$

Do you agree with the formulation? If so, you should analyze its solution below:

```
     OBJECTIVE FUNCTION VALUE
  1)     54555000.

 VARIABLE        VALUE           REDUCED COST
    B         7380000.000000        0.000000
    T         3990000.000000        0.000000
    C           60000.000000        0.000000
    S           93000.000000        0.000000

   ROW          SLACK            DUAL PRICES
    2)         0.0000000           5.500000
    3)         0.0000000           3.500000
    4)         0.0000000         235.000000
    5)         0.0000000         435.000000
```

There is a hint that the formulation is incorrect because the solution is able to magically produce almost four million Tot sets from only 100,000 sticks.

The mistake which was made is a very common one for newcomers to LP, namely trying to describe the features of an activity by a constraint. A constraint can always be thought of as a statement that the usages of some item must be less than or equal to the sources of the item. The last two constraints have this characteristic, but the first two do not.

If one analyzes the dimensions of the components of the first two constraints, one can see that there is trouble. The dimensions (or "units") for the first constraint are:

Term	Units
B	Big sets
30 C	30 [connectors/(Big set)] × connectors
60 S	60 [sticks/(Big Set)] × sticks

Clearly, they have different units but if you are adding items together they must have the same units. Everyone is born with the knowledge that you cannot add apples and oranges. The units of all components of a constraint must be the same.

If one first formulates a problem in words and then converts it to the algebraic form in LINDO, one frequently avoids the above kind of error. In words we wish to:

> Maximize profit contribution
>
> Subject to: Usage of connectors $\leq$ sources of connectors
> Usage of sticks $\leq$ sources of sticks

Converted to algebraic form in LINDO, it is:

```
MAX     5.5 B + 3.5 T
SUBJECT TO
   2)    30 B + 20 T ≤ 60000
   3)    60 B + 30 T ≤ 93000
END
```

The units of the components of the constraint $30B + 20T + \leq 60{,}000$ are:

Term	Units
30 B	30 [connectors/(Big set)] × (Big set) = 30 connectors
20 T	20 [connectors/(Tot set)] × (Tot set) = 20 connectors
60,000	60,000 connectors available

Thus, all the terms have the same units of "connectors." Solving the problem we obtain the sensible solution:

```
        OBJECTIVE FUNCTION VALUE
   1)      10550.00

   VARIABLE      VALUE           REDUCED COST
       B       200.000000          0.000000
       T      2700.000000          0.000000

      ROW       SLACK            DUAL PRICES
       2)      0.000000           0.150000
       3)      0.000000           0.016667
```

The Nonsimultaneity Error

It must be stressed that all the constraints in an LP formulation apply simultaneously. A combination of activity levels must be found which simultaneously satisfy all the constraints. The constraints do not apply in an either/or fashion, even though we might like them to be so interpreted. As an example, suppose that we denote by B the batch size for a production run of footwear. A reasonable policy might be that if a production run is made of at least two dozen units should be made. Thus, B will be either zero or some number greater than or equal to 24. There might be at temptation to state this policy by writing the two constraints:

$B \leq 0$

$B \geq 24.$

The desire is that exactly one of these constraints be satisfied. If these two constraints are part of an LP formulation, the computer will reject such a formulation with a curt remark to the effect that no feasible solution exists. There is not a unique value for B which is simultaneously less than or equal to zero and greater than or equal to 24.

If such either/or constraints are important, then one must resort to integer programming. Such formulations will be discussed in a later section.

Problems

1. The Tiny Timber Company wants to best utilize the wood resources in one of its forest regions. Within this region, there is a sawmill and a plywood mill; thus timber can be converted to lumber or plywood.

   Producing a marketable mix of 1000 board feet of lumber products requires 1000 board feet of spruce and 4000 board feet of Douglas fir. Producing 1000 square feet of plywood requires 2000 board feet of spruce and 4000 board feet of Douglas fir. This region has available 32,000 board feet of spruce and 72,000 board feet of Douglas fir.

   Sales commitments require that at least 5000 board feet of lumber and 12,000 square feet of plywood be produced during the planning period. The profit contributions are $45 per 1000 board feet of lumber products and $60 per 1000 square feet of plywood. Let L be the amount (in 1000 board feet) of lumber produced and P be the amount (in 1000 square feet) of plywood produced. Express the problem as a linear programming model.

2. Shmuzzles, Inc is a struggling toy company that hopes to make it big this year. It makes three fundamental toys: the Shmacrobat, the Shlameleon, and the Jig Saw Shmuzzle. Shmuzzles is trying to unload its current inventories through airline in-flight magazines by packaging these three toys in two different size kits, the Dilettante Shmuzzler kit and the Advanced Shmuzzler kit. The Dilettante sells for $29.95 while the Advanced sells for $39.95. The compositions of these two kits are:

   Dilettante = 6 Shmacrobats plus 10 Shlameleons plus 1 Jig Saw
   Advanced = 8 Shmacrobats plus 18 Shlameleons plus 2 Jig Saws

   Current inventory levels are: 6,000 Shmacrobats, 15,000 Shlameleons and 1,500 Jig Saws. Formulate a model for helping Shmuzzles, Inc. maximize its profits.

3. Ely Provisioners produces, packages and distributes freeze-dried food for the camping and outdoor sportsman market. Ely is ready to introduce a new line of products based on a new drying technology which produces a higher quality, tastier food. The basic ingredients of the current (about to be discontinued) line are dried fruits, dried meat and dried vegetables. There are two products in the current line: the "Weekender" and the "Expedition Pak." The respective profit contribution per package of these two products are $1.25 and $2.75. The makeup of a "Weekender" package equals 3 ounces of dried fruit, plus 7 ounces of dried meat, plus 2 ounces of dried vegetables. The makeup of the "Expedition" package is 5 ounces of dried fruit, plus 18 ounces of dried meat, plus 5 ounces of dried vegetables. Ely would like to deplete its inventories of "old technology" fruit, meat and vegetables before

introducing the new line. The current inventories of these products are respectively 10,000 ounces, 25,000 ounces, and 12,000 ounces. Because there is as yet no "new technology" food on the market, Ely is confident it can sell its current inventories via the "Weekender" and "Expedition Pak" products without lowering prices. Formulate an LP which should be useful in telling Ely how many "Weekender" and "Expedition Pak" packages should be mixed so as to maximize profits from its current inventories.

4. Quart Industries produces a variety of bottled food products at its various plants. At its Americus plant it produces two products, peanut butter and apple butter. There are two scarce resources at this plant: packaging capacity and sterilization capacity. Both have a capacity of 40 hours per week. Production of 1000 jars of peanut butter requires 4 hours of sterilizer time and 5 hours of packaging time, while 1000 jars of apple butter requires 6 hours of sterilizer time and 4 hours of packaging time. The profit contributions per 1000 jars for the two products are $1100 and $1300 respectively. Apple butter preparation requires a boil-down process which is best done in batches of at least 5000 jars. Thus apple butter production during the week should be either 0 or 5000 or more jars. How much should be produced this week of each product?

5

Product Mix Problems

Introduction

Product mix problems are conceptually the easiest to comprehend. The Astro/Cosmo problem considered earlier is an example. Although product mix problems are seldom encountered in their simple textbook form in practice, they very frequently constitute important components of larger problems such as multiperiod planning models.

The features of a product mix problem are that there are a collection of products that compete for a finite set of resources. If there are m resources and n products, then the so-called "technology" is charateried by a table with m rows and n columns of technologic coefficients. The coefficient in row i, column j, is the number of units of resource i used by each unit of product j. The numbers in a row of the table are simply the coefficients of a constraint in the LP. In simple product mix problems these coefficients are nonnegative. Additionally, associated with each product is a profit contribution per unit, and associated with each resource is an availability. The objective is to find how much to produce of each product, i.e., the mix, so as to maximize profits subject to not using more of each resource than is available.

The following product mix example will illustrate not only product mix LP formulations but also: (1) representation of nonlinear profit functions and (2) the fact that most problems have alternative correct LP formulations. Two people may develop ostensibly different formulations of the same problem but both may be correct.

Example

A certain plant can manufacture five different products in any combination. Each product requires time on each of three machines in the following manner (figures in minutes/unit):

	Machine		
Product	1	2	3
A	12	8	5
B	7	9	10
C	8	4	7
D	10	0	3
E	7	11	2

Each machine is available 128 hours per week.

Products A, B, and C are purely competitive, and any amounts made may be sold at respective prices of $5, $4, and $5. The first 20 units of D and E produced per week can be sold at $4 each, but all made in excess of 20 can only be sold at $3 each. Variable labor costs are $4 per hour for machines 1 and 2 and $3 per hour for machine 3. Material costs are $2 for products A and C and $1 for products B, D, and E. You wish to maximize profit to the firm.

The principal complication is that the profit contributions of products D and E are not linear. You may find the following device useful for eliminating this complication. Define two additional products called D_2 and E_2 which sell for $3 per unit. What upper limits must then be placed on the sale of the original products D and E? The decision variables and their profit contributions are as follows:

Decision Variables	Definition	Profit Contribution per Unit
A	Number of units of A produced per week	$5 - 2 = \$3$
B	Number of units of B produced per week	$4 - 1 = \$3$
C	Number of units of C produced per week	$5 - 2 = \$3$
D	Number of units of D not in excess of 20 produced/week	$\$3$
D_2	Number of units of D produced in excess of 20 per week*	$\$2$
E	Number of units of E not in excess of 20 produced/week	$\$3$
E_2	Number of units of E produced in excess of 20	$\$2$
M_1	Hours of machine 1 used per week	$-\$4$
M_2	Hours of machine 2 used per week	$-\$4$
M_3	Hours of machine 3 used per week	$-\$3$

*Total production of product D is $D + D_2$.

In words we want to:

> Maximize   Revenues minus costs
>
> Subject to   Minutes used equals minutes run on each machine,
> At most 20 units each can be produced of products D and E,
> Each machine can be run at most 128 hours

More precisely, the formulation in LINDO is:

```
OBJECTIVE FUNCTION
! Maximize revenue minus costs;
   MAX 3 A + 3 B + 3 C + 3 D + 2 D2 + 3 E + 2 E2 - 4 M1 - 4 M2 - 3 M3
SUBJECT TO
! Machine time used = machine time made available;
     2)    12 A +  7 B + 8 C + 10 D + 10 D2 +  7 E +  7 E2 - 60 M1 = 0
     3)     8 A +  9 B + 4 C +                11 E + 11 E2 - 60 M2 = 0
     4)     5 A + 10 B + 7 C +  3 D +  3 D2 +  2 E +  2 E2 - 60 M3 = 0
! Product limits;
     5)     D ≤ 20
     6)     E ≤ 20
```

```
! Machine availability;
   7)     M1 ≤ 128
   8)     M2 ≤ 128
   9)     M3 ≤ 128
END
```

The first three constraints have the units of "minutes" and specify the hours of machine time as a function of the number of units produced. The next two constraints (5 and 6) place upper limits on the number of high profit units of D and E which may be sold. The final three constraints put upper limits on the amount of machine time which may be used, and have the units of "hours."

Constraint 2 can first be written as

$$\frac{12A + 7B + 8C + 10D + 10D_2 + 7E + 7E_2}{60} = M_1$$

Multiplying by 60 and bringing M_1 to the left gives Constraint 2. The solution is:

```
              OBJECTIVE FUNCTION VALUE
         1)         1777.62

   VARIABLE        VALUE           REDUCED COST
      A           0.00000             1.35833
      B           0.00000             0.18542
      C         942.49999             0.00000
      D           0.00000             0.12917
      D2          0.00000             1.12917
      E          20.00000             0.00000
      E2          0.00000             0.91875
      M1        128.00000             0.00000
      M2         66.49998             0.00000
      M3        110.62501             0.00000

      ROW          SLACK            DUAL PRICES
      2)          0.00000             0.297917
      3)          0.00000             0.0666667
      4)          0.00000             0.05000
      5)         20.00000             0.00000
      6)          0.00000             0.0812497
      7)          0.00000            13.87500
      8)         61.50000             0.00000
      9)         17.37500             0.00000
```

The solution is really quite simple. The units of E which can be sold at the higher price are the most profitable and we make as many as possible (20). After that, product C is most profitable. We make as much as possible until we run out of capacity on machine 1.

This problem is a good example of one for which it is very easy to develop alternative formulations of the same problem. These alternative formulations are all correct but may have more or fewer constraints and variables. For example, the constraint:

$$8A + 9B + 4C + 11E + 11E_2 - 60M_2 = 0$$

can be rewritten as:

$$M_2 = (8A + 9B + 4C + 11E + 11E_2)/60.$$

The expression on the right can be substituted for M_2 wherever M_2 appears in the formulation. Because the expression on the right will always be nonnegative, the nonnegativity constraint on M_2 will automatically be satisfied. Thus, M_2 and the above constraint can be eliminated from the problem if we are willing to do a bit of arithmetic. When similar arguments are applied to M_1 and M_3 and the implied divisions are performed one obtains the formulation:

```
OBJECTIVE FUNCTION
MAX      1.416667 A + 1.433333 B + 1.85 C + 2.183334 D
       + 1.183333 D2 + 1.7 E + .7 E2
SUBJECT TO
  2)   12 A +  7 B + 8 C + 10 D + 10 D2 +  7 E +  7 E2 ≤ 7680
  3)    8 A +  9 B + 4 C +                11 E + 11 E2 ≤ 7680
  4)    5 A + 10 B + 7 C +  3 D +  3 D2 +  2 E +  2 E2 ≤ 7680
  5)    D ≤ 20
  6)    E ≤ 20
END
```

This looks more like a standard product mix formulation. All the constraints are capacity constraints of some sort. Notice that the solution to this formulation is really the same as that of the previous formulation.

```
           OBJECTIVE FUNCTION VALUE
    1)          1777.62

    VARIABLE        VALUE         REDUCED COST
    A              0.00000            1.35833
    B              0.00000            0.18542
    C            942.49999            0.00000
    D              0.00000            0.12917
    D2             0.00000            1.12917
    E             20.00000            0.00000
    E2             0.00000            0.91875

    ROW            SLACK           DUAL PRICE
    2)             0.00000            0.23125
    3)          3690.00000            0.00000
    4)          1042.50000            0.00000
    5)            20.00000            0.00000
    6)             0.00000            0.08125
```

The lazy formulator might give the first formulation while the person who enjoys doing arithmetic might give the second formulation.

Process Selection Product Mix Problems

A not uncommon feature of product mix models is that two or more distinct variables in the LP formulation may actually correspond to alternate methods for producing the same product. In this case, the LP is being used not only to discover how much should be produced of a product but also to select the best process for producing a product.

A second feature that almost always appears with product mix problems is a requirement that a certain amount of a product be produced. This condition takes the problem out of the realm of simple product mix, but let us nevertheless consider a problem with the above two features.

The American Metal Fabricating Company (AMFC) produces various products from steel bars. One of the initial steps is a shaping operation that is performed by rolling machines. There are three machines available for this purpose, the B_3, B_4, and B_5. Their features are given by the following table:

Machine	Speed in Feet per Minute	Allowable Raw Material Thickness in Inches	Available Hours per Week	Labor Cost Per Hour Operating
B_3	150	3/16 to 3/8	35	$10
B_4	100	5/16 to 1/2	35	$15
B_5	75	3/8 to 3/4	35	$17

This kind of combination of capabilities is not uncommon; machines which process larger material operate at a slower speed.

This week there are three products which must be produced. AMFC must produce at least 218,000 feet of 1/4" material, 114,000 feet 3/8" material, and 111,000 feet of 1/2" material. The profit contributions per foot excluding labor for these three products are 0.017, 0.019, and 0.02. These prices apply to all production, e.g., any in excess of the required production. The shipping department has a capacity limit of 600,000 feet per week, regardless of the thickness.

What are the decision variables and constraints for this problem? The decision variables require some thought. There is only one way of producing 1/4" material, three ways of producing 3/8", and two ways of producing 1/8" material, three ways of producing 3/8", and two ways of producing 1/2" Thus, you will want to have at least the following decision variables. For numerical convenience we measure length in thousands of feet.

B_{34} = 1,000's of feet of 1/4" produced on B_3
B_{38} = 1,000's of feet of 3/8" produced on B_3,
B_{48} = 1,000's of feet of 3/8" produced on B_4,
B_{58} = 1,000's of feet of 3/8" produced on B_5,
B_{42} = 1,000's of feet of 1/2" produced on B_4,
B_{52} = 1,000's of feet of 1/2" produced on B_5.

For the objective function we must have the profit contribution including labor costs. When this is done we obtain:

Variable	Profit Contribution per Foot
B_{34}	0.01589
B_{38}	0.01789
B_{48}	0.01650
B_{58}	0.01522
B_{42}	0.0175
B_{52}	0.01622

Clearly, there will be four constraints corresponding to AMFC's three scarce machine resources and its shipping department capacity. There should be three more constraints due to the production requirements in the three products. For the machine capacity constraints we want the number of hours required for 1,000 feet processed. For machine B_3 this figure is $1,000/(60 \text{ min./hr.}) \times (150 \text{ ft./min.}) = 0.111111$ hours per 1,000 ft. Similar figures for B_4 and B_5 are 0.16667 hours per 1,000 ft. and 0.22222 hours per 1,000 ft.

The formulation can now be written:

Maximize $\quad 15.89B_{34} + 17.89B_{38} + 16.5B_{48} + 15.22B_{58} + 17.5B_{42} + 16.22B_{52}$

subject to
$$\left. \begin{array}{l} 0.11111B_{34} + 0.11111B_{38} \leq 35 \\ 0.16667B_{48} + 0.16667B_{42} \leq 35 \\ 0.22222B_{58} + 0.22222B_{52} \leq 35 \end{array} \right\} \text{Machine capacities in hours}$$

$$B_{34} + B_{38} + B_{48} + B_{58} + B_{42} + B_{52} \leq 600 \quad \left\{ \begin{array}{l} \text{Shipping capacity} \\ \text{in 1,000's of feet} \end{array} \right.$$

$$\left. \begin{array}{l} B_{34} \geq 218 \\ B_{38} + B_{48} + B_{58} \geq 114 \\ B_{42} + B_{52} \geq 111 \end{array} \right\} \text{Production requirements in 1,000's of feet}$$

Without the last three constraints the problem is a simple product mix problem.

It is a worthwhile exercise to attempt to deduce the optimal solution just from cost arguments. The ¼″ product can be produced on only machine B_3, so that we know that B_{34} is at least 218. The ⅜″ product is more profitable than the ¼″ on machine B_3; therefore we can conclude that $B_{34} = 218$ and B_{38} will take up the slack. The ½″ and the ⅜″ product can be produced on either B_4 or B_5. In either case, the ½″ is more profitable per foot, so as we know that B_{48} and B_{58} will be no greater than absolutely necessary. The question is: What is "absolutely necessary"? The ⅜″ is more profitably run on B_3 than on B_4 or B_5, so it follows that we will satisfy the ⅜″ demand from B_3 and, if insufficient, the remainder from B_4 and then from B_5. Specifically, we proceed as follows:

Set $B_{34} = 218$.

This leaves a slack of $35 - 218 \times 0.11111 = 10.78$ hours on B_3. This is sufficient to produce 97,000 feet of ⅜″, so we conclude that:

$$B_{38} = 97.$$

The remainder of the ⅜″ demand must be made up from either machine B_4 or B_5. It would appear that it should be done on machine B_4 because the profit contribution for ⅜″ is higher on B_4 than B_5. Note, however, that ½″ is also more profitable on B_4 than B_5 by exactly the same amount. Thus, we are indifferent. Let us arbitrarily use machine B_4 to fill the rest of ⅜″ demand; thus:

$$B_{48} = 17.$$

Now any remaining capacity will be used to produce ½″ product. There are $35 - 17 \times 0.16667 = 32.16667$ hours of capacity on B_4. At this point we should worry about shipping capacity. We still have capacity for $600 - 218 - 97 - 17 = 268$ in 1,000's of feet. B_{42} is more profitable than B_{52}, so we will make it as large as possible, namely, $32.16667/0.16667 = 193$, so:

$$B_{42} = 193.$$

The remaining shipping capacity is 268 − 193 = 75, so:

$B_{52} = 75$.

Any LP is in theory solvable by similar manual economic arguments, but the calculations could be very tedious and prone to errors of both arithmetic and logic. If we take the lazy route and solve it with LINDO we get the same solution as our manual one:

```
         OBJECTIVE FUNCTION VALUE

  1)            10073.85

  VARIABLE        VALUE          REDUCED COST
    B34         218.000000         0.000000
    B38          97.000000         0.000000
    B48          17.000000         0.000000
    B58           0.000000         0.000000
    B42         193.000000         0.000000
    B52          75.000000         0.000000

    ROW          SLACK           DUAL PRICES
     2)         0.000000          24.029995
     3)         0.000000           7.680000
     4)        18.333338           0.000000
     5)         0.000000          16.220000
     6)         0.000000          -2.999999
     7)         0.000000          -1.000000
     8)       157.000000           0.000000

         RANGES IN WHICH THE BASIS IS UNCHANGED
                COST COEFFICIENT RANGES
  VARIABLE      CURRENT        ALLOWABLE        ALLOWABLE
                 COEF          INCREASE         DECREASE
    B34        15.890000        2.999999        INFINITY
    B38        17.890000        INFINITY         2.669999
    B48        16.500000        1.000000         0.000000
    B58        15.220000        0.000000        INFINITY
    B42        17.500000        0.000000         1.000000
    B52        16.220000        1.280000         0.000000

                  RIGHTHAND SIDE RANGES
    ROW         CURRENT         ALLOWABLE       ALLOWABLE
                 RHS            INCREASE        DECREASE
     2         35.000000         1.888888        9.166672
     3         35.000000        12.499996       13.750003
     4         35.000000         INFINITY       18.333338
     5        600.000000        82.500023       74.999978
     6        218.000000        97.000006       16.999994
     7        114.000000       157.000055       16.999994
     8        111.000000       157.000000        INFINITY
```

Notice that the B58 is zero but its reduced cost is also zero, meaning that B58 could be increased (and B48 decreased) without affecting profits. This is consistent with our earlier statement that we were indifferent between using B48 and B58 to satisfy the ⅜″ demand.

Problems

1. Consider a manufacturer that produces two products, Widgets and Frisbees. Each product is made from the two raw materials, Polyester and Polypropylene. The amounts required by each of the two products are given by the following table:

Widgets	Frisbees	Raw Material
3	5	Polyester
6	2	Polypropylene

   Because of import quotas the company is able to obtain only 12 units and 10 units of Polyester and Polypropylene, respectively, this month. The company is interested in planning its production for the next month. For this purpose it is important to know the profit contribution of each product. These contributions have been found to be $3 and $4 for Widgets and Frisbees, respectively. What should be the amounts of Widgets and Frisbees produced next month?

2. The Otto Maddick Machine Tool Company produces two products, muffler bearings and torque amplifiers. One muffler bearing requires ⅛ hour of assembly labor, 0.25 hours in the stamping department and 9 square feet of sheet steel. Each torque amplifier requires ⅓ hour in both assembly and stamping and uses 6 square feet of sheet steel. Current weekly capacities in the two departments are 400 hours of assembly labor and 350 hours of stamping capacity. Sheet steel costs 15 cents per square foot. Muffler bearings can be sold for $8.00 each. Torque amplifiers can be sold for $7 each. Unused capacity in either department cannot be laid off or otherwise fruitfully used.

   (a) Formulate the LP useful in maximizing the weekly profit contribution.

   (b) It has just been discovered that two important considerations had not been included.

      (i) Up to 100 hours of overtime assembly labor can be scheduled at a cost of $5 per hour.

      (ii) The sheet metal supplier only charges 12 cents per square foot for weekly usage in excess of 5000 square feet.

   Which of the above considerations could easily be incorporated in the LP model and how? If one or both cannot be easily incorporated, indicate how you might nevertheless solve the problem.

3. Review the solution to the 5 product, 3 machine product mix problem introduced at the beginning of the chapter.

   (a) What is the marginal value of an additional hour of capacity on each of the machines?

   (b) The current selling price of product A is $5. What would the price have to be before we would produce any A?

   (c) It would be profitable to sell more product E at $4 if you could, but it is not profitable to sell E at $3 per unit even though you can. What is the breakeven price at which you would be indifferent about selling any more E?

(d) It is possible to gain additional capacity by renting by the hour automatic versions of each of the three machines; that is, they require no labor. What is the maximum hourly rate you would be willing to pay to rent each of the three types of automatic machines?

4. The Aviston Electronics company manufactures motors for toys and small appliances. The marketing department is predicting sales of 6,100 units of the Dynamonster motor in the next quarter. This is a new high and meeting this demand will test Aviston's production capacities. A Dynamonster is assembled from three components: a shaft, base, and cage. It is clear that some of these components will have to be purchased from outside suppliers because of limited in-house capacity. The variable in-house production cost per unit is compared with the outside purchase cost in the table below:

Component	Outside Cost	Inside Cost
Shaft	1.21	.81
Base	2.50	2.30
Cage	1.95	1.45

Aviston's plant consists of three departments. The time requirements in hours of each component in each department if manufactured in-house are summarized in the following table. The hours available for Dynamonster production are listed in the last row.

Component	Cutting Department	Shaping Department	Fabrication Department
Shaft	0.04	0.06	0.04
Base	0.08	0.02	0.05
Cage	0.07	0.09	0.06
Capacity	820	820	820

(a) What are the decision variables?
(b) Formulate the appropriate LP.
(c) How many units of each component should be purchased outside?

5. Buster Sod's younger brother, Marky Dee, operates three ranches in Texas. The acreage and irrigation water available for the three farms are shown below:

Farm	Acreage	Water Available (acre feet)
1	400	1500
2	600	2000
3	300	900

Three crops can be grown; however, the maximum acreage which can be grown of each crop is limited by the amount of appropriate harvesting equipment available. The three crops are described below:

Crop	Total Harvesting Capacity (in acres)	Water Requirements (in acre-feet/acre)	Expected Profit (in $/acre)
Milo	700	6	400
Cotton	800	4	300
Wheat	300	2	100

Any combination of crops may be grown on a farm.

(a) What are the decision variables?

(b) Formulate the LP.

6. Review the formulation and solution of the American Metal Fabricating process selection/product mix problem in this chapter. Based on the solution report.

(a) What is the value of an additional hour of capacity on the B_4 machine?

(b) What is the value of an additional 2 hours of capacity on the B_3 machine?

(c) By how much would one have to raise the profit contribution/1,000 ft. of ¼" material before it would be worth producing more of it?

(d) If the speed of machine B_5 could be doubled without changing the labor cost, what would it be worth per week? (Note labor on B_5 is $17/hour.)

6

Covering, Staffing, & Cutting Stock Models

Introduction

Covering problems tend to arise in service industries. The crucial feature is that there are a set of requirements to be covered. We have available to us various activities each of which helps cover some but not all the activities. The qualitative form of a covering problem is:

> Choose a minimum cost set of activities
> Subject to
> > The chosen activities cover all of our requirements.

Some examples of activities and requirement types for various problems are listed below:

Problem	*Requirements*	*Activities*
Staff scheduling	Number of people required on duty each period of the day or week.	Work or shift patterns. Each pattern covers some but not all periods.
Routing	Each customer must be visited.	Various feasible trips, each of which covers some but not all customers.
Cutting of bulk raw material stock, e.g., paper, wood, steel, textiles	Units required of each finished good size.	Cutting patterns for cutting raw material into various finished good size. Each pattern produces some but not every finished good.

In the next sections we look at several of these problems in more detail.

Staff Covering Problems

One part of the management of most service facilities is the scheduling or staffing of personnel, that is, deciding how many people to use on what shifts. This problem exists in the staffing of a telephone company information operators department, a toll plaza, a large hospital and, in general, any facility which must provide service to the public.

The solution process consists of at least three parts: (1) Develop good forecasts of the number of personnel required during each hour of the day or each day of the week during the scheduling period; (2) Identify the possible shift patterns which can be worked based on the personnel available and work agreements and regulations. A particular shift pattern might be to work Tuesday through Saturday and then be off two days; (3) Determine how many people should work each shift pattern so that costs are minimized and the total number of people on duty during each time period satisfy the requirements determined in (1). All three of these steps are difficult. LP can help in solving step 3.

We will illustrate a staff covering LP with a problem which is based on an approach first developed at the New York Port Authority many years ago for analyzing the staffing of toll booths.

Northeast Tollway Staffing Problems

The Northeast Tollway out of Chicago has a toll plaza with the following staffing demands during each 24-hour period:

Hours	Collectors Needed
12 A.M. to 6 A.M.	2
6 A.M. to 10 A.M.	8
10 A.M. to Noon	4
Noon to 4 P.M.	3
4 P.M. to 6 P.M.	6
6 P.M. to 10 P.M.	5
10 P.M. to 12 Midnight	3

Each collector works four hours, is off one hour, and then works another four hours. A collector can be started at any hour. Assuming the objective is to minimize the number of collectors hired, formulate the appropriate LP.

Formulation and Solution

Define the decision variables:

x_1 = number of collectors to start work at 12 midnight
x_2 = number of collectors to start work at 1 A.M.
.
.
.
x_{24} = number of collectors to start work at 11 P.M.

There will be one constraint for each hour of the day, stating that the number of collectors on at that hour be the number required for that hour. The objective will be to minimize the number of collectors hired for the 24-hour period. More formally:

Minimize $x_1 + x_2 + x_3 + \cdots + x_{24}$

subject to

$$x_1 + x_{24} + x_{23} + x_{22} + x_{20} + x_{19} + x_{18} + x_{17} \geq 2 \quad \text{(12 Midnight to 1 A.M)}$$
$$x_2 + x_1 + x_{24} + x_{23} + x_{21} + x_{20} + x_{19} + x_{18} \geq 2 \quad \text{(1 A.M to 2 A.M)}$$
$$\vdots$$
$$x_7 + x_6 + x_5 + x_4 + x_2 + x_1 + x_{24} + x_{23} \geq 8 \quad \text{(6 A.M to 7 A.M)}$$
$$\vdots$$
$$x_{24} + x_{23} + x_{22} + x_{21} + x_{19} + x_{18} + x_{17} + x_{16} \geq 3 \quad \text{(11 P.M. to 12 Midnight)}$$

It may help to see the effect of the one hour off in the middle of the shift by looking at the picture of equation coefficients:

Constraint Row	x_1	x_2	x_3	x_4	x_5	x_6	x_7	x_8	x_9	...	x_{17}	x_{18}	x_{19}	x_{20}	x_{21}	x_{22}	x_{23}	x_{24}	RHS
12 M. to 1 A.M.	1										1	1	1	1		1	1	1	≥ 2
1 A.M. to 2 A.M.	1	1										1	1	1	1		1	1	≥ 2
2 A.M. to 3 A.M.	1	1	1										1	1	1	1		1	≥ 2
3 A.M. to 4 A.M.	1	1	1	1										1	1	1	1		≥ 2
4 A.M. to 5 A.M.		1	1	1	1										1	1	1	1	≥ 2
5 A.M. to 6 A.M.	1		1	1	1	1										1	1	1	≥ 2
6 A.M. to 7 A.M.	1	1		1	1	1	1										1	1	≥ 8
7 A.M. to 8 A.M.	1	1	1		1	1	1	1										1	≥ 8
8 A.M. to 9 A.M.	1	1	1	1		1	1	1	1										≥ 8
9 A.M. to 10 A.M.		1	1	1	1		1	1	1										≥ 8
10 A.M. to 11 A.M.			1	1	1	1		1	1										≥ 4
11 A.M. to 12 A.M.				1	1	1	1		1										≥ 4
12 P.M. to 1 P.M.					1	1	1	1											≥ 3
1 P.M. to 2 P.M.						1	1	1	1										≥ 3
2 P.M. to 3 P.M.							1	1	1										≥ 3
								1	1										≥ 3
					etc.									etc.					

When it is solved we get an objective value of 15.75 with the following variables nonzero.

$x_2 = 5$ $x_5 = 0.75$ $x_{11} = 1$ $x_{16} = 1$
$x_3 = 0.75$ $x_6 = 0.75$ $x_{14} = 1$ $x_{17} = 1$
$x_4 = 0.75$ $x_7 = 0.75$ $x_{15} = 2$ $x_{18} = 1$

The answer is not directly useful because some of the numbers are fractional. The value of 15.75 implies that we must hire at least 16 collectors. It is very easy to round this solution so that we get an integer answer which hires 16, namely, set $x_3 = x_4 = x_6 = x_7 = 1$ and $x_5 = 0$.

If the shifts or duty periods contain no or very few breaks, then the LP solution will tend to be integer without resorting to integer programming.

Cutting Stock and Pattern Selection

In industries such as the paper and textiles a product is manufactured in large economically produced sizes at the outset. These sizes are cut into a variety of smaller more usable sizes as the product nears the consumer. The determination of how to cut the larger sizes into smaller sizes at minimal cost is known as the cutting stock problem. As an example of the so-called one-dimensional cutting stock problem, suppose that machine design dictates that material be manufactured in 72-inch widths. There are a variety of ways of cutting these smaller widths from the 72-inch width, two of which are shown in Figure 6.1.

Pattern 1 has 2 inches of edge waste $[72 - 2 \times (-35) = 2]$, while pattern 2 has only 1 inch of edge waste $(72 - 2 \times 18 - 35 = 1)$. Pattern 2, however, is not very useful unless the number of linear feet of 18-inch material required is about twice the number of linear feet of 35-inch material required. Thus, a compromise must be struck between edge waste and end waste.

The solution of a cutting stock problem can be partitioned into the 3-step procedure discussed earlier: (1) Forecast the needs for the final widths; (2) Construct a large collection of possible patterns for cutting the large manufactured width(s) into the smaller widths; (3) Determine how much of each pattern should be run of each of the patterns in (2) so that the requirements in (1) are satisfied at minimum cost. LP can be used in performing step (3).

Many large paper manufacturing firms have LP based procedures for solving the cutting stock problem. Actual cutting stock problems may involve a variety of cost factors in addition to the edge waste/end waste compromise. The usefulness of the LP based procedure depends upon the importance of these other factors. The following example illustrates the fundamental features of the cutting stock problem with no complicating cost factors.

Example: Cooldot Cutting Stock Problem

The Cooldot Appliance Company produces a wide range of large household appliances such as refrigerators and stoves. A significant portion of the raw material cost is due to the purchase of sheet steel. Currently, sheet steel is purchased in coils in three different widths: 72 inches, 48 inches and 36 inches. In the manufacturing process eight different widths of sheet steel are required: 60, 56, 42, 38, 34, 24, 15 and 10 inches. All uses require the same quality and thickness of steel.

A continuing problem is trim waste. For example, one way of cutting a 72-inch width coil is to slit it into one 38-inch width coil and two 15-inch width coils. There will then be a 4-inch coil of trim waste which must be scrapped.

The prices per linear foot of the three different raw material widths are 15 cents for the 36-inch width, 19 cents for the 48-inch width and 28 cents for the 72-inch width. Simple arithmetic reveals that the costs per inch $\times$ foot of the three widths are $15/36 = 0.416667$ cents/(inch $\times$ foot), 0.395833 cents/(inch $\times$ foot), and 0.388889 cents/(inch $\times$ foot) for the 36", 48" and 72" widths, respectively.

The coils may be slit in any feasible solution. The possible efficient ways of slitting the three raw material widths are tabulated in Table 6.1.

Figure 6.1

Example Cutting Patterns

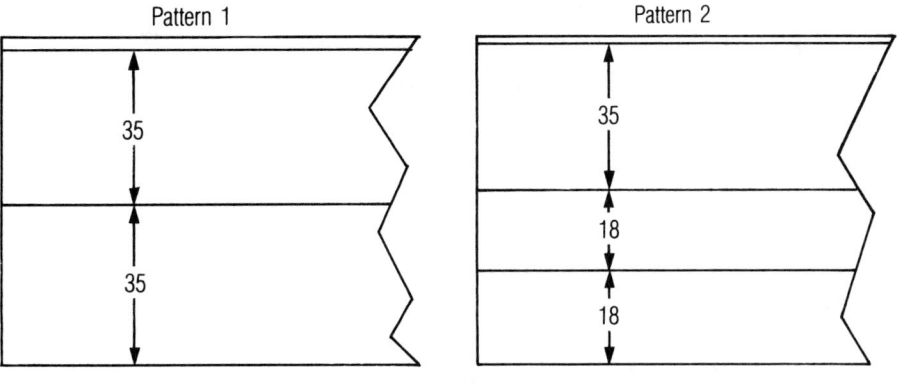

For example, pattern C_4 corresponds to cutting a 72-inch width coil into one 24-inch width and four 10-inch widths with 8 inches left over as trim waste.

The lengths of the various widths required in this planning period are:

Width	60"	56"	42"	38"	34"	24"	15"	10"
Number of feet required	500	400	300	450	350	100	800	1000

The raw material availabilities this planning period are 1600 ft. of the 72-inch coils and 10,000 ft. each of the 48-inch and 36-inch widths.

Formulate a model for determining the number of feet of each pattern which should be cut so as to minimize costs while satisfying the requirements or the various widths. Can you predict beforehand the amount of 36-inch material used?

Formulation and Solution of Cooldot

Let the symbols $A_1, A_2, \ldots, E_4$ appearing in Table 6.1 denote the number of feet to cut of the corresponding pattern.

For accounting purposes it is useful to additionally define:

T_1 = number feet cut of 72-inch patterns,
T_2 = number feet cut of 48-inch patterns,
T_3 = number feet cut of 36-inch patterns,
W_1 = inch × feet of trim waste from 72-inch patterns,
W_2 = inch × feet of trim waste from 48-inch patterns,
W_3 = inch × feet of trim waste from 36-inch patterns,
X_1 = number of feet of excess cut of the 60-inch width,
X_2 = number of feet of excess cut of the 56-inch width,
.
.
.
X_8 = number of feet of excess cut of the 10 inch width.

Table 6.1

Cutting Patterns for Raw Material

Pattern Designation	Number to Cut of the Required Width								Waste in Inches
	60"	56"	42"	38"	34"	24"	15"	10"	
72-Inch Raw Material									
A_1	1	0	0	0	0	0	0	1	2
A_2	0	1	0	0	0	0	1	0	1
A_3	0	1	0	0	0	0	0	1	6
A_4	0	0	1	0	0	1	0	0	6
A_5	0	0	1	0	0	0	2	0	0
A_6	0	0	1	0	0	0	1	1	5
A_7	0	0	1	0	0	0	0	3	0
A_8	0	0	0	1	1	0	0	0	0
A_9	0	0	0	1	0	1	0	1	0
B_0	0	0	0	1	0	0	2	0	4
B_1	0	0	0	1	0	0	1	1	9
B_2	0	0	0	1	0	0	0	3	4
B_3	0	0	0	0	2	0	0	0	4
B_4	0	0	0	0	1	1	0	1	4
B_5	0	0	0	0	1	0	2	0	8
B_6	0	0	0	0	1	0	1	2	3
B_7	0	0	0	0	1	0	0	3	8
B_8	0	0	0	0	0	3	0	0	0
B_9	0	0	0	0	0	2	1	0	9
C_0	0	0	0	0	0	2	0	2	4
C_1	0	0	0	0	0	1	3	0	3
C_2	0	0	0	0	0	1	2	1	8
C_3	0	0	0	0	0	1	1	3	3
C_4	0	0	0	0	0	1	0	4	8
C_5	0	0	0	0	0	0	4	1	2
C_6	0	0	0	0	0	0	3	2	7
C_7	0	0	0	0	0	0	2	4	2
C_8	0	0	0	0	0	0	1	5	7
C_9	0	0	0	0	0	0	0	7	2
48-Inch Raw Material									
D_0	0	0	1	0	0	0	0	0	6
D_1	0	0	0	1	0	0	0	1	0
D_2	0	0	0	0	1	0	0	1	4
D_3	0	0	0	0	0	2	0	0	0
D_4	0	0	0	0	0	1	1	0	9
D_5	0	0	0	0	0	1	0	2	4
D_6	0	0	0	0	0	0	3	0	3
D_7	0	0	0	0	0	0	2	1	8
D_8	0	0	0	0	0	0	1	3	3
D_9	0	0	0	0	0	0	0	4	8
36-Inch Raw Material									
E_0	0	0	0	0	1	0	0	0	2
E_1	0	0	0	0	0	1	0	1	2
E_2	0	0	0	0	0	0	2	0	6
E_3	0	0	0	0	0	0	1	2	1
E_4	0	0	0	0	0	0	0	3	6

It may not be immediately clear what the objective function should be. One might be tempted to calculate a cost of trim waste per foot for each pattern cut and then minimize the total trim waste cost, *i.e.*,

$$\text{Minimize} \quad 0.3888891 W_1 + 0.395833 W_2 + 0.416667 W_3$$

However, such an objective can easily lead to solutions which have very little trim waste but very high cost. This is possible in particular when the cost per square inch is not the same for all raw material widths. A more reasonable objective is to minimize the total cost, that is,

$$\text{Minimize} \quad 28 T_1 + 19 T_2 + 15 T_3.$$

The constraints in either case are:

The supply constraints

(2) $T_1 \leq 1600$
(3) $T_2 \leq 10000$
(4) $T_3 \leq 10000$

Totaling up usage of each of the three raw materials

(5) $T_1 - A_1 - A_2 - A_3 - A_4 - A_5 - A_6 - A_7 - A_8 - A_9$
$- B_0 - B_1 - B_2 - B_3 - B_4 - B_5 - B_6 - B_7 - B_8 - B_9$
$- C_0 - C_1 - C_2 - C_3 - C_4 - C_5 - C_6 - C_7 - C_8 - C_9 = 0$
(6) $T_2 - D_0 - D_1 - D_2 - D_3 - D_4 - D_5 - D_6 - D_7 - D_8 - D_9 = 0$
(7) $T_3 - E_0 - E_1 - E_2 - E_3 - E_4 = 0$

Compute edge waste for each raw material

(8) $-2A_1 - A_2 - 6A_3 - 6A_4 - 5A_6 - 4B_0 - 9B_1 - 4B_2$
$- 4B_3 - 4B_4 - 8B_5 - 3B_6 - 8B_7 - 9B_9 - 4C_0 - 3C_1$
$- 8C_2 - 3C_3 - 8C_4 - 2C_5 - 7C_6 - 2C_7 - 7C_8 - 2C_9 + W_1 = 0$
(9) $- 6D_0 - 4D_2 - 9D_4 - 4D_5 - 3D_6 - 8D_7 - 3D_8 - 8D_9 + W_2 = 0$
(10) $- 2E_0 - 2E_1 - 6E_2 - E_3 - 6E_4 + W_3 = 0$

The demand requirements

(11) $A_1 - X_1 = 500$
(12) $A_2 + A_3 - X_2 = 400$
(13) $A_4 + A_5 + A_6 + A_7 + D_0 - X_3 = 300$
(14) $A_8 + A_9 + B_0 + B_1 + B_2 + D_1 - X_4 = 450$
(15) $A_8 + 2B_3 + B_4 + B_5 + B_6 + B_7 + D_2 + E_0 - X_5 = 350$
(16) $A_4 + A_9 + B_4 + 3B_8 + 2B_9 + 2C_0 + C_1 + C_2 + C_3$
$+ 4C_5 + 3C_6 + 2C_7 + C_8 + D_4 + 3D_6 + 2D_7 + D_8 = 100$
(17) $A_2 + 2A_5 + A_6 + 2B_0 + B_1 + 2B_5 + B_6 + B_9 + 3C_1$
$+ 2C_2 + C_3 + 4C_5 + 3C_6 + 2C_7 + C_8 + D_4 + 3D_6$
$+ 2D_7 + D_8 + 2E_2 + E_3 - X_7 = 800$
(18) $A_1 + A_3 + A_6 + 3A_7 + A_9 + B_1 + 3B_2 + B_4 + 2B_6 + 3B_7$
$+ 2C_0 + C_2 + 3C_3 + 4C_4 + C_5 + 2C_6 + 4C_7 + 5C_8 + 7C_9 + D_1$
$+ D_2 + 2D_5 + D_7 + 3D_8 + 4D_9 + E_1 + 2E_3 + 3E_4 - X_8 = 1000$

Table 6.2
Cutting Stock Solutions

Nonzero Patterns	Feet to Cut	
	Trim Waste Minimizing Solution	Total Cost Minimizing Solution
A_1	500	500
A_2	400	400
A_5	200	171.42865
A_7	135.5	128.57135
A_8	362.5	350
A_9	0	3.57139
B_8	0	32.1429
C_5	0	14.286
D_1	87.5	96.4286
D_3	50	0
Trim Waste Cost	$5.44	$5.55
Total Cost	$474.13	$466.32
X_3	37.5	0
X_5	12.5	0
T_1	1600	1600
T_2	137.5	96.429
T_3	0	0

Constraints (2) through (4) enforce the availability limits of the three raw material widths. Constraints (5) through (7) define variables T_1, T_2, and T_3. Constraints (11) through (18) force the eight demand requirements to be fulfilled. For example, (11) forces the amount of 60-inch width produced to at least equal 500 feet, while (18) enforces a similar requirement for the 10-inch width.

The two different solutions obtained under the two different objectives are compared in Table 6.2.

The key difference in the solutions is that the "Min trim waste" solution uses more of the 48-inch width raw material and cuts it in a way so that the edge waste is minimized. More material of the 42-inch width and the 34-inch width is cut than is needed, however, because the objective function does not count this as waste.

Both solutions involve fractional answers, but the fractional parts are so small relative to the run lengths that in a practical problem most people would be willing to disregard this fact, e.g., by rounding up to the nearest integer if possible.

Generalizations of the Cutting Stock Problem

In large cutting stock problems it may be unrealistic to generate all possible patterns. There is an efficient method for generating only the patterns which have a very high probability of appearing in the optimal solution. It is beyond the scope of this section to discuss this procedure; see Chapter 16 for more details.

In complex cutting stock problems the following additional cost considerations may be important:

1. *Fixed cost of setting up a particular pattern*. This cost consists of lost machine time, labor, etc. This motivates solutions with few patterns.

2. *Value of overage or end waste.* For example, there may be some demand next period for the excess cut this period.
3. *Underage cost.* In some industries you may supply plus or minus, say 5% of a specified quantity. The cost of producing the least allowable amount is measured in foregone profits.
4. *Machine usage cost.* The cost of operating a machine is usually fairly independent of the material being run. This motivates solutions which cut up wide raw material widths.
5. *Material specific products.* It may be impossible to run two different products in the same pattern if they require different materials, e.g., different thickness, quickly, surface finish or type.
6. *Upgrading costs.* It may be possible to reduce setup, edge waste and end waste costs by substituting a higher grade material than required for a particular demand width.
7. *Order splitting costs.* If a demand width is produced from several patterns, then there will be consolidation costs due to bringing the different lots of the output together for shipment.
8. *Stock width change costs.* A setup involving only a pattern change usually takes less time than one involving both a pattern change and a raw material width change. This motivates solutions which use few raw material widths.
9. *Minimum allowable edge waste.* For some materials a very narrow ribbon of edge waste may be very difficult to handle. Therefore, one may wish to restrict attention to patterns which have either zero edge waste or edge waste which exceeds some minimum such as two centimeters.

The most troublesome complications are high fixed setup costs, order-splitting costs and stock width change costs. If they are important, then one will usually be forced to use some ad hoc, manual solution procedure. An LP solution may provide some insight into which solutions are likely to be good, but other methods must be used to determine a final workable solution.

Two-Dimensional Cutting Stock Problems

The one-dimensional cutting stock problem is concerned with the cutting of a raw material which is in coils. The basic idea still applies if the raw material comes in sheets and the problem is to cut these sheets into smaller sheets. For example, suppose that plywood is supplied in 48 by 96 inch rectangular sheets and the end product demand is for sheets with dimensions in inches of 36×50, 24×36, 20×60, and 18×30. Once you have enumerated all possible patterns for cutting a 48×96 sheet into combinations of the 4 smaller sheets, then the problem is exactly as before.

Crew Scheduling Problems

Managing the aircraft and crews of a large airline involves complex scheduling problems. Paying special attention to these scheduling problems can be rewarding. The yearly cost of operating an airliner far exceeds the one time cost of a respectable computer, so devoting some computing resources to make more efficient use of airplanes is attractive. One small part of an airline's scheduling problems is discussed below.

Large airlines face a staffing problem known as the crew scheduling problem. The requirements to be covered are the crew requirements of the flights which the line is committed to fly during the next scheduling period, e.g., one month. A specific crew during its working day typically fly a number of flights, usually, but not necessarily on the same aircraft. The problem is to determine which flights should comprise the day's work of a crew.

The approach taken by a number of airlines is similar to the approach described for staffing problems: (1) Identify the demand requirements, i.e., the flights to be covered; (2) Generate a large number of feasible collections of flights that one crew could cover in a work period; (3) Select a minimum cost subset of the collections generated in (2) so that the cost is minimized and every flight is contained in exactly one of the selected collections.

LP can be used for step (3). Until recently, most large airlines used computerized ad hoc or heuristic procedures for solving (3) because the resulting LP tends to be large and difficult to solve. Marsten, Muller and Killion (1979), however, describe an LP based solution procedure which has been used very successfully by Flying Tiger Airlines. Flying Tiger has a smaller fleet than the big passenger carriers, so the resulting LP can be economically solved and gives markedly lower cost solutions than the ad hoc, heuristic methods. These optimizing methods are now being extended to large airlines.

A drastically simplified version of the crew scheduling problem is given in the following example. This example has only ten flights to be covered. By contrast in 1990, United Airlines had close to 2000 flights per day to be covered.

Example: Sayre-Priors Crew Scheduling

The Sayre-Priors Airline and Stormdoor Company is a small diversified company that operates the following set of scheduled flights:

Flight Number	*Origin*	*Destination*	*Time of Day*
101	Chicago	Los Angeles	Afternoon
410	New York	Chicago	Afternoon
220	New York	Miami	Night
17	Miami	Chicago	Morning
7	Los Angeles	Chicago	Afternoon
13	Chicago	New York	Night
11	Miami	New York	Morning
19	Chicago	Miami	Night
23	Los Angeles	Miami	Night
3	Miami	Los Angeles	Afternoon

The flight schedule is illustrated graphically in Figure 6.2.

The Flight Operations Staff would like to set up a low cost crew assignment schedule. The basic problem is to determine the next flight, if any, that a crew operates after it completes one flight. A basic concept needed in understanding this problem is that of a tour. The characteristics of a tour are as follows:

Figure 6.2
Flight Schedule

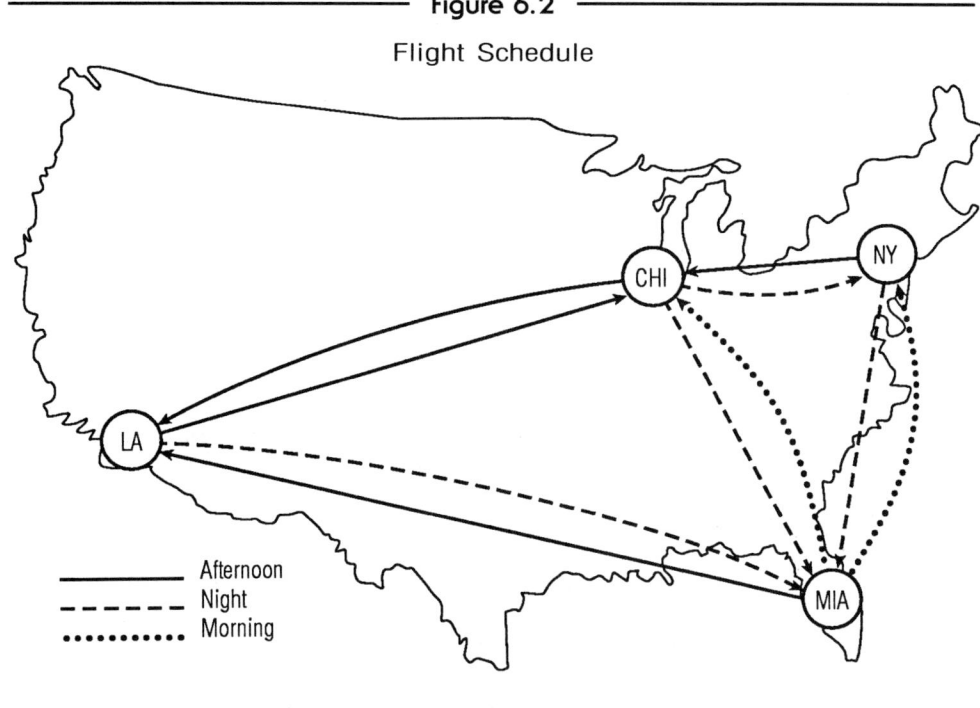

- A tour consists of from 1 to 3 connecting flights.
- A tour has a cost of $2,000 if it terminates in its city of origin.
- A tour which requires "deadheading," i.e., terminates in a city other than the origin city, costs $3,000.

In practice the calculation of the cost of a tour is substantially more complicated than above. In airline parlance a tour is frequently called a "pairing" or a "rotation." The following are examples of acceptable tours:

Tour	Cost
17, 101, 23	$2,000
220, 17, 101	$3,000
410, 13	$2,000

Solving the Sayre/Priors Crew Scheduling Problem

The first thing to do for this small problem is to enumerate all feasible tours. We do not consider a collection of flights which involve an intermediate layover a tour. There are 10 one-flight tours, 14 two-flight tours, and either 37 or 41 three-flight tours depending upon whether one distinguishes the origin city on a nondeadheading tour. These tours are indicated in Table 6.3.

Table 6.3
List of Tours

One-Flight Tours		Cost	Two-Flight Tours		Cost	Three-Flight Tours		Cost
1.	101	$3000	11.	101, 23	$3,000	25.	101, 23, 17	$2,000
2.	410	$3000	12.	410, 13	$2,000	26.	101, 23, 11	$3,000
3.	220	$3000	13.	410, 19	$3,000	27.	410, 19, 17	$3,000
4.	17	$3000	14.	220, 17	$3,000	28.	410, 19, 11	$2,000
5.	7	$3000	15.	220, 11	$2,000	29.	220, 17, 101	$3,000
6.	13	$3000	16.	17, 101	$3,000	30.	220, 11, 410	$3,000
7.	11	$3000	17.	7, 13	$3,000	25.	17, 101, 23	$2,000
8.	19	$3000	18.	7, 19	$3,000	31.	7, 19, 17	$3,000
9.	23	$3000	19.	11, 410	$3,000	32.	7, 19, 11	$3,000
10.	3	$3000	20.	19, 17	$2,000	33.	11, 417, 13	$3,000
			21.	19, 11	$3,000	28.	11, 410, 19	$2,000
			22.	23, 17	$3,000	34.	19, 17, 101	$3,000
			23.	23, 11	$3,000	28.	19, 11, 410	$2,000
			24.	3, 23	$2,000	25.	23, 17, 101	$2,000
						35.	23, 11, 410	$3,000
						36.	3, 23, 17	$3,000
						37.	3, 23, 11	$3,000

Define the decision variables:

$$T_i = \begin{cases} 1 \text{ if tour } i \text{ is used} \\ 0 \text{ if tour } i \text{ is not used} \end{cases} \text{ for } i = 1, 2, \ldots, 37.$$

We do not distinguish the city of origin on nondeadheading three-flight tours. The formulation is (measuring cost in $1,000s):

```
MIN     3 T1  + 3 T2  + 3 T3  + 3 T4  + 3 T5  + 3 T6  + 3 T7  + 3 T8  + 3 T9
      + 3 T10 + 3 T11 + 2 T12 + 3 T13 + 3 T14 + 2 T15 + 3 T16 + 3 T17 + 3 T18
      + 3 T19 + 2 T20 + 3 T21 + 3 T22 + 3 T23 + 2 T24 + 2 T25 + 3 T26 + 2 T27
      + 2 T28 + 3 T29 + 3 T30 + 3 T31 + 3 T32 + 3 T33 + 3 T34 + 3 T35 + 3 T36
      + 3 T37
SUBJECT TO
 F101)   T1  + T11 + T16 + T25 + T26 + T29 + T34 =  1
 F410)   T2  + T12 + T13 + T19 + T27 + T28 + T30 + T33 + T35 =  1
 F220)   T3  + T14 + T15 + T29 + T30 =  1
  F17)   T4  + T16 + T20 + T22 + T25 + T27 + T29 + T31 + T34 + T36 =  1
  F17)   T5  + T17 + T18 + T31 + T32 =  1
  F13)   T6  + T12 + T17 + T33 =  1
  F11)   T7  + T15 + T19 + T21 + T23 + T26 + T28 + T30 + T32 + T33
       + T35 + T37 =  1
  F19)   T8  + T13 + T18 + T20 + T21 + T27 + T28 + T31 + T32 + T34 =  1
  F23)   T9  + T11 + T22 + T23 + T24 + T25 + T26 + T35 + T36 + T37 =  1
   F3)   T10 + T24 + T36 + T37 =  1
END
```

A PICTURE of the coefficients gives a better feel for the structure of the problem and is given below. The first constraint, for example, forces exactly one of the tours which includes flight 101 to be chosen.

```
:PICTURE
                                        T T T T T T T T T T T T T T T T T T T T T T T T T T T
                      T T T T T T T T T 1 1 1 1 1 1 1 1 1 1 2 2 2 2 2 2 2 2 2 2 3 3 3 3 3 3 3
                      1 2 3 4 5 6 7 8 9 0 1 2 3 4 5 6 7 8 9 0 1 2 3 4 5 6 7 8 9 0 1 2 3 4 5 6 7
  1:  3 3 3 3 3 3 3 3 3 3 2 3 3 2 3 3 3 3 2 3 3 3 2 2 3 3 2 3 3 3 3 3 3 3 3 3 3  MIN
  2:  1                 1             1             1 1         1             1              = 1
  3:    1                   1 1             1                 1 1   1       1 1              = 1
  4:      1                     1 1                             1 1                          = 1
  5:        1                             1   1                                              = 1
  6:          1                             1 1                             1 1              = 1
  7:            1           1               1                                 1              = 1
  8:              1               1         1 1 1           1 1 1 1 1         1 1          = 1
  9:                1           1             1 1 1                     1 1     1 1          = 1
 10:                  1 1         1                       1 1 1 1 1               1 1 1      = 1
 11:                    1                                 1                           1 1    = 1
```

When solved as an LP, the solution is conveniently integer with the tours selected being:

Tour	Flights
T17	7,13
T24	3,23
T28	410,19,11
T29	220,17,101

The cost of this solution is $10,000. There may be alternative optima with the same cost.

The dual prices on the constraints are:

ROW	SLACK	DUAL PRICES	Flight
2)	0.000000	−2.000000	(101)
3)	0.000000	0.000000	(410)
4)	0.000000	−2.000000	(220)
5)	0.000000	1.000000	(17)
6)	0.000000	−1.000000	(7)
7)	0.000000	−2.000000	(13)
8)	0.000000	0.000000	(11)
9)	0.000000	−2.000000	(19)
10)	0.000000	−1.000000	(23)
11)	0.000000	−1.000000	(3)

The dual prices suggest that flight 101, 220, 13, and 19 are the most expensive to cover while crew costs could actually be reduced by adding another flight 17 because of the reduced deadheading.

The kind of LP which results from the crew scheduling problem is surprisingly difficult to solve. LPs of this type with more than 500 constraints have proven very difficult to solve. Once they are solved, however, even if the solution is fractional, it is close to the integer optimal.

Problems

1. Certain types of facilities operate seven days each week and face the problem of allocating person power during the week as staffing requirements change as a func-

tion of the day of the week. This kind of problem is commonly encountered in public service and transportation organizations. Perhaps the most fundamental staffing problem involves the assignment of days off to full-time employees. In particular, it is regularly the case that each employee is entitled to two consecutive days off per week. If the number of employees required on each of the seven days of the week is given, then the problem is to find the minimum workforce size which will allow these demands to be met and then to determine the days off for the people in this workforce.

To be specific, let us study the problem faced by the Festus City Bus Company. The number of drivers required for each day of the week are as follows:

Monday	Tuesday	Wednesday	Thursday	Friday	Saturday	Sunday
18	16	15	16	19	14	12

How many drivers should be scheduled to start a five-day stint on each day of the week? Formulate this problem as a linear program. What is the optimal solution to it?

2. Completely unintentionally, several important details were omitted from the Festus City Staffing Problem (see previous question):

   (a) Daily pay is $50 per person on weekdays, $75 on Saturday and $90 on Sunday.

   (b) There are up to three people that can be hired who will work part time, specifically a 3-day week consisting of Friday, Sunday and Monday. Their pay for this 3-day stint is $200.

   Modify the formulation appropriately. Is it obvious whether the part time people will be used?

3. A political organization, Uncommon Result, wants to make a mass mailing to solicit funds. It has identified six "audiences" which it wishes to reach. There are eight mailing lists which it can purchase in order to get the names of the people in each audience. Each mailing list covers only a portion of the audiences. This coverage is indicated in the table below:

Mailing List	M.D.	LL.D.	D.D.S.	Business Executive	Brick Layers	Plumbers	Cost
1	Y	N	N	Y	N	N	$5000
2	N	Y	Y	N	N	N	$4000
3	N	Y	N	N	N	Y	$6000
4	Y	N	N	N	N	Y	$4750
5	N	N	N	Y	N	Y	$5500
6	N	N	Y	N	N	N	$3000
7	N	Y	N	N	Y	N	$5750
8	Y	N	N	N	Y	N	$5250

A "Y" indicates that the mailing list contains essentially all the names in the audience. An "N" indicates that essentially no names in the audience are contained in the mailing list. The costs associated with purchasing and processing a mailing list are given in the far right column. No change in total costs is incurred if an audience is contained in several mailing lists. Formulate a model which will minimize total costs while ensuring that all audiences are reached. Which mailing lists should be purchased?

4. The Pap-Iris Company prints various types of advertising brochures for a wide range of customers. The raw material for these brochures is a special finish paper which comes in 50-inch width rolls. The 50-inch width costs $10 per inch-roll (i.e., $500/roll). A roll is 1,000 feet long. Currently Pap-Iris has three orders. Order number 1 is a brochure which is 16 inches wide with a run length of 400,000 feet. Order number 2 is a brochure which is 30 inches wide and has a run length of 80,000 feet. Order number 3 is a brochure which is 24 inches wide and has a run length of 120,000 feet. The major question is how to slit the larger raw material rolls into widths suitable for the brochures. With the paper and energy shortages, Pap-Iris wants to be as efficient as possible in its use of paper. Formulate an appropriate LP.

5. *Postal Optimality Analysis* (Due to Gene Moore). As part of a modernization effort U.S. Postal Service decided to improve the handling and distribution bulk mail (second, third and fourth class nonpreferential) in the Chicago area. As part of this goal a new processing facility was proposed for the Chicago area. One part of this proposal was development of a low cost operational plan for the staffing of this facility. The plan would recognize the widely fluctuating hourly volume that is characteristic of such a facility and would suggest staffing pattern or patterns that would accomplish the dual objectives of processing all mail received in a day's time while having no idle time.

A bulk mailing processing facility, as the name implies, performs the function of receiving, unpacking, weighing, sorting by destination, and shipping of mail designated as nonpreferential, including second class (bulk rate), third class (parcel post), and fourth class (books). It is frequently designed as a single purpose structure and is typically located in or adjacent to the large metropolitan areas which produce this type of mail in significant volume. Although the trend in such facilities has been increased utilization of automated equipment (including highly sophisticated handling and sorting devices), paid manpower continues to account for a substantial portion of total operating expense.

Mail is received by the facility in mail bags and in containers, both of which are shipped in trucks. It is also received in tied and wrapped packages, which are sent directly to the facility on railroad flatcars. Receipts of mail by the facility tend to be cyclical on a predictable basis throughout the 24 hour working day, resulting in the build-up of an "inventory" of mail during busy hours, which inventory must be processed during less busy hours. A policy decision to have "no idle time" imposes a constraint on the optimal level of staffing.

Once the facility is ready for operations, it will be necessary to implement an operating plan which will include staffing requirements. A number of assumptions regarding such a plan are necessary at the outset. Some of them are based upon existing Postal Service policy while others evolve from functional constraints. These assumptions are as follows:

   i. Pieces of mail are homogeneous in terms of processing effort.

   ii. Each employee can process 1800 pieces per hour.

iii. Only full shifts are worked, i.e., it is impossible to introduce additional labor inputs or reduce existing labor inputs at times other than shift changes.

iv. Shift changes occur at Midnight, 8:00 A.M. and 4:00 P.M, which are the first, second and third shifts, respectively.

v. All mail arrivals occur on the hour.

vi. All mail must be processed the same day it is received, i.e., there may be no "inventory" carryover from the third shift to the following day's first shift.

vii. Labor rates, including shift differential, are given in the following table:

Shift	$/Hour	Daily Rate
1st (Midnight–8 A.M.)	3.90	31.20
2nd (8 A.M.–4 P.M.)	3.60	28.80
3rd (4 P.M.–Midnight)	3.80	30.40

viii. Hourly mail arrival is predictable and is given in the following table.

Cumulative Mail Arrival

1st Shift		2nd Shift		3rd Shift	
Hour	Pieces	Hour	Pieces	Hour	Pieces
0100	56,350	0900	242,550	1700	578,100
0200	83,300	1000	245,000	1800	592,800
0300	147,000	1100	249,900	1900	597,700
0400	171,500	1200	259,700	2000	901,500
0500	188,650	1300	323,400	2100	908,850
0600	193,550	1400	369,950	2200	928,450
0700	210,700	1500	421,400	2300	950,500
0800	220,500	1600	485,100	2400	974,000

(a) Formulate the appropriate LP under the no idle time requirement. Can you predict beforehand the number to staff on the first shift? Will there always be a feasible solution to this problem for arbitrary arrival patterns?

(b) Suppose we allow idle time to occur. What is the appropriate formulation? Do you expect this solution to incur higher cost because it has idle time?

6. In the famous Northeast Tollway staffing problem it was implied that at least a certain specified number of collectors were needed each period of the day. No extra benefit was assumed from having more collectors on duty than specified. You may recall that because of the fluctuations in requirements over the course of the day, the optimal solution did have more collectors than required on duty during certain periods.

In reality, if more collectors are on duty than specified, the extra collectors are not completely valueless. The presence of the extra collectors results in less waiting for the motorists (boaters?). Similarly, if less than the specified number of collectors are on duty, the situation is not necessarily intolerable. Motorists will still be processed but they may have to wait longer.

After much soul searching and economic analysis you have concluded that one full-time collector costs $100/shift. An extra collector on duty for one hour results in $10 worth of benefits to motorists. Further, having one less collector on duty than required during a one-hour period results in a waiting cost to motorists of $50.

Assuming that you wish to minimize total costs (motorists and collectors), show how you would modify the LP formulation. You only need illustrate for one constraint.

7. Some cities have analyzed their street cleaning and snow removal scheduling by methods somewhat analogous to those described for the Sayre-Priors airline problem. After a snowfall each of specified streets must be swept by at least one truck.

   (a) What are the analogs of the flight legs in Sayre-Priors?

   (b) What might be the decision variables corresponding to the tours in Sayre-Priors?

   (c) Should the constraints be equality or inequality in this case and why?

8. The St. Libory Quarry Company (SLQC) sells the rock that it quarries in four grades: limestone, chat, Redi-Mix-Grade, and coarse. A situation that it regularly encounters is one in which it has large inventories of the grades that it does not need and very little inventory in the grades which are needed at the moment. The four grades are produced by processing through a crusher the large rocks removed from the earth. For example, this week it appears that the demand is for 50 tons of limestone, 60 tons of chat, 70 tons of Redi-Mix and 30 tons of coarse. Its on-hand inventories for these same grades are respectively: 5, 40, 30 and 40 tons. For practical purposes one can think of the crusher as having three operating modes: close, medium and coarse. SLQC has done some data gathering and has concluded that one ton of quarried rock gets converted into the following output grades according to the crusher setting as follows:

Crusher Operating Mode	Tons Output per Ton Input				Operating Cost/Ton
	Limestone	Chat	Redi-Mix	Coarse	
Close	0.50	0.30	0.20	0.00	$8
Medium	0.20	0.40	0.30	0.10	$5
Coarse	0.05	0.20	0.35	0.40	$3

SLQC would like to know how to operate its crusher so as to bring inventories up to the equivalent of at least two weeks worth of demand. Provide whatever help that your current circumstanes permit.

9. A certain optical instrument is being designed to selectively provide radiation over the spectrum from about 3500 to 6400 Angstrom units. To cover this optical range, a range of chemicals must be incorporated into the design. Each chemical provides

coverage of a certain range. A list of the available chemicals, the range each covers, and its relative cost is provided below.

Chemical	Range Covered in Angstroms		Relative Cost
	Lower Limit	Upper Limit	
PBD	3500	3655	4
PPO	3520	3905	3
PPF	3600	3658	1
PBO	3650	4075	4
PPD	3660	3915	1
POPOP	3900	4449	6
A–NPO	3910	4095	2
NASAL	3950	4160	3
AMINOB	3995	4065	1
BBO	4000	4195	2
D–STILB	4000	4200	2
D–POPOP	4210	4405	2
A–NOPON	4320	4451	2
D–ANTH	4350	4500	2
4–METHYL–V	4420	5400	9
7–D–4 M	4450	4800	3
ESCULIN	4450	4570	1
NA–FLUOR	5200	6000	9
RHODAMINE–6G	5600	6200	8
RHODAMINE–B	6010	6400	8
ACRIDINE–RED	6015	6250	2

What subset of the available chemicals should be chosen to provide uninterrupted coverage from 3500 to 6400 Angstroms?

7
Networks, Distribution, & PERT/CPM

What's Special About Network Models

A subclass of LP models called network LP's warrant special attention for three reasons:

1. they can be completely described by simple, easily understood graphical figures,
2. under typical conditions they have naturally integer answers, and
3. they are easier to solve than general LP's.

Physical examples that come to mind are pipeline or electrical transmission line networks. Any enterprise producing a product at several locations and distributing it to many warehouses and/or customers may find a network LP a useful device for describing and analyzing the various shipment strategies.

Although not essential, efficient specialized solution procedures may be used to solve network LP's. These procedures may be as much as 100 times faster than the general simplex method. Bradley, Brown and Graves (1977) give a detailed description. Some of these specialized procedures were developed several years before the simplex method was developed for general LPs.

Figure 7.1 illustrates the network representing the distribution system of a firm using intermediate warehouses to distribute a product. The firm has two plants, denoted by A and B, three warehouses, denoted by X, Y, and Z, and four customer areas denoted by 1, 2, 3, 4. The numbers adjacent to each node denote the availability of material at that node. Plant A, for example, has 9 units available to be shipped. Customer 3, on the other hand, has 4 units, which means it requires 4 units to be shipped in.

The number above each arc is the cost per unit shipped along that arc. For example, if 5 of plant A's 9 units are shipped to warehouse Y, then a cost of $5 \times 2 = 10$ will be incurred as a direct result. The problem is to determine the amount shipped along each arc so that total costs are minimized and every customer has his requirements satisfied.

Figure 7.1

Typical Three-Level Distribution Network
Product Distribution System

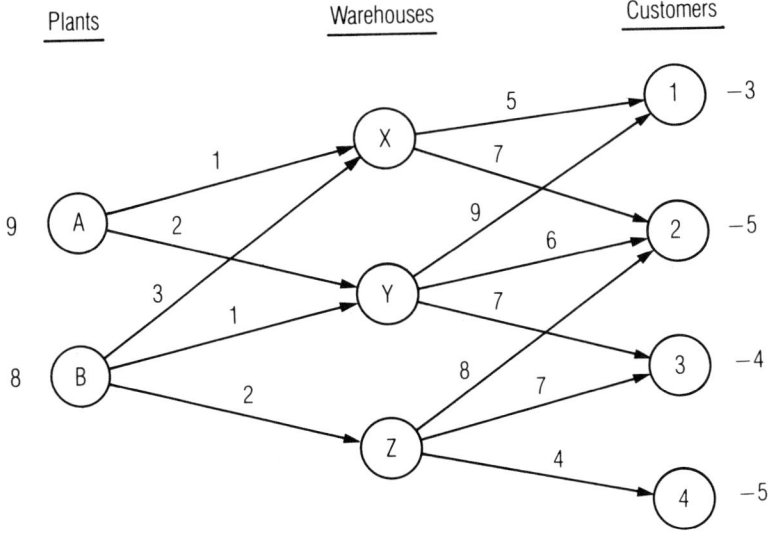

The essential condition on an LP for it to be a network problem is that it be representable as a network. There can be more than three levels of nodes; there can be any number of arcs between any two nodes and there may be upper and lower limits on the amount shipped along a given arc.

Defining variables in an obvious way, the general LP describing this problem is:

```
MIN     AX + 2 AY + 3 BX +   BY + 2BZ + 5 X1 + 7 X2
      + 9 Y1 + 6 Y2 + 7 Y3 + 8 Z2 + 7 Z3 + 4 Z4
SUBJECT TO
    2)       AX +   AY = 9
    3)       BX +   BY +   BZ = 8
    4)     - AX -   BX +   X1 +   X2 = 0
    5)     - AY -   BY +   Y1 +   Y2 +   Y3 = 0
    6)     - BZ +   Z2 +   Z3 +   Z4 = 0
    7)     - X1 -   Y1 = -3
    8)     - X2 -   Y2 -   Z2 = -5
    9)     - Y3 -   Z3 = -4
   10)     - Z4 = -5
END
```

There is one constraint for each node which is of a "sources = uses" form. Constraint 5, for example, is associated with warehouse Y and states that the amount shipped out minus the amount shipped in must equal 0.

A different view of the structure of a network problem is possible by using the PICTURE command of LINDO:

:PICTURE
```
         A A B B B X X Y Y Y Z Z Z
         X Y X Y Z 1 2 1 2 3 2 3 4
  1:     1 2 3 1 2 5 7 9 6 7 8 7 4   MIN
  2:     1 1                         = 9
  3:         1 1 1                   = 8
  4:    -1 -1     1 1                =
  5:    -1 -1         1 1 1          =
  6:            -1         1 1 1     =
  7:               -1 -1             = -3
  8:                  -1 -1 -1       = -5
  9:                        -1 -1    = -4
 10:                              -1 = -5
```

You should notice the key feature of the constraint matrix of a network problem: disregarding any bound constraints on individual variables, each column has exactly two nonzeroes in the constraint matrix, one of which is a +1 while the other is a −1. According to the convention we have adopted the +1 appears in the row of the node from which the arc takes material while the −1 appears in the row of the node to which the arc delivers material. On a problem of this size you should be able to deduce the optimal solution manually simply from examining Figure 7.1. You may check it with the computer solution below:

```
        OBJECTIVE FUNCTION VALUE

   1)         121.0000

 VARIABLE        VALUE         REDUCED COST
   AX          8.000000           0.000000
   AY          1.000000           0.000000
   BX          0.000000           3.000000
   BY          3.000000           0.000000
   BZ          5.000000           0.000000
   X1          3.000000           0.000000
   X2          5.000000           0.000000
   Y1          0.000000           5.000000
   Y2          0.000000           0.000000
   Y3          4.000000           0.000000
   Z2          0.000000           3.000000
   Z3          0.000000           1.000000
   Z4          5.000000           0.000000

   ROW          SLACK          DUAL PRICES
    2)         0.000000          -7.000000
    3)         0.000000          -6.000000
    4)         0.000000          -6.000000
    5)         0.000000          -5.000000
    6)         0.000000          -4.000000
    7)         0.000000          -1.000000
    8)         0.000000           1.000000
    9)         0.000000           2.000000
   10)         0.000000           0.000000
```

This solution exhibits two pleasing features found in the solution to any network problem:

1. If the righthand side coefficients (the capacities and requirements) are integer, then so will be the variables,
2. If the objective coefficients are integer, then so will be the dual prices.

We can summarize network LPs as follows:

1. Associated with each node is a number which specifies the amount of commodity available at that node (negative imples that commodity is required).
2. Associated with each arc are:
   (a) a cost per unit shipped (which may be negative) over the arc,
   (b) a lower bound on the amount shipped over the arc (typically zero),
   (c) an upper bound on the amount shipped over the arc (e.g., infinity in our example).

The problem is to determine the flows which minimize total cost subject to satisfying all the supply, demand, and flow constraints.

Variations of the Network Problem

In order of decreasing generality there are five variations of network problems, namely:

1. *Networks with gains or generalized networks.* This is actually a generalization of the problem just described. This is the most general LP which can still be described graphically as network. The generalization is that there may be a specified gain or loss of material as it is shipped from one node to another. Structurally, these problems are such that every column has at most two nonzeroes in the constraint matrix; however, the requirement that these coefficients be $+1$ and -1 is relaxed. Specialized procedures which are about 20 times faster than the regular simplex method exist for solving these problems.

2. *Network or transshipment problems.* The plant/warehouse/customer problem of the previous section is an example of a network or transshipment problem.

3. *Shortest and longest path problems.* Suppose that one is given the road network of the U.S. and wishes to find the shortest route from Bangor to San Diego. This is equivalent to a special case of a network on transshipment problem in which one unit of material is available at Bangor and one unit is required at San Diego. The cost of shipping over an arc is the length of the arc. Simple, fast procedures exist for solving this problem. An important first cousin of this problem, the longest route problem, arises in the analysis of PERT/CPM projects.

4. *Transportation or distribution problems.* A two-level network problem, where all the nodes at one level are suppliers while the nodes at the other level are customers, is called a transportation or distribution problem.

5. *The assignment problem.* A transportation problem in which the number of suppliers equals the number of customers, and further, each supplier has 1 unit available and each customer requires one unit is called an assignment problem. An efficient specialized procedure exists for its solution.

PERT/CPM Networks and LP

PERT (Project Evaluation and Review Technique) and CPM (Critical Path Method) are two closely related techniques for monitoring the progress of a large project. A key part of PERT/CPM is calculating the critical path, that is, identifying the subset of the activities which must be performed exactly as planned in order for the project to finish on time.

We will show that the calculation of the critical path is a very simple network LP problem. You do not need this fact in order to efficiently calculate the critical path, but it is an interesting observation that becomes useful if you wish to examine a multitude of "crashing" options for accelerating a tardy project.

In the table below we list the activities involved in the simple but nontrivial project of building a house. An activity cannot be started until all of its predecessors are finished.

Activity	Mnemonic	Activity Time	Predecessors (Mnemonic)
Dig Basement	DIG	3	—
Pour Foundation	FOUND	4	DIG
Pour Basement Floor	POURB	2	FOUND
Install Floor Joists	JOISTS	3	FOUND
Install Walls	WALLS	5	FOUND
Install Rafters	RAFTERS	3	WALLS, POURB
Install Flooring	FLOOR	4	JOISTS
Rough Interior	ROUGH	6	FLOOR
Install Roof	ROOF	7	RAFTERS
Finish Interior	FINISH	5	ROUGH, ROOF
Landscape	SCAPE	2	POURB, WALLS

In Figure 7.2 we show the so-called PERT (or activity-on-arrow) network for this project. We would like to calculate the minimum elapsed time to complete this project. Relative to this figure, the number of interest is simply the longest path from left to right in this figure. The project can be completed no sooner than the sum of the times of the successive activities on this path. Verify for yourself that the critical path consists of activities, DIG, FOUND, WALLS, RAFTERS, ROOF, and FINISH and has length 27.

Even though this example can be worked out by hand, almost without pencil and paper, let us derive an LP formulation for solving this problem. Most people attempting this derivation will come up with one of two seemingly unrelated formulations.

The first formulation is motivated as follows. Let variables DIG, FOUND, etc., be either 1 or 0 depending upon whether activities DIG, FOUND, etc. are on or not on the critical path. The variables equal to one will define the critical path. The objective function will be related to the fact that we want to find the maximum length path in PERT diagram.

Our objective is in fact:

```
MAX    3 DIG + 4 FOUND + 2 POURB + 3 JOISTS + 5 WALLS + 3 RAFTERS
     + 4 FLOOR + 6 ROUGH + 7 ROOF + 5 FINISH + 2 SCAPE
```

Figure 7.2

An Activity-on-Arc PERT/CPM Network

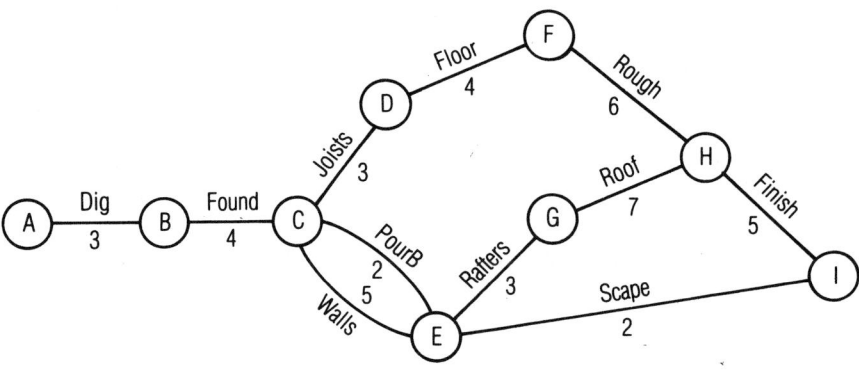

By itself, this objective seems to take the wrong point of view. We do not want to maximize the project length. If, however, we specify the proper constraints we shall see that this objective will seek out the maximum length path in the PERT network. We want to use the constraints to enforce the following:

1. DIG must be on the critical path;
2. An activity can be on the critical path only if one of its predecessors is on the critical path. Further, if an activity is on a critical path exactly one of its successors must be on the critical path, if it has successors;
3. Exactly one of SCAPE or FINISH must be on the critical path.

Convince yourself that the following set of constraints will enforce the above:

```
  - DIG                               = -1
  - FOUND + DIG                       = 0
  - JOISTS - POURB - WALLS + FOUND    = 0
  - FLOOR + JOISTS                    = 0
  - RAFTERS - SCAPE + POURB + WALLS   = 0
  - ROUGH + FLOOR                     = 0
  - ROOF + RAFTERS                    = 0
  - FINISH + ROUGH + ROOF             = 0
  + FINISH + SCAPE                    = +1
```

If you interpret the length of each arc in the network as the scenic beauty of the arc, then the formulation corresponds to finding the most scenic route by which to ship one unit from A to I.

The solution of the problem is:

```
            OBJECTIVE FUNCTION VALUE
      1)          27.0000000
```

```
VARIABLE        VALUE           REDUCED COST
DIG             1.000000        0.000000
FOUND           1.000000        0.000000
POURB           0.000000        3.000000
JOISTS          0.000000        0.000000
WALLS           1.000000        0.000000
RAFTERS         1.000000        0.000000
FLOOR           0.000000        0.000000
ROUGH           0.000000        2.000000
ROOF            1.000000        0.000000
FINISH          1.000000        0.000000
SCAPE           0.000000        13.000000

    ROW         SLACK           DUAL PRICES
     2)         0.000000        0.000000
     3)         0.000000        3.000000
     4)         0.000000        7.000000
     5)         0.000000        10.000000
     6)         0.000000        12.000000
     7)         0.000000        14.000000
     8)         0.000000        15.000000
     9)         0.000000        22.000000
    10)         0.000000        27.000000
```

Notice that the variables corresponding to the activities on the critical path have value 1. What is the solution if the first constraint, $-DIG = -1$, is deleted?

It is instructive to look at the PICTURE of this problem in the following figure.

```
                   R
           J       A           F
      F P O W F F R   I S
      0 0 I A T L O R N C
    D U U S L E O U O I A
    I N R T L R O G O S P
    G D B S S S R H F H E
 1: 3 4 2 3 5 3 4 6 7 5 2 MAX
 2:-1         '       '       '   = -1
 3: 1-1'  '   '   '   '   '   '=
 4:    1-1-1-1    '       '   =
 5:        1   -1         '   =
 6: '  '1 ' 1-1 '     '  '-1'=
 7:         '     1-1     '   =
 8:         '   1 '  -1 '     =
 9: '   '   '    '    ' 1'1-1 '=
10:             '        '    1 1 = 1
```

Notice that each variable has at most two coefficients in the constraints. When two, they are $+1$ and -1. This is the distinguishing feature of a network LP.

Now let us look at the second possible formulation. The motivation for this formulation is to minimize the elapsed time of the project. To do this, realize that each node in the PERT network represents an event, e.g., as follows: *A*, start digging the basement; *C*, complete the foundation; and *I*, complete landscaping and finish interior.

Define variables $A, B, C, \ldots, H, I$ as the time at which these events occur. Our objective function is then

Minimize $I - A$.

These event times are constrained by the fact that each event has to occur later than each of its preceding events, at least by the amount of any intervening activity. Thus, we get one constraint for each activity:

$$
\begin{array}{rl}
B - A \geq 3 & \text{DIG} \\
C - B \geq 4 & \text{FOUND} \\
E - C \geq 2 & \cdot \\
D - C \geq 3 & \cdot \\
E - C \geq 5 & \cdot \\
F - D \geq 4 & \\
G - E \geq 3 & \\
H - F \geq 6 & \\
H - G \geq 7 & \\
I - H \geq 5 & \\
I - E \geq 2 &
\end{array}
$$

The solution to this problem is

```
                OBJECTIVE FUNCTION VALUE

        1)          27.0000000

   VARIABLE         VALUE           REDUCED COST
        A           0.000000        0.000000
        B           3.000000        0.000000
        C           7.000000        0.000000
        D          10.000000        0.000000
        E          12.000000        0.000000
        F          14.000000        0.000000
        G          15.000000        0.000000
        H          22.000000        0.000000
        I          27.000000        0.000000

     ROW            SLACK           DUAL PRICES
        2)          0.000000       -1.000000
        3)          0.000000       -1.000000
        4)          3.000000        0.000000
        5)          0.000000        0.000000
        6)          0.000000       -1.000000
        7)          0.000000       -1.000000
        8)          0.000000        0.000000
        9)          2.000000        0.000000
       10)          0.000000       -1.000000
       11)          0.000000       -1.000000
       12)         13.000000        0.000000
```

Notice that the objective function value equals the critical path length. We can indirectly identify the activities on the critical path by noting the constraints with nonzero dual prices. The activities corresponding to these constraints are on the critical path. This correspondence makes sense. The right-hand side of a constraint is the activity time. If we increase the time of an activity on the critical path, it should increase the project length and thus should have a nonzero dual price. What is the solution if the first variable, A, is deleted?

The PICTURE of the coefficient matrix for this problem appears below:

```
      A  B  C  D  E  F  G  H  I
 1: -1              '        '     1  MIN
 2: -1  1           '        '     > 3
 3:  '-1'1  '       '  '     '     > 4
 4:     -1  '  1    '              > 2
 5:     -1  1                      > 3
 6:  '  -1  '  1'   '        '     > 5
 7:            '-1  1               > 3
 8:        -1       1  '             > 4
 9:  '  '  '  -1    '  1'            > 6
10:            '   -1  1             > 7
11:            '       '-1  1        > 5
12:  '  '  '-1'    '       '1        > 2
```

Notice that the PICTURE of this formulation is essentially the PICTURE of the previous formulation rotated ninety degrees. Even though these to formulations originally were seemingly unrelated, there is really an incestuous relationship between the two; a relationship that mathematicians politely refer to as duality.

Activity-on-Arc vs. Activity-on-Node Network Diagrams

Two conventions are used in practice for displaying project networks: (1) Activity-on-Arc (AOA) and (2) Activity-on-Node (AON). Our previous example used the AOA convention. The characteristics of the two are:

AON

- Each activity is represented by a node in the network.
- A precedence relationship between two activities is represented by an arc or link between the two.
- May be less error prone because it does not need dummy activities or arcs.

AOA

- Each activity is represented by an arc in the network.
- If activity X must precede activity Y, there are X leads into arc Y. The nodes thus represent events or "milestones," e.g., "finished activity X." Dummy activities of zero length may be required to properly represent precedences.
- Historically more popular, perhaps because of its similarity to Gantt charts used in scheduling.

An AON project with six activities is shown in Figure 7.3. The number next to each node is the duration of the activity. By inspection, you can discover that the longest path consists of activities 1, 3, 5 and 6. It has a length of 29. The corresponding AOA network

Figure 7.3

An Activity-on-Node Representation

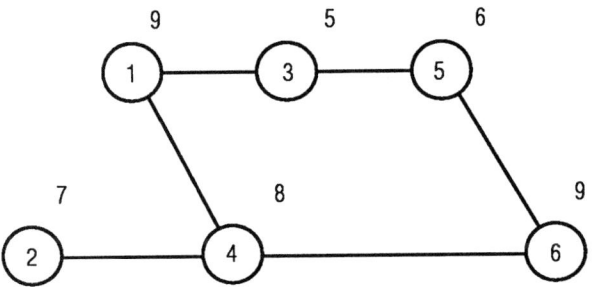

for the same project is shown in Figure 7.4. In the AOA network we have enclosed the activity numbers in circles above the associated arc. The unenclosed numbers below each arc are the activity durations. We have given the nodes, or milestones, arbitrary letter designations, enclosed in squares. Notice that a dummy activity (the dotted arc) between nodes C and D. This is because *a dummy activity will be required in an AOA diagram anytime that two activities*, e.g., 1 and 2, *share some*, e.g., activity 4, *but not all*, e.g., activity 3, *successor activities*.

Crashing of Project Networks

Once the critical path length for a project has been identified, the next question that is invariably asked is: can we shorten the project. The process of decreasing the duration of a project or activity is commonly called crashing. For many construction projects it is common for the customer to pay an incentive to the contractor for finishing the project in a shorter length of time. For example in highway repair projects it is not unusual to have incentives of from $5,000 to $25,000 per day that the project finishes before a target or benchmark date.

The Cost and Value of Crashing

There is value in crashing a project. In order to crash a project we must crash one or more activities. Crashing an activity costs money. Deciding to crash an activity requires us to compare the cost of crashing that activity with the value of the resulting reduction in project length. This decision is frequently complicated by the fact that some negotiation may be required between the party that incurs the cost of crashing the activity (e.g., the contractor) and the party that enjoys the value of the crashed project, (e.g., the customer).

The Cost of Crashing an Activity

The typical activity is crashed by applying more labor to it, e.g., overtime or a second shift. We might typically expect that using second shift labor could cost 1.5 times as much

Figure 7.4

An Activity-on-Arc Representation

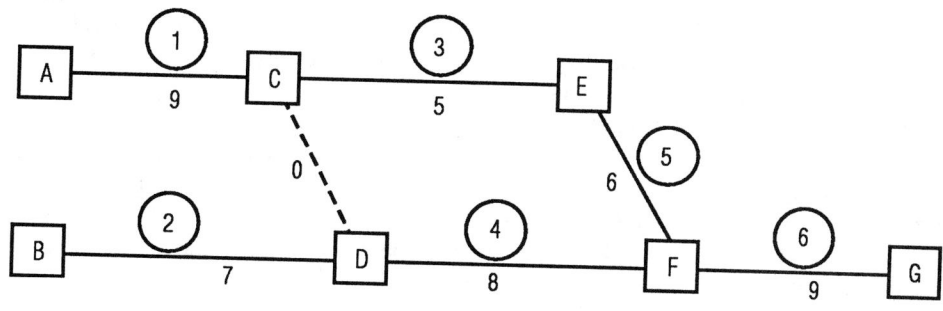

per hour as first shift labor. We might expect third shift labor to cost twice as much as first shift labor.

Consider an activity that can be done in six days if only first shift labor is used and has a labor cost of $6,000. If we allow the use of second shift labor and thus work two shifts per day, the activity can be done in three days for a cost of $3 \times 1000 + 3 \times 1000 \times 1.5 = 7,500$. If third shift labor is allowed then the project can be done in two days by working 3 shifts per day and incurring a total of

$$2 \times 1000 + 2 \times 1000 \times 1.5 + 2 \times 1000 \times 2 = \$9,000$$

Thus, we get a crashing cost curve for the activity as shown in Figure 7.5.

Figure 7.5

Activity Crash Cost Curve

The Value of Crashing a Project

There are two approaches to deciding upon the amount of project crashing: (a) we simply specify a project duration and crash enough to achieve this duration or (b) we estimate the value of crashing it for various days. As an example of (a), in 1987 a new stadium was being built for the Montreal Expos baseball team. The obvious completion target was the first home game of the season.

As an example of (b), consider an urban expressway repair. What is the value per day of completing it early? Suppose that 6,000 motorists are affected by the repair project and each is delayed by 10 minutes each day because of the repair work, e.g., by taking alternate routes or by slower traffic. The total daily delay is 6,000 × 10 = 60,000 minutes = 1000 hours. If we assign an hourly cost of $5/person × hours, the social value of reducing the repair project by one day is $5,000.

Formulation of the Crashing Problem

Suppose we have investigated the crashing possibilities for each activity in our previous project example. These estimates are summarized in the table below:

Activity	Predecessor	Normal Time (Days)	Maximum Crash (Days)	$/Day
1	—	9	5	5000
2	—	7	3	6000
3	1	5	3	4000
4	1,2	8	4	2000
5	3	6	3	3000
6	4,5	9	5	9000

For example, activity 1 could be done in five days rather than nine, however, this would cost us an extra (9 − 5) × 5000 = $20,000.

First consider the simple case where we have a hard due date by which the project must be done, let us say 22 days in this case. How would we decide which activities to crash? Activity 2 is the cheapest to crash per day, however, it is not on the critical path so its low cost is at best just interesting.

Let us define:

EF_i = earliest finish time of activity i, taking into account any crashing that is done,

C_i = number of days by which activity i is crashed.

In words, the LP model will be:

Minimize   Cost of crashing

Subject to

For each activity j and each predecessor i:

earliest finish of j ≥ earliest finish of predecessor i
+ duration of j − crashing of j.

For each activity j:

crashing ≤ normal time − max crash time.

The LINDO formulation is:

```
MIN     5 C1 + 6 C2 + 4 C3 + 2 C4 + 3 C5 + 9 C6
SUBJECT TO
   2)      C1 + EF1             ≥   9
   3)      C2 + EF2             ≥   7
   4)      C3 - EF1 + EF3       ≥   5
   5)      C4 - EF1 + EF4       ≥   8
   6)      C4 - EF2 + EF4       ≥   8
   7)      C5 - EF3 + EF5       ≥   6
   8)      C6 - EF4 + EF6       ≥   9
   9)      C6 - EF5 + EF6       ≥   9
  10)      EF6                  ≤  22
END
SUB       C1       4.00000
SUB       C2       4.00000
SUB       C3       2.00000
SUB       C4       4.00000
SUB       C5       3.00000
SUB       C6       4.00000
```

The SUB's are just compact ways of representing the simple upper bounds, e.g., SUB C1 4.0 is equivalent to C1 ≤ 4.

The solution is:

```
            OBJECTIVE FUNCTION VALUE

     1)          31.0000000

   VARIABLE         VALUE         REDUCED COST
      C1           2.000000         0.000000
      C2           0.000000         5.000000
      C3           2.000000         0.000000
      C4           2.000000         0.000000
      C5           3.000000        -1.000000
      C6           0.000000         3.000000
      EF1          7.000000         0.000000
      EF2          7.000000         0.000000
      EF3         10.000000         0.000000
      EF4         13.000000         0.000000
      EF5         13.000000         0.000000
      EF6         22.000000         0.000000

     ROW      SLACK OR SURPLUS    DUAL PRICES
     2)           0.000000        -5.000000
     3)           0.000000        -1.000000
     4)           0.000000        -4.000000
     5)           0.000000        -1.000000
     6)           0.000000        -1.000000
     7)           0.000000        -4.000000
     8)           0.000000        -2.000000
     9)           0.000000        -4.000000
    10)           0.000000         6.000000
```

Thus, for an additional cost of $31,000 we can meet the 22-day deadline.

Now suppose there is no hard project due date but we do receive an incentive payment of $5000 for each day that we an reduce the project length. Define PCRASH = number of days that the project is finished before the 29th day.

Now the formulation is:

```
MIN      5 C1 + 6 C2 + 4 C3 + 3 C5 + 9 C6 + 9 C6 - 5 PCRASH
SUBJECT TO
  2)         C1 + EF1              ≥  9
  3)         C2 + EF2              ≥  7
  4)         C3 - EF1 + EF3        ≥  5
  5)         C4 - EF1 + EF4        ≥  8
  6)         C4 - EF2 + EF4        ≥  8
  7)         C5 - EF3 + EF5        ≥  6
  8)         C6 - EF4 + EF6        ≥  9
  9)         C6 - EF5 + EF6        ≥  9
 10)         EF6 + PCRASH          = 29
END
SUB        C1       4.00000
SUB        C2       4.00000
SUB        C3       2.00000
SUB        C4       4.00000
SUB        C5       3.00000
SUB        C6       4.00000
```

From the solution we see that we should crash it by 5 days to give a total project length of 24 days.

```
            OBJECTIVE FUNCTION VALUE

       1)        -6.0000000

VARIABLE         VALUE            REDUCED COST
   C1           2.000000            0.000000
   C2           0.000000            6.000000
   C3           0.000000            1.000000
   C4           0.000000            0.000000
   C5           3.000000            0.000000
   C6           0.000000            4.000000
   EF1          7.000000            0.000000
   EF2          7.000000            0.000000
   EF3         12.000000            0.000000
   EF4         15.000000            0.000000
   EF5         15.000000            0.000000
   EF6         24.000000            0.000000
   PCRASH       5.000000            0.000000

   ROW      SLACK OR SURPLUS       DUAL PRICES
    2)         0.000000             -5.000000
    3)         0.000000              0.000000
    4)         0.000000             -3.000000
    5)         0.000000             -2.000000
    6)         0.000000              0.000000
    7)         0.000000             -3.000000
    8)         0.000000             -2.000000
    9)         0.000000             -3.000000
   10)         0.000000              5.000000
```

The excess of the incentive payments over crash costs is $6,000.

Path Formulations

In many network problems it is natural to think of a solution in terms of paths that material takes as it flows through the network. For example, in Figure 7.1 and its associated solution, there were 11 of the 13 possible paths used, namely:

$$A \to X \to 1, \quad A \to X \to 2, \quad A \to Y \to 1, \quad A \to Y \to 1, \quad A \to Y \to 1,$$
$$B \to Y \to 1, \quad B \to Y \to 2, \quad B \to Y \to 3, \quad B \to Z \to 2, \quad B \to Z \to 3,$$
$$B \to Z \to 4.$$

One can in fact formulate decision variables in terms of complete paths rather than just simple links. The motivations for using the path approach are:

1. More complicated cost structures can be represented, e.g., Geoffrion and Graves (1974) uses the path formulation to represent "milling in transit" discount fare structures in shipping food and feed products.

2. Path related restrictions can be incorporated, e.g., regulations allow a truck driver to be on duty for at most 10 hours; thus, in a truckrouting network one would not consider paths longer than 10 hours.

3. The number of rows in the model may be substantially less.

4. In integer programs where some but not all of the problem has a network structure, the path formulation may be easier to solve.

Example

Let us reconsider the first problem, Figure 7.1. Suppose that shipments from A to X are made by the same carrier as shipments from X to 2. This carrier will give a $1/unit "milling-in-transit" discount for each unit that it handles from both A to X and X to 2. Further, the product is somewhat fragile and cannot tolerate a lot of transportation; in particular it cannot be shipped both over link $B \to X$ and $X \to 2$ or both over links $A \to Y$ and $Y \to 1$.

Using the notation AX1 = number of units shipped from A to X to 1, etc., the path formulation is:

```
MIN    6 AX1 + 7 AX2 + 8 AY2 + 9 AY3 + 8 BX1 + 10 BY1 + 7 BY2
       + 8 BY3 + 10 BZ2 + 9 BZ3 + 6 BZ4
SUBJECT TO
   2)     AX1 + AX2 + AY2 + AY3 =     9
   3)     BX1 + BY1 + BY2 + BY3 + BZ2 + BZ3 + BZ4 =    8
   4)     AX1 + BX1 + BY1 =    3
   5)     AX2 + AY2 + BY2 + BZ2 =    5
   6)     AX3 + BY3 + BZ3 =    4
   7)     BZ4 =    5
END
```

Notice that the cost of path AX2 = 1 + 7 − 1 = 7. Also, paths BX2 and AY1 do not appear. This model has only six constraints as opposed to nine in the original formulation. The reduction in constraints arises from the fact that in path formulations one does not need the "sources = uses" constraints for intermediate nodes.

In general, the path formulation will have fewer rows but more decision variables than the corresponding network LP model.

When solved we get:

```
       OBJECTIVE FUNCTION VALUE
  1)           116.000000
  VARIABLE     VALUE
  A1           3.000000
  AX2          5.000000
  AY3          1.000000
  BY3          3.000000
  BZ4          5.000000
```

This is cheaper than the previous solution because the five units shipped over path AX2 go for $1/unit less.

A path formulation need not have a naturally integer solution. If the path formulation, however, is equivalent to a network LP then it will have a naturally integer solution.

The path formulation is popular in long range forest planning, see for example Davis and Johnson (1986), where it is known as the "Model I" approach. The standard network LP based formulation is known as the "Model II" approach. In a forest planning Model II, a link in the network represents a decision to plant an acre of a particular kind of tree in some specified year and harvest it in some future specified year. A node represents a specific harvest and replant decision. A decision variable in Model I is a complete prescription of how to manage (i.e., harvest and replant) a given piece of land over time. Some Model I formulations in forest planning may have just a few hundred constraints but over a million decision variables or paths.

Multicommodity Network Flows

In a network LP the assumption is that a customer is indifferent, except perhaps for cost, to the source from which his product was obtained. The assumption is that there is a single commodity flowing through the network. In many network-like situations there are multiple distinct commodities flowing through the network. If each link has infinite capacity then an independent network flow LP could be solved for each commodity. If, however, a link has a finite capacity which applies to the sum of all commodities flowing over that link, then we have a multicommodity network problem.

The most common setting for multicommodity network problems is in shipping. The network might be a national gas pipeline network and the commodities might be the different fuels shipped over the network. In other shipping problems such as traffic assignment, or overnight package delivery, each origin/destination pair constitutes a commodity.

Figure 7.6

A Phone Company Network Structure

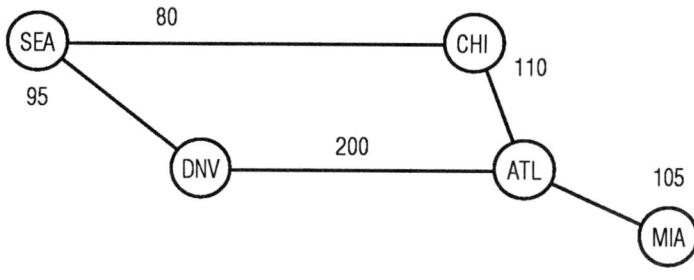

Undirected Networks

In many communications networks the arcs have capacity but are undirected. For example, when you are carrying on a phone conversation with someone in a distant city, the conversation uses capacity on all the links in your connection, however, you cannot speak of a direction of flow of the connection.

A major concern for a long distance communications company is the management of its commmunications network. This becomes particularly important during certain holidays, such as Mother's Day, when not only does the volume of calls increase but also the pattern of calls changes dramatically from that of the business oriented traffic during weekdays of the rest of the year. A communications company faces two problems.

1. *The design problem:* what capacity should be installed on each link; and
2. *The operations problem:* given the installed capacity, how are demands best routed.

The path formulation is an obvious format for modeling an undirected network. The following illustrates the operational problem.

Consider the case of a phone company with the network structure shown in Figure 7.6. The numbers next to each arc are the number of calls that can be in progress simultaneously along that arc. If someone in MIA tries to call his mother in SEA the phone company must first find a path from MIA to SEA such that each arc on that path is not at capacity. It is quite easy to inefficiently use the capacity. Suppose there is a demand for 110 calls between CHI and DNV, and 90 calls between ATL and SEA. Further, suppose that all these calls were routed over the ATL, DNV link. Now suppose we wish to make a call between MIA and SEA. Such a connection is impossible because every path between the two contains a saturated link (i.e., either ATL, DNV or CHI, ATL). If, however, some of the 110 calls between CHI and DNV are routed over the CHI, SEA, DNV links, then one could make calls between MIA and SEA. In conventional voice networks a call cannot be rerouted once it has started. In packet switched data networks and to some extent in cellular phone networks some rerouting is possible.

Example

Suppose that during a certain time period the demands in the table below occur for connections between pairs of cities.

	DNV	CHI	ATL	MIA
SEA	10	20	38	33
DNV		42	48	23
CHI			90	36
ATL				26

Which demands should be satisfied and via what routes so as to maximize the number of connections satisfied?

Solution. If we use the path formulation there will be two paths between every pair of cities except ATL and MIA. We will use the notation $P_{1_{ij}}$ for number of calls using the shorter or more northerly path between cities i and j, and $P_{2_{ij}}$ for the other path if any. There will be two kinds of constraints:

1. for each link a capacity constraint,
2. for each pair of cities an upper limit or the calls between that pair.

The complete formulation is:

```
    MAX     P1SEADNV + P2SEADNV + P1SEACHI + P2SEACHI + P1SEAATL + P2SEAATL
          + P1SEAMIA + P2SEAMIA + P1DNVCHI + P2DNVCHI + P1DNVATL + P2DNVATL
          + P1DNVMIA + P2DNVMIA + P1CHIATL + P2CHIATL + P1CHIMIA + P2CHIMIA
          + P1ATLMIA
    SUBJECT TO
    ! The link capacity constraints;
       LSEADNV)   P1SEADNV + P2SEACHI + P2SEAATL + P2SEAMIA + P1DNVCHI
                + P2DNVATL + P2DNVMIA + P2CHIATL + P2CHIMIA ≤    95
       LSEACHI)   P2SEADNV + P1SEACHI + P1SEAATL + P1SEAMIA + P1DNVCHI
                + P2DNVATL + P2DNVMIA + P2CHIATL + P2CHIMIA ≤    80
       LDNVATL)   P2SEADNV + P2SEACHI + P2SEAATL + P2SEAMIA + P2DNVCHI
                + P1DNVATL + P1DNVMIA + P2CHIATL + P2CHIMIA ≤   200
       LCHIATL)   P2SEADNV + P2SEACHI + P1SEAATL + P1SEAMIA + P2DNVCHI
                + P2DNVATL + P2DNVMIA + P1CHIATL + P1CHIMIA ≤   110
       LATLMIA)   P1SEAMIA + P2SEAMIA + P1DNVMIA + P2DNVMIA + P1CHIMIA
                + P2CHIMIA + P1ATLMIA ≤   105
    ! The demand constraints;
       DSEADNV)   P1SEADNV + P2SEADNV ≤    10
       DSEACHI)   P1SEACHI + P2SEACHI ≤    20
       DSEAATL)   P1SEAATL + P2SEAATL ≤    38
       DSEAMIA)   P1SEAMIA + P2SEAMIA ≤    33
       DDNVCHI)   P1DNVCHI + P2DNVCHI ≤    42
       DDNVATL)   P1DNVATL + P2DNVATL ≤    48
       DDNVMIA)   P1DNVMIA + P2DNVMIA ≤    23
       DCHIATL)   P1CHIATL + P2CHIATL ≤    90
       DCHIMIA)   P1CHIMIA + P2CHIMIA ≤    36
       DATLMIA)   P1ATLMIA ≤   26
    END
```

The structure stands out a little more if it is viewed in PICTURE form:

```
          P P P P P P P P P P P P P P P P
          1 2 1 2 1 2 1 2 1 2 1 2 1 2 1 2 1
          S S S S S S S S D D D D D C C C A
          E E E E E E E E N N N N N H H H T
          A A A A A A A A V V V V V I I I L
          D D C C A A M M C C A A M A M M M
          N N H H T T I I H H T T I I T I I
          V V I I L L A A I I L L A A L A A A

       1: 1 1 1 1 1 1 1 1 1 1 1 1 1 1 1 1 1  MAX
LSEADNV: 1       1     1 ' 1 1 '   1 ' 1      1   ' < B
LSEACHI:   ' 1'1 ' 1'    1    '1 '    '1 ' 1'     1 '1 '     < B
LDNVATL:   1   1       1 ' 1    1 1     1        1    1 '  < C
LCHIATL:   1   1 1       1       1   1 ' 1 1 ' 1     ' < B
LATLMIA: ' '   '    '    1 1'    '     '  1 1'     ' 1'1 1 < C
DSEADNV: 1 1     '          '          '          '   ' < A
DSEACHI:       1 1   '          '          '          ' < B
DSEAATL: '   '   ' 1'1 '   '          '          '   ' < B
DSEAMIA:             '   1 1     '          '          ' < B
DDNVCHI:                 '   1 1     '          '      ' < B
DDNVATL: '   '   '   '     '   1'1 '   '          '   ' < B
DDNVMIA:                     '     '   1 1     '      ' < B
DCHIATL:                         '          '   1 1   ' < B
DCHIMIA: '   '   '   '   '   '   '     '        ' 1'1 ' < B
DATLMIA:                 '          '          '        1 < B
```

When solved we see that we can handle 322 out of the total demand of 366 calls:

```
        OBJECTIVE FUNCTION VALUE

   1)         322.000000

     VARIABLE         VALUE        REDUCED COST
     P1SEADNV        0.000000        0.000000
     P2SEADNV        0.000000        0.000000
     P1SEACHI       20.000000        0.000000
     P2SEACHI        0.000000        2.000000
     P1SEAATL        0.000000        0.000000
     P2SEAATL       38.000000        0.000000
     P1SEAMIA        0.000000        0.000000
     P2SEAMIA        0.000000        0.000000
     P1DNVCHI       42.000000        0.000000
     P2DNVCHI        0.000000        0.000000
     P1DNVATL       48.000000        0.000000
     P2DNVATL        0.000000        2.000000
     P1DNVMIA       23.000000        0.000000
     P2DNVMIA        0.000000        2.000000
     P1CHIATL       75.000000        0.000000
     P2CHIATL       15.000000        0.000000
     P1CHIMIA       35.000000        0.000000
     P2CHIMIA        0.000000        0.000000
     P1ATLMIA       26.000000        0.000000
```

ROW	SLACK OR SURPLUS	DUAL PRICES
LSEADNV)	0.000000	1.000000
LSEACHI)	3.000000	0.000000
LDNVATL)	76.000000	0.000000
LCHIATL)	0.000000	1.000000
LATLMIA)	21.000000	0.000000
DSEADNV)	10.000000	0.000000
DSEACHI)	0.000000	1.000000
DSEAATL)	0.000000	0.000000
DSEAMIA)	33.000000	0.000000
DDNVCHI)	0.000000	0.000000
DDNVATL)	0.000000	1.000000
DDNVMIA)	0.000000	1.000000
DCHIATL)	0.000000	0.000000
DCHIMIA)	1.000000	0.000000
DATLMIA)	0.000000	1.000000

Apparently there are a number of alternate optima. The demand not carried is SEA–DNV: 10, SEA–MIA: 33, and CHI–MIA: 1. One may prefer some of the other optima with the same total number of calls but which spread the service a bit more.

Problems

1. The Slick Oil Company is preparing to make next month's pipeline shipment decisions. The Los Angeles terminal will require 200,000 barrels of oil. This oil can be supplied from either Houston or Casper, Wyoming. Houston can supply oil to L.A. at a transportation cost of $.25/barrel. Casper can supply L.A. at a transportation cost of $.28/barrel. The St. Louis terminal will require 120,000 barrels. St. Louis can be supplied from Houston at a cost of $.18/barrel and from Casper at a cost of $.22/barrel. The terminal at Freshair, Indiana requires 230,000 barrels. Oil can be shipped to Freshair from Casper at a cost of $.21/barrel, from Houston at a cost of $.19/barrel, and from Titusville, Pa. at a cost of $.17/barrel. Casper will have a total of 250,000 barrels available to be shipped. Houston will have 350,000 barrels available to be shipped. Because of limited pipeline capacity no more than 180,000 barrels can be shipped from Casper to L.A. next month and more than 150,000 barrels from Houston to L.A. The Newark, N.J. terminal will require 190,000 barrels next month. It can be supplied only from Titusville at a transportation cost of $.14/barrel. The Atlanta terminal will require 150,000 barrels next month. Atlanta can be supplied from Titusville at a transportation cost of $.16/barrel or from Houston at a cost of $.20/barrel. Titusville will have a total of 300,000 barrels available to be shipped.

    Formulate the problem of finding the minimum transportation cost distribution plan as a linear program.

2. Louis Szathjoseph, proprietor of the Boulangerie Restaurant, knows that he will need 40, 70, and 60 tablecloths on Thursday, Friday, and Saturday respectively for scheduled banquets. He can rent tablecloths for three days for $2 each. A tablecloth must be laundered before it can be reused. He can have them cleaned overnight for

$1.50 each. He can have them laundered by regular one day service (e.g., one used on Thursday could be reused on Saturday) for $.80 each. There are currently 20 clean tablecloths on hand with none dirty or at the laundry. Rented tablecloths need not be cleaned before returning.

(a) What are the decision variables?

(b) Formulate the LP which is appropriate for minimizing the total costs of renting and laundering the tablecloths. For each day you will probably have a constraint requiring the number of clean tablecloths available to at least equal that day's demand. For each of the first two days you will probably want a constraint requiring the number of tablecloths sent to the laundry not to exceed those which have been made dirty. Is it a network LP?

3. The Millersburg Supply Company uses a large fleet of vehicles which it leases from manufacturers. The following pattern of vehicle requirements is forecast for the next eight months:

Month	Jan.	Feb.	Mar.	Apr.	May	June	July	Aug.
Number of Vehicles Required	430	410	440	390	425	450	465	470

Vehicles can be leased from various manufacturers at various costs and for various lengths of time. The best plans available are: 3 month lease: $1,700; 4 month lease: $2,000; 5 month lease: $2,600. A lease can be started in any month. On January 1 there are 200 cars on lease, all of which go off lease at the end of February.

(a) Formulate an approach for minimizing Millersburg's leasing costs over this 8 month period.

(b) Show that this problem is a network problem.

4. Dean P. D. Ghog is in the process of setting up the teaching schedule for his school for the next year. The first thing that Dean Ghog does is require each faculty member to rank courses in order of his preference for each course. A faculty member will give a rank of 1 to the course he would most like to teach, 2 to the next most desirable course, etc. Denote by r_{ij} the rank given by faculty member i to course j. The school schedule (and demand) requires that a certain number of sections of each course be taught each year. Denote by s_j the number of sections of course j which must be taught. Contract requirements are that no faculty member teach more than six courses per year. How would you go about formulating this assignment of faculty members to course sections as a linear program? Consider first of all what would be your decision variables; what would be the constraints; and what would be a reasonable objective function? Why might the solution not be useful?

5. *Aircraft Fuel Ferrying Problem*. A standard problem with any airliner is the determination of how much fuel to take on at each stop. Fuel consumption is minimized if just sufficient fuel is taken on at each stop to fly the plane to the next stop. This policy, however, disregards the fact that fuel prices may differ from airport to the next.

Buying all the fuel at the cheapest stop may not be the cheapest policy either. This might require carrying large fuel loads which would in turn cause large amounts of fuel to be burned.

The stops that a scheduled aircraft must make are numbered in order 1, 2, 3, ..., N. The parameters of the problem are

c_t = cost/liter of fuel at stop t,
d_t = liters of fuel burned from t to $t + 1$ if just sufficient fuel is on board at t to get the craft to $t + 1$,
b = liters of additional fuel burned per excess liter of fuel delivered to $t + 1$ from t.

The problem is to determine P_t, $t = 1, 2, \ldots, N$, the amount of fuel to purchase at stop t. Formulate an LP model for solving this problem. Is it a network LP?

6. Show that any LP can be converted to an equivalent LP in which every column (variable) has at most three nonzero constraint coefficients. What does this suggest about the fundamental complexity of network LPs vs. general LPs?

Figure 7.7
PERT Diagram with Crashing Allowed

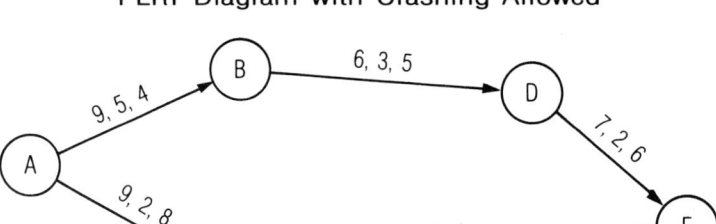

7. In Figure 7.7 is the activity-on-arc diagram showing the precedence relations among the five activities involved in repairing a refinery. The three numbers above each arc represent (from left to right respectively) the normal time for performing the activity in days, the time to perform the activity if crashed to the maximum extent, and the additional cost in $1000 for each day that the activity is shortened. An activity can be partially crashed. It is desired to complete the project in 15 days. Write an LP formulation for determining how much each activity should be crashed.

8. Given n currencies, the one period currency exchange problem is characterized by a beginning inventory vector, an exchange rate matrix, and an ending inventory requirement vector defined as follows:

n_j = amount of cash on hand in currency i, at the beginning of the period measured in units of currency i, for $i = 1, 2, \ldots, n$;
r_{ij} = units of currency j obtainable per unit of currency i for $i = 1, 2, \ldots, n$, $j = 1, 2, \ldots, n$. Note that $r_{ii} = 1$ and in general we can expect that $r_{ij} < 1/r_{ji}$ for $i \neq j$.

e_i = minimum ending inventory requirement for currency i, for $i = 1, 2, \ldots, n$. That is, at the end of the period we must have at least e_i units of currency i on hand.

The decision variables are:

X_{ij} = amount of currency i converted into currency j, for $i = 1, 2, \ldots, n$; $j = 1, 2, \ldots, n$.

Formulate a model for determining an efficient set of values for the X_{ij}. The formulation should have the following features:

(a) If there is a "money pump" kind of arbitrage opportunity, the model will find it.

(b) It should not be biased against any particular currency, e.g., the solution should be independent of which currency is called 1.

(c) If a currency is worthless, you should buy no more of it than that sufficient to meet the minimum requirement. A currency i is worthless if $r_{ij} = 0$ for all $j \neq i$.

8
Multiperiod Planning Problems

Introduction

One of the most important uses of LP is in multiperiod planning. Most of the problems we have considered thus far have been essentially one period problems. The formulations acted as if decisions this period were decoupled from decisions in future periods. Typically, however, if we produce more of a certain product this period than a constraint requires, that extra production will not be worthless but can probably be used next period.

These interactions between periods can be represented very easily within LP models. In fact, most large LPs encountered in practice are multiperiod models. A common synonym for "multiperiod" is "dynamic"; e.g., a multiperiod LP may be referred to as a dynamic model.

Interperiod interactions are usually accounted for in LPs by the introduction of inventory decision variables. These variables "link" adjacent periods. As an example, suppose we have a single explicit decision to make each period, namely, how much to produce of a single product. Call this decision variable for period j, P_j. Further, suppose we have contracts to sell known amounts of this product, d_j, in period j. Define the decision variable I_j as the amount of inventory left over at the end of period j. By this convention the beginning inventory in period j is I_{j-1}. The LP formulation will then contain one "sources of product = uses of product" constraint for each period. For period 2 the sources of product are: beginning inventory, I_1, and production in the period, P_2. The uses of product are: demand, d_2, and end of period inventory, I_2. For example, if $d_2 = 60$ and $d_3 = 40$, then the constraint for period 2 is

$$I_1 + P_2 = 60 + I_2 \text{ or } I_1 + P_2 - I_2 = 60.$$

The constraint for period 3 is

$$I_2 + P_3 - I_3 = 40.$$

Notice how I_2 "links," i.e., appears in both the constraints for period 2 and 3.

In some problems the net outflow need not exactly equal the net inflow into the next period. For example, if the product is cash, then one of the linking variables may be short-term borrowing or lending. For each dollar which is carried over from period 2 by lending, we will enter period 3 with $1.05 if the interest rate is 5% per period.

On the other hand, if the "product" is workforce and there is a predictable attrition rate of 10% per period, then the above two constraints would be modified to

$$0.90I_1 + P_2 - I_2 = 60$$
$$0.90I_2 + P_3 - I_3 = 40.$$

In this case, P_i is the number hired in period i.

The following example provides a simplified illustration of a single product, multi-period planning situation.

A Dynamic Production Problem

A company produces one product for which the demand for the next four quarters is predicted to be:

Spring	Summer	Autumn	Winter
20	30	50	60

Assuming all the demand is to be met, there are two extreme policies which might be followed:

1. "Track" demand with production and carry no inventory.

2. Produce at a constant rate of 40 units per quarter and allow inventory to absorb the fluctuations in demand.

There are costs associated with carrying inventory and costs associated with varying the production level, so one would expect that the least cost policy is probably a combination of (1) and (2), i.e., carry some inventory but also vary the production level somewhat.

For costing purposes the company estimates that changing the production level from one period to the next costs $500 per unit. These costs are often called "hiring and firing" costs. It is estimated that inventory costs can be accurately approximated by charging $800 for each unit of inventory at the end of the period. The initial inventory is zero and the current production level is 55 units per quarter. We require that these same levels be returned to at the end of the winter quarter.

We can now calculate that the cost of the no inventory policy as:

$$\$500 \times (35 + 10 + 20 + 10 + 5) = \$40{,}000.$$

On the other hand, the cost of the constant production policy is

$$\$800 \times (20 + 30 + 20 + 0) + 500 \times (15 + 15) = \$71{,}000.$$

We can find the least cost policy by formulating a linear program.

Formulation

The following definitions of variables will be useful:

P_i = number of units produced in period i, for i = 1, 2, 3, and 4,
I_i = units in inventory at the end of period i,
U_i = increase in production level between period $i - 1$ and i,
D_i = decrease in production level between $i - 1$ and i.

The P_i variables are the obvious decision variables. It is useful to define the I_i, U_i and D_i variables so that we can conveniently compute the costs each period.

To minimize the cost per year we want to minimize the sum of inventory costs:

$$\$800\, I_1 + \$800\, I_2 + \$800\, I_3 + \$800\, I_4$$

plus production change costs:

$$\$500\, U_1 + \$500\, U_2 + \$500\, U_3 + \$500\, U_4 \\ + \$500\, D_1 + \$500\, D_2 + \$500\, D_3 + \$500\, D_4.$$

Constraints

Every multiperiod problem will have a "material balance" or "sources = uses" constraint for each product for each period. The usual form of these constraints in words is:

beginning inventory + production − ending inventory = demand.

Algebraically these constraints for the problem at hand are:

$$P_1 - I_1 = 20 \\ I_1 + P_2 - I_2 = 30 \\ I_2 + P_3 - I_3 = 50 \\ I_3 + P_4 = 60.$$

Notice that I_4 and I_0 do not appear in the first and last constraints because initial and ending inventories are required to be zero.

If the formulation is solved as is, there is nothing to force U_1, D_1, etc. to be greater than zero. Therefore, the solution will be the pure production policy, namely, $P_1 = 20$, $P_2 = 30$, $P_3 = 50$, $P_4 = 60$. This policy implies a production increase at the end of each period but the last. This suggests that a way of forcing U_1, U_2, U_3, U_4 to take the proper values is to append the constraints:

$$U_1 \geq P_1 - 55 \\ U_2 \geq P_2 - P_1 \\ U_3 \geq P_3 - P_2 \\ U_4 \geq P_4 - P_3.$$

Production decreases are still not properly measured. An analogous set of four constraints should take care of this problem, specifically:

$$D_1 \geq 55 - P_1 \\ D_2 \geq P_1 - P_2 \\ D_3 \geq P_2 - P_3 \\ D_4 \geq P_3 - P_4.$$

A Dynamic Production Problem

To incorporate the requirement that the production level be returned to 55 at the end of the winter quarter we add the variables U_5 and D_5 to measure changes at the end of the last quarter. U_5 and D_5 are forced to take on the right values with the constraints:

$$U_5 \geqq 55 - P_4$$
$$D_5 \geqq P_4 - 55.$$

This completes the formulation. When it is solved we get the mixed policy:

$$P_1 = P_2 = 25; \quad P_3 = P_4 = 55.$$

Before moving on we will note that the formulation can be simplified from one with 14 constraints to one with 9 constraints. The key observation is that two constraints like

$$U_2 \geqq P_2 - P_1$$
$$D_2 \geqq P_1 - P_2$$

can be replaced by the single constraint

$$U_2 - D_2 = P_2 - P_1.$$

The argument is more economic than algebraic. The purpose with either formulation is to force $U_2 = P_2 - P_1$ if $P_2 - P_1 \geqq 0$ and $D_2 = P_1 - P_2$ if $P_1 - P_2 \geqq 0$. From economics you can argue that at the optimal solution you will find at most one of U_2 and D_2 are > 0 under either formulation. If both U_2 and D_2 are > 0 under the second formulation then both can be reduced by an equal amount and thus reducing costs without violating any constraints.

The complete, compact formulation is

```
MIN      800 I1 + 800 I2 + 800 I3 + 500 U1
       + 500 U2 + 500 U3 + 500 U4 + 500 D1
       + 500 D2 + 500 D3 + 500 D4 + 500 U5
       + 500 D5
SUBJECT TO
    2)  -  I1 + P1 =     20
    3)     I1 - I2 + P2 =    30
    4)     I2 - I3 + P3 =    50
    5)     I3 + P4 =     60
    6)     U1 - D1 - P1 =  - 55
    7)     U2 - D2 + P1 - P2 =   0
    8)     U3 - D3 + P2 - P3 =   0
    9)     U4 - D4 + P3 - P4 =   0
   10)     U5 - D5 + P4 =    55
END
```

The solution is

```
LP OPTIMUM FOUND
        OBJECTIVE FUNCTION VALUE
   1)      38000.0000
```

VARIABLE	VALUE	REDUCED COST
I1	5.000000	0.000000
I2	0.000000	700.000000
I3	5.000000	0.000000
U1	0.000000	1000.000000
U2	0.000000	100.000000
U3	30.000000	0.000000
U4	0.000000	0.000000
D1	30.000000	0.000000
D2	0.000000	900.000000
D3	0.000000	1000.000000
D4	0.000000	1000.000000
P1	25.000000	0.000000
P2	25.000000	0.000000
P3	55.000000	0.000000
U5	0.000000	800.000000
D5	0.000000	200.000000
P4	55.000000	0.000000

ROW	SLACK	DUAL PRICES
2)	0.000000	900.000000
3)	0.000000	100.000000
4)	0.000000	0.000000
5)	0.000000	−800.000000
6)	0.000000	500.000000
7)	0.000000	−400.000000
8)	0.000000	−500.000000
9)	0.000000	−500.000000
10)	0.000000	300.000000

The mixed policy found by LP is $2,000 cheaper than the best pure policy.

Most realistic multiperiod problems involve more than one product. The next example moves a step in this direction towards realism by considering several products.

Multiperiod Financial Models

In most multiperiod planning problems the management of liquid or cash-like assets is an important consideration. If you are willing to consider cash holdings as an inventory just like an inventory of any other commodity, then it is a small step to incorporate financial management decisions into a multiperiod model. The key feature is that for every period, there is a constraint which effectively says "sources of cash − uses of cash = 0." The following simple but realistic example illustrates the major features of such models.

Example: Cash Flow Matching

Suppose that as a result of a careful planning exercise you have concluded that to meet certain commitments you will need the following amounts of cash for the current plus next 14 years:

Year:	0	1	2	3	4	5	6	7	8	9	10	11	12	13	14
Cash (in $1,000s):	10	11	12	14	15	17	19	20	22	24	26	29	31	33	36

A common example where such a projection is made is in a personal injury lawsuit. Both parties may reach an agreement that the injured party should receive a stream of payments such as above or its equivalent.

For administrative simplicity both parties prefer an immediate single lump sum payment which is "equivalent" to the above stream of 15 payments. The party receiving the lump sum will argue that the lump sum payment should equal the present value of the stream using a low interest rate such as that obtained in a very low risk investment such as a government guaranteed savings account. For example, if an interest rate of 4% is used, the present value of the stream of payments is $230,437. The party which must pay the lump sum, however, would like to argue for a much higher interest rate. To be successful, such an argument must include evidence that such higher interest rate investments are available and are no riskier than savings accounts. The investments usually offered are government securities. Generally a broad spectrum of such investments are available on a given day. For simplicity assume that there are just two such investments available with the following features:

Security	Current Cost	Yearly Return	Years to Maturity	Principal Repayment at Maturity
1	$980	$60	5	$1000
2	$965	$65	12	$1000

The paying party will offer a lump sum now with a recommendation of how much should be invested in securities 1, 2 and in savings accounts such that the yearly cash requirements are met with the minimum lump sum payment.

The following decision variables are useful in solving this problem:

B_1 = amount invested now into security 1, measured in "face value amount,"
B_2 = amount invested now into security 2, measured in "face value amount,"
S_i = amount invested into a savings account in year i,
L = initial lump sum.

The objective function will be to minimize the initial lump sum. There will be a constraint for each year which forces the cash flows to net to zero. If we assume that idle cash is invested at 4% in a savings account and all amounts are measured in $1000, then the formulation is:

```
MIN     L
SUBJECT TO
    2)   L - 0.98 B1 - 0.965 B2 - S0 =            10
    3)   0.06 B1 + 0.065 B2 + 1.04 S0 - S1 =      11
    4)   0.06 B1 + 0.065 B2 + 1.04 S1 - S2 =      12
    5)   0.06 B1 + 0.065 B2 + 1.04 S2 - S3 =      14
    6)   0.06 B1 + 0.065 B2 + 1.04 S3 - S4 =      15
    7)   1.06 B1 + 0.065 B2 + 1.04 S4 - S5 =      17
    8)   0.065 B2 + 1.04 S5 - S6 =                19
    9)   0.065 B2 + 1.04 S6 - S7 =                20
   10)   0.065 B2 + 1.04 S7 - S8 =                22
   11)   0.065 B2 + 1.04 S8 - S9 =                24
   12)   0.065 B2 + 1.04 S9 - S10 =               26
   13)   0.065 B2 + 1.04 S10 - S11 =              29
```

```
 14)    1.065 B2 + 1.04 S11 -   S12 =       31
 15)    1.04 S12 -  S13 =   33
 16)    1.04 S13 -  S14 =   36
END
```

The PICTURE of the constraint coefficients gives a better appreciation of the structure of the problem.

```
                                S S S S S
              B B S S S S S S S S S 1 1 1 1 1
              L 1 2 0 1 2 3 4 5 6 7 8 9 0 1 2 3 4

         1:   1                                     MIN
         2:   1-T-T-1                               = A
         3:     U U A-1                             = B
         4:     U U   A-1                           = B
         5:     U U     A-1                         = B
         6:     U U       A-1                       = B
         7:     A U         A-1                     = B
         8:       U           A-1                   = B
         9:       U             A-1                 = B
        10:       U               A-1               = B
        11:       U                 A-1             = B
        12:       U                   A-1           = B
        13:       U                     A-1         = B
        14:       A                       A-1       = B
        15:                                 A-1     = B
        16:                                   A-1   = B
```

Notice that in row 7 B_1 has a coefficient of 1.06. This represents the principal repayment of $1000 plus the interest payment of $60 measured in $1000s. Variable S_{14}, (investment of funds in a savings account after the final payment is made), appears in the problem even though at first you might think it useless to allow such an option. S_{14} is effectively a surplus cash variable in the final period. Nevertheless, it is not unusual for the solution which minimizes the lump sum payment to have cash left over at the end of the problem. This is because a bond may be the most economical way of delivering funds to intermediate periods. This may cause the big principal repayment at the end of a bond's life to "overpay" the most distant periods. The solution is:

```
              OBJECTIVE FUNCTION VALUE

         1)           195.6837

         VARIABLE         VALUE           REDUCED COST
             L          195.683672            0.000000
             B1          95.795770            0.000000
             B2          90.154735            0.000000
             S0           4.804497            0.000000
             S1           5.604481            0.000000
             S2           5.436464            0.000000
             S3           3.261727            0.000000
             S4           0.000000            0.106979
             S5          90.403574            0.000000
             S6          80.879776            0.000000
             S7          69.975025            0.000000
```

S8	56.634084	0.000000
S9	40.759506	0.000000
S10	22.249944	0.000000
S11	0.000000	0.141246
S12	65.014792	0.000000
S13	34.615385	0.000000
S14	0.000000	0.379637

ROW	SLACK	DUAL PRICES
2)	0.000000	-1.000000
3)	0.000000	-0.961538
4)	0.000000	-0.924556
5)	0.000000	-0.888996
6)	0.000000	-0.854804
7)	0.000000	-0.719063
8)	0.000000	-0.691406
9)	0.000000	-0.664814
10)	0.000000	-0.639244
11)	0.000000	-0.614658
12)	0.000000	-0.591017
13)	0.000000	-0.568286
14)	0.000000	-0.410615
15)	0.000000	-0.394822
16)	0.000000	-0.379637

NO. ITERATIONS=   15

Of the $195,683.70 lump sum payment, $10,000 goes to immediate requirements, $4,804.50 goes into a savings account and $0.98 \times 95{,}795.77 + 0.965 \times 90{,}154.74 = \$180{,}879.20$ goes into longer term securities. By considering a wider range of investments rather than just savings accounts the amount of the lump sum payment has been reduced by about $34,750 or 15%.

In actual solutions one may find that a major fraction of the lump sum is invested in a single security. For example, limiting the amount invested in security 1 to half the initial lump sum is enforced by appending the constraint:

$$0.98B_1 - 0.5L \leqq 0.$$

Such constraints are typically called portfolio constraints.

An additional complication may arise due to integrality requirements on the B_1 and B_2 investments. For example, bonds can be bought only in $1000 increments. Generally, with a modest amount of judgement, the fractional values can be rounded to neighboring integer values with no great increase in lump sum payment. For example, if B_1 and B_2 are set to 96 and 90 in the previous example, the total cost increases to $195,726.50 from $195,683.70. When this is done, S_{14} becomes nonzero; specifically, the last period is overpaid by about $40.

Financial Planning Models with Tax Considerations

The next example treats a slightly more complicated version of the portfolio selection problem and then illustrates how to include and examine the effect of taxes. Winston-

Salem Development Management (WSDM) is trying to complete its investment plans for the next three years. Currently, WSDM has 2 million dollars available for investment. At six month intervals over the next three years, WSDM expects the following income stream from previous investments: $500,000 (6 months from now), $400,000; $380,000; $360,000; $340,000 and $300,000 (at the end of third year). There are three development projects in which WSDM is considering participating. The Foster City Development would, if WSDM participated fully, have the following cash flow stream (projected) at six month intervals over the next three years (negative numbers represent investments, positive numbers represent income): −$3,000,000; −$1,000,000; −$1,800,000; $400,000; $1,800,000; $1,800,000; $5,500,000. The last figure is its estimated value at the end of three years. A second project involves taking over the operation of some old lower-middle income housing on the condition that certain initial repairs to it be made and that it be demolished at the end of three years. The cash flow stream for this project if participated in fully would be: −$2,000,000; −$500,000; $1,500,000; $1,500,000; $1,500,000; $200,000; −$1,000,000.

The third project, the Disney-Universe Hotel, would have the following cash flow stream (six-month intervals) if WSDM participated fully. Again the last figure is the estimated value at the end of the three years: −$2,000,000; −$2,000,000; −$1,800,000; $1,000,000; $1,000,000; $1,000,000; $6,000,000. WSDM can borrow money for half-year intervals at 3.5 percent interest per half year. At most, 2 million dollars can be borrowed at one time, i.e., the total outstanding principal can never exceed 2 million. WSDM can invest surplus funds at 3 percent per half-year.

Initially we will disregard taxes. We will formulate the problem of maximizing WSDM's net worth at the end of three years as a linear program. If WSDM participates in a project at less than 100 percent, all the cash flows of that project are reduced appropriately.

Formulation and Solution of the WSDM Problem

Define: F = fractional participation in the Foster City problem,
M = fractional participation in Lower-Middle;
D = participation in Disney;
B_i = amount borrowed in period i in 1000s of dollars, $i = 1, \ldots, 6$;
L_i = amount lent in period i in 1000s of dollars, $i = 1, \ldots, 6$;
Z = net worth after the six periods in 1000s of dollars.

The problem formally is then (all numbers will be measured in units of 1000):

```
     MAX      Z    ! Max worth at end of final period;
     SUBJECT TO
           ! Sources - uses = demands for cash in each period;
       2)      3000 F + 2000 M + 2000 D - B1 + L1 = 2000
       3)      1000 F +  500 M + 2000 D + 1.035 B1 - 1.03 L1 - B2 + L2 = 500
       4)      1800 F + 1500 M + 1800 D + 1.035 B2 - 1.03 L2 - B3 + L3 = 400
       5)     - 400 F - 1500 M - 1000 D + 1.035 B3 - 1.03 L3 - B4 + L4 = 380
       6)     -1800 F - 1500 M - 1000 D + 1.035 B4 - 1.03 L4 - B5 + L5 = 360
       7)     -1800 F -  200 M - 1000 D + 1.035 B5 - 1.03 L5 - B6 + L6 = 340
       8)      Z - 5500 F + 1000 M - 6000 D + 1.035 B6 - 1.03 L6 = 300
```

```
      ! Borrowing limits;
 9)      B1 ≤   2000
10)      B2 ≤   2000
11)      B3 ≤   2000
12)      B4 ≤   2000
13)      B5 ≤   2000
14)      B6 ≤   2000
      ! We can invest at most 100% in a project;
15)       F ≤   1
16)       M ≤   1
17)       D ≤   1
```

Constraints 2 through 8 are the cash flow constraints for each of the periods. They enforce the requirement that uses of cash − sources of cash = 0 for each period. In the initial period, for example, L1 is a use of cash while B1 is a source of cash.

The solution is

```
                OBJECTIVE FUNCTION VALUE

        1)          7665.179

   VARIABLE         VALUE              REDUCED COST
      Z           7665.179080            0.000000
      F              0.714341            0.000000
      M              0.637210            0.000000
      D              0.000000          452.381714
      B1          1417.443340            0.000000
      L1             0.000000            0.008788
      B2          2000.000000            0.000000
      L2             0.000000            0.334314
      B3          2000.000000            0.000000
      L3             0.000000            0.250956
      B4           448.449000            0.000000
      L4             0.000000            0.005305
      B5             0.000000            0.005150
      L5          2137.484220            0.000000
      B6             0.000000            0.000000
      L6          3954.865110            0.000000

      ROW           SLACK              DUAL PRICES
       2)           0.000000            1.819220
       3)           0.000000            1.757701
       4)           0.000000            1.381929
       5)           0.000000            1.098032
       6)           0.000000            1.060900
       7)           0.000000            1.030000
       8)           0.000000            1.000000
       9)         582.556671            0.000000
      10)           0.000000            0.327404
      11)           0.000000            0.245466
      12)        1551.551010            0.000000
      13)        2000.000000            0.000000
      14)        2000.000000            0.000000
      15)           0.285659            0.000000
      16)           0.362790            0.000000
      17)           1.000000            0.000000
```

SENSITIVITY ANALYSIS:

RANGES IN WHICH THE BASIS IS UNCHANGED
COST COEFFICIENT RANGES

VARIABLE	CURRENT COEF	ALLOWABLE INCREASE	ALLOWABLE DECREASE
Z	1.000000	INFINITY	1.000000
F	0.000000	3043.722050	454.594936
M	0.000000	644.819443	583.692337
D	0.000000	452.381714	INFINITY
B1	0.000000	0.008822	0.409697
L1	0.000000	0.008788	INFINITY
B2	0.000000	INFINITY	0.327404
L2	0.000000	0.334314	INFINITY
B3	0.000000	INFINITY	0.245466
L3	0.000000	0.250956	INFINITY
B4	0.000000	0.005305	0.162487
L4	0.000000	0.005305	INFINITY
B5	0.000000	0.005150	INFINITY
L5	0.000000	0.005150	0.222112
B6	0.000000	0.005000	INFINITY
L6	0.000000	0.005000	0.227865

RIGHTHAND SIDE RANGES

ROW	CURRENT RHS	ALLOWABLE INCREASE	ALLOWABLE DECREASE
2	2000.000000	1415.854160	2526.244390
3	500.000000	775.555534	1887.037060
4	400.000000	1198.599240	942.752693
5	380.000000	448.449009	1551.551030
6	360.000000	INFINITY	2137.484220
7	340.000000	INFINITY	3954.865110
8	300.000000	INFINITY	7665.179080
9	2000.000000	INFINITY	582.556671
10	2000.000000	561.718163	1136.009160
11	2000.000000	1027.054430	296.852333
12	2000.000000	INFINITY	1551.551010
13	2000.000000	INFINITY	2000.000000
14	2000.000000	INFINITY	2000.000000
15	1.000000	INFINITY	0.285659
16	1.000000	INFINITY	0.362790
17	1.000000	INFINITY	1.000000

Interpretation of the Dual Prices

The dual price on each of the first seven constraints is the increase in net worth in the last period resulting from an extra dollar made available in the earliest period. For example, the 1.81922 indicates that an extra dollar available at the start of period 1 would increase the net worth in the last period by about $1.82.

An extra dollar in period 5 is worth $1.0609 at the end because all that we will do with it is invest it for 2 periods at 3 percent. Thus, it will grow to $1.03 \times 1.03 = 1.0609$ at the end.

An extra dollar in period 4 will save us from borrowing a dollar that period; thus, we will be $1.035 richer in period 5. We have already seen the value per extra dollar in period 5, so the value of an extra dollar in period 4 is $1.035 \times 1.0609 = $1.09803.

The dual prices on the borrowing constraints can be reconciled with the rest of the dual prices as follows. Being able to have an additional dollar in period 2 is worth 1.7577. If this dollar were borrowed, then we would have to pay out $1.035 in period 3 which would have an effective cost of 1.035 × 1.38193. Thus, the net value in the last period of being able to borrow an extra dollar in period 2 is $1.7577 - 1.035 \times 1.38193 = 0.3274$, which agrees with the dual price on the borrowing constraint for period 2.

The effective interest rate or cost of capital, i, in any period t can be found from the dual prices by deriving the rate at which one would be willing to borrow. Borrowing one dollar in period t would give us \$1 more in period t but would require us to pay out $1 + i$ dollars in period $t + 1$. We must balance these two considerations. Consider period 1. An extra dollar is worth \$1.81922 at the end of period 6. Paying back $1 + i$ in period 2 would cost $(1 + i)$ \$1.7577 at the end of period 6. Balancing these two:

$$1.81922 = (1 + i)1.7577.$$

Solving,

$$i = 0.035.$$

This is not surprising because we are already borrowing at that rate in period 1, but not to the limit.

Applying similar analysis to the other periods we get the following effective rates:

Period	i	Period	i
1	0.035	4	0.035
2	0.2719	5	0.03
3	0.25855	6	0.03

Accounting for Income Taxes

Suppose we take taxes into account. Let us consider the following simplified situation. There is a tax rate of 50 percent on profit for any period. If there is a loss in a period, 80 percent can be carried forward to the next period. (Typically tax laws put a limit on how many years a loss can be carried forward, but the 80% may be a good approximation.)

Taxable income for each of the prospective projects as well as all existing projects are given in the table below. Note that because of things like depreciation, actual net cash flow may be rather different from taxable income in a period.

		Project		
Period	Foster City	Lower-Middle Housing	Disney Universe	Existing
1	−100,000	−200,000	150,000	0
2	−300,000	−400,000	−200,000	100,000
3	−600,000	−200,000	−300,000	80,000
4	−100,000	500,000	−200,000	76,000
5	500,000	1,000,000	500,000	72,000
6	1,000,000	100,000	800,000	68,000
7	4,000,000	−1,000,000	5,000,000	60,000

To formulate a model in this case we need to additionally define:

P_i = profit in period i.
C_i = loss in period i.

The formulation is affected in two ways. First, we must append some equations which force the P_i's and C_i's to be computed properly and secondly, terms must be added to the cash flow constraints to account for the cash expended in the payment of tax.

In words, one of the tax computation equations is:

Profit − loss = revenue − expense − 0.8 × (last period's loss).

Algebraically in LINDO, this equation for period 2 is:

P2 − C2 = 100 + .03L1 − 300F − 400M − 200D − .035B1 − .8C1

or in standard form:

P2 − C2 − .03L1 + 300F + 400M + 200D + .035B1 + .8C1 = 100.

The entire formulation is:

```
MAX      Z
SUBJECT TO
         ! Cash flow constraints, including the 50% tax usage;
  2)     3000 F + 2000 M + 2000 D - B1 + L1 + 0.5 P1 =      2000
  3)     1000 F + 500 M + 2000 D + 1.035 B1 - 1.03 L1 - B2 + L2
         + 0.5 P2 =    500
  4)     1800 F - 1500 M + 1800 D + 1.035 B2 - 1.03 L2 - B3 + L3
         + 0.5 P3 =    400
  5)     - 400 F - 1500 M - 1000 D + 1.035 B3 - 1.03 L3 - B4 + L4
         + 0.5 P4 =    380
  6)     - 1800 F - 1500 M - 1000 D + 1.035 B4 - 1.03 L4 - B5 + L5
         + 0.5 P5 =    360
  7)     - 1800 F - 200 M - 1000 D + 1.035 B5 - 1.03 L5 - B6 + L6
         + 0.5 P6 =    340
  8)     Z - 5500 F + 1000 M - 6000 D + 1.035 B6 - 1.03 L6 + 0.5 P7
         =    300
         ! The borrowing limits;
  9)     B1 ≤ 2000
 10)     B2 ≤ 2000
 11)     B3 ≤ 2000
 12)     B4 ≤ 2000
 13)     B5 ≤ 2000
 14)     B6 ≤ 2000
         ! The investing limits;
 15)     F ≤ 1
 16)     M ≤ 1
 17)     D ≤ 1
         ! Taxable Profit-Loss for each period;
 18)     100 F + 200 M + 150 D + P1 - C1 =    0
 19)     300 F + 400 M + 200 D + 0.035 B1 - 0.03 L1 + P2 + 0.8 C1 - C2
         =    100
 20)     600 F + 200 M + 300 D + 0.035 B2 - 0.03 L2 + P3 + 0.8 C2 - C3
         =    80
```

21) $100 F - 500 M + 200 D + 0.035 B3 - 0.03 L3 + P4 + 0.8 C3 - C4 = 76$
22) $-500 F - 1000 M - 500 D + 0.035 B4 - 0.03 L4 + P5 + 0.8 C4 - C5 = 72$
23) $-1000 F - 100 M - 800 D + 0.035 B5 - 0.03 L5 + P6 + 0.8 C5 - C6 = 68$
24) $-4000 F + 1000 M - 5000 D + 0.035 B6 - 0.03 L6 + P7 + 0.8 C6 - C7 = 60$

The solution is:

OBJECTIVE FUNCTION VALUE

1)   5899.976

VARIABLE	VALUE	REDUCED COST
Z	5899.975590	0.000000
F	0.487211	0.000000
M	1.000000	0.000000
D	0.000000	945.007523
B1	1461.632140	0.000000
L1	0.000000	0.005112
B2	2000.000020	0.000000
L2	0.000000	0.196093
B3	1046.979320	0.000000
L3	0.000000	0.003168
B4	0.000000	0.002576
L4	991.260727	0.000000
B5	0.000000	0.002537
L5	3221.649020	0.000000
B6	0.000000	0.002500
L6	4359.347720	0.000000
P1	0.000000	0.449947
P2	0.000000	0.379308
P3	0.000000	0.204255
P4	0.000000	0.110749
P5	1072.657820	0.000000
P6	751.860207	0.000000
P7	1139.623200	0.000000
C1	248.721067	0.000000
C2	696.297211	0.000000
C3	1039.364200	0.000000
C4	340.856709	0.000000
C5	0.000000	0.109113
C6	0.000000	0.107500
C7	0.000000	0.500000

ROW	SLACK	DUAL PRICES
2)	0.000000	1.321874
3)	0.000000	1.286092
4)	0.000000	1.067654
5)	0.000000	1.045678
6)	0.000000	1.030225
7)	0.000000	1.015000
8)	0.000000	1.000000
9)	538.367844	0.000000

10)	0.000000	0.192402
11)	953.020706	0.000000
12)	2000.000000	0.000000
13)	2000.000000	0.000000
14)	2000.000000	0.000000
15)	0.512789	0.000000
16)	0.000000	573.561150
17)	1.000000	0.000000
18)	0.000000	−0.210990
19)	0.000000	−0.263738
20)	0.000000	−0.329672
21)	0.000000	−0.412090
22)	0.000000	−0.515113
23)	0.000000	−0.507500
24)	0.000000	−0.500000

Notice that tax considerations cause a substantial change in the solution. More funds are placed into the lower-middle income housing project, M, and less funds are invested in the Foster City, F, project. Project M has cash flows which help to smooth out the stream of yearly profits.

Summary Discussion of Multiperiod Models

Models for planning over time partition time into a number of periods. The portion of the model corresponding to a single period might be some combination of product mix, blending, etc., models. These single period or static models are linked by

1. A link or inventory variable for each commodity and period. The linking variable represents the amount of commodity transferred from one period to the next.

2. A "material balance" or "sources = uses" constraint for each commodity and period. The simplest form of this constraint is "beginning inventory + production = ending inventory + goods sold."

Multiperiod models are usually used in a rolling or sliding format. In this format the model is solved at the beginning of each period. The recommendations of the solution for the first period are implemented. As one period elapses and better data and forecasts become available, the model is slid forward one period. The period which had been number 2 becomes number 1, etc.

There is nothing sacred about having all periods of the same length. For example, when a petroleum company plans production for the coming year, it is sensible to have the periods correspond to the seasons of the year. One possible partition is to have the winter period extend from December 1 to March 15; the spring period extend from March 16 to May 15; the summer period extend from May 16 to September 15, and autumn extend from September 16 to November 30.

Some companies, such as forest products or mineral resources based companies, plan as much as 50 years into the future. In such a case one might have the first two periods be one year each, the next one period two years, the next two periods three years each, the next two periods five years each and the final three periods ten years each.

Problems

1. The Izza Steel Company of Tokyo has predicted delivery requirements of 3,000, 6,000, 5,000 and 2,000 tons of steel in the next four periods. Current workforce is at the 4,000 tons per period level. At the moment there are 500 tons of steel in stock. At the end of the four periods Izza would like its inventory position to be back at 500 tons. Regular time workforce has a variable cost of $100 per ton. Overtime can be hired in any period at a cost of $140 per ton. Regular time workforce size can be increased from one period to the next at a cost of $300 per ton of change in capacity, it can be decreased at a cost of $80 per ton. There is a charge of $5/ton for inventory at the end of each period. Izza would like the regular time workforce to be at the 3000 ton level at the end of the four periods.

    (a) Formulate Izza's problem as a linear program.

    (b) What assumption does your model make about idle workforce?

2. An airline predicts the following pilot requirements for the next 5 quarters: 80, 90, 110, 120, 110. Current staff is 90 pilots. The question of major concern is the number of pilots to hire in each of the next 5 quarters. A pilot must spend the quarter in which she is hired in training. The line's training facilities limit the number of pilots in training to at most 15. Further, the training of pilots requires the services of experienced pilots at the ratio of 5 to 1, e.g., 5 pilots in training require 1 experienced pilot. An experienced pilot so assigned cannot be used to satisfy regular requirements. The cost of hiring and training a pilot is estimated at $20,000 exclusive of the experienced pilot time required. Experienced pilots cost $25,000 per quarter. Company policy does not include firing pilots.

    (a) What are the variables?

    (b) Formulate a model for determining how many pilots to hire in each period.

3. The Toute de Suite Candy Company includes in its product line a number of different mixed nut products. The Chalet nut mix is required to have no more than 25 percent peanuts and no less than 40 percent almonds.

    The nuts available, their prices and their availabilities this month are as follows:

	Price	Availability
Peanuts	20¢/lb.	400 lbs.
Walnuts	35¢/lb.	no limit
Almonds	50¢/lb.	200 lbs.

    The Chalet mix sells for 80 cents per lb. At most 700 lbs. can be mixed per month in questions (a), (b) and (c).

    (a) Formulate the appropriate model for this problem.

    (b) Toute de Suite would like to incorporate into the analysis it second major mixed nut line, the Hovel line. The Hovel mix can contain no more than 60 percent peanuts and no less than 20 percent almonds. Hovel sells for 40 cents per lb. Modify your model appropriately.

(c) Toute de Suite would like to incorporate next month's requirements into the analysis. The expected situation next month is:

	Price	Requirement (Availability)
Peanuts	19¢/lb.	500 lbs.
Walnuts	36¢/lb.	no limit
Almonds	52¢/lb.	180 lbs.
Chalet	81¢/lb.	
Hovel	39¢/lb.	

It costs 2 cents per lb. to store nuts (plain or mixed) for one month. Due to a contract commitment at least 200 lbs. of Chalet mix must be sold next month. Modify your model appropriately.

9

Blending of Input Materials

Introduction

In a blending problem there are:

1. Two or more input raw material commodities;
2. One or more qualities associated with each input commodity;
3. One or more output products to be produced by blending the input commodities so that certain output quality requirements are satisfied.

A good approximation is usually that the quality of the finished product is the weighted average of the qualities of the products that went into it.

Some examples are:

Output Commodity	Qualities	Raw Materials
Food, feed	Protein, carbohydrate, fat content	Corn, oats, soybeans
Gasoline	Octane, volatility, vapor pressure	Types of crude oil refinery products
Metals	Carbon, manganese, chrome content	Metal ore, scrap metals
Grain for export	Moisture, percent foreign material, percent damaged	Grain from various suppliers
Coal for sale	Sulphur, BTU, ash, moisture content	Coal from Illinois, Wyoming, Pennsylvania
Wine	Vintage, variety, region	Pure wines of various regions
Bank balance sheet	Proportion of loans of various types, average duration of loans and investment portfolios	Types of loans and investments available

Blending models are used most frequently in three industries:

1. feed and feed, e.g. the blending of cattle feed, hotdogs, etc.;
2. metals industry, e.g., blending of specialty steels and nonferrous alloys, especially where recycled or scrap materials are used;
3. petroleum industry, e.g., for blending gasolines of specified octanes and volatility.

The market price of a typical raw material commodity may change significantly over the period of a month or even a week. The smart buyer will want to be sure to be buying corn, say, from the cheapest supplier. The even smarter buyer will want to exploit the fact that as the price of corn drops relative to soybeans, s/he may be able to save some money by switching to a blend that uses more corn.

Fields *et al.* (1978) describe a feed blending LP for constructing low cost rations for cattle in a feedlot. This particular model was used at the rate of over 1,000 times/month by feedlot managers.

A recent success story in the steel industry has been the mini-mill. These small mills use mostly recyclable scrap steels to be charged into an electric furnace. The blending problem in this case is to decide what combination of scrap types to use so as to satisfy output quality requirements for specified products such as reinforcing bars, etc.

The first general LP to appear in print was a blending or diet problem formulated by George Stigler (1945). The problem was to construct a "recipe" from about 80 foods so that the mix satisfied about a dozen nutritional requirements; for example, percent protein greater than 5 percent, percent cellulose less than 40 percent, etc. When Stigler formulated this problem the Simplex method for solving LPs did not exist and it was not widely realized that this "diet problem" was just a special case of this wider class of problems. Stigler, realizing its generality, stated ". . . there does not appear to be any direct method of finding the minimum of a linear function subject to linear conditions." The solution he obtained to his specific problem by ingenious arguments was within a few cents of the least cost solution determined later when the Simplex method was invented. Both the least cost solution and Stigler's solution were not exactly haute cuisine. Both consisted largely of cabbage, flour and dried navy beans with a touch of spinach for excitement. It is not clear that anyone would want to exist on this diet or even live with someone who was on it. These solutions illustrate the importance of explicitly including in the formulation constraints which are so obvious that they are forgotten, in this case palatability constraints.

The Structure of Blending Problems

Let us consider a simple feed blending problem. We must produce a batch of cattle feed having a protein content of at least 15%. This feed is produced by mixing corn (which is 6% protein) and soybean meal (which is 35% protein).

If C is the number of bushels of corn in the mix and S is the bushels of soybean meal, then the protein constraint is:

$$\frac{\text{bushels of protein in mix}}{\text{bushels in mix}} \geq 0.15 \qquad \text{(in words)}$$

or
$$\frac{0.06C + 0.35S}{C + S} \geqq 0.15 \qquad \text{(algebraically)}$$

At first glance it looks like we have trouble. This constraint is not linear. If, however, we multiply both sides by $C + S$ we get

$$0.06C + 0.35S \geqq 0.15\,(C + S)$$

or in standard form finally:

$$-0.09C + 0.20S \geqq 0.$$

Constraints on additional characteristics such as fat, carbohydrates and even such slightly nonlinear things as color, taste, and texture can be handled in similar fashion.

The distinctive feature of a blending problem is that the crucial constraints, when written in intuitive form, are *ratios* of linear expressions. They can be converted to linear form by multiplying through by the denominator. Ratio constraints may also be found in "balance sheet" financial planning models where a financial institution may have ratio constraints on the types of loans it makes or on the average duration of its investments.

The formulation is slightly more complicated if the blending aspect is just a small portion of a larger problem in which the batch size is a decision variable. The second example in this section will consider this complication. The first example will consider the situation where the batch size is specified beforehand.

Example: The Pittsburgh Steel Company Blending Problem

The Pittsburgh Steel (PS) Co. has been contracted to produce a new type of steel which has the following tight quality requirements:

	At Least	Not More Than
Carbon Content	3.0%	3.5%
Chrome Content	0.3%	0.45%
Manganese Content	1.35%	1.65%
Silicon Content	2.7%	3.0%

PS has the following materials available for mixing up at batch:

	Cost per Pound	Percent Carbon	Percent Chrome	Percent Manganese	Percent Silicon	Amount Available
Pig Iron 1	0.03	4.0	0	0.9	2.25	unlimited
Pig Iron 2	0.0645	0	10.0	4.5	15.0	unlimited
Ferro-Silicon 1	0.065	0	0	0	45.0	unlimited
Ferro-Silicon 2	0.061	0	0	0	42.0	unlimited
Alloy 1	0.10	0	0	60.0	18.0	unlimited
Alloy 2	0.13	0	20.0	9.0	30.0	unlimited
Alloy 3	0.119	0	8.0	33.0	25.0	unlimited
Carbide (Silicon)	0.08	15.0	0	0	30.0	20 lb.
Steel 1	0.021	0.4	0	0.9	0	200 lb.
Steel 2	0.02	0.1	0	0.3	0	200 lb.
Steel 3	0.0195	0.1	0	0.3	0	200 lb.

A one ton (2000 lb.) batch must be blended which satisfies the quality requirements stated earlier. The problem now is what amounts of each of the eleven materials should be blended together so as to minimize the cost but satisfy the quality requirements. An experienced steel man claims that the least cost mix will not use any more than nine of the eleven available raw materials. What is a good blend? Most of the eleven prices and four quality control requirements are negotiable. Which prices and requirements are worth negotiating?

Note that the chemical content of a blend is simply the weighted average of the chemical content of its components. Thus, for example, if we make a blend of 40% Alloy 1 and 60% Alloy 2, the manganese content is $(0.40) \times 60 + (0.60) \times 9 = 29.4$.

Formulation and Solution of the Pittsburgh Steel Blending Problem

The PS blending problem can be formulated as an LP with 11 variables and 13 constraints. The 11 variables correspond to the 11 raw materials from which we can choose. Four constraints are from the upper usage limits on silicon-carbide and steels. Four of the constraints are from the lower quality limits. Another four constraints are from the upper quality limits. The thirteenth constraint is the requirement that the weight of all materials used must sum to 2000 pounds.

If we let P_1 be the number of pounds of Pig Iron 1 to be used, and similar notation the remaining materials, the problem of minimizing the cost per ton can be stated as:

```
MIN    0.03 P1 + 0.0645 P2 + 0.065 F1 + 0.061 F2 + 0.1 A1 + 0.13 A2
     + 0.119 A3 + 0.08 CB + 0.021 S1 + 0.02 S2 + 0.0195 S3
SUBJECT TO
! Raw material availabilities;
  2)   CB <= 20
  3)   S1 <= 200
  4)   S2 <= 200
  5)   S3 <= 200
! Quality requirements on;
  ! Carbon content;
     6)   0.04 P1 + 0.15 CB + 0.004 S1 + 0.001 S2 + 0.001 S3 >=   60
     7)   0.04 P1 + 0.15 CB + 0.004 S1 + 0.001 S2 + 0.001 S3 <=   70
  ! Chrome content;
     8)   0.1 P2 + 0.2 A2 + 0.08 A3 >=   6
     9)   0.1 P2 + 0.2 A2 + 0.08 A3 <=   9
  ! Manganese content;
    10)   0.009 P1 + 0.045 P2 + 0.6 A1 + 0.09 A2 + 0.33 A3 +
          0.009 S1 + 0.003 S2 + 0.003 S3 >=   27
    11)   0.009 P1 + 0.045 P2 + 0.6 A1 + 0.09 A2 + 0.33 A3 +
          0.009 S1 + 0.003 S2 + 0.003 S3 <=   33
  ! Silicon content;
    12)   0.0225 P1 + 0.15 P2 + 0.45 F1 + 0.42 F2 + 0.18 A1 +
          0.3 A2  + 0.25 A3 + 0.3 CB >=   54
    13)   0.0225 P1 + 0.15 P2 + 0.45 F1 + 0.42 F2 + 0.18 A1 +
          0.3 A2  + 0.25 A3 + 0.3 CB <=   60
! Finish good requirements;
    14)   P1 + P2 + F1 + F2 + A1 + A2 + A3 + CB + S1 + S2 + S3 =    2000
END
```

The general form of this model is:

> Minimize cost of raw materials
>
> subject to (a) Raw material availabilties (rows 2–5)
> (b) Quality requirements (rows 6–13)
> (c) Finish good requirements (row 14)

It is generally good practice to be consistent and group constraints in this fashion.

For this particular example, when writing the quality constraints, we have exploited the knowledge that the batch size is 2000. So for example, 3% of 2000 is 60, 3.5% of 2000 is 70, etc.

When solved, we get the solution:

```
         OBJECTIVE FUNCTION VALUE

   1)          59.5562900

  VARIABLE        VALUE          REDUCED COST
     P1        1474.264000          .000000
     P2          60.000000          .000000
     F1            .000000          .001036
     F2          22.062050          .000000
     A1          14.238860          .000000
     A2            .000000          .020503
     A3            .000000          .019926
     CB            .000000          .003357
     S1         200.000000          .000000
     S2          29.434930          .000000
     S3         200.000000          .000000

    ROW       SLACK OR SURPLUS     DUAL PRICES
    2)          20.000000           .000000
    3)            .000000           .000177
    4)         170.565100           .000000
    5)            .000000           .000500
    6)            .000000          -.183329
    7)          10.000000           .000000
    8)            .000000          -.254731
    9)           3.000000           .000000
   10)            .000000          -.104521
   11)           6.000000           .000000
   12)            .000000          -.098802
   13)           6.000000           .000000
   14)            .000000          -.019503
```

Notice that only 7 of the 11 raw materials were used.

In actual practice, this type of LP was solved on a twice monthly basis. The first solution, including the reduced cost and dual prices, was used by the purchasing agent as a guide in buying materials. The second solution later in the month was mainly for the metallurgist's benefit in making up a blend from the raw materials actually on hand.

Suppose that we can pump oxygen into the furnace. This oxygen combines completely with carbon to produce the gas CO_2 which escapes. The oxygen will burn off carbon at the rate of 12 pounds of carbon burned off for each 32 pounds of oxygen.

Oxygen costs two cents a pound. If you reformulated the problem to include this additional option, would it change the decisions? The oxygen injection option to burn off carbon is clearly uninteresting because in the current solution it is the lower bound constraint rather than the upper bound on carbon which is binding. Thus, burning off carbon, even if by itself it could be done at no expense, would increase the total cost of the solution.

A Blending Problem Within a Product Mix Problem

One additional aspect of blending problem formulation will be illustrated with an example in which the batch size is a decision variable. In the previous example the batch size was specified. In the following example the amount of product to be blended depends upon how cheaply the product can be blended. Thus, it appears that the blending decision and the batch size decision must be made simultaneously.

This example is suggestive of gasoline blending problems faced in a petroleum refinery. We wish to blend gasoline from three ingredients: butane, heavy nephtha and catalytic reformate. Four characteristics of the resultant gasoline and its inputs are important: cost, octane number, vapor pressure and volatility. These characteristics are summarized in the table below.

	Commodity			
Characteristic	Butane (BT)	Catalytic Reformate (CR)	Heavy Naphtha (HN)	Regular Gasoline (RG)
Cost/Unit	7.3	18.20	12.50	?
Octane	120	100	74	≥ 94
Vapor Pressure	60	2.6	4.1	≤ 11
Volatility	105	3	12	≥ 17

The octane rating is a measure of the gasoline's resistance to "knocking" or "pinging." Vapor pressure and volatility are closely related. Vapor pressure is a measure of susceptibility to stalling, particularly on an unusually warm spring day. Volatility is a measure of how easily the engine starts in cold weather.

In this planning period there are only 1,000 units of butane available. The production of gasoline competes with heavy fuel (HF) for production facilities. The sum of gasoline plus heavy fuel production this planning period cannot exceed 12,000 units. Any blending problems associated with production of heavy fuel are disregarded. For this example, heavy fuel is treated as a simple product. At the highest level this is a product mix problem involving the two competiing products, gasoline and heavy fuel.

The profit contribution of heavy fuel is $3.6 per unit, *including* the cost of all ingredients. The profit contribution of regular gasoline is $18.40 per unit *exclusive* of the cost of its ingredients.

A slight simplification assumed in this example is that the interaction between ingredients is linear; e.g. if a "fifty/fifty" mixture of BT and CR is made, then its octane will be $0.5 \times 120 + 0.5 \times 100 = 110$ and its volatility will be $0.5 \times 105 + 0.5 \times 3 = 54$. In reality this linearity is violated slightly, especially if gasoline containing tetraethyl lead is blended.

Formulation

The availability and capacity constraints are straightforward, specifically:

$$BT \leq 1,000$$
$$RG + HF \leq 12,000.$$

The quality constraints require a bit of thought. The fractions of the batch consisting of Butane, Catalytic Reformulate, and Heavy Naphtha are BT/RG, CR/RG and HN/RG, respectively. Thus, if the god of linearity smiles upon us, then the octane constraint of the blend should be the expression:

$$(BT/RG) \times 120 + (CR/RG) \times 100 + (HN/RG) \times 74 \geq 94.$$

Your expression, however, may be a frown because a ratio of variables like BT/RG is definitely not linear. Multiplying through by RG, however, produces the linear constraint:

$$120BT + 100CR + 74HN \geq 94RG$$

or in standard form:

$$120BT + 100CR + 74HN - 94RG \geq 0.$$

Similar arguments can be used to develop the vapor and volatility constraints. Finally, a constraint must be appended which states that the whole equals the sum of its parts, specifically:

$$RG = BT + HN + CR.$$

When all constraints are converted to standard form and the expression for profit contribution is written, we obtain the formulation:

```
MAX     18.4 RG + 3.6 HF - 7.3 BT - 12.5 HN - 18.2 CR
SUBJECT TO
! Raw material and capacity limits
    2)      BT ≤   1000
    3)      RG +   HF ≤    12000
! Octane requirement
    4)   - 94 RG + 120 BT + 74 HN + 100 CR ≥     0
! Vapor pressure requirement
    5)   - 11 RG + 60 BT + 4.1 HN + 2.6 CR ≤     0
! Volatility requirement
    6)   - 17 RG + 105 BT + 12 HN + 3 CR ≥    0
! Batch size of RG
    7)      RG -  BT -  HN -  CR =   0
END
```

The solution is:

```
                    OBJECTIVE FUNCTION VALUE

         1)              43328.84

    VARIABLE            VALUE           REDUCED COST
    RG               7270.296450           0.000000
    HF               4729.703550           0.000000
    BT               1000.000000           0.000000
    HN               2446.991390           0.000000
    CR               3823.304840           0.000000

    ROW               SLACK             DUAL PRICES
     2)              0.000000             0.128845
     3)              0.000000             3.600000
     4)              0.000000            -0.204298
     5)              0.000000             0.258835
     6)          22238.774700             0.000000
     7)              0.000000            -1.556829

    NO. ITERATIONS=       5
```

It is not obvious beforehand that the amount of regular gasoline to produce should be 7,270 units. Can you predict how much gasoline should be produced if there were no heavy fuel competing for production capacity?

LP blending models have been a standard operating tool in refineries for years. Recently there have been some instances where these LP models have been replaced by more sophisticated models which more accurately approximate the nonlinearities in the blending process although they may not optimize as thoroughly as the Simplex method. See DeWitt, Lasdon *et al.* (1989) for a discussion of how Texaco does it.

There are a variety of complications as gasoline blending models are made more detailed. For example, in high quality gasoline the vendor may want the octane to be constant across volatility ranges in the ingredients. The reason is that if you "floor" the accelerator on a non-fuel injected automobile, a shot of raw gas is squirted into the intake. The highly volatile components of the blend will reach the combustion chamber first. If they have low octane you will have knocking, even though the "average" octane rating of the gasoline is high. This may be more important in a station selling gas for city driving as opposed to a station on a cross country highway in Kansas where most driving is at a constant speed.

Proper Choice of Alternate Interpretations of Quality Requirements

Some quality features can be stated either according to some measure of goodness or alternatively according to some measure of undesirability. An example is the efficiency of an automobile. It could be stated in miles per gallon or alternatively in gallons per mile. When considering the quality of a blend of ingredients (e.g., the efficiency of a fleet of cars) it is important to identify whether it is the goodness or the badness measure which is additive over the components of the blend. The next example illustrates.

A federal regulation required that the average of the miles per gallon computed over all automobiles sold by an automobile company in a specific year be at least 18 miles per gallon. Let us consider a hypothetical case for the Ford Motor Company. Assume that

Ford sold only the four car types: Mark V, Ford, Granada, and Fiesta. Various parameters of these cars are listed below:

Car	Miles per Gallon	Marginal Production Cost	Selling Price
Fiesta	30	13,500	14,000
Granada	18	14,100	15,700
Ford	16	14,500	15,300
Mark V	14	15,700	20,000

There is some flexibility in the production facilities so capacities may apply to pairs of car types. These limitations are:

Yearly Capacity in Units	Car Types Limited
250,000	Fiesta
2,000,000	Granadas plus Fords
1,500,000	Fords plus Mark V's

There is a sale capacity limit of 3,000,000 on the total of all cars sold. How many of each car type should Ford plan to sell?

Interpreting the mileage constraint literally results in the following formulation.

```
MAX      500 FIESTA + 1600 GRANADA + 4300 MARKV + 800 FORD
SUBJECT TO
   2)    12 FIESTA - 4 MARKV - 2 FORD ≥ 0
   3)    FIESTA ≤ 250
   4)    GRANADA + FORD ≤ 2000
   5)    MARKV + FORD ≤ 1500
   6)    FIESTA + GRANADA + MARKV + FORD ≤ 3000
END
```

Automobiles and dollars are measured in 1000s. Note that row 2 is equivalent to

$$\frac{30 \text{ Fiesta} + 18 \text{ Granada} + 16 \text{ Ford} + 14 \text{ Mark V}}{\text{Fiesta} + \text{Granada} + \text{Ford} + \text{Mark V}} \geq 18.$$

The solution is:

```
         OBJECTIVE FUNCTION VALUE
   1)       6550000.

   VARIABLE        VALUE           REDUCED COST
   FIESTA       250.000000            0.000000
   GRANADA     2000.000000            0.000000
   MARK V       750.000000            0.000000
   FORD           0.000000         2950.000000

   ROW           SLACK            DUAL PRICES
   2)           0.000000         -1075.000000
   3)           0.000000         13400.000000
   4)           0.000000          1600.000000
   5)         750.000000             0.000000
   6)           0.000000             0.000000
```

Let's look more closely at this solution. Suppose that each car is driven the same number of miles per year regardless of type. An interesting question is whether the ratio of the total miles driven by the above fleet divided by the number of gallons of gasoline used is at least equal to 18. Without loss suppose each car is driven one mile. The gasoline used by a car driven one mile is 1/(miles per gallon). Thus, if all the cars are driven the same distance, then the ratio of miles to gallons of fuel of the above fleet is $(250 + 2000 + 750)/[(250/30) + (2000/18) + (750/14)] = 17.3$ miles per gallon—which is considerably below the mpg we thought we were getting.

The first formulation is equivalent to alloting each automobile the same number of gallons and each automobile then driving until it exhausts its allotment. Thus, the 18 mpg average is attained by having less efficient cars drive fewer miles. A more sensible way of phrasing things is in terms of gallons per mile. In this case the mileage constraint is written:

$$\frac{\text{Fiesta}/30 + \text{Granada}/18 + \text{Ford}/16 + \text{Mark V}/14}{\text{Fiesta} + \text{Granada} + \text{Ford} + \text{Mark V}} \leq 1/18$$

Converted to standard form from this becomes

2) $-.022222 \text{ Fiesta} + .0069444 \text{ Ford} + .015873 \text{ MarkV} \leq 0.$

When this problem is solved with this constraint we get the solution:

```
         OBJECTIVE FUNCTION VALUE
   1)      4830000.

  VARIABLE        VALUE          REDUCED COST
  2)FIESTA       250.000000         0.000000
  2)GRANADA     2000.000000         0.000000
  2)MARKV        350.000000         0.000000
  2)FORD           0.000000      1681.250700
```

Notice that the profit contribution drops noticeably under this second interpretation. The federal regulations could very easily be interpreted to be consistent with the first formulation. Automotive companies, however, wisely implemented the second way of computing fleet mileage rather than leave themselves open to later criticism of implementing what Uncle Sam said rather than what he meant.

Interpretation of Dual Prices for Blending Constraints

The dual price for a blending constraint usually requires a slight reinterpretation in order to be useful. As an example, consider the octane constraint of the gasoline blending problem:

$$-94\text{RG} + 120\text{BT} + 74\text{HN} + 100\text{CR} \geq 0.$$

The dual price of this constraint is the increase in profit if the righthandside of this constraint is changed from 0 to 1. Unfortunately, this is not a change that we would ordinarily consider. More typical changes that might be entertained would be changing the octane rating from 94 to either 93 or 95. A very approximate rule for estimating the effect of a small change of the coefficient in row i of variable RG is to compute the product of the dual price of row i and the value of variable RG. For variable RG and the octane constraint this value is $7270.30 \times (-0.204298) = -1485.31$. This suggests that if the octane requirement is reduced to 93 (increased to 95) from 94 the total profit will increase by about 1485 to 44814 (decrease by about 1485 to 41843). For small changes this approximation will generally understate the true profit after the change. When the LP is actually resolved with an octane requirement of 93 (or 95), the actual profit contribution changes to 44825 (or 43200).

This approximation can be summarized generally as follows: If we wish to change a certain quality requirement of blend by a small amount e, the effect on profit of this change is approximately of the magnitude $e \times$ (dual price of the constraint) $\times$ (batch size). For small changes the approximation tends to understate profit after the change. For large changes the approximation may err in either direction.

Fractional or Hyperbolic Programming

In blending problems we have seen that ratio constraints of the form:

$$\frac{\sum_j q_i X_j}{\sum_j X_j} \geq q_0$$

can be converted to linear form, by rewriting:

$$\sum_j q_j X_j \geq q_0 \sum X_j \quad \text{or} \quad \sum (q_j - q_0) X_j \geq 0$$

Can we handle a similar feature in the objective? That is, can a problem of the following form be converted to linear form?

(1) Maximize $\dfrac{u_0 + \sum_j u_j X_j}{v_0 + \sum_j v_j X_j}$

(2) subject to $\sum_j a_{ij} X_j = b_i$

The $a_{i,j}$, u_0, u_j, v_0, v_j are given constants. For example, we might wish to maximize the fraction of protein in a blend subject to constraints on availability of materials and other quality specifications.

We can make it linear with the following transformations:

Define $r = 1/(v_0 + \sum_j v_j X_j)$

and $y_j = X_j \times r$ We assume that $r > 0$.

Then our objective is:

(1') Maximize $u_0 r + \sum_j u_j y_j$

subject to $r = 1/(v_0 + v_j X_j)$

(1.1') $r v_0 \sum v_j y_j = 1$

Any other constraint i of the form

$$\sum a_{ij} X_j = b_i$$

can be written as

$$\sum A_{ij} X_j r = b_i r$$

or

(2') $$\sum_j a_{ij} y_j - b_i r = 0$$

Problems

1. The Exxoff Company must decide upon the blends to be used for this week's gasoline production. Two gasolines must be blended and their characteristics are listed below:

Gasoline	Vapor Pressure	Octane Number	Selling Price (in $/barrel)
Lo-lead	≤ 7	≥ 80	$9.80
Premium	≤ 6	≥ 100	$12.00

    The characteristics of the components from which the gasoline can be blended are shown below:

Component	Vapor Pressure	Octane Number	Available This Week (in barrels)
Cat-Cracked Gas	8	83	2700
Isopentane	20	109	1350
Straight Gas	4	74	4100

    The vapor pressure and octane number of a blend is simply the weighted average of the coresponding characteristis of its components. Components not used can be sold to "independents" for $9 per barrel.
    (a) What are the decision variables?
    (b) Give the LP formulation.
    (c) How much Premium should be blended?

2. The Blendex Oil Company blends a regular and a premium product from two ingredients, Heptane and Octane. Each liter of regular is composed of exactly 50% Heptane and 50% Octane. Each liter of premium is composed of exactly 40% Heptane and 60% Octane. During this planning period there are exactly 200,000 liters of Heptane and 310,000 liters Octane available. The profit contributions per liter of the regular and premium product this period are $.03 and $.04 per liter respectively.
    (a) Formulate the problem of determining the amounts of the regular and premium products to produce as an LP.
    (b) Determine the optimal amounts to produce without the use of a computer.

3. Hackensack Blended Whiskey Company imports three grades of whiskey: Prime, Choice, and Premium. These unblended grades can be used to make up the following two brands of whiskey with associated characteristics:

Brand	Specifications	Selling Price per Liter
Scottish Club	Not less than 60% Prime. Not more than 20% Premium.	$6.80
Johnny Gold	Not more than 60% Premium. Not less than 15% Prime.	$5.70

The costs and availabilities of the three raw whiskies are:

Whiskey	Available This Week (Number of Liters)	Cost per Litre
Prime	2,000	$7.00
Choice	2,500	$5.00
Premium	1,200	$4.00

Hackensack wishes to maximize this week's profit contribution and feels that it can use linear programming to do so.

4. The Sebastopol Refinery processes two different kinds of crude oil, Venezuelan and Saudi to produce two general classes of products, Light and Heavy. Either crude oil can be processed by either of two modes of processing, Short or Regular. The processing cost and amounts of Heavy and Light produced depend upon the mode of processing used and the type of crude oil used. Costs vary, both across crude oils and across processing modes. The relevant characteristics are summarized in the table below. For example, the short process converts each unit of Venezuelan crude to 0.45 units of Light product, 0.52 units of Heavy product and 0.03 units of waste.

	Short Process		Regular Process	
	Venezuelan	Saudi	Venezuelan	Saudi
Light product fraction	0.45	0.60	0.49	0.68
Heavy product fraction	0.52	0.36	0.50	0.32
Unusable product fraction	0.03	0.04	0.01	0.00

Saudi crude costs $20 per unit while Venezuelan crude costs $19 per unit. The short process costs $2.50 per unit processed while the regular process costs $2.10 per unit. Sebastopol can process 10,000 units of crude per week at the regular rate. When the refinery is running the Short process for the full week, it can process 13,000 units per week.

The refinery may run any combination of short and regular processes in a given week.

The respective market values of Light and Heavy products are $27 and $25 per unit. Formulate the problem of deciding how much of which crudes to buy and which processes to run as an LP. What are the optimal purchasing and operating decisions?

5. There has been a lot of soul searching recently at your company, the Beansoul Coal Company (BCC). Some of its better coal mines have been exhausted and it is having more difficulty selling its coal from remaining mines. One of BCC's most important customers is the electrical utility, Power to the People Company (PPC). BCC sells coal from its best mine, the Becky mine, to PPC. The Becky mine is currently

running at capacity, selling all its 5000 tons/day output to PPC. Delivered to PPC the Becky coal costs BCC $81/ton and PPC pays BCC $86/ton. BCC has four other mines, but you have been unable to get PPC to buy coal from these mines; PPC says that coal from these mines does not satisfy its quality requirements. Upon pressing PPC for details, it has agreed that it would consider buying a mix of coal as long as it satisfies the following quality requirements: sulphur 0.6%; ash 5.9%; BTU 13000 per ton; and moisture 7%. You note that your Becky mine satisfies this in that its quality according to the above four measures is: 0.57%, 5.56%, 13029 BTU, and 6.2%. Your four other mines have the following characteristics:

Mine	BTU Per Ton	Sulphur Percent	Ash Percent	Moisture Percent	Cost Per Ton Delivered to PPC
Lex	14201	0.88	6.76	5.1	73
Casper	10630	0.11	4.36	4.6	90
Donora	13200	0.71	6.66	7.6	74
Rocky	11990	0.39	4.4	4.5	89

The daily capacities of your Lex, Casper, Donora and Rocky mines are 4000, 3500, 3000 and 7000 tons respectively. PPC uses an average about 13000 tons per day.

BCC's director of sales was ecstatic upon hearing of your conversation with PPC. His response was "Great! Now we will be able sell PPC all of the 13,000 tons per day that it needs." Your stock with BCC's newly appointed director of productivity is similarly high. Her reaction to your discussion with PCC was: "Let's see, right now we are making a profit contribution of only $5/ton of coal sold to PPC. I have figured out that we can make a profit contribution of $7.00/ton if we can sell them a mix. Wow! You are an ingenious negotiator!" What do you recommend to BCC?

6. The McClendon Company manufactures two products, bird food and dog food. The company has two departments, blending and packaging. The requirements in each department for manufacturing a ton of either product are as follows:

	Time per Unit in Tons	
	Blending	Packaging
Bird food	0.25	0.10
Dog food	0.15	0.30

Each department has eight hours available per day.

Dog food is made from the three ingredients: meat, fish meal, and cereal. Bird food is made from the three ingredients: seeds, ground stones, and cereal. Descriptions of these five materials are as follows:

	Descriptions of Materials in Percents				
	Protein	Carbohydrates	Trace Minerals	Abrasives	Cost (in $/ton)
Meat	12	10	1	0	600
Fishmeal	20	8	2	2	900
Cereal	3	30	0	0	200
Seeds	10	10	2	1	700
Stones	0	0	3	100	100

The composition requirements of the two products are as follows:

Composition Requirements of the Products in Percents

	Protein	Carbohydrates	Trace Minerals	Abrasives	Seeds
Bird food	5	18	1	2	10
Dog food	11	15	1	0	0

Bird food sells for $750 per ton while dog food sells for $980 per ton. What should be the composition of bird food and dog food and how much of each should be manufactured each day?

7. Recent federal regulations strongly encourage the assignment of students to schools in a city so that the racial composition of any school approximates the racial composition of the entire city. Consider the case of the Greenville city schools. The city can be considered as composed of five areas with the following characteristics:

Area	Fraction Minority	Number of Students
1	0.20	1,200
2	0.10	900
3	0.85	1,700
4	0.60	2,000
5	0.90	2,500

The ruling handed down for Greenville is that a school can have neither more than 75 percent nor less than 30 percent minority enrollment. There are three schools in Greenville with the following capacities:

School	Capacity
Bond	3,900
Pocahontas	3,100
Pierron	2,100

The objective is to design an assignment of students to schools so as to stay within the capacity of each school and satisfy the composition constraints while minimizing the distance traveled by students. The distances in kilometers between areas and schools are:

	Area				
School	1	2	3	4	5
Bond	2.7	1.4	2.4	1.1	0.5
Pocahontas	0.5	0.7	2.9	0.8	1.9
Pierron	1.6	2.0	0.1	1.3	2.2

There is an additional condition that no student can be transported more than 2.6 kilometers. Find the number of students which should be assigned to each school from each area. Assume that any group of students from an area have the same ethnic mix as the whole area.

8. A farmer is raising pigs for market and wishes to determine the quantity of the available types of feed that should be given to each pig to meet certain nutritional

requirements at minimum cost. The units of each type of basic nutritional ingredient contained in a pound of each feed type is given in the following table along with the daily nutritional requirement and feed costs.

Nutritional Ingredient	Pound of Corn	Pound of Tankage	Pound of Alfalfa	Units Required per Day
Carbohydrates	9	2	4	20
Proteins	3	8	6	18
Vitamins	1	2	6	15
Cost (cents/lb.)	7	6	5	

9. Rico-AG is a German fertilizer company which has just received a contract to supply 10,000 tons of 3–12–12 fertilizer. The guaranteed composition of this fertilizer is (by weight) at least 3% nitrogen, 12% phosphorous and 12% potash. This fertilizer can be mixed from any combination of the raw materials described in the table below.

Raw Material	Percent Nitrogen	Percent Phosphorous	Percent Potash	Current World Price per Ton
AN	50%	0%	0%	190 Dm
SP	1	40	5	180 Dm
CP	2	4	35	196 Dm
BG	1	15	17	215 Dm

Rico-AG has in stock 500 tons of SP which is bought earlier for 220 Dm/ton. Rico-AG has a long term agreement with Fledermausguano, SA which allows it to buy already mixed 3–12–12 at 195 Dm/ton.

(a) Formulate a model for Rico-AG which will allow it to decide how much to buy, to mix, and how to mix. State what assumptions you make with regard to goods in inventory.

(b) Can you conclude in advance that no CP and BG will be used because they cost more than 195 Dm/ton?

10. The Albers Milling Company buys corn and wheat and then grinds and blends them into two final products Fast-Gro and Quick-Gro. Fast-Gro is required to have at least 2.5% protein while Quick-Gro must have at least 3.2% protein. Corn contains 1.9% protein while wheat contains 3.8% protein. The firm can do the buying and blending at either the Albers (A) plant or the Bartelso (B) plant. The blended products must then be shipped to the firm's two warehouse outlets, one at Carlyle (C) and the other at Damiansville (D). Current costs per bushel at the two plants are:

	A	B
Corn	10.0	14.0
Wheat	12.0	11.0

Transportation costs per bushel between the plants and warehouses are:

$$\text{Fast-Grow} \qquad \overbrace{\begin{array}{cc} C & D \end{array}}^{To} \qquad\qquad \text{Quik-Grow} \qquad \overbrace{\begin{array}{cc} C & D \end{array}}^{To}$$

$$From \begin{cases} A \\ B \end{cases} \begin{array}{cc} 1.00 & 2.00 \\ 3.00 & 0.75 \end{array} \qquad\qquad From \begin{cases} A \\ B \end{cases} \begin{array}{cc} 3.00 & 3.50 \\ 4.00 & 1.90 \end{array}$$

The firm must satisfy the following demands in bushels at the warehouse outlets:

	Product	
Warehouse	Fast-Gro	Quik-Gro
C	1,000	3,000
D	4,000	6,000

Formulate an LP useful in determining the purchasing, blending, and shipping decisions.

11. A high quality wine is typically identified by three attributes: (a) its vintage, (b) its variety, and (c) its region. For example, the Optima Winery of Santa Rosa, California produces a wine with a label that says 1984, Cabernet Sauvignon, Sonoma County. Regulations vary from country to country but generally the wine in the bottle may be a blend of wines, not all of which need be of the vintage, variety, and region specified on the label. In particular, suppose that to receive the label 1984, Cabernet Sauvignon, Sonoma County, at least 80% of the contents must be of 1984 vintage, at least 70% of the contents must be Cabernet Sauvignon, and at least 65% must be from Sonoma County. How small might be the fraction of the wine in the bottle which is of 1984 vintage *and* of the Cabernet Sauvignon variety *and* from grapes grown in Sonoma County?

10

Decisionmaking Under Uncertainty & Stochastic LP

Introduction

The main reason multiperiod planning is difficult is because of uncertainty about the future. Typically, some action or decision must be taken today which somehow strikes a compromise between the actions which would be, in retrospect, best for each of the possible "futures" which might evolve. For example, if next year the demand for your new product proves to be large and the cost of raw material increases markedly, then buying a lot of raw material today would win you a lot of respect next year as a wise and perspective manager. On the other hand if the market disappears for both your product and your raw material, the company stockholders would probably not be so kind as to call your purchase of lots of raw material bad luck.

We will start by considering planning problems with two periods. These situations consist of the following sequence of events:

1. We make a first period decision,
2. Nature (frequently known as the marketplace) makes a random decision,
3. We make a second period decision which attempts to repair the havoc wrought by nature in (2).

Some types of decisionmaking under uncertainty that have this structure are:

(a) Weather related decisions, e.g.
   - decisions about how much and where to stockpile supplies of fuel and road salt in preparation for the winter;
   - water release decisions in the spring for a river and dam system, taking into account hydroelectric, navigation, and flooding considerations.

(b) Market behavior, e.g.
- stock price movements,
- interest rate movements
(c) Political events, e.g.
- changes of government,
- outbreaks of hostilities.

Methods very similar to those described here have been used in the automotive industry to make plant opening and closing decisions in the face of uncertainty about future demand, and in the utilities industry to make fuel purchase decisions in the face of uncertainties about weather in the next few years.

The Scenario Approach

We will assume that there are only a finite number of decisions which nature can make. We call each of these possible states of nature a "scenario." For example, in practice, most people are satisfied with classifying demand for a product as being either low, medium, or high; or classifying a winter as being either severe, normal, or mild rather than requiring a statement of the average daily temperature and total snowfall measured to six decimal places. General Motors has historically used low, medium, and high scenarios to represent demand uncertainty. The type of model that we will describe for representing uncertainty in the context of LPs is called a "stochastic program."

The first example analyzes a situation in which only steps (1) and (2) are important. A farmer can plant his land to either corn, sorghum or beans. He is willing to classify the growing season as being either wet or dry. For simplicity, assume that the season will be either wet or dry, nothing in between. If it is wet, then corn is more profitable, else beans are more profitable. The specifics are listed in the table below:

Profit as a Function of Decisions

		Our Decision		
		All Corn	All Sorghum	All Beans
Nature's Decision	Wet	$100	$70	$80
	Dry	−$10	$40	$35

In step (1) the farmer decides upon how much to plant of each crop. In step (2) nature decides if the season is wet or dry. Step (3) is trivial; the farmer simply enjoys his profit or suffers his losses.

There is no scenario in which beans are the best crop. You might be tempted to eliminate beans from further consideration. We shall see, however, that this could be wrong.

A situation in which there are exactly two possible decisions by nature can be fruitfully analyzed by the kind of graph appearing in Figure 10.1.

Figure 10.1

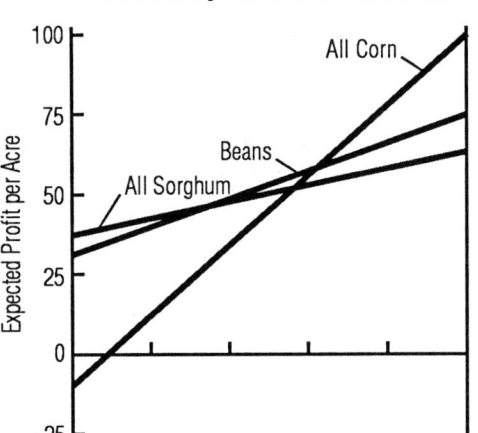

Probability of a Wet Season

The three lines specify expected profit for a given pure policy (all corn, all sorghum, or all soybeans) as a function of the probability of a wet season. If the probability of a wet season is p, then the expected profit for various crops is:

	Corn	Sorghum	Beans
Expected Profit	$-10 + p \times 110$	$40 + 30p$	$35 + 45p$

We are indifferent between sorghum and beans when $p = 1/3$. We are indifferent between beans and corn when $p = 9/13$. Thus, if the probability of a wet season is judged to be less than 1/3, then all sorghum should be planted. If we feel p is greater than 9/13 then all corn should be planted. If $1/3 < p < 9/13$ then all beans should be sown. All of this assumes that the farmer is not risk averse and is interested only in maximizing expected profits. It is important to note that if the farmer is an expected profit maximizer, then the optimal strategy is a pure one: he either plants all corn, all beans or all sorghum.

An approach that one might be tempted to use is to solve for the optimal first stage decision for each of the possible decisions of nature and then implement a first stage decision which is a weighted average of the "conditionally optimal" decisions. For this example the optimal decision if we know nature's decision is "wet" is to plant all corn while planting all sorghum is optimal if we know beforehand that the season will be dry. Suppose that the probability of a wet season is 3/8. Then the "weighted" decision is to plant 3/8 of the acreage in corn and 5/8 in sorghum. The expected profit is $(3/8)[(3/8)100 + (5/8)70] + (5/8)[(3/8)(-10) + (5/8)40] = \$43.75$.

This should be contrasted with the decision which maximizes the expected profit. For a probability of a wet season equal to 3/8 the expected profit of planting all soybeans is $(3/8)80 + (5/8)35 = \$51.875$ per acre. The expected profit from behaving optimally is almost 20% greater than just behaving "reasonably." The qualitative conclusion to draw from this small example is:

> The best decision for today when faced with a number of different outcomes for the future is in general not equal to the "average" of the decisions which would be best for each specific future outcome.

For a problem this simple, one does not need LP; however, let us demonstrate the LP for this problem in preparation for more complex problems. There are three first stage decision variables:

C = acreage planted to corn,
S = acreage planted to sorghum,
B = acreage planted to beans.

Presuming that the probability of a wet season is 3/8, the objective is to

Maximize $(3/8)(100C + 70S + 80B) = (5/8)(-10C + 40S + 35B)$
subject to $C + S + B \leq 1$

The solitary constraint specifies that we are interested only in how to plant one acre. When the expressions in the objective are calculated and simplified we get:

Maximize $31.25C + 51.25S + 51.875B$
subject to $C + S + B \leq 1$.

The solution is clearly to set $B = 1$, i.e., plant all beans.

The coefficients of corn and sorghum in the objective are simply the expected profits of planting one acre of the respective crop. This illustrates a second important point about planning under uncertainty:

> *Certainty Equivalence Theorem:* If the randomness or unpredictability in problem data exists solely in the objective function coefficients, then it is correct to solve the LP in regular form after simply using the expected values for the random coefficients in the objective.

If the randomness exists in a right-hand side or a constraint coefficient, then it is not correct to simply replace the random element by its average or expected value.

A More Complicated Two-Period Planning Problem

The previous example had a trivial second stage decision. There were no decisions left to be made after nature made its decision. The following example requires some nontrivial second stage decisions.

It is late summer in a northern city and the director of streets is making decisions regarding the purchase of fuel and salt to be used in snow removal in the approaching winter. If insufficient supplies are purchased before a severe winter, substantially higher prices must be paid to purchase these supplies quickly during the winter. There are two methods of snow removal: plowing or salting. Salting is generally cheaper, especially during a warm winter; however, excess salt after a warm winter must be carried until next winter. Excess fuel, on the other hand, is readily usable by other city departments, so there is less penalty for stocking too much fuel.

The director of streets classifies a winter as either warm or cold and attaches probabilities 0.4 and 0.6, respectively, to these two possible states of nature. The costs and salvage values of salt and fuel are described in the table below. Decisions made before winter are period 1 decisions while decisions made during or after winter are period 2 decisions. For convenience of the reader all figures will be presented in "truck-days," that is, the amount consumed by one truck in one day.

Cost or Value of Supplies vs. Date of Purchase

		Salt	Fuel	Cost per Truck-Day
Bought in period 1		$20	$70	
Bought in period 2	Warm	$30	$73	$110
	Cold	$32	$73	$120
Salvage value at at end of period 2		$15	$65	

Notice that the second period price of salt is a random variable depending upon the weather. If the winter is cold we expect the price of salt to be higher.

The cost of operating a truck per day, exclusive of fuel and salt, is $110 in a warm winter but $120 in a cold winter. The truck fleet has a capacity of 5,000 truck-days during the winter season. If only plowing but no salting is used, then a warm winter will require 3,500 truck-days of snow removal whereas a cold winter will require 5,100. Salting is a more effective use of trucks than plowing. In a warm winter one truck salting is equivalent to 1.2 trucks plowing while in a cold winter the equivalency drops to 1.1. Thus, in a cold winter the limited truck capacity implies that some salting will be necessary.

At this point it is useful to define variables for the amounts of fuel and salt bought or sold at various times:

BF1 = truck-days of fuel bought in period 1
BS1 = truck-days of salt bought in period 1
BFW = fuel bought in period 2, warm winter
BSW = salt bought in period 2, warm winter
XFW = excess fuel at end of warm winter
XSW = excess salt at end of warm winter
PW = truck-days plowing, warm winter
SW = truck-days spreading salt, warm winter
KW = costs incurred during a warm winter in dollars
BFC = fuel bought in period 2, cold winter
BSC = salt bought in period 2, cold winter
XFC = excess fuel at end of a cold winter
XSC = excess salt at end of a cold winter
PC = truck-days plowing, cold winter
SC = truck-days spreading salt, cold winter
KC = costs incurred during a cold winter in dollars

A More Complicated Two-Period Planning Problem

An important thing to notice is that we have defined unique second stage decision variables for each of the possible states of nature; e.g., salt bought in period 2 is distinguished as to whether bought in a warm rather than cold winter. This is the key to constructing a correct formulation.

The Warm Winter Solution

If the winter is known to be warm, then the relevant LP is:

```
MIN      70 BF1 + 20 BS1 + KW
SUBJECT TO
    2)  -BF1 - BFW + XFW + PW + SW = 0          ! Fuel Usage
    3)  -BS1 - BSW + XSW + SW = 0               ! Salt Usage
    4)  PW + SW ≤ 5,000                         ! Truck Usage
    5)  PW + 1.2SW ≥ 3,500                      ! Snow Removal
    6)  KW - 73 BFW - 30 BSW + 65 XFW - 110 PW - 110 SW = 0  ! Cost
```

When solved, the solution is:

```
            OBJECTIVE FUNCTION VALUE
    1)         583333.3

VARIABLE        VALUE           REDUCED COST
   BF1        2916.666660         0.000000
   BS1        2916.666660         0.000000
   KW       320833.332000         0.000000
   BFW           0.000000         3.000000
   XFW           0.000000         5.000000
   PW            0.000000        13.333334
   SW         2916.666660         0.000000
   BSW           0.000000        10.000000
   XSW           0.000000         5.000000

  ROW          SLACK            DUAL PRICES
   2)           0.000000         70.000000
   3)           0.000000         20.000000
   4)        2083.333340          0.000000
   5)           0.000000       -166.666666
   6)           0.000000         -1.000000
```

The solution is as you would expect if you knew beforehand that the winter is to be warm: buy sufficient fuel and salt in the first period to follow a "pure salt spreading" policy in the second period. No supplies are bought, nor is there any excess in period 2.

The Cold Winter Solution

The corresponding LP if we knew that the winter would be cold is:

```
MIN         70 BF1 + 20 BS1 + KC
SUBJECT TO
    2)  -BF1 - BFC + XFC + PC + SC = 0
    3)  -BS1 + SC - BSC + XSC = 0
    4)  PC + SC ≤ 5,000
    5)  PC + 1.1 SC ≥ 5,100
    6)  KC - 73 BFC + 65 XFC - 120 PC - 120 SC - 32 BSC + 15 XCS = 0
```

The solution is slightly more complicated. In a cold winter the assumptions are such as to make plowing slightly more cost effective than salting. A pure plowing policy cannot be used, however, because of scarce truck capacity. Thus, just sufficient salt is used to make the truck capacity sufficient. This is illustrated below:

```
         OBJECTIVE FUNCTION VALUE
   1)         970000.0

 VARIABLE       VALUE         REDUCED COST
   BF1        5000.0000          0.0000
   BS1        1000.0000          0.0000
   KC       600000.0000          0.0000
   BFC           0.0000          3.0000
   XFC           0.0000          5.0000
   PC         3999.9999          0.0000
   SC         1000.0000          0.0000
   BSC           0.0000         12.0000
   XSC           0.0000          5.0000

   ROW          SLACK         DUAL PRICES
    2)         0.00000          70.000000
    3)         0.00000          20.000000
    4)         0.00000           0.000000
    5)         0.00000        -200.000000
    6)         0.00000          -1.000000
```

The Unconditional Solution

Neither of these two models or solutions, however, is immediately useful by itself because it is not known beforehand whether it will be a cold or warm winter. Part of the problem is that the two solutions recommend different first period purchasing decisions depending upon whether the winter is to be warm or cold whereas in reality the first period decision must be unique, regarding of whether the winter is cold or warm. This is easy to remedy, however; we simply combine the two models into one. Because the same first stage variables, BF1 and BS1 appear in both sets of constraints, this forces the same first stage decision to appear regardless of the severity of the winter.

It remains to specify the appropriate objective function for the combined problem. It is obvious that the cost coefficients of the first stage variables are appropriate as is; however, the second stage costs, KW and KC, are really random variables. With probability 0.4 we want KW to apply and KC to be treated as zero, while with probability 0.6 we want KC to be in the objective and KW be treated as zero. The correct resolution is to apply weights 0.4 and 0.6 to KW and KC, respectively, in the objective. Thus, the complete formulation is:

```
MIN      70 BF1 + 20 BS1 + 0.4 KW + 0.6 KC
SUBJECT TO
   2)   -BF1 - BFW + XFW + PW + SW = 0
   3)   -BS1 + SW - BSW + XSW = 0
   4)    PW + SW ≤ 5,000
   5)    PW + 1.2 SW ≥ 3,500
   6)    KW - 73 BFW + 65 XFW - 110 SW - 110 PW - 30 BSW + 15 XSW = 0
   7)   -BF1 - BFC + XFC + PC + SC = 0
```

```
 8)  -BS1 + SC - BSC + XSC = 0
 9)  PC + SC ≤ 5,000
10)  PC + 1.1 SC ≥ 5,100
11)  KC - 73 BFC + 65 XFC - 120 PC - 120 SC - 32 BSC + 15 XSC = 0
END
```

In order to understand this model it is worth looking at the PICTURE of its coefficients below:

```
          B B| B X     B X| B X     B X
          F S|K F F P S S S|K F F P S S S
          1 1|W W W W W W W|C C C C C C C

  1: B B |T              |T                    MIN
  2:-1   |-1 1 1 1       |                      =
  3:  -1 |      1-1 1    |                      =
  4:     |      1 1      |                     < D
  5:     |        1 A    |                     > D
  6:     |1-B B-C-C-B B  |                      =
  7:-1   |               |-1 1 1 1              =
  8:  -1 |               |      1-1 1           =
  9:     |               |      1 1            < D
 10:     |               |        1 A          > D
 11:     |               |1-B B-C-C-B B        = 0
```

The lines drawn indicate that the model really consists of two submodels, one for a cold winter in the lower right and one for a warm winter above and to the left. These two models would be separate except for the linkage via the common first stage variables BF1 and BS1 on the extreme left. Another way of stating the problem in words is:

Minimize   First stage cost + 0.4(second stage costs for a warm winter)
                            + 0.6(second stage costs for a cold winter)

subject to: The same first decisions applying regardless of whether the winter is warm or cold.

The solution to the complete problem is:

```
         OBJECTIVE FUNCTION VALUE

    1)      819888.3

 VARIABLE        VALUE           REDUCED COST
    BF1       2916.666660           0.0000
    BS1       2916.666660           0.0000
    KW      320833.332000           0.0000
    BFW          0.000000           3.0000
    XFW          0.000000           0.2000
    PW           0.000000           4.6833
    SW        2916.666660           0.0000
    BSW          0.000000           3.5799
    XSW          0.000000           2.4200
    KC      715091.672000           0.0000
    BFC       1891.666690           0.0000
    XFC          0.000000           4.8000
```

```
            PC        1891.666690              0.0000
            SC        2916.666660              0.0000
           BSC           0.000000              7.6200
           XSC           0.000000              2.5799

       ROW           SLACK               DUAL PRICES
        2)           0.000000               26.20000
        3)           0.000000                8.42000
        4)        2083.333340                0.00000
        5)           0.000000              -65.51666
        6)           0.000000               -0.40000
        7)           0.000000               43.80000
        8)           0.000000               11.57999
        9)         191.666645                0.00000
       10)           0.000000             -115.80000
       11)           0.000000               -0.60000
```

The solution is interesting. It recommends buying sufficient salt and fuel in the first period to follow a pure salt spreading policy if the winter is warm. If the winter is cold, extra fuel is bought in the second period to be used for plowing only to gain the needed snow removal capacity. There will be no excess fuel or salt for either outcome.

We are now in position to state the general procedure for developing an LP model of a two-period planning problem under uncertainty:

1. For each possible state of nature formulate the appropriate LP model.
2. Combine these submodels into one super model, making sure that
   (a) the first stage variables are common to all submodels but
   (b) the second stage variables in a submodel appear only in that submodel.
3. The second stage cost for each submodel appears in the overall objective function weighted by the probability that nature will choose the state corresponding to that submodel.

In a typical application there will be a debate about the proper values for the probabilities, and therefore you may wish to examine the sensitivity of the results to changes in the probabilities. The range report on the next page indicates some of these sensitivities.

```
                   RANGES IN WHICH THE BASIS IS UNCHANGED
                           OBJ COEFFICIENT RANGES
       VARIABLE        CURRENT         ALLOWABLE          ALLOWABLE
                        COEF            INCREASE           DECREASE
         BF1         70.000000          3.000000           0.20000
         BS1         20.000000          3.579999           2.42000
         KW           0.400000          0.003077           0.04109
         BFW          0.000000          INFINITY           3.00000
         XFW          0.000000          INFINITY           0.20000
         PW           0.000000          INFINITY           4.68333
         SW           0.000000          5.619999          78.62000
         BSW          0.000000          INFINITY           3.57999
         XSW          0.000000          INFINITY           2.42000
         KC           0.600000          0.002740           0.04109
         BFC          0.000000          0.200000           3.00000
         XFC          0.000000          INFINITY           4.80000
```

PC	0.000000	2.200001	2.34545
SC	0.000000	2.579999	2.42000
BSC	0.000000	INFINITY	7.62000
XSC	0.000000	INFINITY	2.57999

RIGHTHAND SIDE RANGES

ROW	CURRENT RHS	ALLOWABLE INCREASE	ALLOWABLE DECREASE
2	0.000000	2916.666660	1891.666690
3	0.000000	1916.666550	1719.696990
4	5000.000000	INFINITY	2083.333340
5	3500.000000	2063.636380	2299.999760
6	0.000000	INFINITY	320833.332000
7	0.000000	1891.666690	INFINITY
8	0.000000	1719.696990	1916.666550
9	5000.000000	INFINITY	191.666645
10	5100.000000	191.666645	1891.666690
11	0.000000	INFINITY	715091.672000

Notice that the objective coefficient ranges for KW and KC are quite small. Thus, it would appear that modest changes in the probabilities, 0.4 and 0.6, might produce very noticeable changes in the solution.

Expected Value of Perfect Information (EVPI)

Uncertainty has its costs. Therefore it may be worthwhile to invest in research to reduce the uncertainty. This investment might be in better weather forecasts for problems like the one just considered or it might be in test markets or market surveys for problems relating to new product investment. A bound on the value of better forecasts is obtainable by considering the possibility of getting perfect forecasts, so-called perfect information.

We have sufficient information on the snow removal problem to calculate the value of perfect information. For example, if we knew beforehand that the winter would be warm, then we saw from the solution of the warm winter model that the total cost would be 583,333.3. On the other hand, if we knew beforehand that the winter would be cold, we saw that the total cost would be 970,000. Having perfect forecasts will not change the frequency of warm and cold winters. They will presumably still occur with respective probabilities 0.4 and 0.6. Thus, if we had perfect forecasts, the expected cost per season would be:

$$0.4 \times 583{,}333.3 + 0.6 \times 970{,}000 = 815{,}333.3$$

From the solution of the complete model we see that the expected cost per season without any additional information is 819,888.3. Thus, the expected value of perfect information is 819,888.3 − 815,333.3 = 4,555.0. Therefore, if a well-dressed weather forecaster claims prior knowledge of the severity of the coming winter, then an offer of at most 4,555 should be made to learn his forecast. In reality, his forecast is probably worth considerably less than that because it is probably not a perfect forecast.

Risk Aversion

Thus far we have assumed that the decisionmaker is strictly an expected profits maximizer and is neither risk averse nor risk preferring. Casino gamblers who play games such as roulette must be risk preferring if the roulette wheel is not defective because their expected profits are negative. A person is risk averse if he or she attaches more weight to a large loss than expected profits maximization would dictate.

In the context of the snow removal problem the Streets Manager might be embarrassed by a high cost of snow removal in a cold winter even though long-run expected cost minimization would imply an occasional big loss. From the optimal policy for the snow removal problem we can see that the sum of first period plus second period costs if the winter is cold is

$$70*BF1 + 20*BS1 + KC = 977{,}591$$

On the other hand, if it is known beforehand that the winter will be cold, then we have seen that this cost can be reduced to 970,000.

For fear of attracting the attention of a political opponent the Streets Manager might wish to prevent the possibility of a cost more than $5,000 greater than the minimum possible for the cold winter outcome.

The Manager can incorporate his risk aversion into the LP by adding the constraint:

$$70\ BF1 + 20\ BS1 + KC \leq 975{,}000$$

When this is done, the solution is:

```
       OBJECTIVE FUNCTION VALUE

 1)       820061.1

 VARIABLE      VALUE         REDUCED COST
    BF1      3780.557800        0.000000
    BS1      2916.666630        0.000000
    KW     264680.406000        0.000000
    BFW         0.000000        3.199999
    XFW       863.891151        0.000001
    PW          0.000000        4.611111
    SW       2916.666660        0.000000
    BSW         0.000000        3.533333
    XSW         0.000000        2.466667
    KC     652027.609000        0.000000
    BFC      1027.775540        0.000001
    XFC         0.000000        5.333332
    PC       1891.666690        0.000001
    SC       2916.666630        0.000000
    BSC         0.000000        8.466666
    XSC         0.000000        2.866666
```

The expected cost has increased by about $820{,}061 - 819{,}888 = 173$ dollars. A politician might consider this a price worth paying to reduce his worst case (cold winter) cost almost $2,600. Notice, however, that performance in the event of a warm winter does not look as good. The value of XFW indicates that there will be almost 864 units of fuel to be disposed of at the end of a warm winter.

Downside Risk

There are a variety of ways of measuring risk. Variance is probably the most common measure of risk. The variance measure gives equal weight to deviations above the mean as well as below. For a symmetric distribution this is fine but for nonsymmetric distributions this is not attractive. Most people worry a lot more about returns that are below average than about ones that are above average.

Downside risk is a reasonably intuitive way of quantifying risk that looks only at returns that are lower than some threshold. In words, downside risk is the expected amount by which return falls short of a specified target. To explain it more carefully, define:

P_s = probability that scenario s occurs,

T = a target return threshold that we specify,

R_s = the return achieved if scenario s occurs.

D_s = the down side if scenario s occurs,
  = max $\{0, T - R_s\}$.

ER = expected downside risk,
  = $p_1 D_1 + p_2 D_2 + \cdots$

Example

Suppose that the farmer of our earlier acquaintance has made two changes in his assessment of things: (a) he assesses the probability of a wet season as 0.7; and (b) he has eliminated beans as a possible crop so that he has only two choices, corn and sorghum. A reformulation of his model is

```
MAX      0.7 RW + 0.3 RD
SUBJECT TO
    2)   RW - 100 C - 70 S =    0
    3)   RD + 10 C - 40 S =    0
    4)   C + S =    1
END
FREE      RW
FREE      RD
```

The variables RW and RD are the return (i.e., profit) if the season is wet or dry respectively. Notice that both RW and RD were declared as FREE because RD in particular could be negative.

When solved, the recommendation is to plant 100% corn with a resulting expected profit of 67.

```
         OBJECTIVE FUNCTION VALUE

    1)           67.0000000

  VARIABLE          VALUE          REDUCED COST
    RW           100.000000           .000000
    RD           -10.000000           .000000
    C              1.000000           .000000
    S               .000000          6.000000

    ROW      SLACK OR SURPLUS      DUAL PRICES
    2)            .000000            .700000
    3)            .000000            .300000
    4)            .000000          67.000000
```

The solution makes it explicit that if the season is dry, our profits, RD, will be negative. Let us compute the expected downside risk for a solution to this problem. We must choose a target threshold. A plausible value for this target is one such that the most conservative decision available to us just barely has an expected downside risk of zero. For our farmer the most conservative decision is sorghum. A target value of 40 would give sorghum a downside risk of zero. To compute the expected downside risk for our problem we want to add the constraints

$$DW \geq 40 - RW$$
$$DD \geq 40 - RD$$

and

$$ER = .7DW + .3DD$$

The constraint $DW \geq 40 - RW$ effectively sets $DW = \max(0, 40 - RW)$.

When converted to standard form and appended to our model we get:

```
MAX     0.7 RW + 0.3 RD
SUBJECT TO
  2)    RW - 100 C - 70 S =    0
  3)    RD +  10 C - 40 S =    0
  4)    C + S =   1
  5)    RW + DW >=   40
  6)    RD + DD >=   40
  7)  - 0.7 DW - 0.3 DD + ER =    0
END
FREE        RW
FREE        RD
FREE        ER
```

The solution is:

```
          OBJECTIVE FUNCTION VALUE

    1)          67.0000000

   VARIABLE        VALUE          REDUCED COST
     RW          100.000000           .000000
     RD          -10.000000           .000000
      C            1.000000           .000000
      S             .000000          6.000000
     DW             .000000           .000000
     DD           50.000000           .000000
     ER           15.000000           .000000
```

Because we put no constraint on expected downside risk, we get the same solution as before but with the additional information that the expected downside risk is 15.

What happens as we become more risk averse? Suppose we add the constraint $ER \leq 10$. We then get the solution:

```
          OBJECTIVE FUNCTION VALUE

    1)          65.0000000
```

VARIABLE	VALUE	REDUCED COST
RW	90.000000	.000000
RD	6.666668	.000000
C	.666667	.000000
S	.333333	.000000
DW	.000000	.280000
DD	33.333330	.000000
ER	10.000000	.000000

Notice that the recommendation is now to put 1/3 of the land into sorghum. The profit drops modestly to 65 from 67. If the season is dry the profit is now 6.67 rather than -10 as before. Finally, let's constrain the expected downside risk to zero with ER $\leq$ 0. Then the solution is:

OBJECTIVE FUNCTION VALUE

1) 61.0000000

VARIABLE	VALUE	REDUCED COST
RW	70.000000	.000000
RD	40.000000	.000000
C	.000000	.000000
S	1.000000	.000000
DW	.000000	.280000
DD	.000000	.000000
ER	.000000	.000000

Now all the land is planted with sorghum and expected profit drops to 61.

Decisions Under Uncertainty with More than Two Periods

The ideas that were discussed for the two-period problem can be extended to an arbitrary number of periods. The sequence of events in the general case is:

1. We make a decision,
2. Nature makes a random decision,
3. We make a decision,
4. Nature makes a random decision,
5. Etc.

The extension can be made by working backwards through time. For example, if we wished to analyze a three-period problem, we would start with the last two periods and formulate the associated two-period stochastic LP model. When the first period is taken into account, the model just developed for the last two periods is treated as the second period of a two-period problem for which now the true first period is really the first period. This process cannot continue for too many periods because the problem size gets too large rapidly. If the number of periods is n and the number of possible states of nature each period is s, then the problem size is proportional to s^n. Thus, it is unusual to have manageable stochastic LPs with more than two or three periods.

Chance Constrained Programs

A drawback of the methods just discussed is that problem size can grow very large if number of possible states of nature is large. Chance constrained programs do not apply to exactly the same problem and as a result do not become large as the number of possible states of nature gets large. The stochastic programs discussed thus far had the feature that every constraint had to be satisfied by some combination of first- and second-period decisions. Chance constrained programs, however, allow each constraint to be violated with a certain specified probability. An advantage to this approach for tolerating uncertainty is that the chance constrained model has essentially the same size as the LP for a corresponding problem with no random elements.

We will illustrate the idea with the snow removal problem. Under the chance constrained approach there are no second stage decision variables, and we would have to specify a probability allowance for each constraint. For example, we might specify that with probability at least 0.75 we must be able to provide the snow removal capacity required by the severity of the winter. For our problem it is very easy to see that this means that we must provide 5,100 truck-days of snow removal capacity. For example, if only 4,400 truck-days of capacity were provided, then the probability of sufficient capacity would only be 0.4. Let us assume that one truck-day of operation costs $116, and one truck-day of salting equals 1.14 truck-day of plowing; then, the appropriate chance constrained LP is the simple model:

```
MIN     70 BF1 + 20 BS1 + 116 P + 116 S
SUBJECT TO
        -BF1 + P + S = 0
           -BS1 + S       = 0
              P + S       ≤ 5,000
              P + 1.14 S  ≥ 5,100.
```

Problems

1. What is the expected value of perfect information in the corn/soybean/sorghum planting problem?

2. The farmer in the corn/soybean/sorghum problem is reluctant to plant all soybeans because if the season is wet he will make $20 less per acre than he would if he plants all corn. Can you react to his risk aversion and recommend a planting *mix* which has the feature that the profit per acre is never more than $15 from the planting mix that in retrospect would have been best for the particular outcome?

3. Analyze the snow removal problem of this chapter for the situation where the cost of fuel in a cold winter is $80 per truck-day rather than $73 and the cost of salt in a cold winter is $35 rather than $32. Include in your analysis the derivation of the expected value of perfect information.

4. A farmer has 1000 acres available for planting to either corn, sorghum or soybeans. The yields of the three crops, in bushels per acre, as a function of the two possible kinds of season are:

	Corn	Sorghum	Beans
Wet	100	43	45
Dry	45	35	33

The probability of a wet season is 0.6. The probability of a dry season is 0.4. Corn sells for $2/bushel while Sorghum and Beans each sell for $4/bushel. The total production cost for any crop is $100/acre, regardless of type of season. The farmer can also raise livestock. One unit of livestock uses one hundred bushels of corn. The profit contribution of one unit of livestock, exclusive of its corn consumption is $215. Corn can be purchased at any time on the market for $2.20/bushel. The decisions of how much to raise of livestock and each crop must be made before the type of season is known.

(a) What should the farmer do?

(b) Formulate and solve the problem by the scenario based stochastic programming approach.

11

Economic Equilibria as LPs

What Is an Equilibrium

If one is modeling an economy composed of two or more individuals, each acting in his or her own self-interest, there is no obvious overall objective function which should be maximized. In a market, a solution or equilibrium point is a set of prices such that supply equals demand for each commodity. More generally, an equilibrium for a system is a state in which no individual in the system is motivated to change the state. So for example at equilibrium there are no arbitrage possibilities, e.g., buy a commodity in one market and sell it in another market at a higher price at no risk.

Representing Supply and Demand Curves in LPs

The methodology about to be described is the equilibration method used in the PIES (Project Independence Evaluation System) model developed by the Department of Energy. This model and its later versions were extensively used from 1974 onward to evaluate the effect of various U.S. energy policies.

Consider the following example. There is a producer A and a consumer X who have the following supply and demand schedules for a single commodity (e.g., energy):

Producer A		Consumer X	
Market Price per Unit	Amount Willing to Sell	Market Price per Unit	Amount Willing to Buy
$1	2	$9	2
2	4	4.5	4
3	6	3.5	6
4	8	2.25	8

For example, if the price is less than $2 but greater than $1, then the producer will produce 2 units; however, the consumer would like to buy at least 8 units at this

Figure 11.1

Demand and Supply Curves

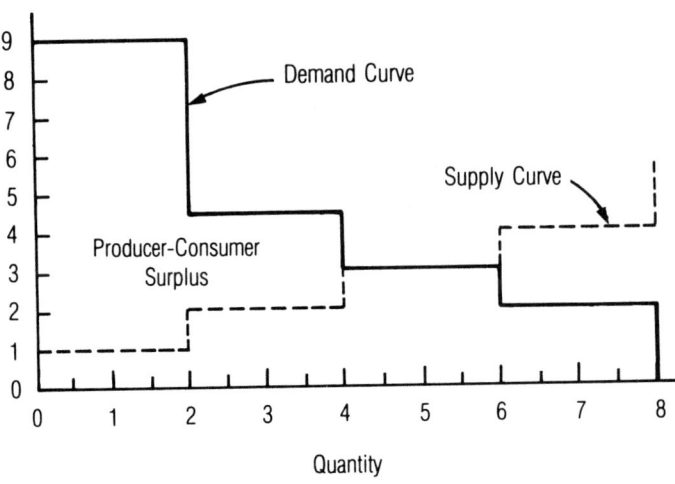

price. By inspection, note that the equilibrium price is $3 and any quantity from 4 to 6 satisfies equilibrium.

It is easy to find an equilibrium in this market by inspection; nevertheless, it is useful to examine the LP formulation that could be used to find it. Although there is a single market clearing price, it is useful to interpret the supply schedule as if the supplier is willing to sell the first 2 units at $1, the next 2 units at $2 each, etc. Similarly, the consumer is willing to pay $9 each for the first 2 units, $4.5 for the next 2 units, etc. To find the market clearing price such that the amount produced equals the amount consumed, we act as if there is a broker who actually buys and sells at these marginal prices, and all transactions must go through the broker. The broker maximizes his profits. The broker will continue to increase the quantity of goods transferred as long as he can sell it at a price higher than his purchase price. At the broker's optimum, the quantity bought equals the quantity sold and price offered by the buyers equals the price demanded by the sellers. This satisfies the conditions for a market equilibrium.

Graphically, the situation is shown in Figure 11.1. The area in the figure marked "producer-consumer surplus" is the profit obtained by the hypothetical broker. In reality, this profit is allocated between the producer and the consumer according to the equilibrium price. In the case where the equilibrium price is $3, the consumer's profit or surplus is the portion of the producer-consumer surplus area above the $3 horizontal line, while the producer's profit or surplus is the portion of the producer-consumer surplus area below $3.

Readers with a mathematical bent may note that the general approach we are using is based on the fact that for almost any problem of finding an equilibrium, one can formulate an objective function, which, when optimized, produces a solution satisfying the equilibrium conditions.

For purposes of the LP formulation, define:

A1 = units sold by producer for $1 per unit
A2 = units sold by producer for $2 per unit
A3 = units sold by producer for $3 per unit
A4 = units sold by producer for $4 per unit
X1 = units bought by consumer for $9 per unit
X2 = units bought by consumer for $4.5 per unit
X3 = units bought by consumer for $3 per unit
X4 = units bought by consumer for $2.25 per unit

The formulation is:

```
MAX     9X1 + 4.5X2 + 3X3 + 2.25X4   ! Maximize broker's revenue
        - A1 - 2A2   - 3A3 - 4A4     ! minus cost
SUBJECT TO
   A1 + A2 + A3 + A4 - X1 - X2 - X3 - X4 = 0   ! Supply = demand
   A1 ≤ 2    A2 ≤ 2    A3 ≤ 2    A4 ≤ 2        ! Steps in supply
   X1 ≤ 2    X2 ≤ 2    X3 ≤ 2    X4 ≤ 2        ! and demand functions
```

The solution is:

```
A1 = A2 = X1 = X2 = 2
A3 = A4 = X3 = X4 = 0
```

The dual price on the first constraint is $3. In general, the dual price on the constraint that sets supply equal to demand is the market clearing price.

Let us complicate the problem by introducing another supplier, B, and another consumer, Y. Their supply and demand curves are, respectively:

Producer B		Consumer Y	
Market Price per Unit	Amount Willing to Sell	MarketPrice per Unit	Amount Willing to Buy
$2	2	$15	2
4	4	8	4
6	6	5	6
8	8	3	8

An additional complication is that it costs $1.5 per unit shipped from A to Y, and $2 per unit shipped from B to X. What will be the clearing price at the shipping door of A, B, X, and Y? How much will each participant sell or buy?

The corresponding LP can be developed if we define B1, B2, B3, B4, Y1, Y2, Y3 and Y4 analogous to A1, X1, etc. Also, we define AX, AY, BX, and BY as the number of units shipped from A to X, A to Y, B to X, and B to Y, respectively. The formulation is:

```
MAX     9X1 + 4.5X2 + 3X3 + 2.25X4 + 15Y1 + 8Y2 + 5Y3 + 3Y4
        - 2BX - 1.5AY - A1 - 2A2 - 3A3 - 4A4 - 2B1 - 4B2 - 6B3 - 8B4
SUBJECT TO
   2)   - AY + A1 + A2 + A3 + A4 - AX = 0   ! Amount shipped from A
   3)   - BX + B1 + B2 + B3 + B4 - BY = 0   ! Amount shipped from B
   4)   - X1 - X2 - X3 - X4 + BX + AX = 0   ! Amount shipped to X
   5)   - Y1 - Y2 - Y3 - Y4 + AY + BY = 0   ! Amount shipped to Y
```

```
 6)   A1 ≤ 2
 7)   A2 ≤ 2
 8)   A3 ≤ 2
 9)   A4 ≤ 2
10)   B1 ≤ 2
11)   B2 ≤ 2
12)   B3 ≤ 2
13)   B4 ≤ 2
14)   X1 ≤ 2
15)   X2 ≤ 2
16)   X3 ≤ 2
17)   X4 ≤ 2
18)   Y1 ≤ 2
19)   Y2 ≤ 2
20)   Y3 ≤ 2
21)   Y4 ≤ 2
```

Notice from the objective function that the broker is charged \$2/unit shipped from B to X, and \$1.5/unit shipped from A to Y. Most of the constraints are simple upper bound (SUB) constraints. In realistic-size problems, several thousand SUB-type constraints can be tolerated without adversely affecting computational difficulty.

The solution is:

```
            OBJECTIVE FUNCTION VALUE

       1)        56.0000000

   VARIABLE       VALUE          REDUCED COST
       X1         2.000000         0.000000
       X2         2.000000         0.000000
       X3         0.000000         0.500000
       X4         0.000000         1.250000
       Y1         2.000000         0.000000
       Y2         2.000000         0.000000
       Y3         2.000000         0.000000
       Y4         0.000000         2.000000
       BX         0.000000         3.500000
       AY         2.000000         0.000000
       A1         2.000000         0.000000
       A2         2.000000         0.000000
       A3         2.000000         0.000000
       A4         0.000000         0.500000
       B1         2.000000         0.000000
       B2         2.000000         0.000000
       B3         0.000000         1.000000
       B4         0.000000         3.000000
       AX         4.000000         0.000000
       BY         4.000000         0.000000

      ROW          SLACK          DUAL PRICES
       2)         0.000000        -3.500000
       3)         0.000000        -5.000000
       4)         0.000000        -3.500000
       5)         0.000000        -5.000000
       6)         0.000000         2.500000
```

7)	0.000000	1.500000
8)	0.000000	0.500000
9)	2.000000	3.000000
10)	0.000000	1.000000
11)	0.000000	0.000000
12)	2.000000	0.000000
13)	2.000000	0.000000
14)	0.000000	5.500000
15)	0.000000	1.000000
16)	2.000000	0.000000
17)	2.000000	0.000000
18)	0.000000	10.000000
19)	0.000000	3.000000
20)	0.000000	0.000000
21)	2.000000	0.000000

From the dual prices on rows 2 through 5 we note that the prices at the shipping door of A, B, X, and Y are \$3.5, \$5, \$3.5, and \$5, respectively. At these prices, A and B are willing to produce 6 and 4 units, respectively, while X and Y are willing to buy 4 and 6 units respectively. A ships 2 units to Y, where the \$1.5 shipping charge causes them to sell for \$5. A ships 4 units to X, where they sell for \$3.5. B ships 4 units to Y, where they sell for \$5.

Auctions as Economic Equilibria

The concept of a broker who maximizes producer-consumer surplus can also be applied to auctions. LP is useful if the auction is complicated by features which might be interpreted as bidders with demand curves. The example which is presented here is based on a design by R. L. Graves for a course-registration system used since 1981 at the University of Chicago in which students bid on courses.

Suppose there are N types of objects to be sold (e.g., courses), and there are M bidders (students). Bidder i is willing to pay up to b_{ij}, $b_{ij} \geq 0$ for one unit of object type j. Further, a bidder is interested in at most one unit of each object type. Let S_j be the number of units of object type j available for sale.

There are a variety of ways of holding the auction. Let us suppose that it is a sealed-bid auction and we want to find a single, market-clearing price, p_j, for each object type j, such that:

(a) at most, S_j units of object j are sold;

(b) any bid for j less than p_j does not buy a unit;

(c) $p_j = 0$ if less than S_j units of j are sold;

(d) any bid for j greater than p_j does buy a unit.

It is easy to determine the equilibrium p_j's by simply sorting the bids and allocating each unit to the higher bidder first. Nevertheless, in order to prepare for more complicated auctions, let us consider how to solve this problem as an optimization problem. Again, we take the view of a broker who sells at as high (buys at as low) a price as possible and maximizes profits.

Define:

$x_{i_j} = 1$ if bidder i buys a unit of object j, else 0.

The LP is:

$$\text{Maximize} \quad \sum_{i=1}^{M} \sum_{j=1}^{N} x_{ij} b_{i_j}$$

$$\text{subject to} \quad \sum_{i=1}^{M} x_{ij} \leq S_j \quad \text{for } j = 1 \text{ to } N$$

$$x_{ij} \leq 1 \quad \text{for all } i \text{ and } j.$$

The dual prices on the first N constraints can be used, with minor modification, as the clearing prices p_j. The possible modifications have to do with the fact that with step function demand and/or supply curves there is usually a small range of acceptable clearing prices. The LP solution will choose one price in this range, usually at one end of the range. One may wish to choose a price within the interior of the range to break ties.

Now we complicate this auction slightly by adding the condition that no bidder wants to buy more than 3 units total. Consider the following specific situation:

Maximum Price Willing to Pay

		Objects				
		1	2	3	4	5
Bidders	1	9	2	8	6	3
	2	6	7	9	1	5
	3	7	8	6	3	4
	4	5	4	3	2	1
Capacity		1	2	3	3	4

For example, bidder 3 is willing to pay up to 4 for one unit of object 5. There are only 3 units of object 4 available for sale.

We want to find a "market clearing" price for each object and an allocation of units to bidders so that each bidder is willing to accept the units awarded to him at the market clearing price. We must generalize the previous condition d to d': a bidder is satisfied with a particular unit if he cannot find another unit with a bigger difference between his maximum offer price and the market clearing price. This is equivalent to saying that each bidder maximizes his consumer surplus.

The associated LP is:

```
MAX    9 X11 + 2 X12 + 8 X13 + 6 X14 + 3 X15 + 6 X21 + 7 X22 + 9 X23
     + X24 + 5 X25 + 7 X31 + 8 X32 + 6 X33 + 3 X34 + 4 X35 + 5 X41
     + 4 X42 + 3 X43 + 2 X44 +   X45                  ! Maximize broker revenues
SUBJECT TO
    2)     X11 + X21 + X31 + X41 ≤ 1            ! Units of object 1 available
    3)     X12 + X22 + X32 + X42 ≤ 2
    4)     X13 + X23 + X33 + X43 ≤ 3
    5)     X14 + X24 + X34 + X44 ≤ 3
    6)     X15 + X25 + X35 + X45 ≤ 4            ! Units of object 5 available
```

```
   7)    X11 + X12 + X13 + X14 + X15 ≤ 3    ! Upper limit on buyer 1 demand
   8)    X21 + X22 + X23 + X24 + X25 ≤ 3
   9)    X31 + X32 + X33 + X34 + X35 ≤ 3
  10)    X41 + X42 + X43 + X44 + X45 ≤ 3    ! Upper limit on buyer 4 demand
  11)    X11 ≤ 1
  12)    X21 ≤ 1
  13)    X31 ≤ 1
  14)    X41 ≤ 1
  15)    X12 ≤ 1
  16)    X22 ≤ 1
  17)    X32 ≤ 1
  18)    X42 ≤ 1
  19)    X13 ≤ 1
  20)    X23 ≤ 1
  21)    X33 ≤ 1
  22)    X43 ≤ 1
  23)    X14 ≤ 1
  24)    X24 ≤ 1
  25)    X34 ≤ 1
  27)    X15 ≤ 1
  28)    X25 ≤ 1
  29)    X35 ≤ 1
  30)    X45 ≤ 1
  END
```

The solution is:

```
              OBJECTIVE FUNCTION VALUE
        1)        65.0000000
       VARIABLE       VALUE        REDUCED COST
         X11        1.000000         0.000000
         X12        0.000000         7.000000
         X13        1.000000         0.000000
         X14        1.000000         0.000000
         X15        0.000000         1.000000
         X21        0.000000         1.000000
         X22        1.000000         0.000000
         X23        1.000000         0.000000
         X24        0.000000         1.000000
         X25        1.000000         0.000000
         X31        0.000000         1.000000
         X32        1.000000         0.000000
         X33        1.000000         0.000000
         X34        0.000000         0.000000
         X35        1.000000         0.000000
         X41        0.000000         0.000000
         X42        0.000000         1.000000
         X43        0.000000         0.000000
         X44        1.000000         0.000000
         X45        1.000000         0.000000
       ROW          SLACK          DUAL PRICES
        2)        0.000000         5.000000
        3)        0.000000         5.000000
        4)        0.000000         3.000000
```

5)	1.000000	0.000000
6)	1.000000	0.000000
7)	0.000000	4.000000
8)	0.000000	2.000000
9)	0.000000	3.000000
10)	1.000000	0.000000
11)	0.000000	0.000000
12)	1.000000	0.000000
13)	1.000000	0.000000
14)	1.000000	0.000000
15)	1.000000	0.000000
16)	0.000000	0.000000
17)	0.000000	0.000000
18)	1.000000	0.000000
19)	0.000000	1.000000
20)	0.000000	4.000000
21)	0.000000	0.000000
22)	1.000000	0.000000
23)	0.000000	2.000000
24)	1.000000	0.000000
25)	1.000000	0.000000
26)	0.000000	2.000000
27)	1.000000	0.000000
28)	0.000000	3.000000
29)	0.000000	1.000000
30)	0.000000	1.000000

The dual prices on the first five constraints essentially provide us with the needed market clearing prices. To avoid ties, we may wish to add or subtract a small number to each of these prices. We claim that acceptable market clearing prices for objects 1, 2, 3, 4 and 5 are 5, 5, 3, 0, and 0, respectively.

Now note that at these prices the market clears. Bidder 1 is awarded the sole unit of object 1 at a price of 5.00. If the price were lower, bidder 4 could claim the unit. If the price were more than 6, then bidder 1's surplus on object 1 would be less than $9 - 6 = 3$, and, therefore, he would prefer object 5 instead, where his surplus is $3 - 0 = 3$. If object 2's price were less than 4, then bidder 4 could claim the unit. If the price were greater than 5, then bidder 3 would prefer to give up his type-2 unit (with surplus $8 - 5 = 3$) and take a type-4 unit, which has a surplus of $3 - 0 = 3$. Similar arguments apply to objects 3, 4, and 5.

Transportation Equilibria

When designing a highway or street system, traffic engineers usually use models of some sophistication to predict the volume of traffic and the expected travel time on each link in the system. For each link the engineers specify estimated average travel time as a (nondecreasing) function of traffic volume on the link.

The determination of the volume on each link is usually based upon a rule called Wardrup's Principle: If a set of commuters wish to travel from A to B, then the commuters will take the shortest route in the travel time sense. The effect of this is that if there are alternative routes from A to B, commuters will distribute themselves over these two routes

Figure 11.2

A Transportation Network

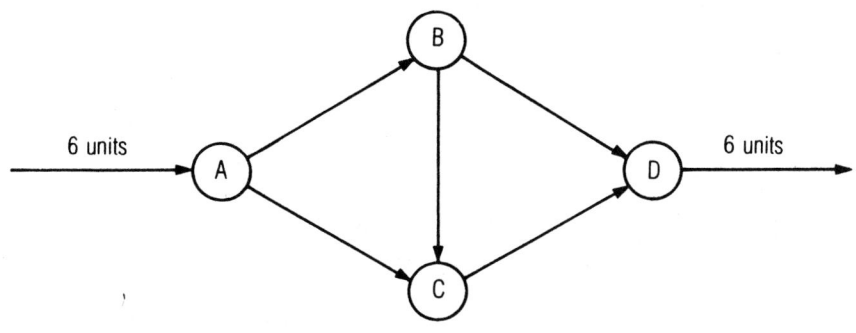

so that either travel times are equal over the two alternates or none of the A to B commuters use the longer alternate.

As an example, consider the network in Figure 11.2. Six units of traffic (e.g., in thousands of cars) want to get from A to B.

The travel time on any link as a function of the traffic volume is given in the table below.

For All Traffic Volumes Less Than or Equal To	Link Travel Time in Minutes				
	AB	AC	BC	BD	CD
2	20	52	12	52	20
3	30	53	13	53	30
4	40	54	14	54	40

The dramatically different functions for the various links might be due to such features as number of lanes, or whether a link has traffic lights or stop signs.

We are interested in how traffic will distribute itself over the three possible routes *ABD*, *ACD*, and *ABCD* if each unit behaves individually optimally. That is, we want to find the flows for which a user is indifferent between the three routes.

This can be formulated as an LP analogous to the previous equilibrium problems if the travel time time schedules are interpreted as supply curves.

Define variables as follows. Two letter variable names, e.g., AB or CD denote the total flow along a given arc, e.g., the arc AB or the arc CD. Variables with a numeric suffix denote the incremental flow along a link, e.g., AB2 measures flow up to 2 units on link $A \to B$; AB3 measures the incremental flow above 2 but less than 3.

The formulation is then:

```
MIN     20 AB2 + 30 AB3 + 40 AB4 + 52 AC2 + 53 AC3 + 54 AC4 + 12 BC2
      + 13 BC3 + 14 BC4 + 52 BD2 + 53 BD3 + 54 BD4 + 20 CD2 + 30 CD3
      + 40 CD4
```

```
SUBJECT TO
    2)   - AB2 -  AB3 -  AB4 +  AB = 0   ! Definition of AB
    3)   - AC2 -  AC3 -  AC4 +  AC = 0
    4)   - BC2 -  BC3 -  BC4 +  BC = 0   !    etc.
    5)   - BD2 -  BD3 -  BD4 +  BD = 0
    6)   - CD2 -  CD3 -  CD4 +  CD = 0
    7)     AB +   AC =   6                ! Flow out of A
    8)     AB -   BC -   BD =   0         ! Flow through B
    9)     AC +   BC -   CD =   0         ! Flow through C
   10)     BD +   CD =   6                ! Flow into D
   11)     AB2 ≤ 2                        ! Definition of the steps in
   12)     AB3 ≤ 1                        ! supply cost schedule
   13)     AB4 ≤ 1
   14)     AC2 ≤ 2
   15)     AC3 ≤ 1
   16)     AC4 ≤ 1
   17)     BC2 ≤ 2
   18)     BC3 ≤ 1
   19)     BC4 ≤ 1
   20)     BD2 ≤ 2
   21)     BD3 ≤ 1
   22)     BD4 ≤ 1
   23)     CD2 ≤ 2
   24)     CD3 ≤ 1
   25)     CD4 ≤ 1
END
```

The solution is:

```
          OBJECTIVE FUNCTION VALUE

    1)        452.0000000

  VARIABLE        VALUE           REDUCED COST
     AB2         2.000000           0.000000
     AB3         1.000000           0.000000
     AB4         1.000000           0.000000
     AC2         2.000000           0.000000
     AC3         0.000000           1.000000
     AC4         0.000000           2.000000
     BC2         2.000000           0.000000
     BC3         0.000000           1.000000
     BC4         0.000000           2.000000
     BD2         2.000000           0.000000
     BD3         0.000000           1.000000
     BD4         0.000000           2.000000
     CD2         2.000000           0.000000
     CD3         1.000000           0.000000
     CD4         1.000000           0.000000
     AB          4.000000           0.000000
     AC          2.000000           0.000000
     BC          2.000000           0.000000
     BD          2.000000           0.000000
     CD          4.000000           0.000000
```

ROW	SLACK	DUAL PRICES
2)	0.000000	40.000000
3)	0.000000	52.000000
4)	0.000000	12.000000
5)	0.000000	52.000000
6)	0.000000	40.000000
7)	0.000000	-92.000000
8)	0.000000	52.000000
9)	0.000000	40.000000
10)	0.000000	0.000000
11)	0.000000	20.000000
12)	0.000000	10.000000
13)	0.000000	0.000000
14)	0.000000	0.000000
15)	1.000000	0.000000
16)	1.000000	0.000000
17)	0.000000	0.000000
18)	1.000000	0.000000
19)	1.000000	0.000000
20)	0.000000	0.000000
21)	1.000000	0.000000
22)	1.000000	0.000000
23)	0.000000	20.000000
24)	0.000000	10.000000
25)	0.000000	0.000000

Notice that 2 units of traffic take each of the three possible routes: *ABD*, *ABCD*, and *ACD*. The travel time on each route is 92 minutes. This agrees with our understanding of an equilibrium, i.e., no user is motivated to take a different route.

Realize that the objective function value has no immediate practical interpretation for this formulation. In this case, the objective function is simply a device to cause Wardrup's principle to hold when the objective is optimized.

The solution approach based on formulating the traffic equilibrium problem as a standard LP was presented mainly for pedagogical reasons. For larger, real world problems there are highly specialized procedures, cf. Florian (1977).

We shall see that for this problem the solution just displayed does not minimize total travel time. In order to minimize total travel time, it is useful to prepare a table of total travel time incurred by users of a link as a function of link volume. This is done in Table 11.1. "Total" is the product of link volume times travel time at that volume.

—————— Table 11.1 ——————

Total and Incremental Travel Time Incurred on a Link

Traffic Volume	AB		AC		BC		BD		CD	
	Total	Rate/Unit	Total	Rate/Unit	Total	Rate/Unit	Total	Rate/Unit	Total	Rate/Unit
2	40	20	104	52	24	12	104	52	40	20
3	90	50	159	55	39	15	159	55	90	50
4	160	70	216	57	56	17	216	57	160	70

The appropriate formulation is:

```
MIN      20 AB2 + 50 AB3 + 70 AB4 + 52 AC2 + 55 AC3 + 57 AC4 + 12 BC2
       + 15 BC3 + 17 BC4 + 52 BD2 + 55 BD3 + 57 BD4 + 20 CD2 + 50 CD3
       + 70 CD4
SUBJECT TO
    2)   - AB2 - AB3 - AB4 +  AB =   0   ! Definition of AB
    3)   - AC2 - AC3 - AC4 +  AC =   0   ! and AC,
    4)   - BC2 - BC3 - BC4 +  BC =   0   ! BC
    5)   - BD2 - BD3 - BD4 +  BD =   0   ! BD
    6)   - CD2 - CD3 - CD4 +  CD =   0   ! and CD
    7)    AB +  AC  =   6                ! Flow out of A
    8)    AB -  BC  -  BD  =   0         ! Flow through B
    9)    AC +  BC  -  CD  =   0         ! Flow through C
   10)    BD +  CD  =   6                ! Flow into D
   11)    AB2 ≤  2                       ! Steps in supply schedule
   12)    AB3 ≤  1
   13)    AB4 ≤  1
   14)    AC2 ≤  2
   15)    AC3 ≤  1
   16)    AC4 ≤  1
   17)    BC2 ≤  2
   18)    BC3 ≤  1
   19)    BC4 ≤  1
   20)    BD2 ≤  2
   21)    BD3 ≤  1
   22)    BD4 ≤  1
   23)    CD2 ≤  2
   24)    CD3 ≤  1
   25)    CD4 ≤  1
END
```

The solution is:

```
         OBJECTIVE FUNCTION VALUE

    1)       498.0000000

   VARIABLE        VALUE           REDUCED COST
      AB2         2.000000           0.000000
      AB3         1.000000           0.000000
      AB4         0.000000          20.000000
      AC2         2.000000           0.000000
      AC3         1.000000           0.000000
      AC4         0.000000           2.000000
      BC2         0.000000           0.000000
      BC3         0.000000           3.000000
      BC4         0.000000           5.000000
      BD2         2.000000           0.000000
      BD3         1.000000           0.000000
      BD4         0.000000           2.000000
      CD2         2.000000           0.000000
      CD3         1.000000           0.000000
      CD4         0.000000          20.000000
      AB          3.000000           0.000000
      AC          3.000000           0.000000
```

BC	0.000000	7.000000
BD	3.000000	0.000000
CD	3.000000	0.000000
ROW	SLACK	DUAL PRICES
2)	0.000000	50.000000
3)	0.000000	55.000000
4)	0.000000	12.000000
5)	0.000000	55.000000
6)	0.000000	50.000000
7)	0.000000	−105.000000
8)	0.000000	55.000000
9)	0.000000	50.000000
10)	0.000000	0.000000
11)	0.000000	30.000000
12)	0.000000	0.000000
13)	1.000000	0.000000
14)	0.000000	3.000000
15)	0.000000	0.000000
16)	1.000000	0.000000
17)	2.000000	0.000000
18)	1.000000	0.000000
19)	1.000000	0.000000
20)	0.000000	3.000000
21)	0.000000	0.000000
22)	1.000000	0.000000
23)	0.000000	30.000000
24)	0.000000	0.000000
25)	1.000000	0.000000

An interesting feature is that no traffic uses link *BC*. Three units each take routes *ABD* and *ACD*. Even more interesting is the fact that the travel time on both routes is 83 minutes. This is noticeably less than the 92 minutes for the previous solution. With this formulation, the objective function measures the total travel time incurred. Note 498/6 = 83.

If link *BC* were removed, this latest solution would also be a user equilibrium because no user would be motivated to switch routes. The interesting paradox is that by adding additional capacity, in this case link *BC*, to a transportation network, the total delay may actually increase. This is known as Braess's Paradox, cf. Braess (1968) or Murchland (1970). Braess claims to have observed this paradox in a German city when a new link was added to its road network. When traffic got worse rather than better with the new link, the new link was removed.

To see why the paradox occurs, consider what happens when link *BC* is added. One of the 3 units taking route *ABD* notices that travel time on link *BC* is 12 and time on link *CD* is 30. This total of 42 minutes is better than the 53 minutes the unit is suffering in link *BD*, so the unit replaces link *BD* in its route by the sequence *BCD*. At this point one of the units taking link *AC* observes that it can reduce its delay in getting to *C* by replacing link *AC* (delay 53 minutes) with the two links *AB* and *BC* (delay of 30 + 12 = 42). Unfortunately (and this is the cause of Braess's paradox), neither of these units which switched took into account the effect of their actions on the rest of the population. The switches increased the load on links *AB* and *CD*, two links for which increased volume dramatically increases the travel time of everyone. The general result is that *when individuals each maximize their own objective function, the obvious overall objective function is not necessarily maximized.*

Problems

1. Producer B in the 2-producer-2-consumer market at the beginning of the chapter is actually a foreign producer. The government of the importing country is contemplating putting a $0.60 per unit tax on units from Producer B.

    (a) How is the formulation changed?

    (b) How is the equilibrium solution changed?

2. An organization is interested in selling five parcels of land, denoted A, B, C, D, and E, which it owns. It is willing to accept offers for subsets of the five parcels. Three buyers, x, y, and z are interested in making offers. In the privacy of their respective offices each buyer has identified the maximum price he would be willing to pay for various combinations. This information is summarized below:

Buyer	Parcel Combination	Maximum Price
x	A, B, D	95
x	C, D, E	80
y	B, E	60
y	A, D	82
z	B, D, E	90
z	C, E	71

    Each buyer wants to buy at most one parcel combination. Suppose the organization is a government and would like to maximize social welfare. What is a possible formulation based on an LP for holding this auction?

3. Commuters wish to travel from points A, B, and C to point D in the network shown in the figure below:

Figure 11.3

A Travel Network

Three units wish to travel from A to D, two units from B to D, and one from C to D. The travel time on the five links as a function of volume are:

For All Traffic Volumes Less Than or Equal To	Link Travel Time in Minutes				
	AD	AC	BC	BD	CD
2	21	50	17	40	12
3	31	51	27	41	13
4	41	52	37	42	14

(a) Display the LP formulation corresponding to a Wardrup's Principle user equilibrium.

(b) Display the LP formulation useful for the total travel time minimizing solution.

(c) What are the solutions to (a) and (b)?

12

Game Theory

Introduction

In most decision making situations our profits (and losses) are determined not only by our decisions but by the decisions taken by outside forces, e.g., our competitors, the weather, etc. A useful classification is whether the outside force is indifferent or mischievous. We will, for example, classify the weather as indifferent because its decision is indifferent to our actions, in spite of how we might feel during a rainstorm after washing the car and forgetting the umbrella. A competitor, however, generally takes into account the likelihood of our taking various decisions and as a result tends to make decisions which are mischievous relative to our welfare. In this chapter we analyze situations involving a mischievous outside force. The standard terminology applied to the problem to be considered is game theory. Situations in which these problems might arise are in the choice of a marketing or price strategy, in international affairs, military combat, and in many negotiation situations. For example, the probability that a competitor executes an oil embargo against us probably depends upon whether we have elected a strategy of building up a strategic petroleum reserve.

Two Person Games

In so-called two person game theory, the key feature is that *each of the two players must make a crucial decision ignorant of the other player's decision*. Only after both players have committed to their respective decisions, then each player learns of the other player's decision and each player receives a payoff that depends solely on the two decisions. Two person game theory is further classified according whether the payoffs are constant sum vs. variable sum. In a constant sum game the total payoff summed over both players is constant. Usually this constant is assumed to be zero so that one player's gain is exactly the other player's loss. The following example illustrates a constant sum game.

A game is to be played between two players called Blue and Gold. It is a single simultaneous move game. Each player must make her single move in ignorance of the other player's move. Both moves are then revealed and then one player pays the other an amount specified by the payoff table below:

Payoff from Blue to Gold

		Blue's Move	
		a	b
Gold's Move	a	4	−6
	b	−5	8
	c	3	−4

Blue must choose one of two moves (a) or (b) while Gold has a choice among three moves (a), (b), or (c). For example, if Gold chooses move (b) and Blue chooses move (a) then Gold pays Blue 5 million dollars. If Gold chooses (c) and Blue chooses (a), then Blue pays Gold 3 million dollars.

The Minimax Strategy

This game does not have an obvious strategy for either player. If Gold is tempted to make move (b) in the hopes of winning the 8 million dollar prize, then Blue will be equally tempted to make move (a) so as to win 5 million from Gold. For this example it is clear that each player will want to consider a random strategy. Any player who follows a pure strategy of always making the same move is easily beaten. Therefore define:

BM_i = probability Blue makes move i, $i = a$ or b,

GM_i = probability Gold makes move i, $i = a, b$, or c.

How should Blue choose the probabilities BM_i? Blue might observe that:

If Gold chooses move (a), my expected loss is:

4 BMA − 6 BMB

If Gold chooses move (b), my expected loss is:

−5 BMA + 8 BMB,

If Gold chooses move (c), my expected loss is:

3 BMA − 4 BMB

So there are three possible expected losses depending upon which decision is made by Gold. If Blue is conservative then a reasonable criterion is to choose the BM_i so as to minimize the maximum expected loss. This philosophy is called the *minimax* strategy. Stated another way, Blue wants to choose the probabilities BM_i such that no matter what Gold does, Blue's maximum expected loss is minimized. If LB is the maximum expected loss to Blue, then her problem can be stated as the LP:

```
       MIN    LB
       SUBJECT TO
          2)    BMA + BMB = 1              ! Probabilities must sum to 1
          3)  - LB + 4 BMA - 6 BMB  < 0    ! Expected loss if Gold chooses (a)
          4)  - LB - 5 BMA + 8 BMB  < 0    ! Expected loss if Gold chooses (b)
          5)  - LB + 3 BMA - 4 BMB  < 0    ! Expected loss if Gold chooses (c)
       END
```

The solution is:

```
                  OBJECTIVE FUNCTION VALUE

       1)            0.2000000

       VARIABLE       VALUE          REDUCED COST
       LB             0.2000000         0.000000
       BMA            0.6000000         0.000000
       BMB            0.4000000         0.000000

       ROW            SLACK          DUAL PRICES
       2)             0.000000         -0.20000
       3)             0.200000          0.00000
       4)             0.000000          0.35000
       5)             0.000000          0.65000
```

The interpretation is that if Blue chooses move (*a*) with probability 0.6 and move (*b*) with probability 0.4 then Blue's expected loss is never greater than 0.2, regardless of Gold's move.

If Gold follows a similar argument but phrases the argument in terms of maximizing the minimum expected profit, PG, instead of minimizing maximum loss, then Gold's problem is:

```
       MAX    PG
       SUBJECT TO
          2)    GMA + GMB + GMC = 1             ! Probabilities sum to 1
          3)  -PG + 4 GMA - 5 GMB + 3 GMC > 0   ! Expected profit if Blue chooses (a)
          4)  -PG - 6 GMA + 8 GMB - 4 GMC > 0   ! Expected profit if Blue chooses (b)
       END
```

The solution to Gold's problem is:

```
                  OBJECTIVE FUNCTION VALUE

                      0.20000000

       VARIABLE       VALUE          REDUCED COST
       PG             0.2000000         0.000000
       GMA            0.0000000         0.000000
       GMB            0.3500000         0.000000
       GMC            0.6500000         0.000000

       ROW            SLACK          DUAL PRICES
       2)             0.000000          0.200000
       3)             0.000000         -0.600000
       4)             0.000000         -0.400000
```

The interpretation is that if Gold chooses move (*b*) with probability 0.35, move (*c*) with probability 0.65 and never move (*a*) then Gold's expected profit is never less than 0.2. Notice that Gold's lowest expected profit equals Blue's highest expected loss. From Blue's point of view the expected transfer to Gold is at least 0.2. The only possible expected transfer is then 0.2. This means that if both players follow the random strategies just derived, then on every play of the game there is an expected transfer of 0.2 units from Blue to Gold. The game is biased in Gold's favor at the rate of 0.2 million dollars per play.

If you look closely at the solutions to Blue's LP and to Gold's LP, you will note a surprising similarity. The dual prices of Blue's LP equal the probabilities in Gold's LP and the negatives of Gold's dual prices equal the probabilities of Blue's LP. Looking more closely you can note that each LP is really the dual of the other one. This is always true for a two-person game of the type just considered, and mathematicians have long been excited by this fact.

Nonconstant-Sum Games Involving Two or More Players

The most unrealistic assumption underlying classical two-person constant-sum game theory is that the sum of the payoffs to all players must sum to zero (actually a constant, without loss of generality). In reality, the total benefits are almost never constant; usually, total benefits increase if the players cooperate. In these nonconstant-sum games, the difficulty then becomes one of deciding how these additional benefits due to cooperation should be distributed among the players.

There are two styles for analyzing nonconstant-sum games. If we restrict ourselves to two persons then so-called *bi-matrix game theory* extends the methods for two-person constant-sum games to nonconstant-sum games. If there are three or more players, then *n-person game theory* can be used in selecting a decision strategy. Bi-matrix games are considered further in Chapter 15. The following example illustrates the essential concepts of *n*-person game theory.

Three property owners, *A*, *B*, and *C*, own adjacent lakefront property on a large lake. A piece of property on a large lake has higher value if it is protected from wave action by a seawall. *A*, *B*, and *C* are each considering building a seawall on their properties. A seawall is cheaper to build on a given piece of property if either or both of the neighbors have seawalls. For our example, *A* and *C* already have expensive buildings on their properties. *B* does not have buildings and separates *A* from *C*; i.e., *B* is between *A* and *C*. The net benefits of a seawall for the three owners are summarized below.

Owners Who Cooperate, i.e., Build While Others Do Not	Net Benefit to Cooperating Owners
A alone	1.2
B alone	0
C alone	1
A and *B*	4
A and *C*	3
B and *C*	4
A, *B*, and *C*	7

Obviously, all three owners should cooperate and build a unified seawall because then their total benefits will be maximized. It appears that B should be compensated in some manner because he has no motivation to build a seawall by himself. Linear programming can provide some help in selecting an acceptable allocation of benefits.

Denote by v_A, v_B, and v_C the net benefits which are to be allocated to owners A, B, and C. No owner or set of owners will accept an allocation which is less than that which they would enjoy if they acted alone. Thus, we can conclude:

$$v_A \geqq 1.2$$
$$v_B \geqq 0$$
$$v_C \geqq 1$$
$$v_A + v_B \geqq 4$$
$$v_A + v_C \geqq 3$$
$$v_B + v_C \geqq 4$$
$$v_A + v_B + v_C \leqq 7$$

That is, any allocation satisfying the above constraints should be self-enforcing. No owner would be motivated to not cooperate. He cannot do better by himself. The above constraints describe what is called the "core" of the game. Any solution satisfying these constraints, $v_A = 3$, $v_B = 1$, $v_C = 3$ is said to be in the core.

Various objective functions might be appended to this set of constraints to give an LP. The objective could take into account secondary considerations. For example, we might choose to maximize the minimum benefit. The LP in this case is:

Maximixe z
subject to $z \leqq v_A$; $z \leqq v_B$; $z \leqq v_C$
$v_A \geqq 1.2$
$v_C \geqq 1$
$v_A + v_B \geqq 4$
$v_A + v_C \geqq 3$
$v_B + v_C \geqq 4$
$v_A + v_B + v_C \leqq 7$

A solution is $v_A = v_B = v_C = 2.3333$.

Note that the core can be empty; that is, there is no feasible solution. This would be true, for example, if the value of the coalition A, B, C was 5.4 rather than 7. This situation is rather interesting. Total benefits are maximized by everyone cooperating; however, total cooperation is inherently unstable when benefits are 5.4. There will always be a pair of players who find it advantageous to form a subcoalition and improve their benefits (at the considerable expense of the player left out). As an example, suppose the allocations to A, B, and C under full cooperation are 1.2, 2.1, and 2.1 respectively. At this point A would suggest to B that the two of them exclude C and cooperate between the two of them. A would suggest to B the allocation of 1.8, 2.2, and 1. This is consistent with the fact that A and B can achieve a total of 4 when cooperating. At this point C might suggest to A that the two of them cooperate and thereby select an allocation of 1.9, 0, 1.1. This is inconsistent with the fact that A and C can achieve a total of 3 when cooperating. At this point B suggests to C, etc. Thus, when the core is empty, it may be that everyone agrees that full cooperation can be better for everyone; there must nevertheless be an enforcement mechanism to prevent "greedy" members from pulling out of the coalition.

Problems

1. By inspection, find the optimal policies for Blue and Gold in the 2-person game described by the following matrix.

   Payment to Blue by Gold as a Function of Both Decisions

		Blue Decision		
		A	B	C
Gold Decision	X	4	8	6
	Y	3	7	4
	Z	5	9	5

2. Formulate an LP for finding the optimal policies for Blue and Gold when confronted with the following game.

   Payment to Blue by Gold as a Function of Both Decisions

		Blue Decision			
		A	B	C	D
Gold Decision	X	3	−2	2	6
	Y	−1	4	5	−1

3. The three neighboring communities of Parched, Cactus and Tombstone are located in the desert and are analyzing their options for improving their water supplies. An aqueduct to the mountains would satisfy all their needs and cost in total $730,000. Alternatively, Parched and Cactus could dig and share an artesian well of sufficient capacity which would cost $580,000. A similar option for Cactus and Tombstone would cost $500,000. Parched, Cactus and Tombstone could each individually distribute shallow wells over their respective surface areas to satisfy their needs for respective costs of $300,000, $350,000 and $250,000.

   Formulate and solve a simple LP for finding a plausible way of allocating the $730,000 cost of an aqueduct among the three communities.

4. Sportcasters say Team I is out of the running if the number of games already won by I plus the number of remaining games for Team I is less than the games already won by the league leader. It is frequently the case that a team is mathematically out of the running even before that point is reached. By Team I mathematically out of the running we mean that there is no combination of wins and losses for the remaining games in the season such that Team I could end the season having won more games than any other team. A third place team might find itself mathematically though not obviously out of the running if the first and second place teams have all their remaining games against each other.

   Formulate a linear program which will not have a feasible solution if Team I is no longer in the running.

The following variables may be of interest:

x_{j_k} = number of times Team j may beat Team k in the season's remaining games and Team I still win more games than anyone else.

The following constants should be used:

R_{j_k} = number of remaining games between Team j and Team k. Note the number of times that j beats k plus the number of times that k beats j must equal R_{j_k}.

T_k = total number of games won by Team k to date. Thus, the number of games won at season's end by team k is T_k plus the number of times it beat other teams.

13

Quadratic Programming

Introduction

Quadratic programming is the name applied to the class of models in which the objective function is a quadratic function and the constraints are linear. Thus, the objective function is allowed to have terms that are products of two variables such as x^2 and $x \times y$. The principal applications of quadratic programming appear mainly in the areas:

1. financial portfolio models,
2. production/demand curve models,
3. constrained least squares regression,
4. two-person, non-constant-sum games.

Strictly speaking, (4) is not a quadratic program, however, essentially the same solution algorithm applies to (4) as to (1), (2) and (3) so we cavalierly include it.

Quadratic programming is computationally appealing because the algorithms for linear programs can be applied to quadratic programming with only modest modifications. Loosely speaking, the reason that only modest modification is required is because the first derivative of a quadratic function is a linear function.

The following sections illustrate the application of quadratic programming to the above problem areas.

The Markowitz Portfolio Model

The portfolio model introduced by Markowitz (1959) assumes that an investor has but two considerations when constructing an investment portfolio, expected return and variance in return. The investor wants the former to be high and the latter to be low. Variance measures the variability in realized return around the expected return, giving equal weight to realizations below the expected and above the expected return. The Markowitz model might be mildly criticized in this regard because the typical investor is probably concerned only with variability below the expected return, so-called downside risk.

The model requires two major kinds of information: (1) the estimated expected return for each candidate asset and (2) the covariance matrix of returns. The covariance matrix characterizes not only the individual variability of an asset's value but also how the value of each asset tends to move with the value of other assets. We assume the reader is familiar with the concepts of variance and covariance as are described in most intermediate statistics texts.

We will take the covariance matrix as given. In an actual application the user should take some care to accurately calculate the covariance matrix. For example, there should be more observations than variables; an accurate formula for computing the covariance matrix should be used.

Example

There are three candidate assets X, Y, and Z for our portfolio. We want to determine what fraction should be devoted to each asset, so that an expected return of at least 12% (equivalently, a growth factor of 1.12) is obtained while minimizing the variance in return and not exceeding the budget constraint. The expected returns of X, Y, and Z are, respectively, 30%, 20%, and 8%. We also have the restriction that any given asset can constitute, at most, 75% of the portfolio.

Suppose the covariance matrix is:

	X	Y	Z
X	3	1	-0.5
Y	1	2	-0.4
Z	-0.5	-0.4	1

Let the symbols X, Y, and Z represent the fraction of the portfolio devoted to each of the three assets. Then the variance can be written as:

$$3X^2 + 2Y^2 + Z^2 + 2X \times Y - X \times Z - 0.8Y \times Z$$

This is to be minimized. The complete problem is then:

Minimize $3X^2 + 2Y^2 + Z^2 + 2X \times Y - X \times Z - 0.8Y \times Z$

subject to
- $X + Y + Z = 1$ (Use exactly 100% of the budget)
- $1.3X + 1.2Y + 1.08Z \geq 1.12$ (Return constraint)
- $X \leq 0.75$
- $Y \leq 0.75$
- $Z \leq 0.75$

If the LINDO computer program is used then this problem must be converted to true linear form by writing the so-called Karush/Kuhn/Tucker/LaGrange first order conditions. To do this, we must introduce a dual variable or LaGrange multiplier for each constraint. For the above five constraints we will use five dual variables denoted, respectively, BUDGET, RETURN, XFRAC, YFRAC, and ZFRAC.

The input procedure for LINDO is LP-based and requires an objective function even though there is no explicit objective listed in the first order conditions. The first row input serves an important purpose, however, in that it is used to identify the order of variables which in turn determines the correspondence between variables and rows. Writing the first order conditions can be done methodically as follows:

1. Write the objective function in minimization form, e.g., multiplying through by -1 if you naturally think of the objective function in the maximization form. The objective function in this form is actually *not* input to LINDO.
2. The first order condition for variable X is composed of
    (a) the derivative of the objective function with respect to X,
    (b) plus the sum over all "<" and "=" rows of X's coefficient in the row times the dual variable of the row,
    (c) minus the sum over all ">" rows of X's coefficient in the row times the dual variable of the row.

LINDO requires that the true constraints, e.g., $X + Y + Z = 1$, $1.3X + 1.2Y + 1.08Z < 1.12$, etc., must appear last.

Finally, the command QCP must be used to specify which constraint is the first of the real constraints.

The complete input of the problem is shown below.

```
MIN     X + Y + Z + BUDGET + RETURN + XFRAC + YFRAC + ZFRAC
SUBJECT TO
    2)      6 X + 2 Y - Z + BUDGET - 1.3 RETURN + XFRAC > 0      ! X
    3)      2 X + 4 Y - 0.8 Z + BUDGET - 1.2 RETURN + YFRAC > 0  ! Y
    4)      - X - 0.8 Y + 2 Z + BUDGET - 1.08 RETURN + ZFRAC > 0 ! Z
    5)      X + Y + Z = 1                                        ! BUDGET
    6)      1.3 X + 1.2 Y + 1.08 Z > 1.12                        ! RETURN
    7)      X < 0.75                                             ! XFRAC
    8)      Y < 0.75                                             ! YFRAC
    9)      Z < 0.75                                             ! ZFRAC
END
QCP
ROW NO. OF FIRST REAL CONSTRAINT:
5
```

The order of the variables in the very first row: MIN X + Y, etc., is important. The so-called complementary slackness conditions require that if X is greater than zero, then the first constraint ($6X + 2Y -$ etc.) must be binding. Similarly, if Y is non-zero, then the constraint ($2X + 4Y -$ etc.) must be binding and so forth. Thus, LINDO must know this correspondence between variables and constraints to enforce these conditions.

We solve the problem as follows.

```
GO
    QP OPTIMUM FOUND AT STEP   7
        OBJECTIVE FUNCTION VALUE
    1)              0.417374880
```

The Markowitz Portfolio Model

```
VARIABLE        VALUE           REDUCED COST
   X            0.154863         0.000000
   Y            0.250236         0.000000
   Z            0.594901         0.000000
BUDGET         -0.834750         0.000000
RETURN          0.000000         0.024098
XFRAC           0.000000         0.595137
YFRAC           0.000000         0.499764
ZFRAC           0.000000         0.155099

   ROW          SLACK           DUAL PRICES
    2)          0.000000        -0.154863
    3)          0.000000        -0.250236
    4)          0.000000        -0.594901
    5)          0.000000        -0.834750
    6)          0.024098         0.000000
    7)          0.595137         0.000000
    8)          0.499764         0.000000
    9)          0.155099         0.000000

NO. ITERATIONS     7
```

The solution recommends that about 15% of the portfolio should be in X, about 25% in Y and about 60% in Z. The expected return of this portfolio is about $0.12 + 0.024 = 0.144$.

It would be an unusual investor that would know exactly the combination of return and variance that he desired. Therefore, it is useful to do some sensitivity or parametric analysis to show how variance increases as the required expected return is increased. In finance terminology we would like to trace out the efficient frontier. The PARA(metric) command in LINDO is useful for doing this. The following illustrates:

```
PARA                ! Execute the PARA command
ROW:                ! It asks for which row we want to vary the RHS
6                   ! We specify the return constraint row
NEW RHS VAL=        ! Vary it up to 1.3
1.3
           VAR     VAR     PIVOT     RHS         DUAL PRICE        OBJ
           OUT     IN      ROW       VAL         BEFORE PIVOT      VAL
                                    1.12000        .000000          .417375
   SLK      6     RETURN    6       1.14410        .000000          .417375
   SLK      7     XFRAC     7       1.26947      -25.8299          2.03651
            Z     ART       0       1.27500      -28.7500          2.18750
                                    1.30000      -INFINITY         INFEASIBLE
```

Recall that row 6 is the constraint on minimum return: $1.3X + 1.2Y + 1.08Z \geq 1.12$. The PARA command has requested that the changes in the portfolio be traced out as the required return is increased to 1.3 from 1.12. One line of output is printed each time one of the following occurs:

(a) a new asset enters the optimal portfolio,

(b) an asset is removed from the optimal portfolio,

(c) a binding constraint becomes nonbinding,

(d) a nonbinding constraint becomes binding.

When our target return was 1.12, it was the case that this constraint was nonbinding, *i.e.*, minimizing the variance in return naturally resulted in a return greater than 12% or a growth factor of 1.12. The first line of output in the parametric report indicates that the return constraint becomes binding (and thus its slack, SLK 6, departs) when the required return is 1.441. As the required return is increased, apparently the investment in asset X is increasing because in the second line of the parametric report the upper bound constraint on X becomes binding (and thus its slack, SLK 7, departs) when the required return is 1.26947. Notice that the variance has increased by almost a factor of five to achieve this return. As the required return is increased still further, the investment in the low return, but also low variance, asset Z is finally driven to zero. The final line of the report indicates that this happens when the required return is 1.275. In fact a higher return of 1.3 is not possible because at most 75% of the portfolio can consist of the high expected return asset X.

If we wish to look in more detail at one of the higher return portfolios we can alter the righthand side of the return constraint as follows:

```
ALTER 6
VAR:
?RHS
NEW COEFFICIENT:
1.27

GO
        QP OPTIMUM FOUND AT STEP       0
            OBJECTIVE FUNCTION VALUE

    1)          2.05034709

    VARIABLE        VALUE          REDUCED COST
        X         0.750000           0.000000
        Y         0.208333           0.000000
        Z         0.041667           0.000000
    BUDGET       29.033337           0.000000
    RETURN       26.111113           0.000000
    XFRAC         0.036109           0.000000
    YFRAC         0.000000           0.541667
    ZFRAC         0.000000           0.708333

    ROW       SLACK OR SURPLUS     DUAL PRICES
    2)           0.000000          -0.750000
    3)           0.000000          -0.208333
    4)           0.000000          -0.041667
    5)           0.000000          29.033337
    6)           0.000000         -26.111113
    7)           0.000000           0.036109
    8)           0.541667           0.000000
    9)           0.708333           0.000000
```

Recall from the parametric analysis that asset X hit its upper bound when the required expected return was raised to 1.26947. Thus, in the above portfolio where the required expected return is 1.27, asset X is very much at its upper bound.

Important Variations of the Portfolio Model

When applying quadratic programming in the straightforward manner to portfolio planning as originally suggested by Markowitz there are at least two complications encountered:

1. For interesting portfolios, the size of the covariance matrix may be overwhelming. For example, 1000 assets implies a covariance matrix of 1,000,000 entries; at least 500,000 if symmetry is exploited. Doing optimization with this many entries or even estimating this many pieces of data is a formidable task.
2. In straightforward form the portfolio model does not consider transaction costs. Thus, every time the model is optimized with new data, a possibly completely different portfolio is recommended. Realistically, one would not wish to adjust his investment level in a particular asset if the transaction cost of making the adjustment exceeds the benefits of making the adjustment.

We now describe simple variations and approximations of the basic portfolio problem which allow us to cope with the above problems.

Scenario Model for Representing Uncertainty

The scenario approach to modeling uncertainty assumes that the possible future situations can be represented by a small number of "scenarios." The smallest number used is typically three, e.g., "optimistic," "most likely," and "pessimistic." See Perold (1984) for a further discussion of this approach. Some of the original ideas underlying the scenario approach come from the approach known as stochastic programming, see Madansky (1962). For a discussion of the scenario approach for large portfolios, see Markowitz and Perold (1981) and Perold (1984). This approach may be appealing in markets such as real estate where the investments are one-of-a-kind and there are no nice historical time series on prices from which covariance matrices can be computed. Each scenario may correspond to different economic events that has major economic significance, such as war breaks out in the Mideast, a Democrat is elected president, our city is awarded the next Olympic games, etc. To make things precise, define:

P_s = Prob {scenario s occurs},

u_{is} = return of asset i if the scenario is s,

X_i = investment in asset i,

m_0 = mean return,
$= \sum_i X_i \sum_s P_s u_{is}$

Y_s = deviation from mean return if the scenario is s,
$= \sum X_i u_{is} - m_0$

Our problem is

Minimize $\sum_s P_s Y_s^2$

subject to $Y_s - \sum_i X_i (u_{is} - m_0) = 0$ (deviation for each scenario, s)

$\sum X_i = 1$ (amount available to invest)

$m_0 = \sum_i X_i \sum_i P_s u_{is}$ (compute mean return)

$m_0 \geq r$ (desired return).

If asset i has an inherent variability, σ_i^2, the objective generalizes to

Minimize $\sum_i X_i^2 \sigma_i^2 + \sum P_s Y_s^2$

The key feature is that even though this formulation has a few more constraints, the number of nonzero coefficients in the model is approximately 2 × (number of assets) × (number of scenarios + 1) + (number of scenarios). For the full Markowitz model the number of nonzeroes is approximately (number of assets)^2. For 500 assets and 9 scenarios the difference is between about 10,000 nonzeroes and about 250,000 nonzeroes.

Factors Model for Simplifying the Covariance Structure

Sharpe (1963) introduced a simple model of portfolio randomness based on the approximation that the movement of the price of a stock or asset consists of just two components (a) a movement perfectly correlated with the random movement of "the market" or some index, and (b) a random movement specific to that stock that is uncorrelated with any other stock. Define the random variables:

r_i = return of asset i,
M = the return of the market index,
e_i = market independent component of asset i returns,

and the constants:

u_i = "excess" expected return of asset i,
b_i = the "beta" of asset i, rate at which asset i moves with the market index,
σ_0^2 = variance of M,
σ_i^2 = variance of e_i.
$m_0 = E(\mathbf{M})$.

Sharpe's approximation assumes that (where $E(\ )$ denotes expected value):

$E(e_i) = 0$
$E(e_i e_j) = 0 \quad$ for $i \neq j$.

Let

X_i = amount invested in asset i.

The variance in return of the portfolio is then:

$$\text{var}[\sum_i X_i(u_i + b_i M + e_i)] = \text{var}(\sum_i X_i b_i M) + \text{var}(\sum_i X_i e_i)$$
$$= (\sum_i X_i b_i)^2 \sigma_0^2 + \sum_i X_i^2 \sigma_i^2$$

Thus, our problem can be written

Minimize $Z^2 \sigma_0^2 + \sum_i X_i^2 \sigma_i^2$
subject to $Z - \sum_i X_i b_i = 0$
$\sum X_i = 1$
$\sum_i X_i(u_i + b_i u_0) \geq r$.

Important Variations of the Portfolio Model

So, at the expense of adding one constraint and one variable, we have reduced a dense covariance matrix to a diagonal covariance matrix.

In practice a generalization of the factors model is often used. The return of asset i is assumed to be correlated with several indices. The indices typically used are based on (a) interest rates, (b) inflation, (c) energy prices, (d) defense spending, (e) gross national product and (f) various industry indices.

The Portfolio Problem with Transaction Costs

The models above do not tell us much about how frequently to adjust our portfolio as new information becomes available, *i.e.*, new estimates of expected return and new estimates of variance. If we applied the above models every time new information become available we would be constantly adjusting our portfolio. This might make our broker happy but that should be at best a secondary objective.

The method we will describe assumes that transaction costs are paid at the end of the period. The interested reader may try to modify the model to represent the situation when transaction costs are paid at the beginning of the period.

If transactions costs are incurred at the end of the period, they are effectively reductions in the return of the portfolio. Thus, if the return on an asset j is 15%, we have none of the asset now, and we pay a transaction fee of 1% for each dollar invested in asset j, then we would treat the return of asset j which is purchased as 14%. This is equivalent to assuming that we do not have to pay the broker until the end of the period. We must distinguish between the asset on hand at the outset and that which is bought or sold. Let A_j = amount of asset j after transactions have taken place, B_j = amount of asset j bought, and S_j = amount of asset j sold. Suppose the level at the outset was 0.35. Then we could write $A_j = 0.35 + B_j - S_j$ or in standard form $A_j - B_j + S_j = 0.35$. If the return of asset j is 15% and the transaction fee for asset j is 2%, then the return computation would contain the expression $15A_j - 2B_j - 2S_j$. Except for the addition of these constraints and the B_j and S_j variables, the formulation is essentially unchanged.

Suppose we currently have three assets 1, 2, and 3. For the next planning period we estimate the rates of return and transaction costs as:

Asset	Rate of Return	Transaction Cost Rate	Current Fraction of Portfolio
1	9.0%	1.0%	0.5
2	13.5%	1.5%	0.3
3	18.0%	2.0%	0.2

If A_1, A_2, and A_3 represent the amount of the new portfolio devoted to assets, 1, 2, and 3, then we further estimate that the variance in return will be

$$25(A_1^2) + 150(A_2^2) + 256(A_3^2) + 5(A_1)(A_2) + 80(A_2)(A_3).$$

The formulation when written in linear form for input to LINDO is

```
MIN    A1 + A2 + A3 + B1 + S1 + B2 + S2              ! The first row simply gives
     + B3 + S3 + R + INV + T1 + T2 + T3              ! the variable order
SUBJECT TO
     50 A1 + 5 A2 - 9 R + INV + T1 > 0               ! First order condition on A1
     5 A1 + 300 A2 + 80 A3 - 13.5 R + INV + T2 > 0   ! First order condition on A2
     80 A2 + 512 A3 - 18 R + INV + T3 > 0            ! First order condition on A3
```

```
        R -  T1 > 0                              ! First order condition on B1
        R +  T1 > 0                              ! First order condition on S1
      1.5 R -  T2 > 0                            ! First order condition on B2
      1.5 R +  T2 > 0                            ! First order condition on S2
        2 R -  T3 > 0                            ! First order condition on B3
        2 R +  T3 > 0                            ! First order condition on S3
                                                 ! Here come the real constraints
      9 A1 + 13.5 A2 + 18 A3 - B1 - S1 - 1.5 B2  ! The desired return
         - 1.5 S2 - 2 B3 - 2 S3 > 9.5
      A1 + A2 + A3 = 1                           ! 100% invested constraint
      A1 - B1 + S1 = 0.5                         ! New Level - Purchases + Sales = Old Level for A1
      A2 - B2 + S2 = 0.3                         ! New Level - Purchases + Sales = Old Level for A2
      A3 - B3 + S3 = 0.2                         ! New Level - Purchases + Sales = Old Level for A3
    END
    QCP 11                                       ! Indicates that row 11 is the first real constraint
```

When solved we have:

```
              OBJECTIVE FUNCTION VALUE

        1)           21.0918300

   VARIABLE         VALUE          REDUCED COST
       A1          0.794909          0.000000
       A2          0.122219          0.000000
       A3          0.082872          0.000000
       B1          0.294909          0.000000
       S1          0.000000          1.975269
       B2          0.000000          2.962904
       S2          0.177781          0.000000
       B3          0.000000          3.950538
       S3          0.117128          0.000000
        R          0.987635          0.000000
      INV        -32.455458          0.000000
       T1          0.987635          0.000000
       T2         -1.481452          0.000000
       T3         -1.975269          0.000000
```

We can examine how the portfolio changes as we demand higher return by doing parametric analysis on the righthand side of the "return" constraint, row 11. Observe:

```
    PARA
    ROW:
    ?11
    NEW RHS VAL =
    ?18
           VAR          VAR         PIVOT      RHS        DUAL         OBJ
           OUT          IN          ROW        VAL        VARIABLE     VAL
                  S3          SLK         10         11.5282    -7.39969     29.5974
                  B1          SLK          5          6         12.1500    -16.4000    35.5400
           SLK    6                       S1         11         12.1500    -16.4000    35.5400
                  S2          SLK          8          9         12.1500    -16.6500    35.5400
           SLK    9                       B3         14         12.1500    -16.6500    35.5400
                  A1          SLK          2          9         15.1500   -236.400    155.740
                  8           SLK         S2         12         15.1500   -236.400    155.740
           SLK    A2          ART                    0          15.4500   -432.000    256.000
```

Notice that the highest possible return of 15.45% is made by selling all A_1 and A_2, and investing the proceeds in asset 3. Thus, the return is

$$0.5(18 - 1 - 2) + 0.3(18 - 1.5 - 2) + 0.2(18) = 15.45.$$

We can look in more detail at one of the higher return portfolios by changing the righthand side of row 11 and resolving as follows:

```
ALTER 11
VAR:
?RHS
NEW COEFFICIENT:
?11.6
GO
    QP OPTIMUM FOUND AT STEP        7
        OBJECTIVE FUNCTION VALUE
            30.1466330

VARIABLE        VALUE           REDUCED COST
A1              0.578571        0.000000
A2              0.221429        0.000000
A3              0.200000        0.000000
B1              0.078571        0.000000
S1              0.000000        15.795919
B2              0.000000        23.693878
S2              0.078571        0.000000
B3              0.000000        26.894897
S3              0.000000        4.696941
R               7.897959        0.000000
INV             -33.147961      0.000000
T1              7.897959        0.000000
T2              -11.846939      0.000000
T3              -11.098978      0.000000
```

Notice that at this target return level, the transaction costs make it unattractive to change the amount of investment in asset 3.

In practice, one may in addition to or instead of the transaction cost feature, have transaction limit constraints. These constraints put limits on the S_i's and B_i's to represent the fact that buying or selling huge amounts of a commodity may affect its price.

Measures of Risk Other Than Variance

The most common measure of risk is variance (or its square root, the standard deviation). This is a reasonable measure of risk for assets that have a symmetric distribution and are traded in a so-called "efficient" market. If these two features do not hold, however, variance has some drawbacks. Consider the four possible growth distributions in Figure 13.1.

Investments A, B, and C are equivalent according to the variance measure because each has an expected growth of 1.10 (an expected return of 10%) and a variance of 0.04 (standard deviation around the mean of 0.20). Risk averse investors would, however,

Figure 13.1
Four Possible Growth Factor Distributions

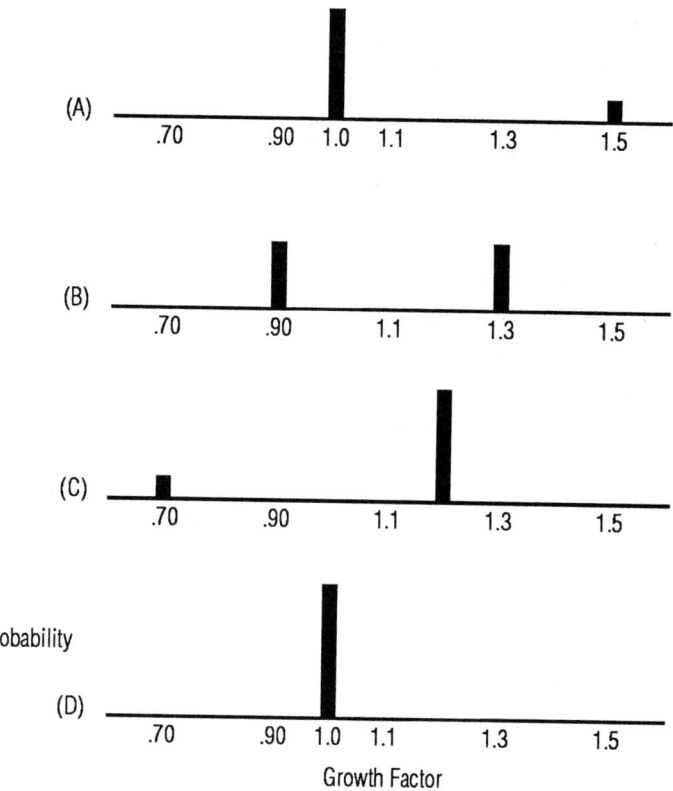

probably not be indifferent among the three. Under distribution (A) you would never lose any of your original investment and there is a 0.2 probability of the investment growing by a factor of 1.5, i.e., a 50% return. Distribution (C) on the otherhand has a 0.2 probability of an investment decreasing to 0.7 of its original value, i.e., a negative 30% return. Risk averse investors would tend to most prefer (A) and least prefer (C). This illustrates that variance need not be a good measure of risk if the distribution of returns is not symmetric.

Investment (D) is an inefficient investment. It is dominated by (A). Suppose the only investments available are (A) and (D) and our goal is to have an expected return of at least 5%, i.e., a growth factor of 1.05, and the lowest possible variance. The solution is to put 50% of our investment in each of (A) and (D). The resulting variance is 0.01 (standard deviation = 0.1) If we invested 100% in (A) the standard deviation would be 0.20. Nevertheless, we would prefer to invest 100% in (A). It is true that the return is more random, however, our profits are always at least as high under every outcome. (If the randomness in profits is an issue we can always give profits to a worthy educational institution when our profits are high so as to reduce the variance). Thus, the variance objective may cause us to choose inefficient investments.

In active markets such as stock markets you will tend to not find investments such as (D) because investors will realize that (A) dominates (D) and thus the market price of (D) will drop until its return approaches that of competing investments. In investment decisions regarding new physical facilities, however, there are no strong market forces making all investment candidates "efficient," so the variance risk measure may be less appropriate in such situations.

Quadratic Programming Applied to Simultaneous Price/Production Decisions

A firm that has the choice of setting either price or quantity for its products may wish to set them simultaneously. If the production process can be modeled as a linear program and the demand curves are linear than the problem of simultaneously setting price and production is a quadratic program. The following example illustrates.

A firm produces and sells two products A and B at price P_A and P_B and in quantities X_A and X_B. Profit maximizing values for P_A, P_B, X_A, and X_B are to be determined. The quantities (sold) are related to the prices by the demand curves:

$$X_A = 60 - 21 P_A + 0.1 P_B,$$
$$X_B = 50 - 25 P_B + 0.1 P_A.$$

Notice that the two products are mild substitutes. As the price of one is raised, it causes a modest increase in the demand of the other item.

The production side has the following features:

	Product	
	A	B
Variable Cost per Unit:	$0.20	$0.30
Production Capacity:	25	30

Further, the total production is limited by the constraint:

$$X_A + 2X_B \leq 50.$$

The problem can be written as:

$$\text{Minimize} \quad -(P_A - 0.20)X_A - (P_B - 0.30)X_B$$

$$\begin{aligned}
\text{subject to} \quad & X_A + 21P_A - 0.1P_B = 60 \quad \text{(Demand curve definition)} \\
& X_B + 25P_B - 0.1P_A = 50 \\
& X_A \leq 25 \quad \text{(Supply restrictions)} \\
& X_B \leq 30 \\
& X_A + 2X_B \leq 50
\end{aligned}$$

Notice that the objective function is quadratic rather than linear because it contains product terms such as $P_A \times X_A$. Also note that we have written it in minimization form.

The problem must be converted to linear form by writing the first order conditions for all the variables. To do this we must introduce dual variables for each of the constraints. We shall associate the dual variables D_A, D_B, C_A, C_B, and C_{AB} with the five original constraints of the model. When we write the first order conditions for the four decision variables, we have a total of nine constraints.

The complete formulation in LINDO style is:

```
MIN     XA + XB + PA + PB + DA + DB + CA + CB + CAB
SUBJECT TO
   2)   - PA + DA + CA + CAB ≥ - 0.2
   3)   - PB + DB + CB + 2CAB ≥ - 0.3
   4)   - XA + 21 DA - 0.1 DB ≥ 0
   5)   - XB + 25 DB - 0.1 DA ≥ 0
   6)   XA + 21 PA - 0.1 PB = 60
   7)   XB - 0.1 PA + 25 PB = 50
   8)   XA ≤ 25
   9)   XB ≤ 30
  10)   XA + 2 XB ≤ 50
END
QCP 6
```

The solution is:

```
          OBJECTIVE FUNCTION VALUE

    1)            -51.9510580

   VARIABLE        VALUE           REDUCED COST
     XA          24.390556           0.000000
     XB          12.804722           0.000000
     PA           1.702805           0.000000
     PB           1.494622           0.000000
     DA           1.163916           0.000000
     DB           0.516845           0.000000
     CA           0.000000           0.609444
     CB           0.000000           7.195278
     CAB          0.338889           0.000000
```

Note that it is the joint capacity constraint $X_A + 2X_B \leq 50$ which is binding. The total profit contribution is $51.951058.

Least Squares Regression

Suppose we are given the following observations:

Observation	X_{i0}	X_{i1}	X_{i2}	Y_i
1	1	2	6	8
2	1	3	9	14
3	1	5	7	12
4	1	7	8	17
5	1	8	10	18

We wish to explain or predict Y_i in terms of X_{i0}, X_{i1}, and X_{i2}. Notice that the column 0 is a constant column of 1's. A common way of doing this is via least squares regression.

The form of the explanatory equation is:

$$Y_i = B_0 X_{i0} + B_1 X_{i1} + B_2 X_{i2} + e_i$$

where e_i is the error in explaining observation Y_i. Because $X_{i0} = 1$ for every observation i, this equation is equivalent to $Y_i = B_0 X_{i0} + B_1 X_{i1} + B_2 X_{i2} + e_i$. Least squares regression chooses B_0, B_1, and B_2 so as to minimize the sum of the squared errors, i.e., $\sum_{i=1}^{5} e_i^2$.

We can rewrite this as

$$\text{Minimize} \sum_{i=1}^{5} (Y_i - B_0 X_{i0} - B_1 X_{i1} - B_2 X_{i2})^2$$

It is convenient to divide by 2 times the number of observations and rewrite as:

$$\text{Minimize} \sum_{i=1}^{5} (Y_i - B_0 X_{i0} - B_1 X_{i1} - B_2 X_{i2})^2 / 10$$

$$= \sum_{i=1}^{5} \frac{[Y_i^2 - 2Y_i(B_0 X_{i0} + B_1 X_{i1} + B_2 X_{i2}) + (B_0 X_{i0} + B_1 X_{i1} + B_2 X_{i2})^2]}{10}$$

The term $\sum_{i=1}^{5} Y_i^2$ is a constant and can be disregarded.

Taking derivations with respect to B_0, B_1, and B_2 gives the first order conditions:

$$\sum_{i=1}^{5} \frac{(B_0 X_{i0} + B_1 X_{i1} + B_2 X_{i2}) X_{i0}}{5} = \sum_{i=1}^{5} Y_i X_{i0} / 5$$

$$\sum_{i=1}^{5} \frac{(B_0 X_{i0} + B_1 X_{i1} + B_2 X_{i2}) X_{i1}}{5} = \sum_{i=1}^{5} Y_i X_{i1} / 5$$

$$\sum_{i=1}^{5} \frac{(B_0 X_{i0} + B_1 X_{i1} + B_2 X_{i2}) X_{i2}}{5} = \sum_{i=1}^{5} Y_i X_{i2} / 5$$

Thus we are interested in means of cross products of the form $\sum_i X_{ij} X_{ik}/5$ and $\sum_i X_{ij} Y_i / 5$. These are tabulated below for our example:

	$\bar{X}_0$	$\bar{X}_1$	$\bar{X}_2$	$\bar{Y}$
$\bar{X}_0$	1	5	8	13.8
$\bar{X}_1$	5	30.2	42	76.2
$\bar{X}_2$	8	42	66	114.8
$\bar{Y}$	13.8	76.2	114.8	203.4

The problem can now be written in LINDO format as:

```
MIN     B0 + B1 + B2
SUBJECT TO
    B0 + 5 B1 + 8 B2 = 13.8
    5 B0 + 30.2 B1 + 42 B2 = 7612
    8 B0 + 42 B1 + 66 B2 = 114.8
END
```

```
QCP
ROW OF FIRST CONSTRAINT =
5
```

Note that row 1, MIN B0 + B1 + B2, simply provides the ordering of the variables. Rows 2, 3 and 4 describe the first order conditions. Because there are no real constraints, the QCP command specifies a row number one more than the total number of rows. When solved we get the solution:

```
GO
         QP OPTIMUM FOUND AT STEP    4
              OBJECTIVE FUNCTION VALUE
     1)              -101.285000
   VARIABLE          VALUE           REDUCED COST
     B0             -1.175000          0.000000
     B1              0.875000          0.000000
     B2              1.325000          0.000000
     ROW        SLACK OR SURPLUS     DUAL PRICES
     2)              0.000000         -1.175000
     3)              0.000000          0.875000
     4)              0.000000          1.325000
```

The proposed form of the regression equation is:

$$Y_i = -1.175 + 0.875 X_{i1} + 1.325 X_{i2}$$

Recall that on the way to developing the formulation we divided the objective by two times the number of observations and subtracted the term $\sum_i Y_i^2$.

Undoing these actions, we find the sum of squares as

$$(-101.285 \times 10) + 203.4 \times 5 = 4.15.$$

Thus far, all we have done is conventional least squares regression and quadratic programming was unneeded.

Constrained Least Squares

Now suppose we have some additional information that causes us to require

$$B_0 + B_1 + B_2 > 1.5$$

A dual variable, SIDEC, associated with this constraint must be added to the formulation. The new formulation is:

```
       MIN    B0 + B1 + B2 + SIDEC
       SUBJECT TO
         2)    B0 + 5 B1 + 8 B2 - SIDEC = 13.8
         3)    5 B0 + 30.2 B1 + 42 B2 - SIDEC = 13.8
         4)    8 B0 + 42 B1 + 66 B2 - SIDEC = 114.8
         5)    B0 + B1 + B2 ≥ 1.5
       END
       QCP 5
```

The solution is:

```
         QP OPTIMUM FOUND AT STEP    5
              OBJECTIVE FUNCTION VALUE
    1)           -101.281015
    VARIABLE         VALUE          REDUCED COST
       B0          -0.641280           0.000000
       B1           0.890728           0.000000
       B2           1.250552           0.000000
       SIDEC        0.016777           0.000000
    ROW       SLACK OR SURPLUS       DUAL PRICES
    2)           0.000000            -0.641280
    3)           0.000000             0.890728
    4)           0.000000             1.250552
    5)           0.000000            -0.016777
    NO. ITERATIONS = 5
```

The sum of squares has increased to

$$101.28105 \times 10 + 203.4 \times 5 = 4.18985$$

Two-Person Nonconstant-Sum Games

There are many situations where the welfare, utility, or profit of one person depends not only on his decisions but on the decisions of others. A two-person game is a special case of the above in which (1) there are exactly two players/decisionmakers, (2) each must make one decision, (3) in ignorance of the other's decision, and (4) the loss incurred by each is a function of both decisions. A two-person constant-sum game (frequently more narrowly called a zero-sum game) is the special case of the above where (4a) the losses to both are in the same commodity, e.g., dollars, and (4b) the total loss is a constant independent of players' decisions. Thus, in a constant-sum game the sole effect of the decisions is to determine how a "constant sized pie" is allocated. Ordinary linear programming can be used to solve two-person constant-sum games.

When (1), (2) and (3) apply but (4b) does not, then we have a two-person nonconstant-sum game. Ordinary linear programming cannot be used to solve these games: however, the algorithm commonly applied to quadratic programs does apply. Sometimes a two-person nonconstant-sum game is also called a bimatrix game.

As an example, consider two firms, each of which is about to introduce an improved version of an already popular consumer product. The versions are very similar so one firm's profit is very much affected by its own advertising decision as well as the decision of its competitor. The major decision for each firm is presumed to be simply the level of advertising. Suppose that the losses (in millions of dollars) as a function of decision are given by the table below. The example illustrates that each player need not have exactly the same kinds of alternatives.

		Firm A		
		No Advertise	Advertise Medium	Advertise High
Firm B	No Advertise	−4 / −4	−3 / −2	−5 / 1
	Advertise	−1 / −5	−2 / −1	−1 / 0

Negative losses correspond to profits.

Prisoner's Dilemma

This cost matrix has the so-called prisoner's dilemma cost structure. This name arises from a setting in which there are two accomplices in crime in jail. If neither prisoner cooperates with the authorities (thus the two cooperate), both will receive a medium punishment. If one of them provides evidence against the other, the other will get severe punishment while the one who provides evidence will get light punishment *if the other does not provide evidence against the first*. If both provide evidence against the other, they both receive severe punishment. Clearly the best thing for the two in a group is for the two to cooperate with each other. However, individually there is a strong temptation to defect.

The same situation exists with our two firms. For example, if A does not advertise but B does, then A makes 1 million and B makes 5 million of profit. Total profit would be maximized if neither advertised; however, if either knew that the other would not advertise, then the one who thought he had such clairvoyance would have a temptation to advertise.

Later, it will be useful to have a loss table with all entries strictly positive. The relative attractiveness of an alternative is not affected if the same constant is added to all entries. The table below was obtained by adding +6 to every entry.

		Firm A		
		No Advertise	Advertise Medium	Advertise High
Firm B	No Advertise	2 / 2	3 / 4	1 / 7
	Advertise	5 / 1	4 / 5	5 / 6

We will henceforth work with this table.

Choosing a Strategy

Our example problem illustrates that we might wish our own choice to be (i) somewhat unpredictable by our competitor and (ii) robust in the sense that regardless of how unpredictable our competitor is, our expected profit is high. Thus, we are lead to the idea of a random strategy. By making our decision random, e.g., by flipping a coin, we tend to satisfy (i). By biasing the coin appropriately we tend to satisfy (ii).

For our example, define a_1, a_2, a_3 as the probability that A chooses the alternative "No advertise," "Advertise Medium," and "Advertise High" respectively. Similarly b_1 and b_2 are the probabilities that B applies to alternatives "No Advertise" and "Advertise" respectively. How should firm A choose a_1, a_2, and a_3? How should firm B choose b_1 and b_2?

For a bimatrix game it is difficult to define a solution which is simultaneously optimum for both. We can, however, define an equilibrium stable set of strategies. A stable solution has the feature that given B's choice for b_1 and b_2, A is not motivated to change his probabilities a_1, a_2, and a_3. Likewise, given a_1, a_2, and a_3, B is not motivated to change b_1 and b_2. There may be bimatrix games with several stable solutions.

What can we say beforehand about a strategy of A's which is stable? Some of the a_i's may be zero while for others we may have $a_i > 0$. An important observation which is not immediately obvious is the following: the expected loss to A of choosing alternative i is the same over all i for which $a_i > 0$. If this were not true, then A could reduce his overall expected loss by increasing the probability associated with the lower loss alternative. Denote the expected loss to A by v_A. Also, the fact that $a_i = 0$ must imply that the expected loss from choosing i is greater than v_A. These observations imply that with regard to A's behavior we must have

$$2b_1 + 5b_2 \geq v_A \quad \text{(with equality if } a_1 > 0\text{),}$$
$$3b_1 + 4b_2 \geq v_A \quad \text{(with equality if } a_2 > 0\text{),}$$
$$b_1 + 5b_2 \geq v_A \quad \text{(with equality if } a_3 > 0\text{).}$$

Symmetric arguments for B imply:

$$2a_1 + 4a_2 + 7a_3 \geq v_B \quad \text{(with equality if } b_1 > 0\text{),}$$
$$a_1 + 5a_2 + 6a_3 \geq v_B \quad \text{(with equality if } b_2 > 0\text{).}$$

We also have the nonnegativity constraints

$$a_i \geq 0 \quad \text{and} \quad b_1 \geq 0, \quad \text{for all alternatives } i.$$

Because the a_i and b_i are probabilities, we wish to add the constraints $a_1 + a_2 + a_3 = 1$ and $b_1 + b_2 = 1$. The above is what is known as a linear complementarity problem.

Formulated for the LINDO computer program we have:

```
MIN     A1 + A2 + A3 + B1 + B2 + VA + VB
SUBJECT TO
    2)    2 B1 + 5 B2 - VA ≥ 0
    3)    3 B1 + 4 B2 - VA ≥ 0
    4)    B1 + 5 B2 - VA ≥ 0
    5)    2 A1 + 4 A2 + 7 A3 - VB ≥ 0
    6)    A1 + 5 A2 + 6 A3 - VB ≥ 0
```

```
     7)    A1 + A2 + A3 = 1
     8)    B1 + B2 = 1
END
QCP 9
```

As before the objective row serves only to specify an order for the decision variables consistent with the constraint order. There are and can be no real constraints, only first order conditions in a bimatrix game, so the QCP 9 indicates that the problem is a "quadratic/complementary pivoting" problem.

When solved we get the following solution:

VARIABLE	VALUE	REDUCED COST
A1	0.000000	0.333333
A2	0.500000	0.000000
A3	0.500000	0.000000
B1	0.333333	0.000000
B2	0.666667	0.000000
VA	3.666667	0.000000
VB	5.500000	0.000000

The solution indicates that firm A should not use option 1 and should randomly choose with equal probability between options 2 and 3. Firm B should choose its option 2 twice as frequently as it chooses its option 1.

The objective function value, reduced costs and dual prices can be disregarded. Using our original loss table we can calculate the following:

Situation			Weighted Contribution To Total Loss of	
A	B	Probability	A	B
No Ads	No Ads	$0 \times 1/3$	0	0
No Ads	Ads	$0 \times 2/3$	0	0
Advertise Medium	No Ads	$1/2 \times 1/3$	$(1/6) \times (-3)$	$(1/6) \times (-2)$
Advertise Medium	Ads	$1/2 \times 2/3$	$(1/3) \times (-2)$	$(1/3) \times (-1)$
Advertise High	No Ads	$1/2 \times 1/3$	$(1/6) \times (-5)$	$(1/6) \times (1)$
Advertise High	Ads	$1/2 \times 2/3$	$(1/3) \times (-1)$	$(1/3) \times (0)$
			-2.333	-0.5

Thus, following the randomized strategy suggested, A would have an expected profit of 2.33 million while B would have an expected profit of 0.5 million. Contrast this with the fact that if A and B cooperated, they could each have an expected profit of 4 million.

Bimatrix Games with Several Solutions

When a nonconstant-sum game has several stable solutions, life gets more complicated. The essential observation is that we must look outside our narrow definition of "stable solution" to decide which of the stable solutions, if any, would be selected in reality.

Consider the following nonconstant sum two person game:

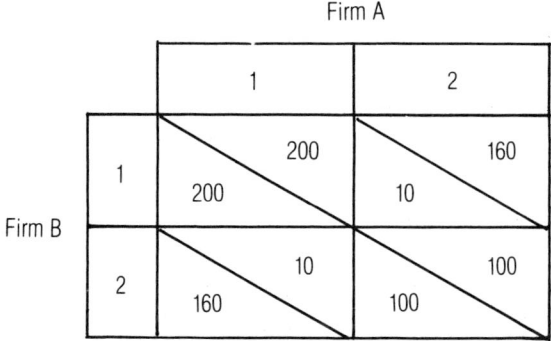

As before the numbers represent losses.

First observe that one solution that is stable according to our definition: (I) Firm *A* always choose option 1 and Firm *B* always chooses option 2. Firm *A* is not motivated to switch to 2 because his losses would increase to 100 from 10. Similarly, *B* would not switch to 1 from 2 because his losses would increase to 200 from 160. The game is symmetric in the players so similar arguments apply to the solution (II): *B* always chooses 1 and *A* always chooses 2.

Which solution would result in reality? It probably depends upon such things as the relative wealths of the two firms. Suppose (i) *A* is the wealthier firm, (ii) the game is repeated week after week, and (iii) currently the firms are using solution II. After some very elementary analysis, *A* concludes that it much prefers solution I. To move things in this direction *A* switches to option 1. Now it becomes what applied mathematicians call a game of "chicken." Both players are taking punishment at the rate of 200 per week. Either player could improve his lot by 200 − 160 = 40 by unilaterally switching to his option 2; however, his lot would be improved a lot more, i.e., 200 − 10 = 190 if his opponent unilaterally switched. At this point a rational *B* would probably take a glance at *A*'s balance sheet and decide that *B* switching to option 2 is not such a bad decision.

If it is not clear which firm is wealthier, then the two firms may decide that a cooperative solution is best, e.g., alternate between solutions I and II on alternate weeks. At this point, however, federal antitrust authorities might express a keen interest in this bimatrix game.

We conclude that a "stable" solution is stable only in a local sense. When there are multiple stable solutions we should really look at all of them and take into account other considerations in addition to the loss matrix.

Problems

1. You are considering three stocks, IBM, GM, and Georgia-Pacific (GP), for your stock portfolio. The covariance matrix of the yearly percentage returns on these stocks is estimated to be:

	IBM	GM	GP
IBM	10	2.5	1
GM	2.5	4	1.5
GP	1	1.5	9

Thus, if equal amounts were invested in each, the variance would be proportional to $10 + 4 + 9 + 2(2.5 + 1 + 1.5)$. The predicted yearly percentage returns for IBM, GM, and GP are 9, 6 and 5 respectively. Find a minimum variance portfolio of these three stocks for which the yearly return is at least 7, at most 80% of the portfolio is invested in IBM and at least 10% is invested in GP.

2. Modify your formulation of problem 1 to incorporate the fact that your current portfolio is 50% IBM and 50% GP. Further, transactions costs on a buy or sell transaction are 1% of the amount traded.

3. The manager of an investment fund hypothesizes that three different scenarios might characterize the economy one year hence. These scenarios are denoted Green, Yellow and Red and subjective probabilities 0.7, 0.1, and 0.2 are associated with them. The manager wishes to decide how a model portfolio should be allocated among stocks, bonds, real estate and gold in the face of these possible scenarios. His estimated returns in percent per year as a function of asset and scenario are given in the table below:

	Stocks	Bonds	Real Estate	Gold
Green	9	7	8	−2
Yellow	−1	5	10	12
Red	10	4	−1	15

Formulate and solve the asset allocation problem of minimizing the variance in return subject to having an expected return of at least 6.5.

4. Conglomerate Motors (CM) manufacturers and sells three sizes of automobiles: Rambler, Mercury and Cadillac. CM's operations research department has just completed an extensive market analysis. One of the results of that study is a set of demand curves for the three products. If sales are measured in thousands of cars and price/car is measured in thousands of dollars, then the demand curves can be written as

$$Q_R = 1600 - 100P_R + 4P_M,$$
$$Q_M = 495 - 13P_M + 3P_R + P_C,$$
$$Q_C = 180 - 4P_C + 2P_M,$$

where Q_R = number of Ramblers sold in 1000's, P_R = the price of the Rambler in 1000's, etc.

Federal regulations regarding "fleet mileage" place a restriction on the mix of cars that CM may manufacture. Specifically, the average miles per gallon (mpg) taken over all cars manufactured must be greater than or equal to 24. The Rambler, Mercury, and Cadillac have mpg ratings of 29, 23, and 19 respectively. The average is based on the presumption that all cars are driven equal distance. CM has five plants. Plant D can manufacture only Ramblers. The variable cost/unit is $7000 and it has a capacity of 500,000 cars/year. Plant E can manufacture either Ramblers or Mercurys in any mix totaling no more than 100,000 cars/year. The variable cost of a car in this plant is $800 for a Rambler and $12,000 for a Mercury. Plant F can produce only Mercury's. It has a capacity of 200,000 cars per year and the variable cost/car is $10,500. Plant G can produce either Mercurys or Cadillacs in any mix totaling no more than 50,000 cars/year. The variable costs of Mercurys and Cadillacs in this plant are $12,500 and $17,000 per car respectively. Plant H can produce only Cadillacs. The variable cost per unit is $15,600. The yearly capacity is 50,000. How many cars of each type should CM produce? At what price should CM plan to sell each type?

5. Two not necessarily friendly nations, Blue and Gold, are contemplating their military options for the next few years. Each has three general options: Aggressive, Defensive, and Minimal. The losses to each as a function of option chosen are summarized in the table below.

		Gold		
		A	D	M
Blue	A	10 / 11	4 / 8	11 / −5
	D	3 / 5	4 / 6	1 / 5
	M	−6 / 12	2 / 1	1 / 1

Find a strategy for each country which is stable in the game theory sense.

6. From time to time a department store will reallocate some space among its various departments. One simple approach is to approximate the average profit per square meter per year for a department as a linear function of the space allocated to the department. One then tries to find an allocation which maximizes the total profit. Suppose that we have a modest little store with but two departments: Odds and Ends. The managers of these departments were asked to each give two point estimates of the yearly profit per square meter as a function of the number of square meters allocated. These are shown below:

	Odds		Ends	
	Square Meters of Space	Profits per Square Meter per Year	Square Meters of Space	Profits per Square Meter per Year
min space	9	$12,000	12	$15,000
max space	50	$5,000	45	$4,000

There are a total of 65 square meters of space to be allocated. Further, each department will be allocated neither less than the minimum space shown for it in the above table nor more than the max space. It is assumed that between the min and max allocations the average profit per square meter per year is a linear function of space allocated.

(a) Formulate this allocation problem as a quadratic program.

(b) Solve it.

(c) Suppose that any space not allocated to Odds and Ends can be rented out for a constant $800 per square meter per year of profit. Now what should be the allocation?

(d) How would you motivate managers to give accurate estimates of the numbers needed in the table above?

7. In each round of the game of Even/Odd, player A writes one of the numbers 2, 4, or 6 while player B writes one of the numbers 1, 3, or 5. Both players then reveal their selection. If the difference is greater than 1 then the player with the lower number pays the other player the difference. If the difference is exactly 1 then the player with the higher number pays the other player the sum of the two numbers.

(a) Write the loss matrix.

(b) Write the conditions for a stable solution.

(c) Is the implied solution likely to be good in the sense that globally optimizing players would in fact settle upon a solution satisfying the conditions in (b)?

(d) Which player seems to have the advantage?

14

Formulation of Integer Programs

Introduction

In most applications of LP one would really like the decision variables to be restricted to integer values. One is likely to tolerate a solution recommending that GM produce 1,524,328.37 Chevrolets. No one will mind if this recommendation is rounded up or down. If, however, a different study recommends that the optimum number of aircraft carriers to build is 1.37, then a lot of people around the world will be very interested in how this number is rounded. It is clear that the validity and value of many LP models could be improved markedly if one could restrict selected decision variables to integer values.

All good commercial LP modeling systems are augmented with a capability which allows the user to restrict certain decision variables to integer values. The manner in which the user informs the program of this requirement varies from program to program. For example, in LINDO one way of indicating that variable X is to be restricted to integer values 0 or 1 is to type the command INTEGER X. The important point is that it is straightforward to specify this restriction. We shall see later that even though easy to specify, sometimes it may be difficult to solve problems with this restriction. The methods for formulating and solving problems with integrality requirements are called Integer Programming.

The integrality enforcing capability is perhaps more powerful than the reader at first realizes. A frequent use of an integer variable in a model is as a zero/one variable to represent a go/no-go decision. It is probably true that the majority of real world integer programs are of the zero/one variety.

Computational Difficulty of Integer Programs

Integer programs can be very difficult to solve. This is in marked contrast to LP problems. The solution time for an LP is fairly predictable. For an LP the time increases approximately proportionally with the number of variables and approximately with the square of the number of constraints. For a given IP problem the time may in fact decrease as the number of constraints is increased. As the number of integer variables is increased the solution time may increase dramatically. Some small IPs, e.g., 60 constraints, 60 variables are extremely difficult to solve.

Just as with LPs, there may be alternate IP formulations of a given problem. With IPs, however, the solution time generally depends critically upon the formulation. Producing a good IP formulation requires skill. For many of the problems in the remainder of this chapter, the difference between a good formulation and a poor formulation may be the difference between whether the problem is solvable or not.

Types of Variables

One general classification is according to types of variables:

(a) *Pure vs. mixed*. In a pure integer program, all variables are restricted to integer values, whereas in a mixed formulation only certain of the variables are integer, while the rest are allowed to be continuous.

(b) *0/1 vs. general*. In many applications the only integer values allowed are 0/1, therefore some integer programming codes assume that integer variables are restricted to the values 0 or 1.

Exploiting of the IP Capability, Standard Applications

You will frequently encounter problems which are LPs with the exception of just a few combinatorial complications. Many of these complications are fairly standard. The next several sections describe many of the standard complications along with the methods for incorporating them into an IP formulation. It is interesting to notice that most of these complications only require the 0/1 capability rather than the general integer capability.

Minimum Batch Size Constraints

When there are substantial economies of scale in undertaking an activity regardless of its level, many decision makers will specify a minimum "batch" size for the activity. For example, a large brokerage firm may require that if you buy any bonds from the firm, you must buy at least 100. A zero/one variable can enforce this restriction as follows. Let

x = activity level to be determined, e.g., no. of bonds purchased,
y = a zero/one variable = 1, if and only if $x > 0$,
B = minimum batch size for x, e.g., 100, and
U = known upper limit on the value of x.

The following two constraints enforce the minimum batch size condition:

$x \leq Uy$
$By \leq x$.

If $y = 0$, then the first constraint forces $x = 0$, while if $y = 1$, the second constraint forces x to be at least B. Thus, y acts as a switch which forces x to be either 0 or greater

Figure 14.1

Typical Fixed Plus Linear Cost Curve

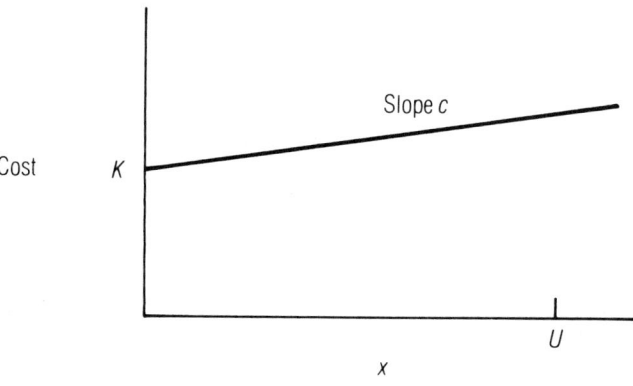

than B. The constant U should be chosen with care. For reasons of computational efficiency, it should be as small as validly possible.

Fixed Charge Problems

A situation closely related to the minimum batch size situation is one where the cost function for an activity is of the fixed plus linear type indicated in Figure 14.1. Define x, y, and U as before and let K be the fixed cost incurred if $x > 0$. Then the following components should appear in the formulation:

$$\text{Minimize} \quad Ky + cx + \cdots$$
$$\text{subject to} \quad x \leqq Uy$$
$$\vdots$$

The constraint and the term Ky in the objective imply that x cannot be greater than 0 unless a cost K is incurred. Again, for computational efficiency, U should be as small as validly possible.

The Simple Plant Location Problem

The Simple Plant Location Problem (SPL) is a commonly encountered form of fixed charge problem. It is specified as follows:

n = the number of sites at which a plant may be located or opened,

m = the number of customer or demand points, each of which must be assigned to a plant,

k = the number of plants which may be opened,

f_i = the fixed cost (e.g., per year) of having a plant at site i, for $i = 1, 2, \ldots, n$,

c_{ij} = cost (e.g., per year) of assigning customer j to a plant at site i, for $i = 1, 2, \ldots, n$ and $j = 1, 2, \ldots, m$.

The goal is to determine the set of sites at which plants should be located and which site should service each customer.

A situation giving rise to the SPL problem is the lockbox location problem encountered by a firm with customers scattered over a wide area. The plant sites in this case correspond to sites at which the firm might locate a postal lockbox which is managed by a bank at the site. The customer points would correspond to the, 100 say, largest metropolitan areas in the firm's market. A customer would mail his or her monthly payments to the closest lockbox. The reason for resorting to multiple lockboxes rather than having all payments mailed to a single site is that several days of mail time may be saved. Suppose that a firm receives $60 million per year through the mail, the yearly cost of capital to the firm is 10% per year and it could reduce the mail time by two days. This reduction has a yearly value of about $30,000.

The f_i for a particular site would equal the yearly cost of having a lockbox at site i regardless of the volume processed through the site. The cost term c_{ij} would approximately equal the product: (daily cost of capital) × (mail time in days between i and j) × (yearly dollar volume mailed from area j).

Define the decision variables:

$y_i = 1$ if a plant is located at site i, else 0,

$x_{ij} = 1$ if the customer j is assigned to a plant site i, else 0.

A compact formulation of this problem as an IP is:

$$\text{Minimize} \quad \sum_{i=1}^{n} f_i y_i + \sum_{i=1}^{n} \sum_{j=1}^{m} c_{ij} x_{ij} \tag{1}$$

$$\text{subject to} \quad \sum_{i=1}^{n} x_{ij} = 1 \quad \text{for } j = 1 \text{ to } m, \tag{2}$$

$$\sum_{j=1}^{m} x_{ij} \leq m y_i \quad \text{for } i = 1 \text{ to } n, \tag{3}$$

$$\sum_{i=1}^{n} y_i = k, \tag{4}$$

$$y_i = 0 \text{ or } 1 \quad \text{for } i = 1 \text{ to } n, \tag{5}$$

$$x_{ij} = 0 \text{ or } 1 \quad \text{for } i = 1 \text{ to } n, j = 1 \text{ to } m. \tag{6}$$

Constraints (2) force each customer j to be assigned to exactly one site. Constraints (3) force a plant to be located at site i if any customer is assigned to site i.

The reader should be cautioned against trying to solve a problem formulated in this fashion because the solution process may require embarrassingly much computer time for all but the smallest problem. The difficulty arises because when the problem is solved as an LP, i.e., with conditions (5) and (6) deleted, the solution tends to be highly fractional and with little similarity to the optimal IP solution.

A "tighter" formulation which frequently produces an integer solution naturally when solved as an LP is obtained by replacing constraints (3) by the constraints:

$$x_{ij} \leq y_i \quad \text{for } i = 1 \text{ to } n, j = 1 \text{ to } m. \tag{3'}$$

At first glance, replacing (3) by (3') may seem counterproductive. If there are 20 possible plant sites and 60 customers, then the set (3) would contain 20 constraints whereas set (3') would contain 20 × 60 = 1,200 constraints. Empirically, however, it appears to be the rule rather than the exception that when the problem is solved as an LP with (3') rather than (3), the solution is naturally integer.

The Capacitated Plant Location Problem (CPL)

The CPL problem arises from the SPL problem if the volume of demand processed through a particular plant is an important consideration. In particular, the CPL problem assumes that each customer has a known volume and each plant site has a known volume limit on total volume assigned to it. The additional parameters to be defined are:

D_j = volume or demand associated with customer j,

K_i = 1 capacity of a plant located at i.

The IP formulation is:

$$\text{Minimize} \quad \sum_{i=1}^{n} f_i y_i + \sum_{i=1}^{n} \sum_{j=1}^{m} c_{ij} x_{ij} \tag{7}$$

$$\text{subject to} \quad \sum_{i=1}^{n} x_{ij} = 1 \quad \text{for } j = 1 \text{ to } m, \tag{8}$$

$$\sum_{j=1}^{m} D_j x_{ij} \leq K_i y_i \quad \text{for } i = 1 \text{ to } n, \tag{9}$$

$$\sum_{i=1}^{n} y_i = k, \tag{4}$$

$$x_{ij} \leq y_i \quad \text{for } i = 1 \text{ to } n, j = 1 \text{ to } m. \tag{10}$$

$$y_i = 0 \text{ or } 1 \quad \text{for } i = 1 \text{ to } n, \tag{11}$$

$$x_{ij} = 0 \text{ or } 1 \quad \text{for } i = 1 \text{ to } n, j = 1 \text{ to } m. \tag{12}$$

This is the "single-sourcing" version of the problem. Because the x_{ij} are restricted to 0 or 1, each customer must have all of its volume assigned to a single plant. If "split-sourcing" is allowed, then the x_{ij} are allowed to be fractional with the interpretation that x_{ij} is the fraction of customer j's volume assigned to plant site i. In this case condition (12) is dropped.

Example: Capacitated Plant Location

Some of the points just mentioned will be illustrated with the following example.

The Zzyzx Company of Zzyzx, California currently has a warehouse in each of the following cities: (A) Baltimore, (B) Cheyenne, (C) Salt Lake City, (D) Memphis and (E) Wichita. These warehouses supply customer regions throughout the U.S. It is convenient to aggregate customer areas and consider the customers to be located in the following cities: (1) Atlanta, (2) Boston, (3) Chicago, (4) Denver, (5) Omaha and (6) Portland, Oregon. There is some feeling that Zzyzx is "overwarehoused"; that is, it may be able to save substantial fixed costs by closing some warehouses without unduly increasing transportation and service costs. Relevant data have been collected and assembled on a "per month" basis and are displayed below.

Cost per Ton-Month Matrix

Warehouse	Demand City						Monthly Supply Capacity in Tons	Monthly Fixed Cost
	1	2	3	4	5	6		
A	$1675	$400	$685	$1630	$1160	$2800	18	$7,650
B	1460	1940	970	100	495	1200	24	3,500
C	1925	2400	1425	500	950	800	27	5,000
D	380	1355	543	1045	665	2321	22	4,100
E	922	1646	700	508	311	1797	31	2,200
Monthly Demand in Tons	10	8	12	6	7	11		

For example, closing the warehouse at A (Baltimore) would result in a monthly fixed cost saving of $7,650. If 5 (Omaha) gets all of its monthly demand from E (Wichita), then the associated transportation cost for supplying Omaha is $7 \times 311 = \$2,177$ per month. A customer need not get all of its supply from a single source. Such "multiple sourcing" may result from the limited capacity of each warehouse; e.g., Cheyenne can only process 24 tons per month. Should Zzyzx close any warehouses and, if so, which ones?

We will compare the performance of four different methods for solving this problem:

1. Loose formulation of the IP,
2. Tight formulation of the IP,
3. Greedy open heuristic: start with no plants open and sequentially open the plant giving the greatest reduction in cost until it is worthless to open further plants.
4. Greedy close heuristic: start with all plants open and sequentially close the plant saving the most money until it is worthless to close further plants.

The advantage of heuristics 3 and 4 is that they are easy to apply. The performance of the four methods is as follows.

Method	Solution: Best Solution	Computing Time in Seconds	Plants Open	Cost of LP Solution
Loose IP	46,031	3.38	A,B,D	35,662
Tight IP	46,031	1.67	A,B,D	46,031
Greedy Open Heuristic	46,943	nil	A,B,D,E	—
Greedy Close Heuristic	46,443	nil	A,C,D,E	—

Notice that even though the loose IP finds the same optimum as the tight formulation (as it must), it takes about twice as much computing time. For large problems the difference becomes much more dramatic.

Dynamic Lotsizing

The single product dynamic lotsizing problem is described by the following parameters:

n = number of periods for which production is to be planned for a product
D_j = predicted demand in period j, for $j = 1, 2, \ldots, n$
f_i = fixed cost of making a production run in period i
h_i = cost per unit of product carried from period i to $i + 1$

This problem can be cast as a simple plant location problem if we define:

$$c_{ij} = D_j \sum_{t=i}^{j-1} h_t,$$

that is, c_{ij} is cost of supplying period j's demand from period i production. Each period can be thought of as both a potential plant site (period for a production run) and a customer.

If, further, there is a finite production capacity, K_i, in period i, then this capacitated dynamic lotsizing problem is a special case of the capacitated plant location problem.

Representing General Cost Curves

The fixed-plus linear cost curve seen in plant location models is a special case of the more general cost curve such as that shown in Figure 14.2.

The slopes of the three segments are c_1, c_2, and c_3. The intercepts K_2 and K_3 are determined from the formula $K_{i+1} = K_i + c_i U_i - c_{i+1} U_i$. If $c_{i+1} \leq c_i$, the cost curve represents an activity with economies of scale. We are faced with a similar cost curve if we are buying from a vendor that gives quantity discounts.

There are several methods for representing such cost curves. The first method we describe is an extension of the approach used to represent the simple fixed plus linear curve. This method is satisfactory if there are only a few such curves in the overall models or if each such curve has only one or two breakpoints.

———————————————— Figure 14.2 ————————————————
Piecewise Linear Cost Curve (Solid Curve)

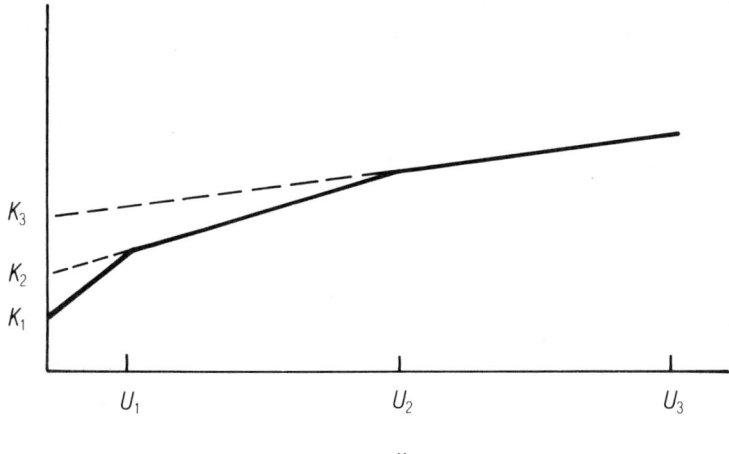

Define:

$$y_i = \begin{cases} 1 & \text{if } U_{i-1} < x \leq U_i \\ 0 & \text{otherwise.} \end{cases}$$

$$x_i = \begin{cases} x & \text{if } U_{i-1} < x \leq U_i \\ 0 & \text{otherwise.} \end{cases}$$

The formulation should include the terms:

Minimize $K_1 y_1 + K_2 y_2 + K_3 y_3 + c_1 x_1 + c_2 x_2 + c_3 x_3 + \cdots$

subject to (a)
$$x_1 \leq U_1 y_1$$
$$x_2 \leq U_2 y_2$$
$$x_3 \leq U_3 y_3$$

(b) $y_1 + y_2 + y_3 \leq 1$
$$x_2 \geq U_1 y_2$$
$$x_3 \geq U_2 y_3$$
$$\vdots$$

Anywhere that x appears in the remainder of the formulation it should be replaced by $x_1 + x_2 + x_3$. If the y_i are required to be 0 or 1, then the above will cause the cost function to be correctly represented. Constraint set (b) is not needed if the cost curve is concave (has economies of scales everywhere) and the upper limit on x is not binding.

Example

One part of a larger problem involves the determination of the order quantity for a supplier that gives a quantity discount. The relevant facts are: There is a fixed cost of $150 for placing an order; the first 1,000 gallons of the product can be purchased for $2 per gallon; the price drops to $1.90 per gallon for anything in excess of 1,000 gallons; at most 5,000 gallons will be purchased. The parameters can be now computed as

$K_1 = 150$
$U_1 = 1,000$
$K_2 = 150 + 1,000 \times 2 - 1,000 \times 1.90 = 250$
$U_2 = 5,000$

Define the variables:

$y_1 = 1$ if more than 0 but no more than 1,000 gallons are purchased, else 0;
$y_2 = 1$ if more than 1,000 gallons are purchased, else 0;
$x_1 = $ gallons purchased if no more than 1,000 gallons are purchased;
$x_2 = $ gallons purchased if more than 1,000 gallons are purchased.

The formulation would include:

Minimize $\quad 150y_1 + 250y_2 + 2x_1 + 1.9x_2 + \cdots$

subject to $\quad x_1 \leqq 1{,}000y_1$

$\quad\quad\quad\quad\quad x_2 \leqq 5{,}000y_2$

$\quad\quad y_1 + y_2 \leqq 1 \quad\quad\quad y_1$ and y_2 are required to be integer.

Alternative Representation of Nonlinear Cost Curves

An alternative method for representing nonlinear cost curves is illustrated with the cost curve in Figure 14.3. The function is assumed to be linear between the breakpoints $x = U_1$, $x = U_2$, etc. The value of the function at the ith breakpoint is denoted by v_i, i.e., $v_i = f(U_i)$.

Such a function with n breakpoints can be represented in a linear integer program if we:

1. Append the constraint $w_1 + w_2 + \cdots + w_n = 1$.
2. Replace each occurrence of x by the expression $w_1U_1 + w_2U_2 + \cdots + w_nU_n$.
3. Replace each occurrence of $f(x)$ by the expression $w_1v_1 + w_2v_2 + \cdots + w_nv_n$.
4. Allow at most two w_is to be nonzero and then only if adjacent.

The new variable w_i specifies the weight to be applied to point U_i. If the function $f(x)$ is linear between the two adjacent points $x = U_i$ and $x = U_{i+1}$ and $x = w_iU_i + w_{i+1}U_{i+1}$ with $w_i + w_{i+1} = 1$ then $f(x) = w_if(U_i) + w_{i+1}f(U_{i+1}) = w_iv_i + w_{i+1}v_{i+1}$.

Restriction (4) can be enforced in several ways. A number of IP codes allow constraints such as (1) to be identified as so-called "Special Ordered Sets of Type 2" or

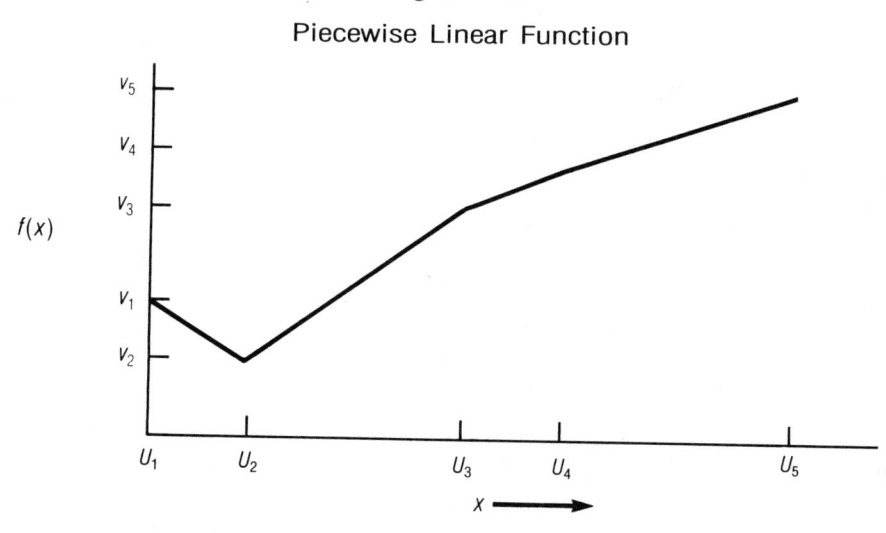

Figure 14.3

Piecewise Linear Function

simply "SOS2." The IP code will guarantee that restriction (4) is satisfied for each constraint identified as SOS2.

If we have a standard IP code but without the SOS2 feature, then restriction (4) can be enforced by adding the following constraints:

$$w_1 \leq z_1$$
$$w_2 \leq z_1 + z_2$$
$$w_3 \leq z_2 + z_3$$
$$\vdots$$
$$w_{n-1} \leq z_{n-2} + z_{n-1}$$
$$w_n \leq z_{n-1}$$
$$z_1 + z_2 + \cdots + z_{n-1} = 1$$
$$z_i = 0 \text{ or } 1.$$

Summarizing, each nonlinear term results in the addition of at least one constraint and n variables. If the SOS2 feature is not available, then to this one must further add n constraints and $n - 1$ variables.

The general approach just described is sometimes called the lambda method.

Outline of Integer Programming Methods

The time that a computer requires to solve an IP may depend dramatically on how you formulated it. It is therefore worthwhile to know a little about how IP's are solved. There are two general approaches for solving IP's: "cutting plane" methods and "branch and bound" (B & B) method. The B & B method has thus far proven to be the most reliable. All commercial IP codes use the B & B method, perhaps aided by some cutting plane features. Fortunately for the reader, the B & B method is the easier to describe. In most general terms B & B is a form of intelligent enumeration.

More specifically, B & B first solves the problem as an LP. If the LP solution is integer valued in the integer variables, then no more work is required. Otherwise, B & B resorts to an intelligent search of all possible ways of rounding the fractional variables.

We shall illustrate the application of the Branch-and-bound method to the following problem.

```
MAX     75 X1 +  6 X2 +  3 X3 + 33 X4
SUBJECT TO
   2)      774 X1 + 76 X2 + 22 X3 + 42 X4 ≦ 875
   3)       67 X1 + 27 X2 + 794 X3 + 53 X4 ≦ 875
        X1, X2, X3, X4  restricted to 0, 1.
```

The search process that a computer follows in finding an integer optimum is illustrated in Figure 14.4. First the problem is solved as an LP with the constraints X1, X2, X3, X4 ≤ 1. This solution is summarized in the box labeled 1. The solution has fractional values for X2 and X3 and is therefore unacceptable. At this point X2 is arbitrarily selected and the following reasoning is applied. At the integer optimum X2 must equal either 0 or 1.

CHAPTER 14: Formulation of Integer Programs   **225**

— **Figure 14.4** —

Branch-and-Bound Search Tree

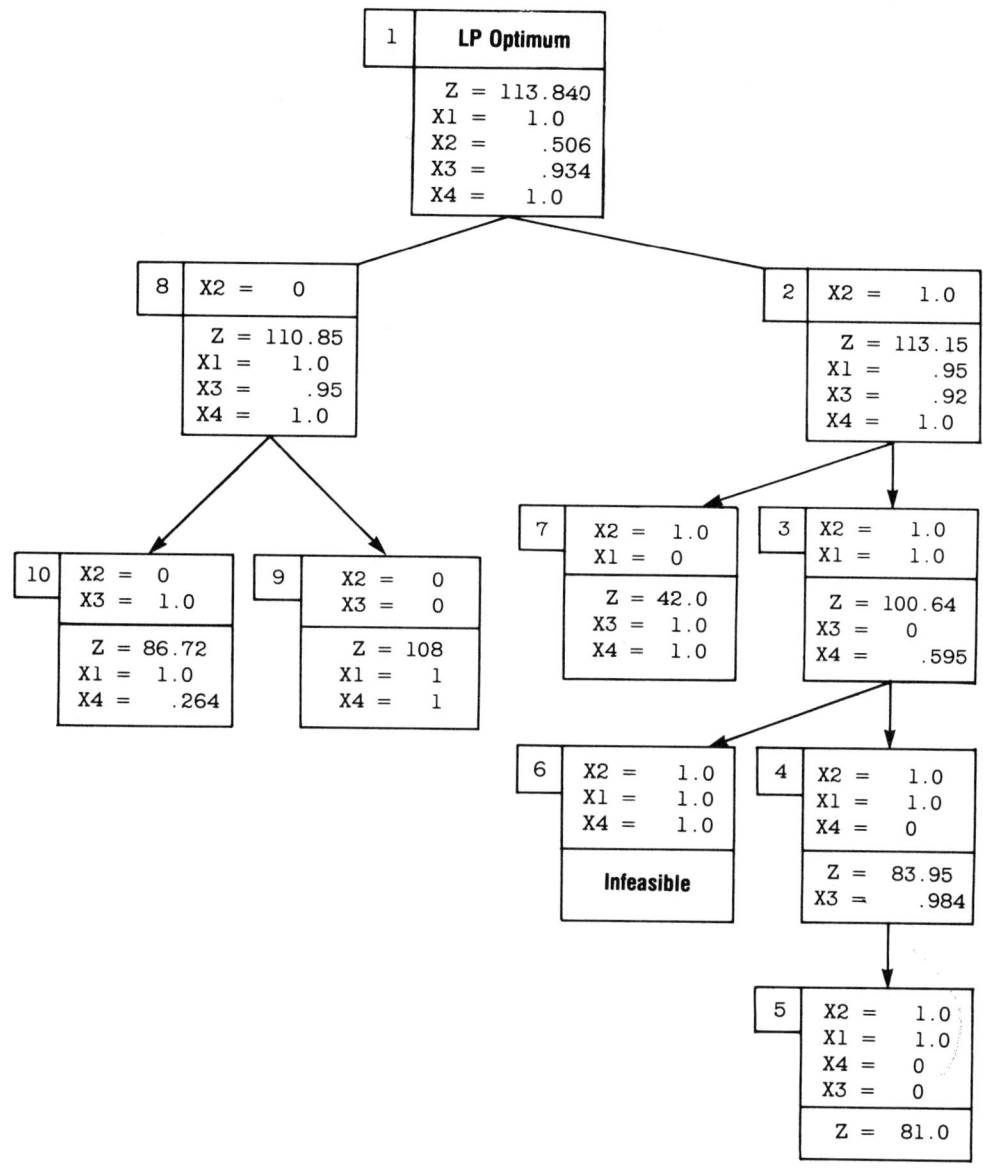

Therefore, replace the original problem by two new subproblems, one with X2 constrained equal 1 (Box or node 2) and the other with X2 constrained to equal 0 (node 8). If we solve both of these new IPs, then the better solution must be the best solution to the original problem. This reasoning is the motivation for using the term "branch." Each subproblem created corresponds to a branch in an enumeration tree.

The numbers to the upper left of each node indicate the order in which the nodes (or equivalently, subproblems) are examined. The variable Z is the objective function value. When the subproblem with X2 constrained to 1 (node 2) is solved as an LP, we find that X1 and X3 take fractional values. Arguing as before but now with variable X1, two new subproblems are created: one with X1 constrained to 0 (node 7) and one with X1 constrained to 1 (node 3). This process is repeated with X4 and X3 until node 5. At this point an integer solution with $Z = 81$ is found. We do not know that this is the optimum integer solution, however, because we must still look at subproblems 6 through 10. Subproblem 6 need not be pursued further because there are no feasible solutions having all of X2, X1, and X4 equal to 1. Subproblem 7 need not be pursued further because it has a Z of 42 which is worse than an integer solution already in hand.

At node 9 a new and better integer solution with $Z = 108$ is found when X3 is set to 0. Node 10 illustrates the source for the "bound" part of "branch-and-bound." The solution is fractional; however, it is not examined further because the Z-value of 86.72 is less than the 108 associated with an integer solution already in hand. The Z-value at any node is a bound on the Z-value at any offspring node. This is true because an offspring node or subproblem is obtained by appending a constraint to the parent problem. Appending a constraint can only hurt. Interpreted in another light, this means that the Z-values cannot improve as one moves down the tree. The tree presented in the preceding figure was only one illustration of how the tree might be searched. Other trees could be developed for the same problem by playing with the following two degrees of freedom:

(a) Choice of next node to examine, and
(b) Choice of branching variable when splitting a node.

For example, if nodes 8 and then 9 were examined immediately after node 1 then the solution with $Z = 108$ would have been found quickly. Further, nodes 4, 5, and 6 could then have been skipped because the Z-value at node 3 (100.64) is worse than a known integer solution (108) and therefore no offspring of node 3 would need examination.

In the example tree the first node is split by branching on the possible values for X2. One could have just as well chosen X3 or even X1 as the first branching variable.

The efficiency of the search is closely related to how wisely the choices are made in (a) and (b) above. In (b) one wants to choose variables which are "decisive." In general, the computer will make intelligent choices and the user need not be aware of the details of the search process. The user should, however, keep the general B & B process in mind when formulating a model. If the user has a priori knowledge that an integer variable x is decisive, then for the LINDO program it is useful to place x early in the formulation to indicate its importance. This general understanding should drive home the importance of a "tight" LP formulation. A tight LP formulation is one which, when solved, has an objective function value close to the IP optimum. The LP solutions at the subproblems are used as bounds to curtail the search. If the bounds are poor, many early nodes in the tree may be explicitly examined because their bounds look good even though in fact these nodes have no good offspring.

Problems with Naturally Integer Solutions and the Prayer Algorithm

The solution algorithms for IP are generally based on first solving the IP as an LP by disregarding the integrality requirements and praying that the solution is naturally integer. For example, if x is required to be 0 or 1, the problem is first solved by replacing this requirement by the requirement that simply $0 \leq x \leq 1$. When initiating the analysis of a problem in which integer answers are important, it is useful to know beforehand whether the resulting IP will be easy to solve. After the fact one generally observes that the IP was easy to solve if the objective function values for the LP optimum and the IP optimum were close. About the only way we can predict beforehand that the objective function values of the LP and IP will be close is if we know beforehand that the LP solution will be almost completely integer valued. Thus, we are interested in knowing what kind of LPs have naturally integer solutions.

The classes of LP problems for which we know beforehand that there is a naturally integer optimum have integer righthandsides and are in one of the classes:

(a) Network LP's,

(b) MRP or Integral Leontief LP's,

(c) Problems that can be transformed to (a) or (b) by either row operations or taking the dual.

We first review the distinguishing features of network and MRP LP's.

Network LP's Revisited

A LP is said to be network LP if, disregarding simple upper and lower bound constraints such as $x \leq 3$, each column has at most two nonzeroes, if two they are +1 and −1, if one it is either +1 or −1.

Result: If the right-hand side is integer then there is an integer optimum. If the objective coefficients are all integer then there is an optimum with integral dual prices.

Integral Leontief Constraints

A constraint set is said to be *integral Leontief* or MRP (for Material Requirements Planning) if:

(a) Each constraint is an equality,

(b) Every column has exactly one positive coefficient and it is a +1,

(c) Each column has 0 or more negative coefficients, every one of which is integer.

(d) Each RHS coefficient is a nonnegative integer.

Result: An LP whose complete constraint set is an MRP set has an optimal solution that is integer. Further, if the objective coefficients are all integer, then there is an optimal solution with integral dual prices.

Example: A One Period MRP Problem

The Schwindle Cycle Company makes three products: Unicycles (U), Regular Bicycles (R), and Twinbikes (T). Each product is assembled from a variety of components including: seats (S), wheels (W), hubs (H), spokes (P), chains (C), and links (L). The full bills of materials for each product are shown below. The numbers in parentheses specify how many units of the child are required per parent.

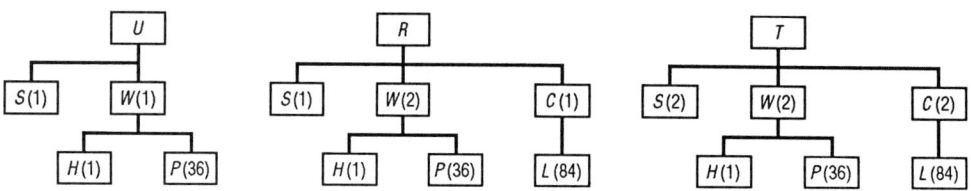

Current inventories are zero. Schwindle needs to supply 100 Unicycles, 500 Regular bicycles and 200 Twinbikes. Finished products and complete subassemblies can be either manufactured or bought at the following prices

Item	U	R	T	S	W	C	H	P	L
Bought Price	2.60	5.2	3.10	0.25	1.40	0.96	0.19	0.07	0.05
Assembly Cost	1.04	1.16	1.90	0.20	0.22	0.26	0.16	0.04	0.03

Note that the assembly cost is the immediate cost at the level of assembly; it does not include the cost of the components going into the assembly. How many units of each item should be made or bought so as to satisfy demand at minimum price?

An LP formulation is:

```
MIN     1.04 UM + 2.6 UB + 1.16 RM + 5.2 RB + 1.9 TM + 3.1 TB
      + 0.2 SM + 0.25 SB + 0.22 WM + 1.4 WB + 0.26 CM + 0.96 CB
      + 0.16 HM + 0.19 HB + 0.04 PM + 0.07 PB + 0.03 LM + 0.05 LB
SUBJECT TO
 UNICYCLE)    UM + UB =     100
  REGULAR)    RM + RB =     500
 TWINBIKE)    TM + TB =     200
    SEATS) - UM - RM - 2 TM + SM + SB =    0
   WHEELS) - UM - 2 TM + 2 TM + WM + WB =  0
   CHAINS) - RM - 2 TM + CM + CB =    0
     HUBS) - WM + HM + HB =    0
   SPOKES) - 36 WM + PM + PB =    0
    LINKS) - 84 CM + LM + LB =    0
END
```

In the PICTURE of the formulation in the figure below, notice that it has the MRP structure.

```
                    U U R T T S S W W C C H H P P L L
                    M B M B M B M B M B M B M B M B
           1:  A A A A A A T T A T T T U U U U  MIN
  UNICYCLE:  1 1  '    '      '     '            = B
   REGULAR:  '  '1 1 '  '   '   '   '   '   '    = C
  TWINBIKE:     '  1 1 '       '                 = C
     SEATS: -1 -1 '-2  1 1  '       '            =
    WHEELS: -1 -2 '-2'  ' '1 1  '   '   '   '    =
    CHAINS:    -1 '-2   '  '1 1 '       '        =
      HUBS:        '      -1 '    1 1   '        =
    SPOKES:  '  '   '   '  -B '   '   ' '1 1  '  =
     LINKS:        '      '      '-B  '   ' '1 1 =
```

The solution is:

```
         1)        3440.0000

   VARIABLE         VALUE         REDUCED COST
       UB         100.000000        0.000000
       RM         500.000000        0.000000
       TB         200.000000        0.000000
       SM         500.000000        0.000000
       WB        1000.000000        0.000000
       CB         500.000000        0.000000
```

Notice that it is naturally integer. Thus we should buy all the unicycles and twinbikes (and paste our own brand name on them). We assemble our own regular bicycles. They are assembled from manufactured seats and bought wheels and chains.

If we put an upper limit of 300 on the number of links manufactured by adding the constraint LM ≤ 300, we will get a fractional solution, because this constraint violates the MRP structure.

Transformations to Naturally Integer Formulations

A *row operation* consists of either of the following:

(a) multiplication through an equation by some non-zero constant,

(b) adding a finite multiple of one equation to another.

A row operation changes neither the feasible region nor the set of optimal solutions to a problem. Thus, if we can show that a model can be transformed to either a network LP or an MRP LP by row operations, then we know there is an integer optimum. We do not actually need to do the transformation to get the solution.

Similarly, if we have a model with integer righthandside and we can show that it is the dual of either a network LP or an MRP LP, then we know the model has an integer optimum.

Example

Consider the following LP that arose in planning how much to produce in each of four periods:

```
          P P P P P P P P P
          1 1 1 1 2 2 2 3 3 4
          4 3 2 1 4 3 2 4 3 4
   1:     9 6 4 3 6 4 3 4 3 3  MIN
   2:     1 1 1 1                  = 1
   3:     1 1 1     1 1 1          = 1
   4:     1 1       1 1     1 1    = 1
   5:     1         1       1   1  = 1
```

When solved as an LP we obtained the following naturally integer solution:

P12 = P34 = 1;   all others 0.

Could we have predicted a naturally integer solution beforehand? If we perform the row operations: (5') = (5) − (4); (4') = (4) − (3); (3') = (3) − (2), we obtain the equivalent LP:

```
          P P P P P P P P P
          1 1 1 1 2 2 2 3 3 4
          4 3 2 1 4 3 2 4 3 4
   1:     9 6 4 3 6 4 3 4 3 3  MIN
   2:     1 1 1 1                  = 1
   3:          −1    1 1 1         = 0
   4:       −1      −1      1 1    = 0
   5:     −1      −1      −1   1   = 0
```

This is a network LP, so it has a naturally integer solution.

Example

In trying to find the minimum elapsed time for a certain project composed of seven activities, the following LP was constructed (in PICTURE form):

```
         A  B  C  D  E  F
   1: −1          '     1  MIN
   AB:−1  1       '        > 3
   AC:−1     '1'  '        > 2
   BD:   −1      1         > 5
   BE:   −1         ' 1    > 6
   CF:   '  −1  '      '1  > 4
   DF:          −1     1   > 7
   EF:              '−1 1  > 6
```

This is neither a network LP, e.g., consider columns A, B, or F, nor an MRP LP, e.g., consider columns A or F. Nevertheless, when solved we get the naturally integer solution:

```
         OBJECTIVE FUNCTION VALUE

    1)          15.0000000

  VARIABLE        VALUE         REDUCED COST
     A           .000000            .000000
     B          3.000000            .000000
     C          2.000000            .000000
     D          8.000000            .000000
     E          9.000000            .000000
     F         15.000000            .000000
```

```
         ROW      SLACK OR SURPLUS       DUAL PRICES
         AB)              .000000         -1.000000
         AC)              .000000           .000000
         BD)              .000000         -1.000000
         BE)              .000000           .000000
         CF)             9.000000           .000000
         DF)              .000000         -1.000000
         EF)              .000000           .000000
```

Could we have predicted a naturally integer solution beforehand? If we look at the PICTURE of the model we see that each constraint has exactly one +1 and one −1, thus its dual model is a network LP, and expectation of integer answers is justified.

The Assignment Problem and Related Sequencing and Routing Problems

The assignment problem is a simple LP problem which is frequently encountered as a major component in more complicated practical problems.

The assignment problem is:

Given a matrix of costs:

$$c_{ij} = \text{cost of assigning object } i \text{ to object } j,$$

and variables:

$$x_{ij} = 1 \text{ if object } i \text{ is assigned to object } j.$$

Then we want to

Minimize $\sum_i \sum_j c_{ij} x_{ij}$

subject to $\sum_i x_{ij} = 1$ for each object i,

$\sum_j x_{ij} = 1$ for each object i,

$x_{ij} \geq 0$.

This problem is easy to solve as an LP and the x_{ij} will be naturally integer.

There are a number of problems in routing and sequencing which are closely related to the assignment problem.

Example: The Assignment Problem

Large airlines tend to base their route structure around the hub concept. An airline will try to have a large number of flights arrive at the hub airport during a certain short interval of time, e.g., 9 A.M. to 10 A.M., and then have large number of flights depart the hub shortly thereafter, e.g., 10 A.M. to 11 A.M. This allows customers of that airline to travel between a large combination of origin/destination cities with one stop and at most one change of planes. For example, United Airlines uses Chicago as a hub, Delta Airlines uses Atlanta, TWA uses St. Louis, and American uses Dallas/Fort Worth.

A desirable goal in using a hub structure is to minimize the amount of changing of planes (and the resulting moving of baggage) at the hub. The following little example illustrates how the assignment model applies to this problem.

A certain airline has six flights arriving at O'Hare airport between 9 and 9:30 A.M. The same six airplanes depart on different flights between 9:40 and 10:20 A.M. The average number of people transferring between incoming and leaving flights appear in the table below:

	L01	L02	L03	L04	L05	L06
I01	20	15	16	5	4	7
I02	17	15	33	12	8	6
I03	9	12	18	16	30	13
I04	12	8	11	27	19	14
I05	0	7	10	21	10	32
I06	0	0	0	6	11	13

Flight I05 arrives too late to connect with L01. Similarly, I06 is too late for flights L01, L02, and L03.

All the planes are identical. A decision problem is which incoming flight should be assigned to which outgoing flight. For example, if incoming flight *I02* is assigned to leaving flight *L03*, then 33 people (and their baggage) will be able to remain on their plane at the stop at O'Hare. How should incoming flights be assigned to leaving flights so that a minimum number of people need to change planes at the O'Hare stop?

This problem can be formulated as an assignment problem if we define

$$x_{ij} = \begin{cases} 1 & \text{if incoming flight } i \text{ is assigned to outgoing flight } j, \\ 0 & \text{otherwise.} \end{cases}$$

The objective is to maximize the number of people that do not have to change planes. A formulation is:

```
MAX      20 X11 + 15 X12 + 16 X13 + 5 X14 + 4 X15 + 7 X16
       + 17 X21 + 15 X22 + 33 X23 + 12 X24 + 8 X25 + 6 X26
       + 9 X31 + 12 X32 + 18 X33 + 16 X34 + 30 X35 + 13 X36
       + 12 X41 + 8 X42 + 11 X43 + 27 X44 + 19 X45 + 14 X46
       + 7 X52 + 10 X53 + 21 X54 + 10 X55 + 32 X56 + 6 X64
       + 11 X65 + 13 X66
SUBJECT TO
    2)   X11 + X21 + X31 + X41 + X51 =           1
    3)   X12 + X22 + X32 + X42 + X52 =           1
    4)   X13 + X23 + X33 + X43 + X53 + X63 =     1
    5)   X14 + X24 + X34 + X44 + X54 + X64 =     1
    6)   X15 + X25 + X35 + X45 + X55 + X65 =     1
    7)   X16 + X26 + X36 + X46 + X56 + X66 =     1
    8)   X11 + X12 + X13 + X14 + X15 + X16 =     1
    9)   X21 + X22 + X23 + X24 + X25 + X26 =     1
   10)   X31 + X32 + X33 + X34 + X35 + X36 =     1
   11)   X41 + X42 + X43 + X44 + X45 + X46 =     1
   12)   X52 + X53 + X54 + X55 + X56 =           1
   13)   X64 + X65 + X66 =         1
END
```

A solution is:

```
         OBJECTIVE FUNCTION VALUE
   1)          135.00000
```

VARIABLE	VALUE	REDUCED COST
X11	1.000000	.000000
X23	1.000000	.000000
X32	1.000000	.000000
X44	1.000000	.000000
X56	1.000000	.000000
X65	1.000000	.000000

Notice that each incoming flight except *I03* is able to be assigned to its most attractive outgoing flight.

The Traveling Salesman Problem

One of the more famous optimization problems is the traveling salesman problem (TSP). It is an assignment problem with the additional condition that the assignments chosen must constitute a tour. Lawler *et al.* (1985) present a tour-de-force on this fascinating problem.

The constraint sets are:

(1) Each city j must be entered exactly once:
$$\sum_{\substack{i=1 \\ i \neq j}}^{n} x_{ij} = 1 \qquad \text{for } j = 1 \text{ to } n,$$

(2) Each city i must be exited exactly once:
$$\sum_{\substack{j=1 \\ j \neq i}}^{n} x_{ij} = 1 \qquad \text{for } i = 1 \text{ to } n,$$

(3) No subtours are allowed for any subset of cities S not including city 1:
$$\sum_{i,j \in S} x_{ij} \leq |S| - 1 \qquad \text{for every subset } S, \text{ where } |S| \text{ is the size of } S,$$

(4) Alternatively (3) may be replaced by
$$u_j \geq u_i + 1 - (1 - x_{ij})n \qquad \text{for } j = 2, 3, 4, \ldots; j \neq i.$$

Effectively, u_j is the sequence number of city j on the trip. Note that (3) is much tighter than (4). Large problems may be computationally intractable if (3) is not used. On the other hand there are the order of 2^n constraints of type (3) but only $n - 1$ constraints of type (4). Even though there are a huge number of constraints in (3) only a few of them, e.g., those equal to or greater than n, will be binding at the optimum. Thus, an iterative approach which adds violated constraints of type (3) as needed, works surprisingly well. Padberg and Rinaldi (1987) used essentially this iterative approach and were able to solve to optimality problems with over 2000 cities. The solution time was several hours on a large computer.

For practical problems it may be important to get good but not necessarily optimal answers in just a few seconds or minutes rather than hours. The most commonly used heuristic for the traveling salesman problem is due to Lin and Kernighan (1973). This heuristic tries to improve a given solution by clever reorderings of cities in the tour. For practical problems, e.g., in operation sequencing on computer controlled machines, the heuristic seems to always find solutions no more than 2% more costly than the optimum. Problems with up to 14,464 "cities" arising from the sequencing of operations on a computer controlled machine are described by Bland and Shallcross (1989). In no case was the Lin-Kernighan heuristic more than 1.7% from the optimal for these problems.

Example of a Traveling Salesman Problem

P. Rose, currently unemployed, has hit upon the following scheme for making some money. He will guide a group of 18 people on a tour of all the baseball parks in the National League. He is betting his life savings on this scheme so he wants to keep the cost of the tour as low as possible. The tour will start and end in Cincinnati. The following distance matrix has been constructed:

	Atl	Chi	Cin	Hou	LA	Mon	NY	Phi	Pit	StL	SD	SF
Atlanta	0	702	454	842	2396	1196	864	772	714	554	2363	2679
Chicago	702	0	324	1093	2136	764	845	764	459	294	2184	2187
Cincinnati	454	324	0	1137	2180	798	664	572	284	338	2228	2463
Houston	842	1093	1137	0	1616	1857	1706	1614	1421	799	1521	2021
Los Angeles	2396	2136	2180	1616	0	2900	2844	2752	2464	1842	95	405
Montreal	1196	764	798	1857	2900	0	396	424	514	1058	2948	2951
New York	864	845	664	1706	2844	396	0	92	386	1002	2892	3032
Philadelphia	772	764	572	1614	2752	424	92	0	305	910	2800	2951
Pittsburgh	714	459	284	1421	2464	514	386	305	0	622	2512	2646
St. Louis	554	294	338	799	1842	1058	1002	910	622	0	1890	2125
San Diego	2363	2184	2228	1521	95	2948	2892	2800	2512	1890	0	500
San Francisco	2679	2187	2463	2021	405	2951	3032	2951	2646	2125	500	0

Solution

We can exploit the fact that the distance matrix is symmetric. Define the decision variables:

$$Y_{ij} = \begin{cases} 1 & \text{if the link between cities } i \text{ and } j \text{ is used, regardless of the direction of travel;} \\ 0 & \text{otherwise.} \end{cases}$$

Thus, YATLCHI = 1 if the link between Atlanta and Chicago is used. Each city or node must be connected to two links. In words the formulation is:

> Minimize   the cost of links selected;
>
> subject to   for each city, number of links connected to it that are selected = 2;
> each link can be selected at most once.

A fragment of the LINDO formulation is shown below.

```
MIN    702 YATLCHI + 454 YATLCIN + 842 YATLHOU + 2396 YATLLAX
     + 1196 YATLMON + 864 YATLNYK + 772 YATLPHI + 714 YATLPIT
     + 554 YATLSTL + 2363 YATLSND + 2679 YATLSNF + 324 YCHICIN
     + 1093 YCHIHOU + 2136 YCHILAX + 764 CHIMON + 845 YCHINYK
     + 764 YCHIPHI + 459 YCHIPIT + 294 YCHISTL + 2184 YCHISND
     + 2187 YCHISNF
                             .
                             .
                             .
```

```
          + 2512 YPITSND + 2646 YPITSNF + 1890 YSTLSND + 2125 YSTLSNF
          + 500 YSNDSNF
     SUBJECT TO
       ATL)  YATLCHI + YATLCIN + YATLHOU + YATLLAX + YATLMON + YATLNYK
           + YATLPHI + YATLPIT + YATLSTL + YATLSND + YATLSNF =     2
       CHI)  YATLCHI + YCHICIN + YCHIHOU + YCHILAX + YCHIMON + YCHINYK
           + YCHIPHI + YCHIPIT + YCHISTL + YCHISND + YCHISNF =     2
                                  .
                                  .
       SNF)  YATLSNF + YCHISNF + YCINSNF + YHOUSNF + YLAXSNF + YMONSNF
           + YNYKSNF+ YPHISNF + YPITSNF + YSTLSNF + YSNDSNF =     2
     END
     SUB  YATLCHI   1.00
     SUB  YATLCIN   1.00
     SUB  YATLHOU   1.00
     SUB  YATLLAX   1.00
     SUB  YATLMON   1.00
                .
                .
     SUB  YSNDSNF   1.00
```

When this model is solved *as an LP*, we get the solution:

```
     VARIABLE      VALUE
     YATLCIN       1.000000
     YATLHOU       1.000000
     YCHICIN       1.000000
     YCHISTL       1.000000
     YHOUSTL       1.000000
     YLAXSND       1.000000
     YLAXSNF       1.000000
     YMONNYK       1.000000
     YMONPIT       1.000000
     YMONPHI       1.000000
     YPHIPIT       1.000000
     YSNDSNF       1.000000
```

This has a cost of 5020 miles. Graphically it corresponds to the Figure 14.5. Unfortunately, the solution has three subtours. We decide to cut off the smallest subtour by adding the constraint

$$YLAXSND + YLAXSNF + YSNDSNF \leq 2$$

Now when we solve it *as an LP* we get a solution with cost 6975, corresponding to the Figure 14.6. We cut off the subtour in the southwest by adding the constraint:

$$YLAXSND + YLAXSNF + YSNDSNF + YHOULAX + YHOUSND + YHOUSNF \leq 3$$

We continue in this fashion adding subtour elimination cuts:

$$YMONNYK + YMONPHI + YMONPIT + YNYKPHI + YNYKPIT + YPHIPIT \leq 3$$

and

$$YMONNYK + YMONPHI + YNYKPHI \leq 2$$

Figure 14.5

Figure 14.6

Figure 14.7

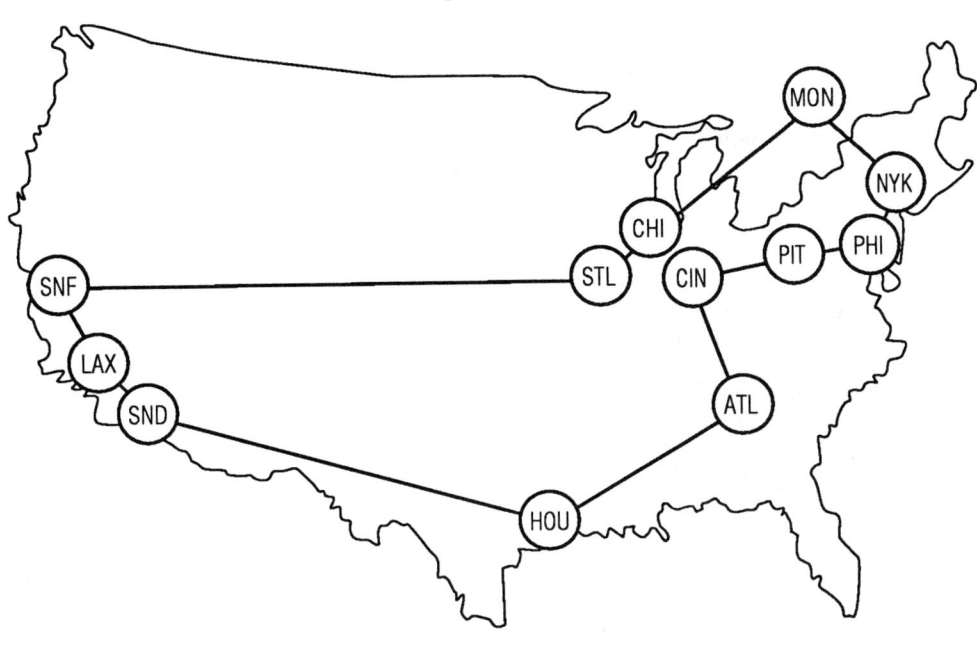

After the above are all added we get the solution shown in the Figure 14.7. It is a complete tour with cost 7577. Note that only LP's were solved. No branch and bound was required.

Could P. Rose have done as well by trial and error? The most obvious heuristic is the "closest unvisited city" heuristic. If one starts in Cincinnati and next goes to the closest unvisited city at each step and finally returns to Cincinnati, the total distance is 8015 miles; about 6% worse than the optimum.

The Optional Stop TSP

If we drop the requirement that every stop must be visited, we then get the optional stop TSP. Let:

$y_j = 1$ if city j is visited, 0 otherwise.

If v_j is the value of visiting city j, then the objective is:

Minimize $\sum_i \sum_j c_{ij} x_{ij} - \sum v_j y_j$.

The constraint sets are:

(1) Each city j can be visited at most once

$$\sum_{i \neq j} x_{ij} = y_j$$

(2) If we enter city j, then we must exit it:

$$\sum_{k \neq j} x_{jk} = y_j$$

(3) No subtours allowed for each subset, S, of cities not including the home base 1.

$$\sum_{i,j \in S} x_{ij} \leq |S| - 1, \text{ where } |S| \text{ is the size of } S.$$

For example, if there are n cities, including the home base, then there are $(n-1)(n-2)/(3 \times 2)$ subsets of size 3.

(4) Alternatively, (3) may be replaced by

$$u_j \geq u_i + 1 - (1 - x_{ij})n \quad \text{for } j = 2, 3, \ldots n.$$

Effectively, u_j is the sequence number of city j in its tour. Constraint set (3) is much tighter than (4).

Capacitated Multiple TSP/Vehicle Routing Problems

An important practical problem is the routing of vehicles from a central depot. An example is the routing of delivery trucks for a metropolitan newspaper. You can think of this as a multiple traveling salesman problem with finite capacity for each salesperson. A formulation is:

Given

$V = $ capacity of a vehicle

$d_j = $ demand of city or stop j

(1) Each city, j, must be visited once for $j > 1$.

$$\sum_{j} x_{ij} = 1$$

(2) Each city $i > 1$, must be exited once

$$\sum_{j} x_{ij} = 1$$

(3) No subtours

$$\sum_{i,j \in S} x_{ij} \leq |S| - 1,$$

(4) No overloads: For each set of cities T, including 1, which constitute more than a truckload:

$$\sum_{i,j \in T} x_{ij} \leq |T| - k, \text{ where } k = \text{minimum number of cities which must be dropped from } T \text{ to reduce it to one load.}$$

This formulation can solve to optimality modest sized problems of say, 25 cities. For larger or more complicated practical problems the heuristic method of Clarke and Wright (1964) is a standard starting point for quickly finding good but not necessarily optimal solutions.

Minimum Spanning Tree

A spanning tree of n nodes is a collection of $n - 1$ arcs so that there is exactly one path between every pair of nodes. A minimum cost spanning tree might be of interest, for example, in designing a communications network.

Assume that node 1 is the root of the tree. Let $x_{ij} = 1$ if the path from 1 to j goes through node i immediately before node j, else $x_{ij} = 0$.

A formulation is

$$\text{Minimize} \quad \sum_i \sum_j c_{ij} x_{ij}$$

$$\text{subject to} \quad \sum_i \sum_j x_{ij} = n - 1$$

$$(*) \quad \sum_{i,j \in S} x_{ij} \leq |S| - 1 \quad \text{for every subset } S.$$

$$x_{ij} = 0 \quad \text{or} \quad 1$$

An alternative to (*) is

$$u_j \geq u_i + 1 - (1 - x_{ij})n \quad \text{for } j = 2, 3, 4, \ldots, n.$$
$$u_j \geq 0$$

In this case, u_j is number of arcs between node j and node 1.

If one has a pure spanning tree problem, then the "greedy" algorithm of Kruskal (1956) is a fast way of finding optimal solutions.

The Linear Ordering Problem

A variation of the TSP is the linear ordering problem. One wants to find a strict ordering of n objects. Applications are to ranking in sports tournaments, product preference ordering in marketing, job sequencing on one machine, ordering of industries in an input-output matrix, ordering of historical objects in archeology and others.

The crucial input data are cost entries c_{ij}. If object i appears *anywhere* before object j in the proposed ordering, then c_{ij} is the resulting cost. The decision variables are:

$x_{ij} = 1$ if object i precedes object j, either directly or indirectly for all $i \neq j$.

The problem is

$$\text{Minimize} \quad \sum_i \sum_j c_{ij} x_{ij}$$

$$\text{subject to} \quad (1) \quad x_{ij} + x_{ji} = 1 \quad \text{for all } i \neq j$$

If i precedes j and j precedes k then we want to imply that i precedes k. This is enforced with the constraints

$$(2) \quad x_{ij} + x_{jk} + x_{ki} \leq 2 \quad \text{for all } i, j, k \text{ with } i \neq j, i \neq k, j \neq k.$$

The size of the formulation can be cut in two by noting that $x_{ij} = 1 - x_{ji}$. Thus, we substitute out x_{ji} for $j > i$. Constraint set (1) becomes simply $0 \leq x_{ij} \leq 1$. Constraint set (2) becomes

$$(2') \quad x_{ij} + x_{jk} - x_{ik} + s_{ij} = 1 \quad \text{for all } i < j < k. \ 0 \leq s_{ijk} \leq 1$$

Quadratic Assignment Problem

The quadratic assignment problem has the same constraint set as the linear assignment, however, the objective function contains products of two variables. Notationally it is

$$\text{Minimize} \quad \sum_i \sum_j \sum_k \sum_l c_{ijkl} x_{ij} x_{kl}$$

subject to   for each j: $\sum_i x_{ij} = 1$

subject to   for each i: $\sum_j x_{ij} = 1$

Some examples of this problem are:

1. *Facility layout.* If d_{jl} is the physical distance between room j and room l, s_{ik} is the communication traffic between department i and k, and $x_{ij} = 1$ if department i is assigned to room j, then we want to minimize $\sum_i \sum_j \sum_k \sum_l x_{ij} x_{kl} d_{jl} s_{ik}$.

2. *Radio frequency assignment.* If d_{ij} is the physical distance between transmitters i and j. s_{kl} is the distance in frequency k and l, p_i is the power of transmitter i, we want $\max\{p_i, p_j\} (1/d_{ij})(1/s_{kl})$ to be small if transmitter i is assigned frequency k and transmitter j is assigned frequency.

3. *Type wheel design.* Arrange letters and numbers on a type wheel so that (a) most frequently used characters appear together (b) characters that tend to get typed together, e.g., qu, appear close together on the wheel.

4. *Disk file allocation.* If w_{ij} is the interference if files i and j are assigned to the same disk we want to assign files to disk so that total interference is minimized.

The quadratic assignment problem is a notoriously difficult problem. If someone asks you to solve such a problem, you should make every effort to show that the problem is not really a quadratic assignment problem. One indication of its difficulty is that the solution is not naturally integer.

Small quadratic assignment problems can be converted to linear integer programs by the transformation:

(a) Replace the product $x_{ij} x_{kl}$ by z_{ijkl}

(b) If $c_{ijkl} > 0$, add the constraint

$$z_{ijkl} \geq x_{ij} + x_{kl} - 1$$

(c) If $c_{ijkl} \leq 0$, add the constraints:

$$z_{ijkl} \leq x_{ij}$$
$$z_{ijkl} \leq x_{kl}$$

Problems of Grouping: Matching, Covering, Partitioning and Packing

There is a class of problems which have the following essential structure:

(a) there is a set of m objects and
(b) they are to be grouped into subsets so that some criterion is optimized.

Some example situations are:

	Objects	Group	Criteria for a Group
(i)	Dormitory inhabitants	Roommates	At most two to a room no smokers with nonsmokers.
(ii)	Deliveries to customers	Trip	Total weight assigned to trip is less than or equal to capacity, customers in same trip are close together.
(iii)	Sessions at a scientific meeting	Sessions scheduled for same time slot	No two sessions on same general topic; enough rooms of sufficient size.
(iv)	Exams to be scheduled	Exams scheduled for same time slot	No student has more than one exam in the time slot.
(v)	Sportsmen	Foursome, e.g., in golf or tennis doubles	Members are of comparable ability, appropriate combination of sexes as in tennis mixed doubles.
(vi)	States on map to be colored	All states of a given color	States in same group/color cannot be adjacent.

If each object can belong to at most one group, it is called a *packing* problem. If each object must belong to exactly one group it is called a *partitioning* problem. If every object must belong to at least one group it is called a *covering* problem. A packing or partitioning problem with group sizes limited to two or less is called a *matching* problem. Specialized and fast algorithms exist for matching problems. A problem that is closely related to covering problems is the cutting stock problem. It arises in paper, printing, textile, and steel industries. In this problem we want to determine cutting patterns to be used in cutting up large prices of raw material into finished good size pieces. This problem was discussed in Chapter 6.

Although grouping problems may be very easy to state, it may be very difficult to find a proveably optimal solution.

There are two common approaches to formulating grouping problems: (1) assignment style, or (2) the partition method. The former is convenient for small problems but it quickly becomes useless as the number of objects gets large.

Formulation as an Assignment Problem

The most obvious formulation for the general grouping problem is based around the following definition 0/1 decision variables:

$X_{ij} = 1$ if object j is assigned to group i, 0 otherwise.

A drawback of this formulation is that there are many alternate optimal solutions, all of which essentially are identical. For example, assigning golfers A, B, C, and D to group 1 and golfers E, F, G, and H to group 2 is essentially the same assigning golfers E, F, G, and H to group 1 and golfers A, B, C and D to group 2. These alternate optima make the typical integer programming algorithm take much longer than necessary.

We can eliminate these alternate optima with no loss of optimality if we agree to the following restrictions: (a) object 1 can only be assigned to group 1; (b) object 2 can only be assigned to groups 1 or 2 and only to 1 if object 1 is not assigned; (c) object 3 can only be assigned to groups 1, 2 or 3, and only to groups 1 or 2 if object 2 is not assigned to group 2, and only to group 1 if neither object 1 nor object 2 are assigned; (d) etc.

This restriction can be enforced with the following 2 sets of constraints:

(1) For each object $j = 2, 3, \ldots, N$:

$$X_{i,j-1} + X_{j+1,j-1} + \cdots X_{M,j-1} = 0$$

(You do not actually add this constraint, rather just do not bother to generate the variables in it.)

You may also add the constraints for $i = 2, 3, \ldots N, j = 2, 3, \ldots, \min\{i, M\}$:

(2) $\quad X_{ij} \leq X_{i-1,1} + X_{i-1,2} + X_{i-1,j-1}.$

In words, if object j is assigned to group i, then some lower numbered object must be assigned to group $i - 1$.

Even with constraints (1) and (2) this formulation tends to be hard to solve if the number of groups is greater than about a half dozen.

Formulation as a Packing Problem

An alternative approach is to first enumerate either all possible or all interesting feasible groups and then solve an optimization problem of the form:

> Maximize value of the groups selected,
>
> subject to each object is in at most one of the selected groups.

The advantage of this formulation is that, when it can be used, it typically can be solved more easily then the assignment formulation. The disadvantages are that it may have a huge number of decision variables, especially if the typical group size is more than three. For example, if there are 21 objects, all groups are of size three and all groups of size three are feasible then the problem is to choose the best set of 7 groups out of a set of 1330 groups.

Example: Packing Financial Instruments

A financial services firm has financial objects, e.g., mortgages, that it wants to "package" and sell. One of the features of a package is that it must contain a combination of objects whose values total at least one million dollars. For our purposes we will assume that this is the only qualification in synthesizing a package. Suppose we have nine objects with the values:

Object:	A	B	C	D	E	F	G	H	I
Value in $1000:	910	870	810	640	550	250	120	95	55

We want to maximize the number of packages that we form.

The packing approach to formulating a model for this problem constructs all possible packages or groups that just satisfy the one million minimum. The general form of the LP/IP is:

Maximize number of packages selected,

subject to each object appears in at most one selected package.

In the actual formulation below we will use variable names like AB, BGH, etc. to represent packages of (A and B), (B, G, and H). The resulting LP/IP model in PICTURE form is:

```
                                              D E
                              B B B       C   D F F
      A A A A A A B B B B G G H C C C G D F H G
      B C D E F G H C D E F H I I D E F H E G I H
   1: 1 1 1 1 1 1 1 1 1 1 1 1 1 1 1 1 1 1 1 1 1 1 MAX
   A: 1 1 1 1 1 1 1       '       '      '         '    '   < 1
   B: 1 ' ' ' ' '1'1 1 1'1 1 1' ' ' ' ' ' ' < 1
   C:     1 '      ' 1 '       ' 1 1 1 1 '     ' < 1
   D:       1 '     ' 1 '       ' 1 '   1 1 1 ' < 1
   E: ' ' 1 ' ' ' 1 ' ' ' 1 ' 1  ' 1 < 1
   F:       ' 1 '    ' 1 '    ' 1 ' 1 1 1 < 1
   G:         ' 1 '  ' 1 1     ' 1 ' 1   1 < 1
   H: ' ' ' ' 1 ' ' '1 ' 1' ' '1 ' '1 1 < 1
   I:         '     '    ' 1 1  '   ' 1 ' < 1
```

When solved as an LP it produces the following naturally integer solution:

```
       OBJECTIVE FUNCTION VALUE

  1)          4.00000000

  VARIABLE        VALUE           REDUCED COST
     AH         1.000000             0.000000
     BGI        1.000000             0.000000
     CF         1.000000             0.000000
     DE         1.000000             0.000000
```

Thus, four packages are constructed, namely: AH, BGI, CF, and DE. It happens that every object appears in some package. There are alternate packings of all the objects into four groups. Thus, one may wish to consider secondary criteria for choosing one alternate optimum over another, e.g., the largest package should be as close as possible to one million in size.

Linearizing Products of Variables

We have previously seen that products of 0/1 variables, such as $y_1 \times y_2$ and y_1^2 can be represented as linear expressions by means of a simple transformation. This transformation generalizes to the case of the product of a 0/1 variable and a continuous variable.

To illustrate, suppose the product $x \times y$ appears in a model, where y is 0/1 while x is nonnegative continuous. We want to replace this nonlinear component by a (somewhat bigger) linear component. If we have an upper bound, M_x, on the value of x, an upper bound, M_y, on the product $x \times y$, and we define $P = x \times y$, then the following linear constraints will cause P to take on the correct value:

$$P \leq x$$
$$P \leq M_y \times y$$
$$P \geq x - M_x \times (1 - y)$$

Hanson and Martin (1990) show how this approach is useful in setting prices for products when we allow bundling of products. Bundle pricing is a form of quantity discounting. Examples of products that might be bundled are (a) airfare, hotel, rental car, tours, and meals or (b) computer, monitor, printer, and hard disk. Stigler (1963) showed how a movie distributor might improve profits by leasing bundles of movies rather than leasing individual movies. Bundling assumes that it is easy for the seller to assemble the bundle and difficult for a buyer to unbundle. Else a reseller could buy the bundle at a discount and then sell the individual components at a markup.

Example: Bundling of Products

Microland Software has recently acquired an excellent word processing product to complement its own recently developed spreadsheet product. Microland is contemplating offering the combination of the two products for a discount. After demonstrating the products at a number of diverse professional meetings, Microland developed the following characterization of the market.

Market Segment	Size in 10,000	Maximum Price Market Segment Is Willing To Pay for Various Bundles		
		Spreadsheet Only	Wordprocessor Only	Both
Business/Scientific	7	450	110	530
Legal/Administrative	5	75	430	480
Educational	6	290	250	410
Home	4.5	220	380	390

We will refer to each market segment as simply a "customer." Economic theory suggests that a customer will buy the product which gives it the greatest consumer surplus, where consumer surplus is defined as the price the customer is willing to pay for the product (the "reservation price") minus the market price for the product. For example, if the prices for the three bundles: spreadsheet only, word processor only, and both together were set respectively at 400, 150, and 500, then the Business/Scientific market would buy the spreadsheet alone because the consumer surplus is 50 vs. -40, and 30 for the other two bundles.

To give a general model of this situation, define:

R_{ij} = reservation price of customer i for bundle j,
N_i = "size of customer" i, i.e., number of individual customers in segment i,
s_i = consumer surplus achieved by customer i,
y_{ij} = 1 if customer i buys bundle j, 0 otherwise,
x_j = price of bundle j set by the seller.

We will treat the empty bundle as just another bundle so that we can say that every customer buys exactly one bundle.

The seller, Microland, would like to choose the s_j to:

Maximize $\sum_i \sum_j N_i y_{ij} x_j$

The fact that each customer will buy exactly one bundle is enforced with:

For each customer i:

$$\sum_j y_{ij} = 1$$

For each customer i its achieved consumer surplus is:

$$s_i = (R_{ij} - x_j) y_{ij}$$

Customer i will buy only that bundle j for which its consumer surplus, s_i is maximum. This is enforced by the constraints:

For each customer i and bundle j:

$$s_i \geq R_{ij} - x_j$$

A difficulty with the objective function and the consumer surplus constraints is that they involve the product $y_{ij} x_j$. Let us follow our previous little example and replace the product $y_{ij} x_j$ by P_{ij}. If M_j is an upper bound on x_j, then proceeding as before, to enforce the definition that $P_{ij} = y_{ij} x_j$ we need the constraints:

$$P_{ij} \leq x_j$$
$$P_{ij} \leq R_{ij} y_{ij}$$
$$P_{ij} \geq x_j - (1 - y_{ij}) M_j.$$

Making these adjustments to the model, we get:

Maximize $\sum_i \sum_j N_i P_{ij}$

subject to For each customer i

$$\sum_j y_{ij} = 1;$$

For each customer i, bundle j:

$$s_i \geq R_{ij} - x_j$$

For each customer i:

$$s_i = \sum_j (R_{ij} y_{ij} - P_{ij}).$$

and to enforce the nonlinear condition $P_{ij} = y_{ij} x_j$ we have for each i and j:

$$P_{ij} \leq x_j$$
$$P_{ij} \leq R_{ij} y_{ij}$$
$$P_{ij} \geq x_j - (1 - y_{ij}) M_j.$$

For all i and j

$$y_{ij} = 0 \text{ or } 1$$

In explicit form the LINDO model is:

```
MAX     7 PBZZ + 7 PBSZ + 7 PBZW + 7 PBSW +
        5 PLZZ + 5 PLSZ + 5 PLZW + 5 PLSW +
        6 PEZZ + 6 PESZ + 6 PEZW + 6 PESW +
        4.5 PHZZ + 4.5 PHSZ + 4.5 PHZW + 4.5 PHSW
SUBJECT TO
 ! Each customer buys exactly one bundle;
    2)    YBZZ + YBSZ + YBZW + YBSW =    1
    3)    YLZZ + YLSZ + YLZW + YLSW =    1
    4)    YEZZ + YESZ + YEZW + YESW =    1
    5)    YHZZ + YHSZ + YHZW + YHSW =    1
 ! Each customer's achieved surplus, S, must be at least
 ! as good as that possible from every bundle
    6)    XSZ + SB ≤    450
    7)    XZW + SB ≤    110
    8)    XSW + SB ≤    530
    9)    XSZ + SL ≤     75
   10)    XZW + SL ≤    430
   11)    XSW + SL ≤    480
   12)    XSZ + SE ≤    290
   13)    XZW + SE ≤    250
   14)    XSW + SE ≤    410
   15)    XSZ + SH ≤    220
   16)    XZW + SH ≤    380
   17)    XSW + SH ≤    390
 ! Compute the achieved surplus for each customer;
   18) - 450 YBSZ - 110 YBZW - 530 YBSW + PBZZ + PBSZ + PBZW
         + PBSW + SB =    0
   19) - 75 YLSZ - 430 YLZW - 480 YLSW + PLZZ + PLSZ + PLZW
         + PLSW + SL =    0
   20) - 290 YESZ - 250 YEZW - 410 YESW + PEZZ + PESZ + PEZW
         + PESW + SE =    0
   21) - 220 YHSZ - 380 YHZW - 390 YHSW + PHZZ + PHSZ + PHZW
         + PHSW + SH =    0
 ! Each product variable Pij must be..
 !    ≥ Xj
 !    ≥ Rij * Yij
 !    ≤ Xj - M + M * Yij
   22)    PBZZ ≥    0    ! Empty bundle must have price = 0;
   23) - 600 YBZZ + PBZZ ≤ - 600
   24)    PBSZ - XSZ ≥    0
   25) - 450 YBSZ + PBSZ ≥    0
   26) - 600 YBSZ + PBSZ - XSZ ≤ - 600
   27)    PBZW - XZW ≥    0
   28) - 110 YBZW + PBZW ≥    0
   29) - 600 YBZW + PBZW - XZW ≤ - 600
   30)    PBSW - XSW ≥    0
   31) - 530 YBSW + PBSW ≥    0
   32) - 600 YBSW + PBSW - XSW ≤ - 600
   33)    PLZZ ≥    0
   34) - 600 YLZZ + PLZZ ≤ - 600
   35)    PLSZ - XSZ ≥    0
   36) - 75 YLSZ + PLSZ ≥    0
```

37) − 600 YLSZ + PLSZ − XSZ ≤ − 600
38)   PLZW − XZW ≥ 0
39) − 430 YLZW + PLZW ≥ 0
40) − 600 YLZW + PLZW − XZW ≤ − 600
41)   PLSW − XSW ≥ 0
42) − 480 YLSW + PLSW ≥ 0
43) − 600 YLSW + PLSW − XSW ≤ − 600
44)   PEZZ ≥ 0
45) − 600 YEZZ + PEZZ ≤ − 600
46)   PESZ − XSZ ≥ 0
47) − 290 YESZ + PESZ ≥ 0
48) − 600 YESZ + PESZ − XSZ ≤ − 600
49)   PEZW − XZW ≥ 0
50) − 250 YEZW + PEZW ≥ 0
51) − 600 YEZW + PEZW − XZW ≤ − 600
52)   PESW − XSW ≥ 0
53) − 410 YESW + PESW ≥ 0
54) − 600 YESW + PESW − XSW ≤ − 600
55)   PHZZ ≥ 0
56) − 600 YHZZ + PHZZ ≤ − 600
57)   PHSZ − XSZ ≥ 0
58) − 220 YHSZ + PHSZ ≥ 0
59) − 600 YHSZ + PHSZ − XSZ ≤ − 600
60)   PHZW − XZW ≥ 0
61) − 380 YHZW + PHZW ≥ 0
62) − 600 YHZW + PHZW − XZW ≤ − 600
63)   PHSW − XSW ≥ 0
64) − 390 YHSW + PHSW ≥ 0
65) − 600 YHSW + PHSW − XSW ≤ − 600
! Price of bundle should be ≥ sum of component prices;
66) − XSZ − XZW + XSW ≥ 0
! Price of bundle should be ≤ price of any component;
67) − XSZ + XSW ≤ 0
68) − XZW + XSW ≤ 0
END
! Make the "pick a bundle" variables 0/1
INTEGER   YBZZ
INTEGER   YBSZ
INTEGER   YBZW
INTEGER   YBSW
INTEGER   YLZZ
INTEGER   YLSZ
INTEGER   YLZW
INTEGER   YLSW
INTEGER   YEZZ
INTEGER   YESZ
INTEGER   YEZW
INTEGER   YESW
INTEGER   YHZZ
INTEGER   YHSZ
INTEGER   YHZW
INTEGER   YHSW

For the Microland problem, the solution is to set the following prices:

	Spreadsheet Only	Word Processing Only	Both
Bundle Price:	410	380	410

Thus, the business, legal and educational markets will buy the bundle of both products. The home market will buy only the word processor. Total revenues obtained by Microland are 90,900,000. The interested reader may show that if bundling is not possible, then the highest revenue that Microland can achieve is only 67,150,000.

Problems

1. The following problem is known as a segregated storage problem. A feed processor has various amounts of four different commodities which must be stored in seven different silos. Each silo can contain at most one commodity. Associated with each commodity and silo combination is a loading cost. Each silo has a finite capacity so some commodities may have to be split over several silos. The following table contains the data for this problem.

Loading Cost per Ton

Commodity	Silo 1	2	3	4	5	6	7	Amount of Commodity To Be Stored
A	$1	$2	$2	$3	$4	$5	$5	75 tons
B	2	3	3	3	1	5	5	50 tons
C	4	4	3	2	1	5	5	25 tons
D	1	1	2	2	3	5	5	80 tons
Silo Capacity in Tons	25	25	40	60	80	100	100	

(a) Present a formulation for solving this class of problems.

(b) Find the minimum cost solution for this particular example.

(c) How would your formulation change if additionally there was a fixed cost associated with each silo which is incurred if anything is stored in the silo?

2. You are the scheduling coordinator for a small growing airline. You must schedule exactly one flight out of Chicago to each of the following cities: Atlanta, Los Angeles, New York, and Peoria. The available departure slots are 8 A.M., 10 A.M. and 12 noon. Your airline has only two departure lounges so at most two flights can be scheduled per slot. Demand data suggests the following expected profit contribution per flight as a function of departure time:

Expected Profit Contribution in $1000s

	Time		
Destination	8	10	12
Atlanta	10	9	8.5
Los Angeles	11	10.5	9.5
New York	17	16	15
Peoria	6.4	2.5	−1

Formulate a model for solving this problem.

3. A problem faced by an electrical utility each day is that of deciding which generators to start up. The utility in question has three generators with the following characteristics:

Generator	Fixed Startup Cost	Fixed Cost per Period of Operation	Cost per Period per Megawatt Used	Maximum Capacity in Megawatts Each Period
A	3000	700	5	2100
B	2000	800	4	1800
C	1000	900	7	3000

There are two periods in a day and the number of megawatts needed in the first period is 2900. The second period requires 3900 megawatts. A generator started in the first period may be used in the second period without incurring an additional startup cost. All major generators, e.g., A, B, and C above are turned off at the end of each day.

(a) First assume that fixed costs are zero and thus can be disregarded. What are the decision variables?

(b) Give the LP formulation for the case where fixed costs are zero.

(c) Now take into account the fixed costs. What are the additional (zero/one) variables to define?

(d) What additional terms should be added to the objective function? What additional constraints should be added?

4. (Crude Integer Programming.) Recently *U.S.* Government began to sell crude oil from its Naval Petroleum Reserve in sealed bid auctions. There are typically six commodities or products to be sold in the auction, corresponding to the crude oil at the six major production and shipping points. A "bid package" from a potential buyer consists of (a) a number indicating an upper limit on how many barrels the buyer is willing to buy overall in this auction and (b) any number of "product bids." Each product bid consists of a product name and three numbers representing respectively the bid price per barrel of this product, the minimum acceptable quantity of this product at this price and, the maximum acceptable quantity of this product at this price. Not all product bids of a buyer need be successful. The government usually places an arbitrary upper limit, e.g., 20%, on the percentage of the total bbls over all six products that one firm is allowed to purchase.

To illustrate the principle ideas let us simplify slightly and suppose there are only two supply sources/products which are denoted by A and B. There are 17,000 bbls available at A while B has 13,000. Also, there are only two bidders, the Mobon and the Exxil companies. The government arbitrarily decides that either one can purchase at most 65% of the total available crude. The two bid packages are as follows.

Mobon:

Maximum desired = 16,000 bbls. total.

Product	Bid per Barrel	Minimum Barrels Accepted	Maximum Barrels Wanted
A	43	9000	16000
B	51	6000	12000

Exxil

Maximum desired = No limit.

Product	Bid per Barrel	Minimum Barrels Accepted	Maximum Barrels Wanted
A	47		10000
B	50	5000	10000

Formulate and solve an appropriate IP for the seller.

5. A certain state allows a restricted form of branch banking, specifically a bank can do business in a county i if the bank has a "principal place of business" in county i or in a county sharing a nonzero length border with county i. Below is a map of the state in question:

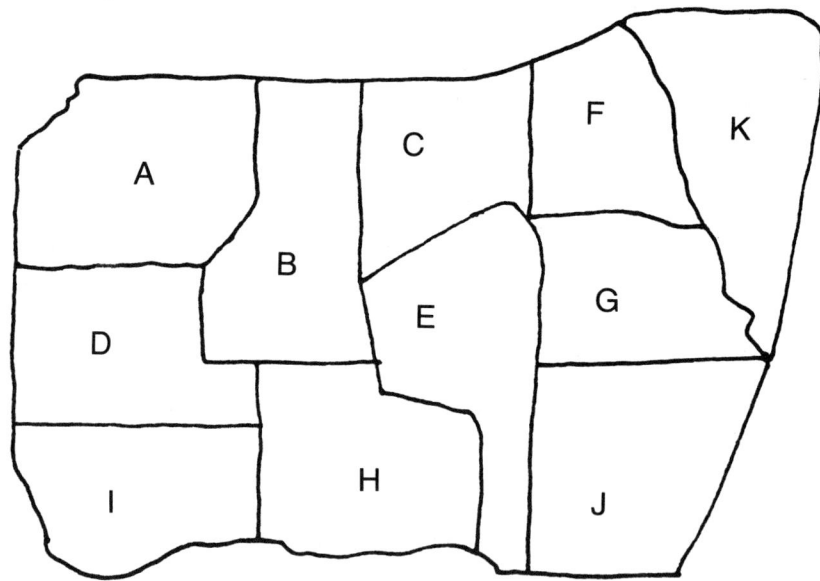

Formulate the problem of locating a minimum number of principal places of business in the state so that a bank can do business in every county in the state. If the problem is formulated as a covering problem, how many rows and columns will it have? What is an optimal solution? Which formulation is tighter, set covering or simple plant location?

6. (Data Set Allocation Problem). There are 10 datasets, each of which is to be allocated to 1 of 3 identical disk storage devices. A disk storage device has 885 cylinders of capacity. Within a storage device a dataset will be assigned to a contiguous set of cylinders. Dataset sizes and interactions between datasets are shown in the table below. Two datasets with high interaction rates should not be assigned to the same device. For example, if datasets C and E are assigned to the same disk, then an interaction cost of 46 is incurred. If they are assigned to different disks there is no interaction cost between C and E.

Dataset for Interaction (Seek Transition) Rates

	A	B	C	D	E	F	G	H	I	J	Dataset Size In Cylinders
A											110
B	43										238
C	120	10									425
D	57	111	188								338
E	96	78	46	88							55
F	83	58	421	60	63						391
G	77	198	207	109	73	74					267
H	31	50	43	47	51	21	88				105
I	38	69	55	21	36	391	47	96			256
J	212	91	84	53	71	40	37	35	221		64
											2250

Find an assignment of datasets to disks so that total interaction cost is minimized and no disk capacity is exceeded.

7. The game of mastermind pits two players, a "coder" and a "decoder" against each other. The game is played with a pegboard and a large number of colored pegs. The pegboard has an array of 4 × 12 holes. For our purposes we assume that there are only six colors: red, blue, clear, purple, gold and green. Each peg has only one

color. The coder starts the game by selecting four pegs and arranging them in a fixed order, all out of sight of the decoder. This ordering remains fixed throughout the game and is called the code. At each play of the game the decoder tries to match the coder's ordering by placing four pegs in a row on the board. The coder then provides two pieces of information about how close the decoder's latest guess is to the coder's order:

(a) The number of pegs in the correct position, *i.e.*, color match the coder's peg in that position, and

(b) The maximum number of pegs which would be in correct position if the decoder were allowed to permute the ordering of the decoder's latest guess.

Call these two numbers m and n. The object of the decoder is to discover the code in a minimum number of plays.

The decoder may find the following IP of interest.

```
MAX      XRED1
SUBJECT TO
    2)   XRED1 + XBLUE1 + XCLEAR1 + XPURP1 + XGOLD1 + XGREEN1 = 1
    3)   XRED2 + XBLUE2 + XCLEAR2 + XPURP2 + XGOLD2 + XGREEN2 = 1
    4)   XRED3 + XBLUE3 + XCLEAR3 + XPURP3 + XGOLD3 + XGREEN3 = 1
    5)   XRED4 + XBLUE4 + XCLEAR4 + XPURP4 + XGOLD4 + XGREEN4 = 1
    6)   XRED1 + XRED2  + XRED3 + XRED4 - RED = 0
    7)   XBLUE1 + XBLUE2 + XBLUE3 + XBLUE4 - BLUE = 0
    8)   XCLEAR1 + XCLEAR2 + XCLEAR3 + XCLEAR4 - CLEAR = 0
    9)   XPURP1 + XPURP2 + XPURP3 + XPURP4 - PURP = 0
   10)   XGOLD1 + XGOLD2 + XGOLD3 + XGOLD4 - GOLD = 0
   11)   XGREEN1 + XGREEN2 + XGREEN3 + XGREEN4 - GREEN = 0
END
```

All variables are required to be integer. The interpretation of the variables are as follows. XRED1 = 1 if a red peg is in position 1, otherwise 0; etc., XGREEN4 = 1 if a green peg is in position 4, otherwise 0. Rows 2 through 5 enforce the requirement that exactly one peg be placed in each position. Rows 6 through 11 are simply accounting constraints which count the number of pegs of each color. For example, RED = the number of red pegs in any position 1 through 4. The objective is unimportant. All variables are (implicitly) required to be nonnegative.

At each play of the game the decoder can add new constraints to this IP to record the information gained. Any feasible solution to the current formulation is a reasonable guess for the next play. An interesting question is what constraints can be added at each play.

To illustrate, suppose the decoder guesses the solution XBLUE1 = XBLUE2 = XBLUE3 = XRED4 = 1, and the coder responds with the information that $m = 1$ and $m - n = 1$, that is, one peg is in the correct position, and if permutations were allowed, at most two pegs would be in the correct position. What constraints can be added to the IP to incorporate the new information?

8. The Mathematical Football League (MFL) is composed of M teams (M is even). In a season of $2(M - 1)$ consecutive Sundays each team will play $(2M - 1)$ games. Each team must play each other team twice, once at home and once at the other team's home stadium. Each Sunday, k games from the MFL are televised. We are

given a matrix $\{v_{ij}\}$ where v_{ij} is the viewing audience on a given Sunday if a game between teams i and j playing at team j's stadium is televised.

(a) Formulate a model for generating a schedule for the MFL which maximizes the viewing audience over the entire season. Assume that viewing audiences are additive.

(b) Are some values of k easier to accommodate than others? How?

9. The typical automobile has close to two dozen electric motors, however, if you examine these motors you will see that only about a half dozen distinct motor types are used. For inventory and maintenance reasons the automobile manufacturer would like to use as few distinct types as possible. For cost, quality, and weight reasons one would like to use as many distinct motor types as possible so that the most appropriate motor can be applied to each application. The table below describes the design possibilities for a certain automobile:

24-Month Failure Probability

Application	Number Required	Motor Type				
		A	B	C	D	E
Head lamps	2	0.002	0.01		0.01	0.007
Radiator fan	2		0.01	0.002		0.004
Wipers	2				0.007	
Seat	4	0.003			0.006	0.008
Mirrors	2			0.004	0.001	
Heater fan	1		0.006	0.001		
Sun roof	1	0.002			0.003	0.009
Windows	4	0.004	0.008	0.005		
Antenna	1	0.003		0.003	0.002	
Weight		2	3	1.5	1	4
Cost per Motor		24	20	36	28	39

For example, two motors are required to operate the head lamps; if type D motors are used for head lamps, then the estimated probability of a head lamp motor failure in two years is about 0.01. If no entry appears for a particular combination of motor type and application it means that the motor type is inappropriate for that application, e.g., because of size.

Formulate a solvable linear integer program for deciding which motor type to use for each application so that at most M motor types are used, the total weight of the motors used is less than W, total cost of motors used is less than or equal to K, and probability of any failure in two years is approximately minimized.

10. We have a rectangular three dimensional container that is $30 \times 50 \times 50$. We want to pack in it rectangular three dimensional boxes of the three different sizes:

(a) $5 \times 5 \times 10$, (b) $5 \times 10 \times 10$, (c) $5 \times 15 \times 25$.

A particular packing of boxes into the container is undominated if there is no other packing which contains at least as many of each of the three box types and strictly more of one of the box types.

Show that there are no more than 3101 undominated packings.

11. Given the following:

Checkerboard and *Domino*

If two opposite corners of the checkerboard are made unavailable, prove that there is no way of exactly covering the remaining grid with 17 domino's.

15

Application to Statistical Estimation

Introduction

LP can be used for linear regression in much the same way that least squares is used. Classical least squares estimation finds the prediction formula which minimizes the sum of squared differences between the observed and the prediction. LP is applicable if instead of minimizing the sum of squared errors one wishes to either:

(a) Minimize the sum of the absolute errors.

(b) Minimize the maximum absolute error.

(c) Minimize the error in predicting the ranking of item, so-called ordinal regression.

A standard notation we shall use is:

n = number of observations,

k = number of explanatory variables,

d_i = value of the dependent variable in observation i, for $i = 1, 2, \ldots n$,

e_{ij} = value of the jth dependent variable in observation i, for $i = 1, 2, \ldots, n$ and $j = 1, 2, \ldots, k$.

We want to determine:

x_j = prediction coefficient applied to the jth explanatory variable,

w_i = error of the forecast formula applied to the ith observation.

Least squares regression then finds values for the x_j's which:

$$\text{Minimize} \quad w_1^2 + w_2^2 + \cdots + w_n^2$$

$$\text{subject to} \quad w_i = d_i - x_0 - \sum_{j=1}^{k} e_{ij} x_j$$

$$x_j, w_i \quad \text{unconstrained in sign.}$$

Least Absolute Deviations (LAD) Estimation

An alternative objective might be to minimize the sum of the absolute values of the errors, that is:

$$\text{Minimize} \quad |w_1| + |w_2| + |w_3| + \cdots + |w_n|.$$

A LAD regression is less affected by extreme outliers. Thus, it is appropriate to use if the data contain a few extreme observations which would otherwise affect the predictions more than is deemed proper.

Linear programming can be applied to this problem if we define:

$$u_i - v_i = w_i.$$

The difference, $u_i - v_i$, is introduced because w_i is unconstrained in sign whereas LP is designed for variables constrained to be nonnegative. The problem of minimizing the sum of absolute errors can now be written:

$$\text{Minimize} \quad u_1 + v_1 + u_2 + v_2 + \cdots + u_n + v_n$$

$$\text{subject to} \quad u_i - v_i = d_i - x_0 - \sum_{j=1}^{k} e_{ij} x_j \quad \text{for } i = 1, 2, \ldots, n.$$

x_j unconstrained in sign.

Example

We have five observations on a single explanatory variable.

d_i	e_{i1}
2	1
3	2
4	4
5	6
8	7

The plot of d_i versus e_{i1} appears in Figure 15.1. With the exception of the last point $(8, 7)$, a straight line would provide a good fit.

The LP specific for this problem is:

```
        MIN       U1 + V1 + U2 + V2 + U3 + V3 + U4 + V4 + U5 + V5
        SUBJECT TO
           2)     U1 - V1 + X0 + X1  =   2
           3)     U2 - V2 + X0 + 2 X1 =  3
           4)     U3 - V3 + X0 + 4 X1 =  4
           5)     U4 - V4 + X0 + 6 X1 =  5
           6)     U5 - V5 + X0 + 7 X1 =  8
        END
```

Figure 15.1
Observations on One Independent and One Dependent Variable

The PICTURE of the matrix is more revealing of the problem's structure:

```
PICTURE
   U V U V U V U V U V X X
   1 1 2 2 3 3 4 4 5 5 0 1

1: 1 1 1 1 1 1 1 1 1 1         MIN
2: 1-1                 1 1  = 2
3:     1-1             1 2  = 3
4:         1-1         1 4  = 4
5:             1-1     1 6  = 5
6:                 1-1 1 7  = 8
```

The solution is:

```
LP OPTIMUM FOUND
       OBJECTIVE FUNCTION VALUE
  1)           2.666667
```

VARIABLE	VALUE	REDUCED COST
U1	0.000000	1.333333
V1	0.000000	0.666667
U2	0.333333	0.000000
V2	0.000000	2.000000
U3	0.000000	1.666667
V3	0.000000	0.333333
U4	0.000000	2.000000
V4	0.333333	0.000000
U5	2.000000	0.000000
V5	0.000000	2.000000
X0	1.333333	0.000000
X1	0.666667	0.000000

ROW	SLACK	DUAL PRICES
2)	0.000000	0.333333
3)	1.000000	-1.000000
4)	0.000000	0.666667
5)	0.000000	1.000000
6)	0.000000	-1.000000

NO. ITERATIONS= 6

The values for X0 and X1 specify the prediction formula specifically:

$$y_i = 1.3333 + 0.666667 e_{i1}.$$

Measuring Goodness of Fit for LAD

In classical least-squares the goodness of fit is measured by a statistic usually called the R^2. This statistic equals the fraction of the variability in the d_is which is explained or eliminated by the prediction model. An analogous statistic can be computed for the LAD regression if we define m to be the median of the d_i. For example, in our example data, $m = 4$. The analogous R^2 (the so-called "adjusted") is then:

$$1 - \frac{(u_1 + v_1 + \cdots + u_n + v_n)/(n - k - 1)}{(|d_1 - m| + \cdots + |d_n - m|)/(n - 1)}.$$

For our example this statistic is:

$$1 - \frac{(2.66667)/3}{(2 + 1 + 0 + 1 + 4)/4} = 0.55556.$$

For reference we will present the least squares solution to this prediction problem. It is:

$$d_i = 1.015 + 0.846 e_{i1}.$$

The adjusted R^2 for this formula is 0.8374.

Least Maximum (LMAX) Deviation Regression

LMAX regression is at the opposite end of the spectrum from LAD regression. LMAX minimizes the worst error of forecast that occurs on any observation. A single extreme observation will have dramatic effect upon the estimates derived. The general form of an LP model for an LMAX regression is:

Minimize z

subject to $x_0 + e_{i1}x_1 + e_{i2}x_2 + \cdots + e_{ik}x_k + u_i - v_i = d_i$ for $i = 1, 2, \ldots, n$.

$z - u_i - 2v_i \geqq 0$ for $i = 1, 2, \ldots, n$.

x_j unconstrained in sign.

This formulation exploits the fact that at an optimal solution at most of one of u_i and v_i will be nonzero. Therefore, $z \geqq v_i$ and $z \geqq v_i$ is equivalent to $z \geqq u_i + v_i$. For our example problem the formulation is:

```
MIN    Z
SUBJECT TO
    2)   X0 - Y0 +   X1 + U1 - V1 =   2
    3)   X0 - Y0 + 2 X1 + U2 - V2 =   3
    4)   X0 - Y0 + 4 X1 + U3 - V3 =   4
    5)   X0 - Y0 + 6 X1 + U4 - V4 =   5
    6)   X0 - Y0 + 7 X1 + U5 - V4 =   8
    7)   Z - U1 - V1 ≧ 0
    8)   Z - U2 - V2 ≧ 0
    9)   Z - U3 - V3 ≧ 0
   10)   Z - U4 - V4 ≧ 0
   11)   Z - U5 - V5 ≧ 0
END
```

Notice that the variable X0 has been replaced by the difference X0 − Y0 because the original X0 is unconstrained in sign.

The PICTURE of the matrix reveals more of the structure of this formulation:

```
PICTURE
     X Y X U V U V U V U V
     Z 0 0 1 1 2 2 3 3 4 4 5 5
 1:  1                              MIN
 2:    1-1 1 1-1                    = 2
 3:    1-1 2     1-1                = 3
 4:    1-1 4         1-1            = 4
 5:    1-1 6             1-1        = 5
 6:    1-1 7                 1-1    = 8
 7:  1      -1-1                    >
 8:  1          -1-1                >
 9:  1              -1-1            >
10:  1                  -1-1        >
11:  1                      -1-1    >
```

The solution is:

```
LP OPTIMUM FOUND

    OBJECTIVE FUNCTION VALUE

    1)            1.000000

VARIABLE        VALUE           REDUCED COST
    Z           1.000000          0.000000
    X0          0.000000          0.000000
    Y0          0.000000          0.000000
    X1          1.000000          0.000000
```

U1	1.000000	0.000000
V1	0.000000	0.000000
U2	1.000000	0.000000
V2	0.000000	0.200000
U3	0.000000	0.000000
V3	0.000000	0.000000
U4	0.000000	1.000000
V4	1.000000	0.000000
U5	1.000000	0.000000
V5	0.000000	0.800000

ROW	SLACK	DUAL PRICES
2)	0.000000	0.000000
3)	0.000000	−0.000000
4)	0.000000	0.000000
5)	0.000000	0.500000
6)	0.000000	−0.400000
7)	0.000000	0.000000
8)	0.000000	−0.100000
9)	0.000000	0.000000
10)	0.000000	−0.500000
11)	0.000000	−0.400000

NO. ITERATIONS=   9

The values of X0 − Y0 and X1 reveal that the prediction formula is:

$$y_i = e_{i1}.$$

Measuring Goodness of Fit, LMAX Case

Define r to be equal to the range of the d_i's, that is, $\max\{d_i\} - \min\{d_i\}$. The analog of the adjusted R^2 is then:

$$1 - \frac{\max\{u_i + v_i\}/(n - k - 1)}{r/(n - 1)}.$$

For our example this statistic equals:

$$1 - \frac{1/3}{(8 - 2)/4} = 0.778.$$

The three different prediction curves resulting from the three different methods applied to the example data are displayed in Figure 15.2. Notice that Least Maximum Deviation is most affected by the outlier at (8, 7) while Least Absolute Deviation is least affected by the outlier.

Exploiting the Dual to Obtain a More Compact Formulation

The amount of work required to solve an LP is much more highly correlated with the number of rows than with the number of columns. Because the solution to the dual problem provides the same information as the solution to the primal, one may wish to solve the dual if it has fewer rows.

Figure 15.2

Prediction Line According to Error Measure

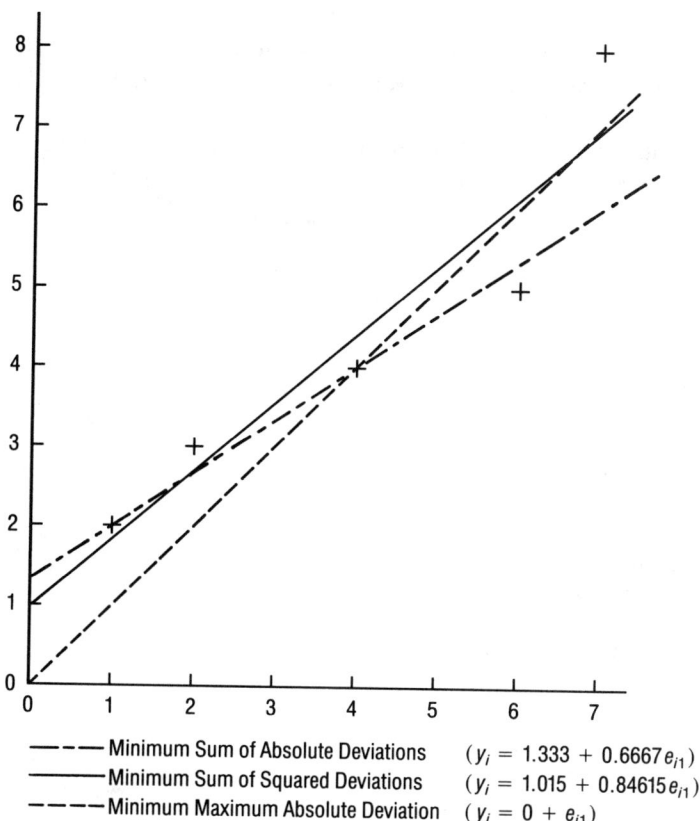

– – – Minimum Sum of Absolute Deviations   ($y_i = 1.333 + 0.6667 e_{i1}$)
———— Minimum Sum of Squared Deviations ($y_i = 1.015 + 0.84615 e_{i1}$)
– - – - Minimum Maximum Absolute Deviation ($y_i = 0 + e_{i1}$)

Dual of LAD Formulation

First we will examine the Least Absolute Deviations problem. The dual of the previous formulation is:

$$\begin{aligned}
\text{Maximize} \quad & \lambda_1 d_1 = \lambda_2 d_2 + \cdots + \lambda_n d_n \\
\text{subject to} \quad & \lambda_1 e_{1j} + \lambda_2 e_{2j} + \cdots + \lambda_n e_{nj} \leq 0 \quad \text{for } j = 1, \ldots, k, \\
& \lambda_i \leq 1 \\
& \lambda_i \geq -1.
\end{aligned}$$

This formulation simplifies slightly if we define:

$$L_i = \lambda_i + 1 \quad \text{so} \quad \lambda_i = L_i - 1.$$

When this substitution is made the formulation becomes:

Maximize $L_1 d_1 + L_2 d_2 + \cdots + L_n d_n - d_1 - d_2 - \cdots - d_n$
subject to $L_1 e_{1j} + L_2 e_{2j} + \cdots + L_n e_{nj} \leq e_{1j} + e_{2j} + \cdots + e_{nj}$ for $j = 0, 1, \ldots, k$,
$L_i \leq 2$ for $i = 1, 2, \ldots, n$.

This formulation has $n + k$ rows as compared to only n in the primal formulation; however, n of the constraints are of the very simple form $L_i \leq 2$. Most LP codes exploit this simple form.

This formulation and its shorthand picture appear below. The constant $-d_1 - d_2 - \cdots - d_n$ in the objective function has no effect, so it is not included.

```
MAX     2 L1 + 3 L3 + 4 L3 + 5 L4 + 8 L5
SUBJECT TO
    2)      L1 +  L3 +  L3 +  L4 +  L5 ≤     5
    3)      L1 + 2 L3 + 4 L3 + 6L4 + 7L5 ≤    20
    4)      L1 ≤  2
    5)      L2 ≤  2
    6)      L3 ≤  2
    7)      L4 ≤  2
    8)      L5 ≤  2
END

PICTURE
        L L L L L
        1 2 3 4 5

1:      2 3 4 5 8 MAX
2:      1 1 1 1 1 < 5
3:      1 2 4 6 7 < B
4:      1         < 2
5:        1       < 2
6:          1     < 2
7:            1   < 2
8:              1 < 2
```

The solution is:

```
LP OPTIMUM FOUND
        OBJECTIVE FUNCTION VALUE
    1)          24.66667

VARIABLE        VALUE           REDUCED COST
    L1          0.666667        0.000000
    L2          2.000000        0.000000
    L3          0.333333        0.000000
    L4          0.000000        0.333333
    L5          2.000000        0.000000

ROW             SLACK           DUAL PRICES
    2)          0.000000        1.333333
    3)          0.000000        0.666667
    4)          1.333333        0.000000
    5)          0.000000        0.333333
    6)          1.666667        0.000000
    7)          2.000000        0.000000
    8)          0.000000        2.000000

NO. ITERATIONS=         5
```

The dual prices on constraints (2) and (3), 1.3333 and 0.6667 correspond to X_0 and X_1. Notice that only five iterations were required to solve it as compared to six iterations for the primal formulation.

The Dual of the LMAX Formulation

The dual of the Least Maximum Deviation Formulation is:

$$\text{Maximize } \sum_i \lambda_i d_i \quad \text{(Primal Variable)}$$

subject to
$$\sum_i \lambda_i e_{ij} = 0 \quad (x_j)$$
$$\lambda_i - \alpha_i \leq 0 \quad (u_i)$$
$$-\lambda_i - \alpha_i \leq 0 \quad (v_i)$$
$$\sum_i \alpha_i \leq 1$$

λ_i unconstrained in sign.

This formulation can be rearranged to a more convenient form if we define the variables g_i and h_i such that:

$$g_i + h_i = \alpha_i$$
$$g_i - h_i = \lambda_i,$$

with g_i and h_i unconstrained in sign.

Substituting for both α_i and λ_i the formulation becomes:

$$\text{Maximize } \sum_i (g_i - h_i) d_i$$

subject to
$$\sum_i (g_i - h_i) e_{ij} = 0$$
$$g_i - h_i - (g_i + h_i) \leq 0 \quad \text{or} \quad -2h_i \leq 0 \quad \text{or} \quad h_i \geq 0$$
$$-(g_i - h_i) - (g_i + h_i) \leq 0 \quad \text{or} \quad -2g_i \leq 0 \quad \text{or} \quad g_i \geq 0$$
$$\sum (g_i + h_i) \leq 1$$

The nonnegativity constraints $h_i \geq 0$ and $g_i \geq 0$ are assumed by any LP code so they need not be explicitly stated.

The formulation and PICTURE applied to the example data are given below.

```
MAX    2 G1 - 2 H1 + 3 G2 - 3 H2 + 4 G3 - 4 H3 + 5 G4
     - 5 H4 + 8 G5 - 8 H5
SUBJECT TO
2)     G1 - H1 + G2 - H2 + G3 - H3 + G4 - H4 + G5 - H5 =   0
3)     G1 - H1 + 2 G2 - 2 H2 + 4 G3 - 4 H3 + 6 G4 - 6 H4
     + 7 G5 - 7 H5 =   0
4)     G1 + H1 + G2 + H2 + G3 + H3 + G4 + H4 + G5 + H5 ≤   0
END
PICTURE
   G H G H G H G H G H
   1 1 2 2 3 3 4 4 5 5
1: 2-2 3-3 4-4 5-5 8-8 MAX
2: 1-1 1-1 1-1 1-1 1-1 =
3: 1-1 2-2 4-4 6-6 7-7 =
4: 1 1 1 1 1 1 1 1 1 1 < 1
```

The solution is:

```
 LP OPTIMUM FOUND

     OBJECTIVE FUNCTION VALUE

        1)         1.000000

      VARIABLE      VALUE         REDUCED COST
        G1         0.083333         0.000000
        H1         0.000000         2.000000
        G2         0.000000         0.000000
        H2         1.000000         2.000000
        G3         1.000000         1.000000
        H3         0.000000         1.000000
        G4         0.000000         2.000000
        H4         0.500000         0.000000
        G5         0.416667         0.000000
        H5         0.000000         2.000000

        ROW         SLACK         DUAL PRICES
        2)         0.000000         0.000000
        3)         0.000000         1.000000
        4)         0.000000         1.000000

      NO. ITERATIONS=    3
```

The dual prices for rows (2) and (3) are the values of X0 and X1.

Notice that this formulation had only three rows and required three iterations as compared to ten constraints and nine iterations for the primal formulation.

Ordinal Regression

The regression methods discussed in the previous section apply when all the data are in numeric form. Sometimes, however, data are found in a more subjective or qualitative form. Consider, for example, a marketing study in which you are trying to predict what determines consumer preferences for various products in a class, e.g., breakfast foods. The data from a consumer survey might consist simply of preference statements of the form "I prefer Wheaties to Cheerios." There is available additional independent quantitative data on each breakfast food describing its characteristics, e.g., sweetness, nutritional value, price, etc. The desire is to determine how ranking by consumers depends upon the product characteristics.

This problem can be attacked via LP. Consider the following example. Five different cars, denoted by B, C, F, L, and M have been evaluated by a consumer panel. These evaluations are in the form of eight different pairwise comparisons by different members of the panel. The results are shown in the table at the top of the next page.

For example, the first comparison indicates that some consumer preferred an L to a C, while that last comparison indicates that some consumer preferred an F to a B.

Although one could, we have not required that these pairwise rankings be consistent or transitive. Indeed, if these rankings are collected from a number of people we would expect some inconsistency among them. For example, you can note an inconsistency among rankings (3), (6), (2), and (5). Ranking (3) says F is inferior to L; however, rankings (6), (2) and (5) suggest that L is inferior to F.

Five Car Consumer Panel Evaluation Results

Comparison Number	Less Preferred Car	More Preferred Car
1.	C	L
2.	M	B
3.	F	L
4.	F	C
5.	B	F
6.	L	M
7.	M	C
8.	M	F

We suspect that consumer preferences are affected by the four characteristics: price, weight, length, and mpg. These characteristics for the five cars are listed below:

Car	Price (1,000s)	Weight (1,000s)	Length (Feet)	MPG
B	9	4	15	17
C	6	3	13	21
F	7	2.8	13.5	20
L	10	4.2	15.5	16
M	8	3.9	14	18

Can you develop a scoring formula based on these characteristics such that higher scoring cars will tend to be the more preferred ones? Such a formula would help in identifying the relative importance of various characteristics. The following is an approach for developing such a scoring formula.
Define:

e_{ij} = value of characteristic j for car i,

x_j = scoring weight to be applied to characteristic j, i.e., the score of car i is $x_1 e_{i1} + x_2 e_{i2} + \cdots + x_4 e_{i4}$,

z_k = the scoring error on the kth observation.

We want to choose the x_j's so that the resulting scores agree as much as possible with the eight preference rankings given previously. We will say the scoring agrees with the first of the eight rankings, for example, if car L receives a higher score than car C; and it agrees with the last ranking if car F receives a higher score than car B. To see how to compute the scoring error, z_k, suppose that car F is preferred to car L in the kth preference; then the following constraint will cause z_i to take on the proper value:

$$(e_{F1} - e_{L1})x_1 + (e_{F2} - e_{L2})x_2 + \cdots + (e_{F4} - e_{L4})x_4 + z_k \geq 0.$$

The left-hand side of this constraint is the score of F minus the score of $L + z_k$.
A reasonable objective is then to:

Minimize $z_1 + z_2 + \cdots + z_8$.

Ordinal Regression

Using a right-hand side of zero only forces the scores of F to at least equal the score of L; it does not force the score of F to exceed the score of L. If this is desired, then the zero might be replaced by a small positive number, .e.g., .001. This is illustrated in a later example.

We need a "normalizing" constraint to prohibit the useless solution: $x_1 = x_2 = x_3 = x_4 = 0$. The simplest possible normalizing constraint is $x_1 + x_2 + x_3 + x_4 = 1$. This, however, ignores the fact that the various characteristics have different units, e.g., mpg may range from 10 to 40 whereas price may have a much higher range of from 2,000 to 20,000. Thus, you probably want to use different weights on the x_j's. A reasonable weighted normalizing constraint is:

$$\sum_{j=1}^{4} \sum_{i=1}^{8} (e_{rj} - e_{sj}) x_j = 1.$$

Realize that the x_j's are unconstrained in sign; therefore, in the LP formulation the x_j's will be replaced by the difference $x_j - y_j$. The complete formulation and PICTURE for our example is given below.

```
       MIN    Z1 + Z2 + Z3 + Z4 + Z5 + Z6 + Z7 + Z8
       SUBJECT TO
          2)      Z1 + 4 X1 - 4 Y1 + 1.2 X2 - 1.2 Y2 + 2.5 X3 - 2.5 Y3
                  - 5 X4 + 5 Y4 ≥    0
          3)      Z2 + X1 - Y1 + 0.1 X2 - 0.1 Y2 + X3 - Y3 - X4
                  - Y4 ≥    0
          4)      Z3 + 3 X1 - 3 Y1 + 1.4 X2 - 1.4 Y2 + 2 X3
                  - 2 Y3 - 4 X4 + 4 Y4 ≥    0
          5)      Z4 - X1 + Y1 + 0.2 X2 - 0.2 Y2 - 0.5 X3
                  + 0.5 X3 + X4 - Y4 ≥    0
          6)      Z5 - 2 X1 + 2 Y1 - 1.2 X2 + 1.2 Y2 - 1.5 X3
                  + 1.5 Y3 + 3 X4 - 3 Y4 ≥    0
          7)      Z6 - 2 X1 + 2 Y1 - 0.3 X2 + 0.3 Y2 - 1.5 X3
                  + 1.5 Y3 + 2 X4 - 2 Y4 ≥    0
          8)      Z7 - 2 X1 + 2 Y1 - 0.9 X2 + 0.9 Y2 - X3 + Y3
                  + 3 X4 - 3 Y4 ≥    0
          9)      Z8 - X1 + Y1 - 1.1 X2 + 1.1 Y2 - 0.5 X3
                  + 0.5 Y3 + 2 X4 - 2 Y4 ≥    0
         10)      - 0.6 X2 + 0.6 Y2 + 0.5 X3 - 0.5 Y3 + 3 X4 - 3 Y4 =       1
       END

       PICTURE
              Z Z Z Z Z Z Z Z X Y X Y X Y X Y
              1 2 3 4 5 6 7 8 1 1 2 2 3 3 4 4
          1:  1 1 1 1 1 1 1 1                          MIN
          2:  1                     4-4 A-A A-A-5 5 >
          3:    1                   1-1 U-U 1-1-1-1 >
          4:      1                 3-3 A-A 2-2-4 4 >
          5:        1              -1 1 T-T-T T 1-1 >
          6:          1             -2 2-A A-A A 3-3 >
          7:            1           -2 2-T T-A A 2-2 >
          8:              1         -2 2-T T-1 1 3-3 >
          9:                1-1 1-A A-T T 2-2 >
         10:                         -T T T-T 3-3 = 1
```

The solution report is:

```
LP OPTIMUM FOUND
   OBJECTIVE FUNCTION VALUE
     1)            0.07692308
   VARIABLE       VALUE          REDUCED COST
     Z1          0.000000          0.576923
     Z2          0.000000          0.500000
     Z3          0.000000          1.000000
     Z4          0.000000          1.000000
     Z5          0.000000          1.000000
     Z6          0.076923          0.000000
     Z7          0.000000          1.000000
     Z8          0.000000          0.807692
     X1          0.461538          0.000000
     Y1          0.000000          0.000000
     X2          0.384615          0.000000
     Y2          0.000000          0.000000
     X3          0.000000          0.000000
     Y3          0.076923          0.000000
     X4          0.423077          0.000000
     Y4          0.000000          1.000000
   ROW           SLACK           DUAL PRICES
     2)          0.000000         -0.423077
     3)          0.000000         -0.500000
     4)          0.076923          0.000000
     5)          0.076923          0.000000
     6)          0.000000          0.000000
     7)          0.000000         -1.000000
     8)          0.076923          0.000000
     9)          0.000000         -0.192308
    10)          0.000000         -0.076923
   NO. ITERATIONS=     7
```

The implication of the report is that the scoring formula for a car should be (for the case of a zero right-hand side for constraints 2 to 9):

Score = 0.461538 Price + .384615 Weight − 0.076923 Length + 0.423077 MPG.

Whereas the formula with a RHS of 0.001 for constraints (2) through (9) is:

Score = 0.461385 Price + 0.381154 Weight − 0.076231 Length + 0.422269 MPG.

The resulting scores for the five cars are:

	Score	
Car	(RHS = 0.000)	(RHS = 0.001)
B	11.73077	11.71219
C	11.80769	11.78842
F	11.73077	11.71319
L	11.80769	11.78942
M	11.73077	11.71119

Observe that the scores are in the correct order for all eight of the pairwise rankings except for the sixth one, "*M* is preferred to *L*."

Goodness of Ordinal Fit

If we let z be the optimal objective function value, n the number of ranking observations, and k the number of parameters estimated for the ordinal regression, then a measure of goodness of fit somewhat analogous to the adjusted R^2 of least squares regression is:

$$1/[1 + z/(n - k)].$$

For our example the goodness of fit is:

$$1/[1 + 0.0769/(8 - 4)] = 0.981.$$

Exploiting the Dual to Reduce the Formulation Size

As with other LP regression formulations, the dual tends to be easier to solve. The primal formulation in general form is below. In all of the following, r is the object preferred to object s in the ith pairwise ranking.

$$\text{Minimize} \quad z_1 + z_2 + \cdots + z_n$$

$$\text{subject to} \quad \sum_{j=1}^{k}(e_{rj} - e_{sj})x_j + z_i \geq 0 \quad \text{where } r \text{ is preferred to } s \text{ in the } i\text{th observation, } i = 1, 2, \ldots, n$$

$$\sum_{j=1}^{k}\sum_{i=1}^{n}(e_{rj} - e_{sj})x_j = 1$$

x_j unconstrained in sign.

The dual is:

$$\text{Maximize} \quad u$$

$$\text{subject to} \quad \sum_{i=1}^{n}(e_{rj} - e_{sj})v_i + \sum_{i=1}^{n}(e_{rj} - e_{sj})u = 0 \quad \text{for } j = 1, 2, \ldots, k$$

$$v_i \leq 1 \quad \text{for } i = 1, 2, \ldots, n.$$

u unconstrained in sign.

This formulation has a lot of constraints; however, the majority of them, n out of $n + k$, are of the simple upper bound variety.

The dual formulation for the example problem follows. Note that the unconstrained variable u is replaced by the difference $u_1 - u_2$.

```
MAX      U1 - U2
SUBJECT TO
  2)    4 V1 + V2 + 3 V3 - V4 - 2 V5 - 2 V6 - 2 V7 - V8 =    0
  3)   - 0.6 U1 + .6 U2 + 1.2 V1 + 0.1 V2 + 1.4 V3 + 0.2 V4
       - 1.2 V5 - 0.3 V6 - 0.9 V7 - 1.1 V8 =    0
  4)    0.5 U1 - 0.5 U2 + 2.5 V1 + V2 + 2 V3 - 0.5 V4 - 1.5 V5
       - 1.5 V6 - V7 - 0.5 V8 =    0
  5)    3 U1 - 3 U2 - 5 V1 -   V2 - 4 V3 + V4 + 3 V5 + 2 V6
       + 3 V7 + 2 V8 =    0
  6)    V1 ≤    1
```

```
 7)    V2 ≤  1
 8)    V3 ≤  1
 9)    V4 ≤  1
10)    V5 ≤  1
11)    V6 ≤  1
12)    V7 ≤  1
13)    V8 ≤  1
END
```

It is helpful to compare the PICTURE of this formulation with that of the primal.

```
?:PICTURE
       U U V V V V V V V V
       1 2 1 2 3 4 5 6 7 8
  1: 1-1                         MAX
  2:      4 1 3-1-2-2-2-1 =
  3:-T T A U A T-A-T-T-A  =
  4: T-T A 1 2-T-A-A-1-T  =
  5: 3-3-5-1-4 1 3 2 3 2  =
  6:     1                  < 1
  7:       1                < 1
  8:         1              < 1
  9:           1            < 1
 10:             1          < 1
 11:               1        < 1
 12:                 1      < 1
 13:                   1  < 1
```

The solution of the dual is:

LP OPTIMUM FOUND

OBJECTIVE FUNCTION VALUE

1)   0.07692308

VARIABLE	VALUE	REDUCED COST
U1	0.076923	0.000000
U2	0.000000	0.000000
V1	0.423077	0.000000
V2	0.692308	0.000000
V3	0.000000	0.076923
V4	0.000000	0.076923
V5	0.192308	0.000000
V6	1.000000	0.000000
V7	0.000000	0.076923
V8	0.000000	0.000000

ROW	SLACK	DUAL PRICES
2)	0.000000	0.461538
3)	0.000000	0.384615
4)	0.000000	-0.076923
5)	0.000000	0.423077
6)	0.576923	0.000000
7)	0.307692	0.000000
8)	1.000000	0.000000
9)	1.000000	0.000000

10)	0.807692	0.000000
11)	0.000000	0.076923
12)	1.000000	0.000000
13)	1.000000	0.000000

NO. ITERATIONS= 6

Notice that it took only six iterations as compared to seven for the primal. The dual variables on constraints (2)-(5) provide the values for the x_j variables of the primal formulation. The scoring formula is again:

Score = 0.461538 Price + 0.384615 Weight − 0.076923 Length + 0.423077 MPG.

For a further discussion of ordinal linear regression, see Srinivasan (1976).

Problems

1. A table of statistical data contains a small fraction of data transcription errors, e.g., typing mistakes. These errors in the data are very difficult to track down. Which type of regression, LAD, LMAX or least squares would be least affected by these outlier type errors?

2. In the simple linear regression model the ith observation is written in the form:

$$r_i = a + bs_i + e_i$$

where r_i, s_i, and e_i are respectively the dependent variable, the explanatory variable, and the error term which regression model LAD, LMAX, or least squares is most appropriate if the e_i are (a) uniformly distributed over a finite but unknown range, (b) Normal distribution, (c) distributed according to a distribution with fatter tails than the Normal?

3. Consider the following table for a multiple regression problem:

r	s	t
7	3	12
10	4	11
11	7	9
13	8	8

Formulate and solve the relevant LP for regressing the dependent variable r on the two explanatory variables s and t using (a) LMAX regression, (b) LAD regression.

16

Design & Implementation of Optimization Based Decision Support Systems

General Structure of the Modeling Process

The overall modeling process is one of:

1. Developing the model,
2. Implementing the model.

If the purpose of the model is to do a one time analysis, e.g., to decide whether or not to make a certain investment, then step (2) will be relatively less laborious.

Developing the Model: Detail and Maintenance

Whether the model is intended for a one-time study or is to be used regularly, has some influence on how you develop the model. If the model is to be used regularly, then you want to worry especially about the following:

Problem: The real world changes rapidly, e.g., prices, company structure, suppliers. We must be able to update the model just as fast.

Resolution: There are two relevant philosophies.
1. Keep worthless detail out of the model, follow the KISS (Keep It Simple, . . .) admonition.
2. Put as much of the model as possible into data tables rather than hardcoded into the model structure.

Appropriate Level of Detail, Verification and Validation

If unimportant details are kept out of the model, the model should be not only easier to modify but also easier to use.

Example

In developing a long range ship scheduling model, a question of appropriate unit of time arose. Tides follow a roughly 13 hour cycle and this is an important consideration in the scheduling of ships into shallow ports. Deep draft ships can enter a shallow port only at high tide. Thus, in developing a multiperiod model for ship scheduling it appeared that 13 hours should be the length of a period.

We found, however, that ship travel times were sufficiently random that scheduling to the day was satisfactory. Thus, to model a month of activity, 30 time periods rather than about 60 was satisfactory. Halving the number of periods greatly simplified the computations. The moral perhaps is that when it comes to incorporating detail into the model, a little bit of selective laziness may be a good thing.

Simplifying approximations can be categorized roughly as follows.

1. *Approximations*

    If there is an art to modeling, this is it: identifying the simplifications or approximations that can be made without sacrificing the useful accuracy of the model.

    1.1 *Functional*, e.g., use a linear function to approximate a slightly nonlinear one.

    1.2 *Aggregation*

        1.2.1 *Temporal* aggregation, e.g., all events occurring during a given day (or week, month, etc.) are treated as having occurred at the end of the day.

        1.2.2 *Cross-sectional* aggregation, e.g., all customers in a given mail code region are lumped together to be treated as one large customer, or in a consumer products firm all detergents are treated as a single product.

    1.3 *Statistical*, e.g., replace a random variable by its expectation. For example, even though future sales are a random variable, most planners use a single number forecast in planning.

    1.4 *Decomposition*. If a system is overwhelming in its complexity, then decomposition is an approach that may be useful for simplifying the structure. Under this approach a sequence of models are solved, each nailing down more detail of the complete solution.

Verification and Validation

The term *verification* is usually applied to the process of verifying that the model as implemented is actually doing what we think it should. Effectively, verification is checking that the model has no unintentional "bugs." *Validation* is the process of demonstrating that the approximations to reality that are intentionally incorporated in the model do not sully the quality of the results from the model.

Verification should begin with understanding the real world that is to be modeled. A common problem is that the people willing to speak most authoritatively about the process to be modeled are not always the most informed. A good rule of thumb is to always check your "facts" with a second source. Rothstein (1985) mentions that in a conversation with a vice president of a major airline, the vice president assured him that the airline did not engage in overbooking at all. A short time later in a discussion with operating personnel he learned that in fact overbooking was practiced everywhere in that airline.

Separation of Data and System Structure

With regard to separating data from model structure, there are two reasons for doing it:

(a) it allows us to easily and quickly adjust the model to changes in the real world,

(b) the person responsible for making day-to-day changes in the data need not be familiar with the technical details of the model structure.

A flexible system is table driven. In LINDO, essentially all data are "in the model." In more powerful systems such as LINGO and *What's Best* things such as interest rates can be input at a single place by a clerk, even though they appear numerous places in the model structure.

System Structure

In the typical case, a model will be used regularly, e.g., weekly in an operational environment. In this case the model system can be thought as having the following structure.

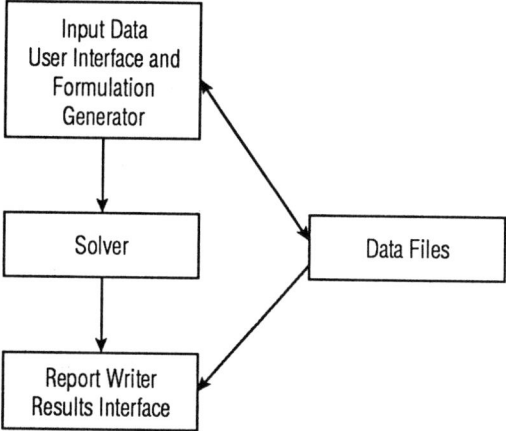

The success of spreadsheet programs such as Lotus 1-2-3 is due in part to the fact that they incorporate all the above components in a relatively seamless fashion.

Marketing the Model

It is important to keep in mind: "Who will be the users/clients?"
Frequently there are two types of clients in a single organization:

1. The model champion, e.g., a CEO,
2. Actual user, e.g., a foreman working 12 hours/day and whose major concern is getting the work out and meeting deadlines.

Client (1) will commit to model development based on expected profit improvement. Client (2) will actually use the model if it simplifies his/her life. He may get fired if he misses a production deadline. There is a modest probability of a raise if he improves profitability and takes the trouble to document it. Thus, for client (2) the input and output user interfaces are very important.

Reports

A model has an impact largely via the reports it produces. If a standard report already exists in the organization, try to use it. The model simply puts better numbers in it.

Example. An LP-based scheduling system was developed for shoe factories. It was a success in the first factory where it was tried. Production improved by about 15%. The system never got off the ground in a second factory. The reason for the difference in success was apparently as follows. The first factory had an existing scheduling report or work order. This report was retained. The results of the LP scheduling model simply put better numbers in it. The second factory had been using an informal scheduling system. The combination of installing both a new reporting and a new scheduling systems was too big a barrier to change.

Designing Reports

The proper attitude in designing reports is to ask: How will the results be used?

In operations settings there frequently are three types of reports implied by the results of a model run:

(a) Raw material acquisition recommendations, e.g., in extreme cases the model might generate purchase orders directly,

(b) Production orders, e.g., how are the raw materials to be processed into finished goods,

(c) Finished goods summaries. If the production process is complicated, e.g., several different alternative processes are used to achieve the total production of a specific product, then it may not be clear from (a) and (b), how much of a particular finished good was produced.

Example: Reports in a Blending Facility. In a facility that blends raw materials into finished goods, reports of the following type might be appropriate.

(a)

Raw Material Purchases			
Raw Material	Total Required	Beginning Inventory	Required Purchases

(b)

Production			
Batch 1. Product:		**Batch 2.** Product:	
Inputs:		Inputs:	
Raw Material	Amount	Raw Material	Amount

(c)

Finished Goods Summary				
Product	Beginning Inventory	Goods Produced	Total Required	Surplus

Dimensional View of Reports

A more mechanical view of report generation is to take a dimensional view of a system, *i.e.*, a problem and its solution has a number of dimensions. Each report is a sort and summary by dimensions.

Example: *Multiperiod Shipping*

Dimensions: Origins, Destinations, Time Periods. The major decision variables might be of the form X_{ijt}, where X_{ijt} is the number of tons to be shipped from supplier i, to customer j in time period t. The types of reports might be:

Suppliers Report: Sorted by Origin, Time, Destination
(or summed over destination).

Shipping Manager: Sorted by Time, Origin, Destination.

Customer's Report: Sorted by Destination, Time, Origin
(or perhaps summed over origin).

Most spreadsheets and database systems have multi-level sorting capability.

Report Details/Passing the Snicker Test

Results should be phrased in terms that the user finds easy to use. For example, reporting that a steel bar should be cut to a length of 58.36 inches may cause snickers in some places because "everybody knows" that this commodity (like U.S. stock prices) is measured in multiples of 1/8, inches or dollars, as the case may be. So it would be better to round the result to 58.375 inches, or even better, report it as 58 and 3/8 inches.

Other examples: Dates should be reported not only in day of the month (taking into account leap years) but also day of the week. Different parts of the world use different formats for displaying dates, e.g., 14 March 1991 vs. 3/14/1991, etc. Use a format appropriate for the location where used.

Example: Vehicle Routing/Passing the Snicker Test

Customers are grouped into trips so that customers on the same trip are served by the same vehicle. The actual model decomposed the problem into two phases:

1. Allocate to trips   ←   Big savings here
2. Sequence each trip   ←   Users notice this the most.

If your system does an excellent job of allocating customers to trips (where the big savings exist) but does not always get the optimal sequence of customers within a trip, users may notice the latter weakness. Even though there may be no big savings possible by improving the sequence, users may have less faith in the system because of this small weakness.

Models Should Always Have Feasible Solutions

In a large model where the input data are prepared by many people there may be no assurance that the data are perfectly consistent. For example, production capacity as estimated by the production department may be insufficient to satisfy sales forecasts as estimated by the marketing department. If the model has a constraint that requires production to equal forecasted sales, then there may be no feasible solution. The terse message: "No feasible solution" is not very helpful.

A better approach is to have in the model a *superworker* or superfacility that can make any product at infinite speed but at a rather high cost. There will always be feasible solutions although some parts of the solution may look somewhat funny.

Another device is to allow *demand to be backlogged* at a high cost.

In each case the solution will give sensible indications of where one should install extra capacity or cut back on projected sales, etc.

A model may be fundamentally good but incomplete in certain minor details. As a result, some of its recommendations may be slightly but blatantly incorrect.

For example, in reality almost every activity has a finite upper bound.

Similarly there may be obvious *bounds on the dual* prices of certain resources. For example, if land is a scarce resource in the real world then its dual price should never be zero. You should *include sellout or buy activities* corresponding to such things as renting out excess land to put lower and upper bounds on dual prices.

"Signing Off" on System Structure

If a prospective model (a) is likely to be complicated and (b) the group that will use the model is distinct from the group that will design the model, then it will be worthwhile to have beforehand a written document describing exactly what the model does. Effectively, the "User's Manual" is written before the system is implemented. The prospective users should "sign off" on the design, e.g., by providing a letter that says "Yes, this is what we want *and we will accept* if it provides this."

The structure of this document would include things like

(a) form in which input will be provided,

(b) form in which output will be provided,

(c) test data sets that must be successfully processed. The model will be accepted if and only if these are satisfied.

Reducing Model Size

Practical LP models tend to be large. Thus, it makes sense to talk about the management of these models. Some of the important issues are:

1. Choosing an appropriate formulation. Frequently there are two conflicting considerations: (a) the model should be large enough to capture all important details of reality and (b) the model should be solveable in reasonable time.
2. What input data are needed? How is it collected?
3. How do we create an explicit model from the current data? This process has traditionally been called matrix generation.
4. How is the model solved? Is it solveable in reasonable time? In reality some optimization program must be selected. For our purposes we assume LINDO has been chosen.

In this section we discuss issues (1) and (3). The selection of an appropriate formulation also has implications for how easily a model is solved (issue 4).

We begin our discussion with how to choose a formulation which is small and thus more easily solved (usually).

The computational difficulty of an LP is closely related to three features of the LP: the number of rows, the number of columns, and the number of nonzeroes in the constraint matrix. For linear programs, the computation time tends to increase with the square of the number of nonzeroes. Thus, there is some motivation to (re)formulate LP models so that they are small in the above mentioned three dimensions.

A number of commercial LP solvers have built-in commands with names like REDUCE, which will mechanically do simple kinds of algebraic substitutions and eliminations necessary for reduction. Brearley, Mitra, and Williams (1975) give a thorough description of these reductions.

Reducing the Number of Rows and Columns: Reduction by Substitution

The standard method for reducing the number of rows and columns is to use a row (for simplicity we assume the last row) to solve for one of the columns (say the last one) and then use this row to substitute out the last variable in all the other rows. That, if there are currently m rows and n columns, write the last row as:

$$X_n = \sum_{j=1}^{n-1} a_{mj} X_j + a_{m0}$$

In rows 1 through $m - 1$, every occurence of X_n is replaced by the righthandside in the above equation. Now row m and column n can be dropped if (a) there are no implicit constraints, such as $X_n \geqq 0$ which might be violated as a result, and (b) X_n is not an integer variable. One should further note that this substitution, although it reduces the number of rows and columns by one, may increase the number of nonzeroes. Also, some parametric analyses may be invalidated by this substitution.

Frequently, the constraint on which the substitution is based starts out as an inequality constraint. The simplest example is a constraint of the form:

$$ay \leqq X$$

where the constant $a > 0$ and the variable $y \geqq 0$. In this case the constraint $X \geqq 0$ cannot be binding because the expression ay is always nonnegative. Adding a slack variable we have:

$$ay + s = X$$
$$y \geqq 0, s \geqq 0, X \geqq 0$$

Every occurrence of X in the model can be replaced by $ay + s$ and the constraint $ay + s = X$ can be dropped. Thus, the number of constraints is reduced by 1, at the expense of generating $k - 1$ additional nonzeroes, where k is the original number of nonzeroes in the X column.

Example

This reduction can be significant. Certain electrical distribution models (cf. Dutton, Hinman, and Millham [1974]) have essentially the following structure. Parameters (all $\geqq 0$) are: c_{ij}, d_{ij}, e_j, p_j, S_i, Q_i, a_{ij} and b_{ij}. The decision variables are: X_{ij} is the electrical energy supplied from i to j, and Y_{ij} is the peak power supplied from i to j.

$$\text{Minimize} \quad \sum_{i=1}^{m} \sum_{j=1}^{n} (c_{ij} X_{ij} + d_{ij} Y_{ij})$$

subject to   For each demand area $j = 1, 2, \ldots, n$:

Energy requirements:

$$\sum_i X_{ij} = e_j$$

Peak power requirements:

$$\sum_i Y_{ij} = p_j$$

For each supply station i, $i = 1, 2, \ldots, m$:

Energy availability:

$$\sum_i X_{ij} \leqq S_i$$

Peak power availability:

$$\sum_i Y_{ij} \leqq Q_i$$

For each shipment combination: $i = 1, 2, \ldots, m$ and $j = 1, 2, \ldots, n$: Peak power and energy must be loosely related:

$$a_{ij} Y_{ij} \leqq X_{ij}$$
$$X_{ij} \leqq b_{ij} Y_{ij}$$

$$X_{ij} \geq 0$$
$$Y_{ij} \geq 0$$

If there are 10 supply points and 100 demand areas, then this model has 2120 constraints. This is not prohibitive in size but it would be nice if it were smaller. What can we do to reduce the size? Introducing a slack variable s_{ij}, all occurences of X_{ij} can be replaced by $a_{ij}Y_{ij} + s_{ij}$. The explicit constraint $a_{ij}Y_{ij} \leq X_{ij}$ is replaced by $s_{ij} \geq 0$. The constraint $X_{ij} \leq b_{ij}$ becomes $a_{ij}Y_{ij} + s_{ij} \leq b_{ij}Y_{ij}$ or $s_{ij} \leq (b_{ij} - a_{ij})Y_{ij}$. Repeating the process by adding the slack variable U_{ij}, we have:

$$s_{ij} + U_{ij} = (b_{ij} - a_{ij})Y_{ij}$$

Now all occurrences of Y_{ij} can be replaced by:

$$s_{ij}/(b_{ij} - a_{ij}) + U_{ij}/(b_{ij} - a_{ij}).$$

When all substitutions are completed the new model is:

$$\text{Minimize} \quad \sum_{i=1}^{m} \sum_{j=1}^{n} \frac{(c_{ij}b_{ij} + d_{ij})}{(b_{ij} - a_{ij})} s_{ij} + \frac{(c_{ij}a_{ij} + d_{ij})}{(b_{ij} - a_{ij})} u_{ij}$$

subject to   For $j = 1, 2, \ldots, n$:
$$\sum_i (b_{ij}s_{ij} + a_{ij}u_{ij})/(b_{ij} - a_{ij}) = e_j$$
$$\sum_i (s_{ij} + u_{ij})/(b_{ij} - a_{ij}) = p_j$$
For $i = 1, 2, \ldots, m$:
$$\sum_j (b_{ij}s_{ij} + a_{ij}u_{ij})/(b_{ij} - a_{ij}) \leq S_i$$
$$\sum_j (s_{ij} + u_{ij})/(b_{ij} - a_{ij}) \leq Q_i$$
For $i = 1, 2, \ldots, m$ and $j = 1, 2, \ldots, n$:
$$0 \leq s_{ij}$$
$$0 \leq u_{ij}$$

The non-negativity constraints are not carried explicitly.

The original formulation has $2n + 2m + 2mn$ explicit constraints while the new formulation has $2n + 2m$ explicit constraints. For example, if $m = 10$ and $n = 20$, then the original formulation has 460 constraints while the new formulation has 60 constraints. The latter is small enough to be solved on a small personal computer.

Reduction by Aggregation

We say that we aggregate a set of variables if we replace a set of variables by a single variable. We aggregate a set of constraints if we replace a set of constraints by a single constraint. If we do aggregation we must resolve several issues:

1. After solving the LP there must be a postprocessing/disaggregation phase to deduce the disaggregate values from the aggregate values.
2. If row aggregation was performed, the solution to the aggregate problem may not be feasible to the true disaggregate problem.

3. If variable aggregation was performed, the solution to the aggregate problem may not be optimal to the true disaggregate problem.

To illustrate (2), consider the LP:

Maximize $2x + y$
subject to $x \leq 1$
$y \leq 1$
$x, y \geq 0$

The optimal solution is $x = y = 1$; with objective value equal to 3. We could aggregate the rows to get:

Maximize $2x + y$
subject to $x + y \leq 2$
$x, y \geq 0$

The optimal solution to this aggregate problem is $x = 2, y = 0$; with objective value equal to 4. This solution, however, is not feasible to the original problem.

To illustrate (3), consider the LP:

Minimize $x_1 + x_2$
subject to $x_1 \geq 2$
$x_2 \geq 1$
$x_1, x_2 \geq 0$

The optimal solution is $x_1 = 2, x_2 = 1$; with objective value equal to 3. We could aggregate variables to get the LP:

Minimize $2x$
subject to $x \geq 2$
$x \geq 1$
$x \geq 0$

The optimal solution to the aggregate problem is $x = 2$; with objective value equal to 4. This solution is, however, not optimal for the original, disaggregate LP.

Example: The Room Scheduling Problem

We will illustrate both variable and constraint aggregation with a problem that confronts any large hotel which has extensive conference facilities for business meetings. The hotel has r conference rooms available for various sizes. Over the next t time periods, e.g., days, the hotel must schedule g groups of people into these rooms. Each group has a hard requirement for a room of at least a certain size. Each group may also have a preference of certain time periods over others. Each group requires a room for exactly one time period. The obvious formulation is:

V_{gtr} = value of assigning group g to time period t in room r. This value is provided by group g, presumable as a ranking. The decision variables are:

$X_{gtr} = 1$ if group g is assigned to room r in time period t. This variable is defined for each group g, each time period t, and each room r which is big enough to accommodate group g.

$\qquad = 0$ otherwise.

The constraints are:

$$\sum_t \sum_r x_{gtr} = 1, \qquad \text{for each group } g$$
$$\sum_g x_{gtr} \leq 1, \qquad \text{for each room } r, \text{ time period } t$$
$$x_{gtr} = 0 \quad \text{or} \quad 1, \qquad \text{for all } g, t, \text{ and } r$$

The objective is:

$$\text{Maximize} \quad \sum_g \sum_t \sum_r V_{gtr} x_{gtr}$$

The number of constraints in this problem is $g + r \times t$. The number of variables is approximately $g \times t \times r/2$. The $r/2$ is based on the assumption that for a typical group, about one half of the rooms will be big enough.

A typical problem instance might have $g = 250$, $t = 10$, and $r = 30$. Such a problem would have 550 constraints and about 37,500 variables. A problem of that size is nontrivial to solve, so we might wish to work with a smaller formulation.

Aggregation of variables can be used validly if a group is indifferent between rooms b and c, as long as both rooms b and c are large enough to accommodate the group. In terms of our notation, $V_{gtb} = V_{gtc}$ for every g and t if both rooms b and c are large enough for g. More generally, two variables can be aggregated if in each row of the LP they have the same coefficients. Two constraints in an LP can be validly agggregated if in each variable they have the same coefficients. We will do constraint aggregation by aggregating together all rooms of the same size. This aggregation process is representative of a fundamental modeling principle: when it comes to solving the model, *do not distinguish things that do not need distinguishing*.

The aggregate formulation can now be defined:

$K =$ number of distinct room sizes

$N_k =$ number of rooms of size k or larger

$S_k =$ the set of groups which require a room of size k or larger

$V_{gt} =$ value of assigning group g to time period t

$x_{gt} = 1$ if group g is assigned to a room in time period t

$\qquad = 0$ otherwise

The constraints are:

$$\sum_t x_{gt} = 1, \qquad \text{for each group } g$$
$$\sum_{g \in S_k} x_{gt} \leq N_k, \qquad \text{for each room size } k.$$

The objective is

$$\text{Maximize} \quad \sum_g \sum_t V_{gt} x_{gt}$$

This formulation will have $g + k \times t$ constraints and $g \times t$ decision variables. For the case $g = 250$, $t = 10$, and $r = 30$, we might have $k = 4$. Thus, the aggregate formulation would have 290 constraints and 2500 variables, compared with 550 constraints and 37500 variables for the disaggregate formulation.

The post processing required to extract a disaggregate solution from an aggregate solution to our room scheduling problem is straightforward. For each time period, the groups assigned to that time period are ranked from largest to smallest. The largest group is assigned to the largest room, the second largest group to the second largest room, etc. Such an assignment will always be feasible as well as optimal to the original problem.

Example 2: Reducing Rows by Adding Additional Variables

If two parties, A and B, in a financial agreement want the agreement to be treated as a lease for tax purposes, the payment schedule typically must satisfy certain conditions specified by the taxing agency. Suppose that P_i is the payment that A is scheduled to make to B in month i of a seven year agreement. Parties A and B want to choose at the outset a set of P_j's that satisfy a tax regulation that no payment in any given month can be less than two thirds of the payment in any earlier month. If there are T periods, the most obvious way of writing these constraints is:

For $i = 2, T$:
    For $j = 1, i - 1$:
        $P_i \geqq 0.66666 P_j$

This would require $T(T - 1)/2$ constraints. A less obvious approach would be to define PM_i as the largest payment occurring any period before i. The requirement could be enforced with:

$PM_1 = 0$

For $i = 2$ to T:
    $P_i \geqq 0.66666 PM_i$
    $PM_i \geqq PM_{i-1}$
    $PM_i \geqq P_{i-1}$.

This would require $3T$ constraints rather than $T(T - 1)/2$. For $T = 84$ the difference is between 3486 constraints and 252.

Reducing the Number of Nonzeroes

If a certain linear expression is used more than once in a model, you may be able to reduce the number of nonzeroes by substituting it out. For example, consider the two sided constraints which are frequently encountered in metal blending models:

$$L_i \leqq \frac{\sum_j q_{ij} X_j}{\sum_j X_j} \leqq U_i \quad \text{for each quality characteristic } i.$$

In these situations L_k and U_k are lower and upper limits on the ith quality requirement, and q_{ij} is the quality of ingredient j with respect to the ith quality. The "obvious" way of writing this constraint in linear form is:

$$\sum_j (q_{ij} - L_i) X_j \geqq 0,$$
$$\sum_j (q_{ij} - U_k) X_j \leqq 0.$$

By introducing a batch size variable B and a slack variable s_i, things can be rewritten:

$$B - \sum_j X_j = 0$$
$$\sum_j q_{ij} X_j + s_i = U_i \times B$$
$$s_i \leq (U_k - L_i) \times B.$$

If there are m qualities and n ingredients, the original formulation had $2 \times m \times n$ nonzeroes. The modified formulation has $n + 1 + m \times (n + 2) + m \times 2 = n + 1 + m \times (n + 4)$ nonzeroes. For large n, the modified formulation has approximately 50% fewer nonzeroes.

Reducing the Number of Nonzeroes in Covering Problems

A common feature in some covering and some multiperiod financial planning models is that each column will have the same coefficient, e.g., $+1$, in a large number of rows. A simple transformation may substantially reduce the number of nonzeroes in the model. Suppose that row i is written:

$$\sum_{j=1}^{n} a_{ij} X_j = a_{i0}.$$

Now suppose we subtract row $i - 1$ from row i, so that row i becomes:

$$\sum_{j=1}^{n} (a_{ij} - a_{i-1,j}) X_j = a_{i0} - a_{i-1,0}.$$

If $a_{ij} = a_{i-1,j} \neq$ for most j, then the number of nonzeroes in row i is substantially reduced.

Example

Suppose that we must staff a facility around the clock with people who work eight hour shifts. A shift can start at the beginning of any hour of the day. If r_i is the number of people required to be on duty from hour i to hour $i + 1$, X_i is the number of people starting a shift at the beginning of hour i, and s_i is the surplus variable for hour i, then the constraints are:

$$X_1 + X_{18} + X_{19} + X_{20} + X_{21} + X_{22} + X_{23} + X_{24} - s_1 = r_1$$
$$X_1 + X_2 + X_{19} + X_{20} + X_{21} + X_{22} + X_{23} + X_{24} - s_2 = r_2$$
$$X_1 + X_2 + X_3 \phantom{+ X_{18}} + X_{20} + X_{21} + X_{22} + X_{23} + X_{24} - s_3 = r_3$$

Suppose we subtract row 23 from row 24, row 22 from row 23, etc. The above constraints will be tranformed to:

$$X_1 + X_{18} + X_{19} + X_{20} + X_{21} + X_{22} + X_{23} + X_{24} - s_1 = r_1$$
$$ X_2 - X_{18} \phantom{+ X_{19} + X_{20} + X_{21} + X_{22} + X_{23} + X_{24}} + s_1 - s_2 = r_2 - r_1$$
$$X_1 \phantom{+ X_2 + X_3 + X_{18}} - X_{19} \phantom{+ X_{20} + X_{21} + X_{22} + X_{23} + X_{24}} + s_2 - s_3 = r_3 - r_2$$

Thus, a typical constraint will have four nonzeroes rather than 9.

The pattern of nonzeroes for the X variables in the original formulation is shown in Figure 16.1. The pattern of the nonzeroes for the X variables in the transformed formulation

Figure 16.1

Nonzero Pattern for X Variables in Original Formulation

X variables

		1 2	3 4	5 6	7 8	9 10	11 12	13 14	15 16	17 18	19 20	21 22	23 24
	1	+								+	+ +	+ +	+ +
	2	+ +									+ +	+ +	+ +
	3	+ +	+								+	+ +	+ +
	4	+ +	+ +									+ +	+ +
	5	+ +	+ +	+								+	+ +
	6	+ +	+ +	+ +									+ +
	7	+ +	+ +	+ +	+								+
	8	+ +	+ +	+ +	+ +								
	9	+	+ +	+ +	+ +	+							
	10		+ +	+ +	+ +	+ +							
Rows	11		+	+ +	+ +	+ +	+						
	12			+ +	+ +	+ +	+ +						
	13			+	+ +	+ +	+ +	+					
	14				+ +	+ +	+ +	+ +					
	15				+	+ +	+ +	+ +	+				
	16					+ +	+ +	+ +	+ +				
	17					+	+ +	+ +	+ +	+			
	18						+ +	+ +	+ +	+ +			
	19						+	+ +	+ +	+ +	+		
	20							+ +	+ +	+ +	+ +		
	21							+	+ +	+ +	+ +	+	
	22								+ +	+ +	+ +	+ +	
	23								+	+ +	+ +	+ +	+
	24									+ +	+ +	+ +	+ +

is shown in Figure 16.2. The total constraint nonzeroes for X and s variables in the original formulation is 216. The analogous count for the transformed formulation is 101, a very attractive reduction.

Matrix Generators

In large LPs it is impractical to manually enter all the coefficients of the LP. In these situations one writes an auxiliary computer program called a matrix generator. This program reads the problem description in an arbitrary format from either a file or the user's terminal and then generates the corresponding LP formulation.

There are two approaches to writing the matrix generator program: (1) use a general purpose programming language such as FORTRAN or PL/1 or (2) use a special purpose language designed expressly for generating LP formulations. These special purpose languages are frequently available from vendors of LP optimization packages.

Figure 16.2
Nonzero Pattern for X Variables in Transformed Formulation

	1 2	3 4	5 6	7 8	9 10	11 12	13 14	15 16	17 18	19 20	21 22	23 24
1	+								+	+ +	+ +	+ +
2	+								−			
3		+							−			
4		+								−		
5			+								−	
6			+									−
7				+							−	
8				+								−
9	−				+							
10	−				+							
11		−				+						
12		−				+						
13			−				+					
14			−				+					
15				−				+				
16				−				+				
17					−				+			
18					−				+			
19						−				+		
20						−				+		
21							−				+	
22							−				+	
23								−				+
24								−				+

On-the-Fly Column Generation

There are a number of generic LP models which have a modest number of rows, e.g., a hundred or so, but a large number of columns, e.g., a million or so. This is frequently the case in cutting stock problems. This could also be the case in staffing problems, where there might be many thousands of different work patterns that people could work. Explicitly generating all these columns is not a task taken lightly. An alternative approach is motivated by the observation that at an optimum there will be no more positive columns than there are rows.

The basic idea is described by the following iterative process.

1. Generate and solve an initial LP which has all the rows of the full model defined but only a small number (perhaps even zero) of the columns explicitly specified.

2. Given the dual prices of the current solution, generate one or more columns which price out attractively. That is, if a_{0j} is the cost of column j, a_{ij} is its

usage of resource i, i.e., its coefficient in rows i for $i = 1, \ldots, m$, and p_i is the dual price of row i, then generate or find a new column j such that $a_{0j} + p_{1j}a_{ij} + p_2 a_{2j} + \cdots + p_m a_{mj} < 0$. If no such column exists, then stop.

3. Solve the LP with the new column(s) from (2) added.
4. Go to (2).

The crucial step is (2). To use column generation for a specific problem you must be able to solve the column generation subproblem in (2). In mathematical programming form the subproblem in (2) is:

Given $\{p_j\}$, solve

Minimize $a_{0j} + p_1 a_{1j} + p_2 a_{2j} + \cdots + p_m a_{mj}$

subject to the a_{ij} satisfy the conditions defining a valid column.

Example of Column Generation Applied to a Cutting Stock Problem

A common problem encountered in flat goods industries such as paper, textiles and steel, is the cutting of large pieces of raw material into smaller pieces needed for producing a finished product. Suppose that raw material comes in 72-inch widths and it must be cut up into eight different finished good widths described by the following table.

Product	Width in Inches	Linear Feet Required
1	60	500
2	56	400
3	42	300
4	38	450
5	34	350
6	24	100
7	15	800
8	10	1000

We start the process somewhat arbitrarily by defining the eight pure cutting patterns. A pure pattern produces only one type of finished good width. Let P_i = number of feet raw material to cut according to the pattern i. We want to minimize the total number of feet cut. The LP with these patterns is

```
MIN     P001 + P002 + P003 + P004 + P005 + P006 + P007 + P008
SUBJECT TO
    2)      P001 ≥  500         ! 60 inch width
    3)      P002 ≥  400         ! 56 inch width
    4)      P003 ≥  300         ! 42 inch width
    5)      P004 ≥  450         ! 38 inch width
    6)    2 P005 ≥  350         ! 34 inch width
    7)    3 P006 ≥  100         ! 24 inch width
    8)    4 P007 ≥  800         ! 15 inch width
    9)    7 P008 ≥ 1000         ! 10 inch width
END
```

The solution is

```
            OBJECTIVE FUNCTION VALUE

    1)          2201.19000

  VARIABLE       VALUE         REDUCED COST
    P001        500.000000        .000000
    P002        400.000000        .000000
    P003        300.000000        .000000
    P004        450.000000        .000000
    P005        175.000000        .000000
    P006         33.333330        .000000
    P007        200.000000        .000000
    P008        142.857100        .000000

    ROW      SLACK OR SURPLUS   DUAL PRICES
    2)           .000000        -1.000000
    3)           .000000        -1.000000
    4)           .000000        -1.000000
    5)           .000000        -1.000000
    6)           .000000         -.500000
    7)           .000000         -.333333
    8)           .000000         -.250000
    9)           .000000         -.142857
```

The dual prices provide information about which finish goods are currently expensive to produce. A new pattern to add to the problem can be found by solving the problem:

Minimize $1 - y_1 - y_2 - y_3 - y_4 - 0.5y_5 - 0.333333y_6 - 0.25y_7 - 0.142857y_8$

subject to $60y_1 + 56y_2 + 42y_3 + 38y_4 + 34y_5 + 24y_6 + 15y_7 + 10y_8 \leq 72$

$y_i = 0, 1, 2, \ldots$ for $i = 1, \ldots, 8$.

Note that the objective can be rewritten as

Maximize $y_1 + y_2 + y_3 + y_4 + 0.5y_5 + 0.333333y_6 + 25y_7 + 0.142857y_8$.

This is a knapsack problem. Although knapsack problems are theoretically difficult to solve, there are algorithms which are quite efficient on typical practical knapsack problems. An optimal solution to this knapsack problem is $y_4 = 1$, $y_7 = 2$, i.e., a pattern which cuts one 38-inch width and two 15-inch widths. When this column, P009, is added to the LP we get the formulation (in PICTURE form):

```
    P P P P P P P P P
    0 0 0 0 0 0 0 0 0
    0 0 0 0 0 0 0 0 0
    1 2 3 4 5 6 7 8 9
 1: 1 1 1 1 1 1 1 1 1 MIN
 2: 1 ' ' ' ' ' ' ' '  > C
 3: ' 1' ' ' ' ' ' ' '  > C
 4:     1 ' ' ' ' '    > C
 5:       1   '   1    > C
 6: ' '  ' 2' ' '       > C
 7:        3 '          > B
 8:         ' 4   2     > C
 9: ' ' ' ' ' 7'        > C
```

The solution is

OBJECTIVE FUNCTION VALUE

1)   2201.19000

VARIABLE	VALUE	REDUCED COST
P001	500.000000	.000000
P002	400.000000	.000000
P003	300.000000	.000000
P004	50.000000	.000000
P005	175.000000	.000000
P006	33.333330	.000000
P007	.000000	1.000000
P008	142.857100	.000000
P009	400.000000	.000000

ROW	SLACK OR SURPLUS	DUAL PRICES
2)	.000000	−1.000000
3)	.000000	−1.000000
4)	.000000	−1.000000
5)	.000000	−1.000000
6)	.000000	−.500000
7)	.000000	−.333333
8)	.000000	−.000000
9)	.000000	−.142857

The column generation subproblem is

Minimize $y_1 + y_2 + y_3 + y_4 + .5y_5 + 0.333333y_6 + 0.142857y_8$

subject to $60y_1 + 56y_2 + 42y_3 + 38y_4 + 34y_5 + 24y_6 + 15y_7 + 10y_8 \leq 72$

$y_i = 0, 1, 2, \ldots$ for $i = 1, 2, \ldots, 8.$

An optimal solution to this knapsack problem is $y_4 = 1$, $y_5 = 1$, i.e., a pattern which cuts one 38-inch width and one 34-inch width.

We continue generating and adding patterns for a total of eight iterations. At this point the LP formulation is:

```
    P P P P P P P P P P P P P P
    0 0 0 0 0 0 0 0 0 0 0 0 0 0
    0 0 0 0 0 0 0 0 1 1 1 1 1 1
    1 2 3 4 5 6 7 8 9 0 1 2 3 4 5
1:  1 1 1 1 1 1 1 1 1 1 1 1 1 1  MIN
2:  1               '       1  > C
3:  ' 1'      '  '  '  '1 '  ' > C
4:       1 '       '  ' 1  '1   > C
5:         1  '  1 1    1       > C
6:  '  '  ' 2' '  ' 1  '  '  '  > C
7:           '  3 '     '   1   > B
8:           '    4  2 ' 2 1 '  > C
9:  '  '  '  '  ' 7' '  ' 1 3'1 > C
```

The solution is:

OBJECTIVE FUNCTION VALUE

1)   1664.28600

```
VARIABLE          VALUE              REDUCED COST
P001              .000000            .142857
P002              .000000            .214285
P003              .000000            .428571
P004              .000000            .476191
P005              .000000            .047619
P006              .000000            .000000
P007              .000000            .142857
P008            14.285710            .000000
P009              .000000            .047619
P010           350.000000            .000000
P011           200.000000            .000000
P012           400.000000            .000000
P013           100.000000            .000000
P014           100.000000            .000000
P015           500.000000            .000000

  ROW         SLACK OR SURPLUS       DUAL PRICES
   2)             .000000             -.857143
   3)             .000000             -.785714
   4)             .000000             -.571429
   5)             .000000             -.523809
   6)             .000000             -.476191
   7)             .000000             -.333333
   8)             .000000             -.214285
   9)             .000000             -.142857
```

The relevant knapsack problem is:

$$\text{Maximize} \quad 0.857143y_1 + 0.785714y_2 + 0.571429y_3 + 0.523809y_4$$
$$+ 0.476191y_5 + 0.333333y_6 + 0.214285y_7 + 0.142857y_8$$
$$\text{subject to} \quad 60y_1 + 56y_2 + 42y_3 + 38y_4 + 34y_5 + 24y_6 + 15y_7 + 10y_8 \leq 72$$
$$y_i = 0, 1, 2, \ldots \quad \text{for} \quad i = 1, 2, \ldots, 8.$$

The optimal solution to the knapsack problem has an objective function value less than or equal one. Because each column when added to the LP has a "cost" of one in the LP objective, when the proposed column is priced out with the current dual prices it is unattractive to enter. Thus, the previous LP solution specifies the optimal amount to run of all possible patterns. There are in fact 29 different efficient patterns possible, where efficient means the edge waste is less than 10." Thus, the column generation approach allowed us to avoid generating the majority of the patterns.

If an integer solution is required then a simple rounding up heuristic tends to work moderately well. In our example we know that the optimal integer solution costs at least 1665. By rounding P008 up to 15 we obtain a solution with cost 1665.

Column Generation and Integer Programming

Column generation can be used to easily find an optimum solution to an LP. This is not quite true with IP's. The problem is that with an IP there is no simple equivalent to dual prices. Dual prices may be printed in an IP solution but they have an extremely limited interpretation. For example, it may be that all dual prices are 0 in an IP solution.

Thus, the usual approach when column generation is used to attack IP's is to use column generation only to solve the LP relaxation. A standard IP algorithm is then applied to the problem comprised of only the columns generated during the LP. It may be, however, that a true IP optimum includes one or more columns which were not generated during the LP phase. The LP solution nevertheless provides a bound on the optimum LP solution. In our previous cutting stock example this bound was tight.

There is a fine point to be made with regard to the stopping rule. We stop, *not* when the previous column added led to no improvement in the LP solution, but rather when the latest column generated prices out unattractively.

Row Generation

An analogous approach can be used if the problem intrinsically has many thousands of constraints even though only a few of them will be binding. The basic approach is

1. Generate some of the constraints.
2. Solve the problem with the existing constraints.
3. Find a constraint that has not been generated but is violated. If none, we are done.
4. Add the violated constraint and go to (2).

17

Multiple Criteria & Goal Programming

Introduction

Until now we have assumed a single objective or criterion. In reality, however, there may be two or more measures of goodness. Our life becomes more difficult, or at least more interesting, if these multiple criteria are incommensurate, *i.e.*, it is difficult to combine them into a single criterion. The overused phrase used in lamenting the difficulty of such situations is that "You can't mix apples and oranges."

Some examples of incommensurate criteria are:

- risk vs. return on investment,
- short term profits vs. long term growth of a firm,
- cost vs. service by a government agency,
- the treatment of different individuals under some policy of an administrative agency, e.g., rural vs. urban citizens, residents near an airport vs. travelers using an airport, fisherman vs. water transportation companies vs. farmers using irrigation near a large lake.

Multi-criteria situations can be classified into several categories.

1. Criteria are intrinsically different (e.g. risk vs. return, cost vs. service),
   (a) Weights or trade-off rates can be determined,
   (b) Criteria can be strictly ordered by importance. We have so-called pre-emptive objectives.
2. Criteria are intrinsically similar, i.e., in some sense they should have equal weight.

Alternate Optima and Multicriteria

If you have a model with alternate optimal solutions, this is nature's way of telling you that you have multiple criteria. You should probably look at your objective function more closely and add more detail. Users do not like alternate optima. If there are alternate optima, the solution method will usually choose among them essentially randomly. If people's jobs or salaries depend upon the "flip of a coin" in your analysis they are going to be unhappy. Even if careers are not at stake, alternate optima are at least a nuisance. People find it disconcerting if they get different answers (albeit with the same objective value) when they solve the same problem on different computers.

One resolution of alternate optima that might occur to some readers is to take the average of all distinct alternate optima produced by the simplex method and use it as the final, unique, well defined answer. Unfortunately, this is usually not practical because:

(a) it may be difficult to enumerate all alternate optima, and

(b) the average solution may be unattractive or even infeasible because the answer may involve fractional values.

Approaches to Multicriteria Problems

Pareto Optimal Solutions and Multiple Criteria

A solution to a multi-criteria problem is said to be *Pareto optimal* if there is no other solution which is at least as good according to all criteria and strictly better according to at least one criterion. A Pareto optimal solution is not dominated by any other solution. Clearly we want to consider only Pareto optimal solutions. If we do not choose our criteria carefully we might find ourselves recommending solutions that are not Pareto optimal. There are computer programs for multicriteria linear programming that will generate all the undominated extreme solutions. For a small problem a decisionmaker could simply choose the most attractive extreme solution based on subjective criteria. For large problems the number of undominated extreme solutions may easily exceed 100 and so this approach may be overwhelming.

Utility Function Approach

A solution of the multicriterion problem that is superficially attractive is the definition of a utility function. If the decision variables are $x_1, x_2, \ldots, x_n$ we "simply" construct the utility function $u(x_1, x_2, \ldots, x_n)$ which computes the value or utility of any possible combination of values for the vector $x_1, x_2, \ldots, x_n$. This is a very useful approach for *thinking* about optimization but it has several practical limitations: (a) it may take a lot of work to construct it and (b) it will probably be highly nonlinear. Feature (b) means that we probably cannot use LP to solve the problem.

Trade-Off Curves

If we have only two or three criteria then the trade-off curve approach has most of the attractive features of the utility function approach but is also fairly practical. We simply construct a curve, the so-called "efficient frontier," which shows how we can trade-off one criterion for another. One of the most well known settings in which a trade-off curve

Figure 17.1

Trade-Off Curve for Risk and Return

is used is to describe the relationship between two criteria is in a financial portfolio. The two criteria are expected return on investment and risk. We want return to be high and risk to be low. Figure 17.1 shows the typical relationship between risk and return. Each point on the curve is Pareto optimal. That is, for any point on the curve there is no other point with higher expected return and lower risk.

Even though a decisionmaker has not gone through the trouble of constructing his utility function, he may be able to look at this trade-off curve and perhaps say: "Gee, I am comfortable with an expected return of 8% with standard deviation of 3%."

Example: Advertising Media Selection

The number of exposures obtained in each of seven markets per dollar of advertising in each of five media is given in the table below. In the first row below the table is listed a minimum required number of exposures in each of the seven markets. The feeling is that we must reach this minimum number of readers/viewers, regardless of the cost. The second row of numbers is the saturation level for each market. The feeling is that exposures beyond this level are of no value. Exposures between these two limits will be termed useful exposures.

Exposure Statistics for Ad Lib Marketing

	Exposure in 1000's per $1000 Spent						
	Market Group						
	1	2	3	4	5	6	7
Times		10	4	50	5		2
Mirror		10	30	5	12		
Tribune	20				5	3	
Herald	8				6	10	
Post		6	5	10	11	4	
Minimum Number of Exposures needed in 1,000's	25	40	60	120	40	11	15
Saturation Level in 1,000's of Exposures	60	70	120	140	80	25	55

How much money should be spent on advertising in each medium? There are really two criteria: (a) cost, (which we want to be low) and (b) useful exposures (which we want to be high). At the outset we arbitrarily decided that we will spend no more than $11,000.

A useful model can be formulated if we define:

Decision variables:

$\quad$ TIMES, MIRROR, etc. = dollars spent in 1,000's on advertising in the *Times*, *Mirror*, etc.;

$\quad$ UX1, UX2, etc. = number of useful excess exposures obtained in market 1, 2, etc., beyond the minimum, i.e., min {saturation level, actual exposures} − minimum required;

$\quad$ COST = total amount spent on advertising,

$\quad$ USEFULX = total useful exposures.

There will be two main sets of constraints, one set which says:

$\quad$ exposures in a market $\geq$ minimum required + useful excess exposure beyond minimum

The other saying:

$\quad$ useful excess exposures in a market $\leq$ saturation level − minimum required.

The explicit formulation is:

```
MAX       USEFULX              ! Maximize useful exposures;
SUBJECT TO
  LIMCOST)   COST ≤ 11          ! With a limit of 11 (in $1,000) on cost;
  LIMEXP)    USEFULX ≥ 0
  DEFCOST)  - COST + TIMES + MIRROR + TRIBUNE + HERALD + POST = 0
  DEFEXP)   - USEFULX + UX1 + UX2 + UX3 + UX4 + UX5 + UX6 + UX7 = 0
  MKT1)     20 TRIBUNE + 8 HERALD - UX1 ≥ 25
  MKT2)     10 TIMES + 10 MIRROR + 6 POST - UX2 ≥ 40
  MKT3)     4 TIMES + 30 MIRROR + 5 POST - UX3 ≥ 60
  MKT4)     50 TIMES + 5 MIRROR + 10 POST - UX4 ≥ 120
  MKT5)     5 TIMES + 12 MIRROR + 11 POST - UX5 ≥ 40
  MKT6)     5 TRIBUNE + 6 HERALD + 4 POST - UX6 ≥ 11
  MKT7)     2 TIMES + 3 TRIBUNE + 10 HERALD - UX7 ≥ 15
  RANGE1)   UX1 ≤ 35
  RANGE2)   UX2 ≤ 30
  RANGE3)   UX3 ≤ 60
  RANGE4)   UX4 ≤ 20
  RANGE5)   UX5 ≤ 40
  RANGE6)   UX6 ≤ 14
  RANGE7)   UX7 ≤ 40
END
```

The following is part of the solution to this model.

$\quad\quad\quad$ OBJECTIVE FUNCTION VALUE

$\quad\quad$ 1)$\quad\quad$ 196.762600

VARIABLE	VALUE	REDUCED COST
USEFULX	196.762600	.000000
COST	11.000000	.000000
TIMES	1.997602	.000000
MIRROR	3.707434	.000000
TRIBUNE	2.908873	.000000
HERALD	.227818	.000000
POST	2.158273	.000000
UX1	35.000000	.000000
UX2	30.000000	.000000
UX3	60.000000	.000000
UX4	20.000000	.000000
UX5	38.218220	.000000
UX6	13.544360	.000000
UX7	.000000	.007194

ROW	SLACK OR SURPLUS	DUAL PRICES
LIMCOST)	.000000	21.438850
LIMEXP)	196.762600	.000000
DEFCOST)	.000000	21.438850
DEFEXP)	.000000	−1.000000

Notice that we advertise up to the saturation level in markets 1 to 4. In market 7 we advertise just enough to achieve the minimum required.

If you change the cost limit (initially at 11) to various values ranging from 6 to 14, and plot the maximum possible number of useful exposures, you get a tradeoff curve, or efficient frontier like that shown in the Figure 17.2.

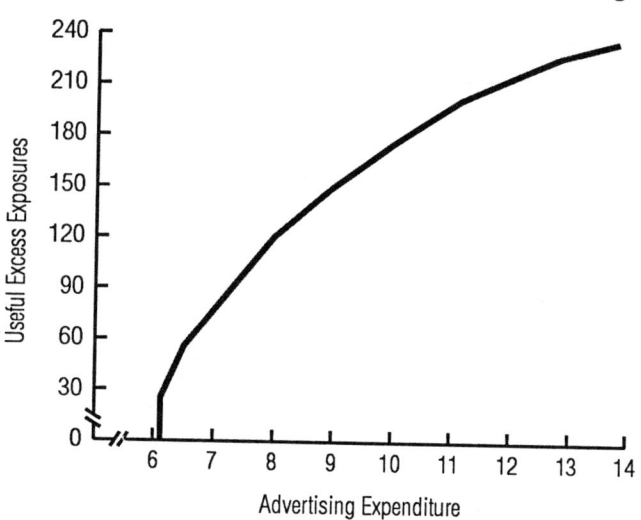

Figure 17.2

Useful Excess Exposures vs. Advertising

Goal Programming and Soft Constraints

Goal Programming is closely related to the concept of multicriteria as well as a simple idea that we dub "soft constraints." Soft constraints and Goal Programming are a response to the following two "laws of the real world":

In the real world,

1. there is always a feasible solution,
2. there are no alternate optima.

In practical terms (1) means that a good manager (or one wishing to at least keep a job) never throws up his or her hands in despair and says "no feasible solution." Law (2) means that a typical decisionmaker will never be indifferent between two proposed courses of action. There are always sufficient criteria to distinguish some course of action as better than all others.

From a model perspective these two laws mean that a well formulated model (a) always has a feasible solution and (b) does not have alternate optima.

Example: Secondary Criterion to Choose Among Alternate Optima

Here is a standard, seven day/week staffing problem similar to that discussed in Chapter 6.

```
MIN      9 M + 9 T + 9 W + 9 R + 9 F + 9 S + 9 N
SUBJECT TO
    MON)  M         + R + F + S + N ≥ 3
    TUE)  M + T         + F + S + N ≥ 3
    WED)  M + T + W         + S + N ≥ 8
    THU)  M + T + W + R         + N ≥ 8
    FRI)  M + T + W + R + F         ≥ 8
    SAT)      T + W + R + F + S     ≥ 3
    SUN)          W + R + F + S + N ≥ 3
END
```

When solved we get the following solution.

```
            OBJECTIVE FUNCTION VALUE

     1)       72.0000000

  VARIABLE        VALUE          REDUCED COST
     M          3.000000          0.000000
     T          0.000000          0.000000
     W          5.000000          0.000000
     R          0.000000          9.000000
     F          0.000000          9.000000
     S          0.000000          0.000000
     N          0.000000          0.000000

    ROW     SLACK OR SURPLUS     DUAL PRICES
    MON)       0.000000           0.000000
    TUE)       0.000000           0.000000
    WED)       0.000000          -9.000000
    THU)       0.000000           0.000000
    FRI)       0.000000           0.000000
    SAT)       2.000000           0.000000
    SUN)       2.000000           0.000000
```

Notice that there may be alternate optima, e.g., the zero slack and zero dual price in row "MON." This solution puts all the surplus capacity on Saturday and Sunday. The different optima might distribute the surplus capacity in different ways over the days of the week. Saturday and Sunday have a lot of excess capacity while the very similar days, Monday and Tuesday have no surplus capacity.

In terms of multiple criteria we might say:

(a) our most important criterion is to minimize total staffing cost.

(b) Your secondary criterion is to have a little extra capacity, specifically one unit, each day if it will not increase criterion 1.

To encourage more equitable distribution we add some "excess" variables, XM, XT, etc. which give a tiny credit of -1 for each surplus up to at most 1 on each day. The modified formulation is:

```
MIN      9 M + 9 T + 9 W + 9 R + 9 F + 9 S + 9 N
         - XM  - XT  - XW  - XR  - XF  - XS  - XN
SUBJECT TO
  MON)   M                 + R   + F   + S   + N   - XM ≥   3
  TUE)   M   + T                 + F   + S   + N   - XT ≥   3
  WED)   M   + T   + W                 + S   + N   - XW ≥   8
  THU)   M   + T   + W   + R                 + N   - XR ≥   8
  FRI)   M   + T   + W   + R   + F                 - XF ≥   8
  SAT)        T    + W   + R   + F   + S           - XS ≥   3
  SUN)             + W   + R   + F   + S   + N     - XN ≥   3
    9)   XM ≤  1
   10)   XT ≤  1
   11)   XW ≤  1
   12)   XR ≤  1
   13)   XF ≤  1
   14)   XS ≤  1
   15)   XN ≤  1
END
```

The solution now is:

```
          OBJECTIVE FUNCTION VALUE

   1)       68.000000

VARIABLE        VALUE           REDUCED COST
    M          4.000000             0.000000
    T          0.000000             0.000000
    W          4.000000             0.000000
    R          0.000000             4.000000
    F          0.000000             4.000000
    S          0.000000             0.000000
    N          0.000000             0.000000
   XM          1.000000             0.000000
   XT          1.000000             0.000000
   XW          0.000000             4.000000
   XR          0.000000             0.000000
   XF          0.000000             0.000000
   XS          1.000000             0.000000
   XN          1.000000             0.000000
```

Notice that just as before we still hire a total of eight people but now the surplus is evenly distributed over the four days M, T, S, and N. This should be a more attractive solution.

Minimizing the Maximum Hurt, or Unordered Lexico Minimization

There are some situations in which there are a number of parties that in some sense are equal. There may be certain side conditions, however, that prevent us from treating them exactly equal. An example is representation in a house of representatives. Ideally, we would like each state to have the number of representatives in a state be exactly proportional to the population of the state. The fact that the house of representatives is typically limited to a fixed size and that we cannot have fractional representatives (although some voters may feel they have encountered such an anomaly) we will find that some states have more citizens per representative than others.

In more general settings, an obvious approach for minimizing such inequities is to choose things so that we minimize the maximum inequity or "hurt." Once we have minimized the worst hurt, the obvious next thing is to minimize the second highest hurt, etc. Such a minimization we will refer to as Unordered Lexico Minimization. For example, if there are four parties and (10, 13, 8, 9) is the vector of taxes to be paid then we would say that the vector (13, 8, 9, 9) is better in the unordered lexico-min sense. The highest tax is the same for both solutions but the second highest tax is lower for the second solution.

Example

This example is based on one in Sankaran (1989). There are six parties and x_i is the assessment to be paid by party i to satisfy a certain community building project. The x_i must satisfy the set of constraints:

A) $X1 + 2\ X2 + 4\ X3 + 7\ X4 \geq 16$
B) $2.5\ X1 + 3.5\ X2 + 5.2\ X5 \geq 17.5$
C) $0.4\ X2 + 1.3\ X4 + 7.2\ X6 \geq 12$
D) $2.5\ X2 + 3.5\ X3 + 5.2\ X5 \geq 13.1$
E) $3.5\ X1 + 3.5\ X4 + 5.2\ X6 \geq 18.2$

The interested reader may try to improve upon the following set of assessments:

$X1 = 1.5625$
$X2 = 1.5625$
$X3 = .305357$
$X4 = 1.463362$
$X5 = 1.5625$
$X6 = 1.463362$

There is no other solution in which

- the highest assessment is less than 1.5625 and
- the second highest assessment is less than 1.5625 and
- the third highest assessment is less than 1.5625 and
- the fourth highest assessment is less than 1.463362, etc.

Finding the Unique Solution Minimizing the Maximum

A quite general approach to finding a unique unordered lexico minimum exists when the feasible region is convex, e.g., there are no integer variables. Let the vector $\{x_1, x_2, \ldots, x_n\}$ denote the cost allocated to each of n parties.

If the feasible region is convex, then there is a unique solution and the following algorithm will find it. Maschler, Peleg, and Shapley (1979) discuss this idea in the game theory setting. If the feasible region is not convex, e.g., the problem has integer variables, then the following method is not guaranteed to find the solution. Let S be the original set of constraints on the x's.

(1) Let $J = \{1, 2, \ldots n\}$, and $k = 0$;
(Note: J is the set of parties for whom we do not yet know the final x_i)

(2) Let $k = k + 1$;

(3) Solve the problem:

$$\text{Minimize } Z$$
$$\text{subject to } x \text{ feasible to } S \text{ and,}$$
$$Z \geq x_j \quad \text{for } j \text{ in } J;$$

(Note: this minimizes the maximum hurt among parties for which we have not yet fixed the x_j's.)

(4) Set $Z_k = Z$, of (3) and add to S the constraints:

$$x_j \leq Z_k \quad \text{for all } j \text{ in } J:$$

(5) Set $L = \{j \text{ in } J \text{ for which } x_j = Z_k \text{ in } (3)\}$; For each j in L, solve:

$$\text{Minimize } x_j$$
$$\text{subject to } x \text{ feasible to } S;$$

If $x_j = Z_k$, then set $J = J - j$, and append to S the constraint

$$x_j = Z_k$$

(6) If J is not empty, go to (2), else we are done.

To find the minimum maximum assessment for our example problem we solve the following problem:

```
MIN     Z
SUBJECT TO
 ! The physical constraints on the X's;
    A)      X1 + 2 X2 + 4 X3 + 7 X4 ≥ 16
    B)      2.5 X1 + 3.5 X2 + 5.2 X5 ≥ 17.5
    C)      0.4 X2 + 1.3 X4 + 7.2 X6 ≥ 12
    D)      2.5 X2 + 3.5 X3 + 5.2 X5 ≥ 13.1
    E)      3.5 X1 + 3.5 X4 + 5.2 X6 ≥ 18.2
 ! Constraints to compute the max hurt  Z;
    H1)     Z - X1 ≥ 0
    H2)     Z - X2 ≥ 0
    H3)     Z - X3 ≥ 0
```

```
       H4)      Z - X4 ≥ 0
       H5)      Z - X5 ≥ 0
       H6)      Z - X6 ≥ 0
   END
```

Its solution is:

```
             OBJECTIVE FUNCTION VALUE

       1)          1.56250000

   VARIABLE        VALUE           REDUCED COST
      Z           1.562500          0.000000
      X1          1.562500          0.000000
      X2          1.562500          0.000000
      X3          1.562500          0.000000
      X4          1.562500          0.000000
      X5          1.562500          0.000000
```

Thus, at least one party will have a "hurt" of 1.5625. Which party or parties will it be? Because all six x_i's equal 1.5625, we solve a series of six problems like the following:

```
   MIN   X1
   SUBJECT TO
   ! The physical constraints on the X's;
      A)     X1 + 2 X2 + 4 X3 + 7 X4 ≥ 16
      B)     2.5 X1 + 3.5 X2 + 5.2 X5 ≥ 17.5
      C)     0.4 X2 + 1.3 X4 + 7.2 X6 ≥ 12
      D)     2.5 X2 + 3.5 X3 + 5.2 X5 ≥ 13.1
      E)     3.5 X1 + 3.5 X4 + 5.2 X6 ≥ 18.2
   ! Constraints for finding the minmax hurt, Z;
      H1)    + X1 ≤ 1.5625
      H2)    + X2 ≤ 1.5625
      H3)    + X3 ≤ 1.5625
      H4)    + X4 ≤ 1.5625
      H5)    + X5 ≤ 1.5625
      H6)    + X6 ≤ 1.5625
   END
```

The solution for the case of X1 is:

```
             OBJECTIVE FUNCTION VALUE

       1)          1.56250000

   VARIABLE        VALUE           REDUCED COST
      X1          1.562500          .000000
      X2          1.562500          .000000
      X3          1.562500          .000000
      X4          1.562500          .000000
      X5          1.562500          .000000
      X6          1.562500          .000000
```

Thus, there is no solution with all the X_i's $\leq$ 1.5625 but with X1 strictly less than 1.5625. So we can fix X1 at 1.5625. Similar observations turn out to be true for X2 and X5.

So now we wish to solve the following problem:

```
MIN    Z
SUBJECT TO
  ! The physical constraints on the  X's;
    A)      X1 + 2 X2 + 4 X3 + 7 X4 ≥ 16
    B)      2.5 X1 + 3.5 X2 + 5.2 X5 ≥ 17.5
    C)      0.4 X2 + 1.3 X4 + 7.2 X6 ≥ 12
    D)      2.5 X2 + 3.5 X3 + 5.2 X5 ≥ 13.1
    E)      3.5 X1 + 3.5 X4 + 5.2 X6 ≥ 18.2
  ! Constraints for finding the minmax hurt, Z;
    H1)         X1 = 1.5625
    H2)         X2 = 1.5625
    H3)      - Z + X3 ≤ 0
    H4)      - Z + X4 ≤ 0
    H5)         X5 = 1.5625
    H6)      - Z + X6 ≤ 0
END
```

Upon solution we see that the second highest "hurt" is 1.463362:

```
        OBJECTIVE FUNCTION VALUE

   1)         1.46336200

 VARIABLE        VALUE           REDUCED COST
    Z           1.463362           .000000
    X1          1.562500           .000000
    X2          1.562500           .000000
    X3          1.463362           .000000
    X4          1.463362           .000000
    X5          1.562500           .000000
    X6          1.463362           .000000
```

Any or all of X3, X4 or X6 could be at this value in the final solution. Which ones? To find out, we solve the following kind of problem for X3, X4 and X6.

```
MIN    X3
SUBJECT TO
  ! The physical constraints on the  X's;
    A)      X1 + 2 X2 + 4 X3 + 7 X4 ≥ 16
    B)      2.5 X1 + 3.5 X2 + 5.2 X5 ≥ 17.5
    C)      0.4 X2 + 1.3 X4 + 7.2 X6 ≥ 12
    D)      2.5 X2 + 3.5 X3 + 5.2 X5 ≥ 13.1
    E)      3.5 X1 + 3.5 X4 + 5.2 X6 ≥ 18.2
  ! Constraints for finding the minmax hurt, Z;
    H1)      X1 = 1.5625
    H2)      X2 = 1.5625
    H3)      X3 ≤ 1.463362
    H4)      X4 ≤ 1.463362
    H5)      X5 = 1.5625
    H6)      X6 ≤ 1.463362
END
```

The solution when we minimize X3 is:

```
        OBJECTIVE FUNCTION VALUE

   1)          .305357300
```

VARIABLE	VALUE	REDUCED COST
X3	.305357	.000000
X1	1.562500	.000000
X2	1.562500	.000000
X4	1.463362	.000000
X5	1.562500	.000000
X6	1.463362	.000000

Thus, X3 need not be as high as 1.463362 in the final solution. We do find, however that X4 and X6 can be no smaller than 1.463362.

So the final problem we want to solve is:

```
MIN    Z
SUBJECT TO
 ! The physical constraints on the X's;
  A)      X1 + 2 X2 + 4 X3 + 7 X4   ≥ 16
  B)    2.5 X1 + 3.5 X2 + 5.2 X5    ≥ 17.5
  C)    0.4 X2 + 1.3 X4 + 7.2 X6    ≥ 12
  D)    2.5 X2 + 3.5 X3 + 5.2 X5    ≥ 13.1
  E)    3.5 X1 + 3.5 X4 + 5.2 X6    ≥ 18.2
 ! Constraints for finding the minmax hurt, Z;
  H1)     X1 = 1.5625
  H2)     X2 = 1.5625
  H3) - Z + X3 = 0
  H4)     X4 = 1.463362
  H5)     X5 = 1.5625
  H6)   + X6 = 1.463362
END
```

We already know that the solution will be:

OBJECTIVE FUNCTION VALUE

1)   .305357300

VARIABLE	VALUE	REDUCED COST
Z	.305357	.000000
X1	1.562500	.000000
X2	1.562500	.000000
X3	.305357	.000000
X4	1.463362	.000000
X5	1.562500	.000000
X6	1.463362	.000000

The above solution minimizes the maximum X value, as well as the number of X's at that value. Given that maximum value (of 1.5625), it minimizes the second highest X value, as well as the number at that value; etc.

The approach described requires us to solve a sequence of linear programs. It would be nice if we could formulate a single mathematical program for finding the unordered lexico-min. There are a number of such formulations; unfortunately all of them suffer from numerical problems when implemented on real computers. The formulations assume that arithmetic is done with infinite precision whereas most computers do arithmetic with at most 15 decimal digits of precision.

Comparing Performance with Data Envelope Analysis

Data Envelope Analysis (DEA) was originated by Charnes, Cooper, and Rhodes (1978) as a means of evaluating the performance of decisionmaking units. Examples of decisionmaking units might be hospitals, banks, airports, schools, and managers. For example, Bessent, Bessent, Kennington and Reagan (1982) used the approach to evaluate the performance of 167 schools around Houston, TX. This kind of problem is a multi-criteria problem in that we are concerned with the performance of a number of units. DEA seems most appropriate for units that deliver a multidimensional service.

Simple comparison can be misleading because different units are probably operating in different environments. For example, a school that is operating in a wealthy neighborhood will probably have higher test scores than a school in a poor neighborhood, even though the teachers in the poor school are working harder and require more skill than the teachers in the wealthy school. Also, different decisionmakers may have different skills. If the teachers in school (A) are well trained in science while those in school (B) are well trained in fine arts, then a scoring system that applies a lot of weight to science may make the teachers in (B) appear to be inferior, even though they are doing an outstanding job at what they do best.

DEA circumvents both difficulties in clever fashion. If the arts teachers were choosing the performance measures they would choose one that placed a lot of weight on arts, while the science teachers would probably choose a different one. DEA follows the philosophy of a popular fast food chain, that is, "Have it your way." DEA will derive an "efficiency" score between 0 and 1 for each unit by solving the following problem:

For each unit k:

    choose a scoring function

so as to:

    maximize   score of unit k

    subject to   for every unit j (including k):

        score$_j \leq 1$.

Thus, unit k may choose a scoring function that makes it look as good as possible subject to no other unit getting a score greater than 1 when that same scoring function is applied to the other unit. If a unit k gets a score of 1.0, it means there is no other unit strictly dominating k.

In the version of DEA we consider, the allowed scoring functions are limited to ratios of weighted outputs to weighted inputs, *i.e.*,

$$\text{score} = \frac{\text{weighted sum of outputs}}{\text{weighted sum of inputs}}.$$

We can normalize weights so

    weighted sum of inputs = 1,

then "score ≤ 1" is equivalent to:

    weighted sum of outputs $\leq$ weighted sum of inputs.

Algebraically, the DEA model is:

Given
$$n = \text{decisionmaking units,}$$
$$m = \text{number of inputs,}$$
$$s = \text{number of outputs,}$$

Observed data:
$$c_{ij} = \text{level of } j\text{th input for unit } i,$$
$$r_{ij} = \text{level of } j\text{th output for unit } i,$$

Variables in the model:
$$w_j = \text{weight applied to the } j\text{th input,}$$
$$v_j = \text{weight (or value) applied to the } j\text{th output.}$$

For unit k, the model to compute the best score is:

Maximize $\sum_{j=1}^{s} v_j r_{kj}$

subject to $\sum_{j=1}^{m} w_j c_{kj} = 1.$

For each unit i (including k):

$$\sum_{j=1}^{s} v_j r_{ij} \leq \sum_{j=1}^{m} w_j c_{ij}$$

This model will tend to have more constraints than decision variables, thus if implementation efficiency is a major concern, then one may wish to solve the dual of this model rather than the primal.

Problems

1. In the example staffing problem of this chapter, the primary criterion was minimizing the number of people hired. The secondary criterion was to spread out any excess capacity as much as possible. The primary criterion received a weight of 9 while the secondary criterion received a weight of 1. The minimum number of people required (primary criterion) was 8. How much could the weight on the secondary criterion be increased before the number of people hired increases to more than 8?

2. Reconsider the advertising media selection problem of this chapter.
   (a) Reformulate it so that we achieve at least 197 (in 1000s) useful exposures at minimum cost.
   (b) Predict the cost before looking at the solution.

3. A description of a "project crashing" decision appears on pages 102 and 103 of Chapter 7. In this case there are two criteria, project length and project cost. Trace out the efficient frontier describing the tradeoff between length and cost.

18

Parametric Analysis

Motivation for Parametric Analysis

The advantage and perhaps the major motivation for using "seat-of-the-pants" decision making is that it obscures the assumptions made in arriving at a decision. If no one knows the assumptions upon which you based your decision, then even though they may be uneasy with the decision they will have a difficult time criticizing your assumptions or decisions.

When a formal model is used in decision making, the assumptions are more apparent to everyone. Therefore, "what if" questions are more likely to be asked. What happens if the assumptions are changed? In an LP model the most obvious assumptions are the values of each of the coefficients in the model. These coefficients may represent such things as demand for a product, machine capacity, raw material cost, and labor rates. There may be considerable disagreement regarding the exact value of some of these coefficients. The standard LP solution report gives some indication of how the solution is affected by *small* changes in each of the objective function and right-hand side coefficients.

Parametric analysis or parametric programming is the term applied to tracing out how the solution changes as a specific coefficient (the parameter) changes over a *wide* range. Many LP computer programs have special commands for performing this analysis.

Types of Parametric Analysis

Parametric procedures found in computer packages typically allow two kinds of parametric changes: (1) cost or objective coefficients parametrics and (2) right-hand side parametrics. With objective function parametrics one could, for example, trace out how total profit varies as the selling price of a product is varied over a wide range. With right-hand side parametrics one could similarly trace out profit as the projected sales (a right-hand side number) of a product is varied over a wide range.

Types of Paarametric Analysis

There are three different perspectives from which one might wish to view the effect of a parametric change:

1. How does total profit or cost change as the parameter changes?
2. How does the optimal value and the reduced cost of a specific decision variable change as the parameter changes?
3. How does the dual price and slack of a specific constraint change as the parameter changes?

The following model will be used to illustrate parametric analysis:

$$\text{Maximize } 20A + 30C$$

subject to
2) $A \leq 60$
3) $C \leq 50$
4) $A + 2C \leq 120$
5) $2A + 5C \leq 280$
6) $A - C \geq -40$

We will examine two changes:

(a) Varying the right-hand side of row (2) from 60 to 0.
(b) Varying the objective function coefficient A from 20 down to whatever level is required to drive A from the solution.

The results of a parametric analysis are usually presented in graphic form. Therefore, let us immediately display the results in this form and then talk about how these results were obtained. Figure 18.1 shows the effect on the total profit and the dual price of row (2) of varying the right-hand side of row 2.

Notice that the total profit is a piecewise linear function of the right-hand side of row (2). The dual price of the constraint is a step function of the right-hand side. In fact, any plot of optimal objective function value and dual price of a constraint as a function of the right-hand side of the constraint will have the following features:

1. The objective function value curve will be piecewise linear and continuous, i.e., without steps or breaks. It will be a straight line between the finite number of points where it bends.
2. The dual price will be a decreasing step function.
3. The objective function value will be concave for Max problems (convex for Min problems); that is, for a Max problem the steepness of the curve diminishes as the right-hand side increases. The slope may in fact go negative. Practically speaking, this is exactly the same as saying that the less you have of something the more valuable is each unit.
4. For a given value of the right-hand side, the slope of the objective function curve equals the level of the dual price curve. As the right-hand side increases to 60 from 40, the objective function curve has slope $(2100 - 2000)/20 = 50$.

Figure 18.1

Righthand Side Value, b, of the Constraint A ≦ b

The dual price over this interval is also 50. Feature (4) with feature (2) implies feature (3).

Each point where the slope changes corresponds to what is called a basis change in the solution. Specifically, as the parameter is increased (or decreased), all variables which are nonzero change in value smoothly (i.e., linearly) until one of the variables hits zero. At this point a variable which had been zero now starts to increase. When this so-called basis change occurs there is a bend in the objective function curve or a step in the dual price curve.

The Simplex method for solving LPs requires only a minor modification to allow it to trace out the sequence of break points or basis change points in these curves. Even though the method is ostensibly solving as many different LP's as there are break points, the amount of work involved to move from one point to the next is roughly equivalent to doing only one iteration of the Simplex method.

The kind of report produced by a typical computer program for doing parametric analysis on the example problem described earlier might look as follows.

Parametric Analysis on the RHS of Constraint 2

Entering Variable	Departing Variable	RHS Value	New Value of Dual Price	Objective Value
—	—	60	5	2100
Slack(4)	Slack(5)	40	8	2000
Slack(5)	Slack(3)	15	20	1800
Slack(3)	Slack(6)	10	50	1700
Slack(6)	A	0	∞	1200

The graph in Figure 18.1 was produced from this table. Right to left in Figure 18.1 corresponds to top to bottom in this table.

Graphical Derivation of Parametric Profit Curve (Right-hand Side)

On a problem with but two variables, a graph of the constraint set can clearly show how the specific shape of the parametric profit curve comes about. Figure 18.2 graphs the constraint set for our example problem. Positions of the constraint $A \leq b$ for the parameter b equal to certain key values are indicated by the vertical dashed lines. The slope of the objective function is indicated by the slanted dashed line. The rightmost vertical line corresponds to the constraint $A \leq 60$. The optimal solution in this case is at the intersection of the two dashed lines. As the constraint $A \leq 60$ is tightened, i.e., as b is decreased from 60, the vertical dashed line moves to the left and the optimal point moves with it to the left along the top of the feasible region. The specific vertical dashed lines in Figure 18.2 correspond to points at which the breaks occur in the curves in Figure 18.1. The breaks occur at the points where the set of binding constraints changes.

One can also observe from Figure 18.2 which variables enter and leave the solution as the constraint $A \leq b$ is tightened. When $b = 60$ the slack in row (5): $2A + 5C \leq 280$ is in the solution at value 10. As b decreases to the breakpoint $b = 40$ the slack in row (4): $A + 2C \leq 120$ begins to increase from zero.

At each breakpoint the solution is degenerate, that is, the number of strictly positive variables (both original and slack) is less than the number of constraints. For example, at $b = 40$ we have $A = 40$, $C = 40$, slack (4) = 0, slack (5) = 0, slack (2) = 0, slack (3) = 10 and slack (6) = 40. There are only 4 nonzero variables even though

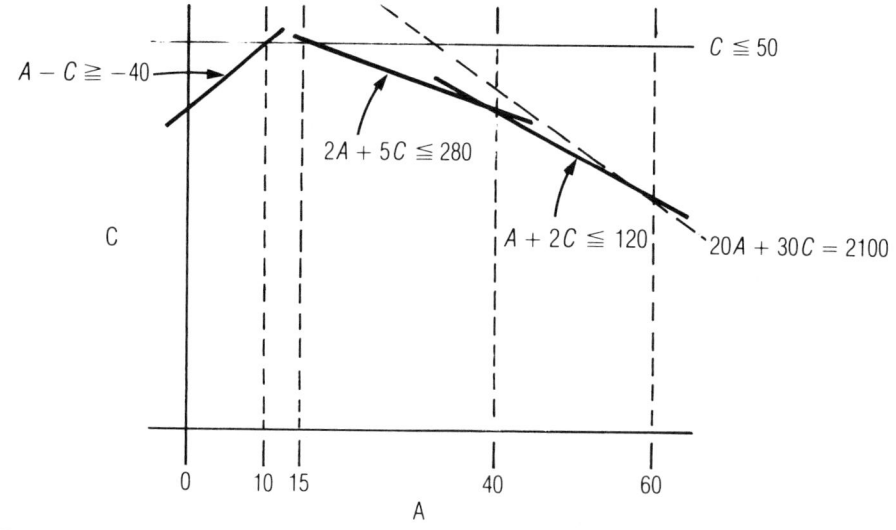

Figure 18.2

Feasible Region and Optimal Solution as RHS of $A \leq b$ Changes

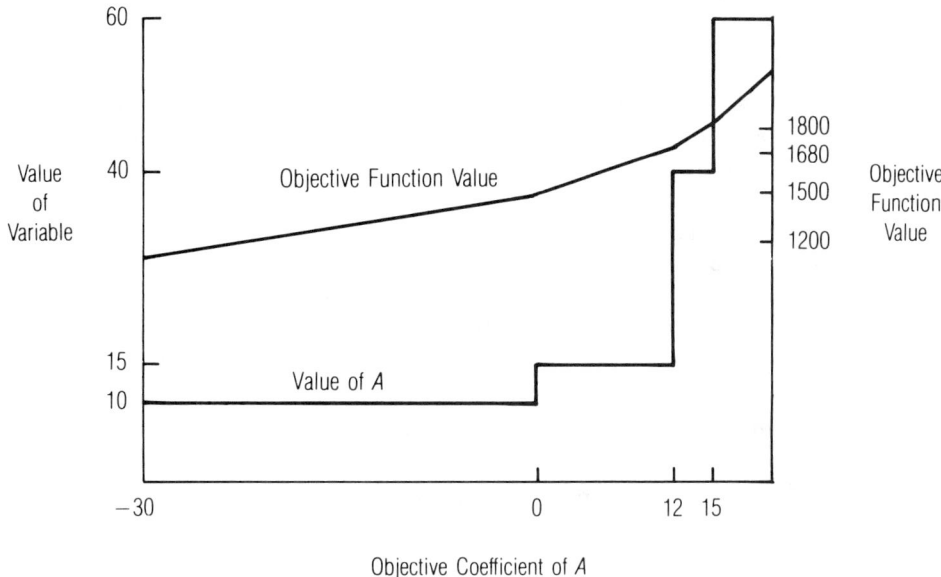

Figure 18.3

Parameterized Objective

there are 5 constraints. Figure 18.3 shows how the optimal objective function value and the value of the variable A change as the profit contribution of A is reduced.

Again, the total profit is a piecewise linear function of the profit contribution of A. In fact, the plot of the optimal objective value and the value of a decision variable as a function of the profit contribution of that decision variable for any LP will have the following features:

1. The objective value will be piecewise linear;
2. The decision variable's value will be an increasing step function as the profit contribution of the variable is increased;
3. The objective value curve will be convex for Max problems (concave for Min). Practically speaking, this is the same as saying that if the profit contribution per unit of a product is very small, e.g., negative, then increasing the per unit contribution by a fixed amount will have small effect on total profit. This is because at the optimum we produce very little of the product. If, however, the contribution per unit is large, then we tend to produce a lot of the product; therefore improving the per unit contribution of the product by a fixed amount will tend to produce a large improvement in total profit. Stated another way, reducing the production cost of a Chevrolet by $1 will have a much more dramatic effect on total profits of GM than reducing the production cost of a Cadillac Seville by $1 because so many Chevrolets are produced.

4. For a given value of the coefficient in the objective, the slope of the objective function curve equals the level of decision variable curve (see Figure 18.3). As the profit contribution of A increases from 15 to 20, the objective curve has slope $(2100 - 1800)/5 = 60$. The value of A over this interval is 60. Feature (4) with feature (2) implies feature (3).

As with changes in a right hand side coefficient, the set of nonzero variables remains the same between breakpoints. As the parameter is changed past a breakpoint some variable decreases to zero and is replaced by a variable which had been zero but increases from zero as the breakpoint is passed.

The Simplex method requires only minor modifications to trace out the effect of changing an objective coefficient. The computational work in moving from one breakpoint to the next is roughly equivalent to one iteration of the Simplex method.

The kind of report produced by a typical program for doing the parametric analysis of an objective coefficient for the previous example might look at follows:

Parametric Analysis on the Objective Coefficient of Variable A

Entering Variable	Departing Variable	Objective Coefficient Value	New Value of Variable	Objective Value
—	—	20	60	2100
Slack(2)	Slack(5)	15	40	1800
Slack(4)	Slack(3)	12	15	1680
Slack(5)	Slack(6)	0	10	1500
Slack(3)	A	−30	0	1200

Graphical Derivation of Parametric Profit Curve (Objective Coefficient)

Figure 18.4 shows the constraint set for our example problem. The dotted line shows the slope of the objective function $20A + 30C$. The line as drawn passes through the optimal solution $A = 60$, $C = 30$. As the coefficient of A is decreased the relative appeal of C increases and the dotted line rotates or rolls counterclockwise around the boundary of the feasible region. When the coefficient of A is 15, the dotted line is parallel to the constraint line $A + 2C \leq 120$. In this case the point $A = 40$, $C = 40$ with profit 1800 becomes an optimal solution. Note that the point $A = 60$, $C = 30$ is also optimum. Indeed, at every breakpoint there will be alternate optima when objective coefficient parameterizing is done. Compare this with right-hand side parameterizing in which case there is degeneracy at each breakpoint. When the coefficient of A is decreased to 12 the dotted line is parallel to the middle slanted line corresponding to the constraint $2A + 5C \leq 280$. In this case the point $A = 15$, $C = 50$ with profit 1680 becomes an optimal solution.

When the profit contribution of A is reduced to zero the dotted line becomes horizontal and the point $A = 10$, $C = 50$ with profit 1500 becomes optimal.

Finally, when the profit contribution of A is reduced to -30, the point $A = 0$, $C = 40$ with profit 1200 becomes optimal.

Figure 18.4
Optimal Solution as the Objective Coefficient of A is Changed

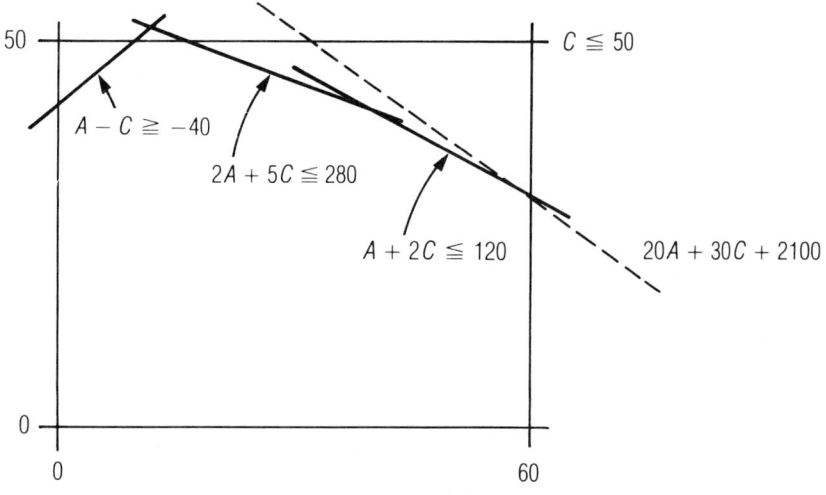

Changing Several Coefficients Simultaneously

Our discussion thus far has been in terms of changing only one coefficient at a time. One can additionally examine the effect of simultaneously varying several coefficients if the change in each parameter is linearly dependent upon a single parameter.

One application in which one might wish to consider changing several coefficients at once is in multiperiod planning. Each period might have a constraint defining plant capacity. Changing the plant capacity would entail changing the right-hand side of the plant capacity constraint in each of the periods in the model.

To illustrate simultaneous changes, suppose that in the Astro/Cosmo problem we want to examine the effect of simultaneously increasing the prices of both Astros and Cosmos. Specifically, for each dollar increase in Astro price we will increase the Cosmo price by three dollars. You can think of there being a second objective function which receives an adjustable weight f. The problem can be written

$$
\begin{aligned}
\text{Maximize} \quad & 20A + 30C \\
& + f(A + 3C) \\
\text{subject to} \quad & A \leq 60 \\
& C \leq 50 \\
& A + 2C \leq 120
\end{aligned}
$$

When $f = 0$ the original problem is obtained; when $f = 1$ the profit contributions of A and C are 21 and 33 respectively; when $f = 2$, the profit contributions are 22 and 36 respectively, etc.

Some computer packages allow you to enter a second objective as above and then trace out the optimal solutions as f is varied. For this example, the row $A + 3C$ is known as a change row.

Alternatively, one can introduce a new variable z and the parametric problem can be written

$$\text{Maximize} \quad 20A + 30C + fz$$
$$\begin{aligned}
\text{subject to} \quad A + 3C - z &= 0 \\
A &\leq 60 \\
C &\leq 50 \\
A + 2C &\leq 120
\end{aligned}$$

This form is compatible with changing only one objective coefficient, f, at once. This illustrates the fact that the crucial feature for parametric analysis is the ability to vary a single coefficient. It is convenient but not essential to be able to specify a change row to be applied parametrically to the original objective.

A similar situation holds for simultaneously changing several right-hand side coefficients. Suppose we want to examine the effect of decreasing capacities of both the Astro line capacity by two units.

We could write the problem as

$$\text{Maximize} \quad 20A + 30C$$
$$\text{subject to} \quad \begin{aligned} A &\leq 60 \\ C &\leq 50 \\ A + 2C &\leq 120 \end{aligned} - f \begin{Bmatrix} 2 \\ 1 \\ 0 \end{Bmatrix}$$

Alternatively, one can introduce a new variable Y and the parametric problem can be written

$$\text{Maximize} \quad 20A + 30C$$
$$\begin{aligned}
\text{subject to} \quad A \phantom{{}+C} + 2Y &\leq 60 \\
C + Y &\leq 50 \\
 + 2C \phantom{{}+Y} &\leq 120 \\
Y &= f
\end{aligned}$$

where f is the parameter to be varied.

Again, the problem has been reduced to analyzing the effect of changing a single right-hand side coefficient, f.

Supply and Demand Curves Derived via Parametric Analysis

Parametric analysis provides a way of approximating the supply and/or demand curve of a firm for a specific product. A demand (supply) curve specifies how much of a material a firm is willing to buy (sell) of the given material as a function of the material's price. A firm that is able to set the price of a product which it buys or sells will find it useful to know the supply or demand curve of its supplier or customer. Setting the price of a

Figure 18.5

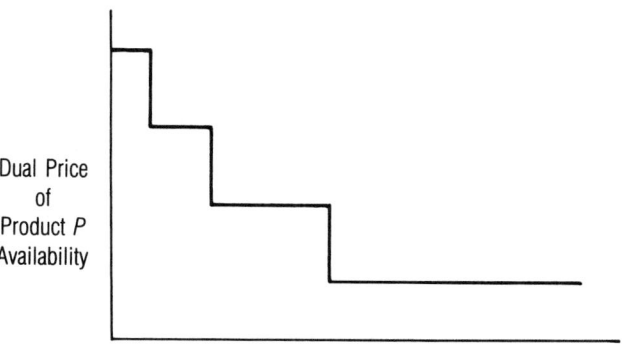

Price of product *P* vs. Amount Available

product it sells to the highest possible value will not necessarily maximize a firm's profit. The firm must know how much it can sell at a given price in order to maximize profits.

Suppose that firm X buys a specific product P from firm Y and that firm X uses an LP to make its allocation decisions. Firm Y can take this LP and if necessary add a constraint which puts an upper limit on how much of product P can be bought. If parametric analysis is performed on the right-hand side of this constraint a curve such as in Figure 18.5 will be obtained.

This curve is effectively firm X's demand curve for product P. There is some indication that petroleum companies have used this methodology occasionally to set the price of crude oil supplied to their refinery customers.

Similarly if, firm X sells a product S, a constraint could be added to its LP which placed a lower limit on the amount produced of this product. Because this constraint is of $\geqq$ type it will have a nonpositive dual price. If parametric analysis is performed on the right-hand side of this constraint and the negative of the dual is plotted, a curve such as in Figure 18.6 is obtained. This curve is effectively firm X's supply curve for product S.

Economics texts usually draw supply and demand curves as smooth curves. This is for aesthetic and statistical reasons, e.g., conventional statistical regression produces smooth curves. The realities of technology suggest, however, that the curves have small steps as shown here. For example, there may be a threshold price for some product above which it is profitable to produce it by a different technology. Once this technology switch is made a supplier may be willing to produce dramatically more of the product.

Parametric Programming and Tracing Out the Efficient Frontier in Multi-Objective Problems

A cliché commonly heard in business decision making (and perhaps more in cocktail conversation) is "What's the bottom line?" Implicit in this is that all considerations can be converted to a single unit of measure, dollars. The fact that this single measure of

Figure 18.6

Marginal Cost vs. Production

Marginal Cost of Producing One More Unit of Product S. (Negative of Dual Price on Product S Production Requirement)

Production Requirement for Product S

performance is frequently not an accurate measure of reality is borne out by the frequent repetition of another cliché: "You can't compare apples and oranges." In the latter case we say we have multiple criteria or multiple objectives.

Frequently the multiple objectives are conflicting. In assembling an investment portfolio there are the conflicting objectives of minimizing risk and maximizing expected return. In a service organization there are the conflicting objectives of minimizing costs and maximizing some measure of service. Planning in a typical firm involves the long-range objective of increasing market share which conflicts with the short-range objective of maximizing profit. A key feature of the above examples is that the two objectives in each case were measured in different units, e.g., portfolio variance vs. dollars, dollars vs. service level, and percent share vs. dollars.

Parametric programming is frequently recommended in situations with two incommensurate objectives. Loosely speaking, the objective is to

$$\text{Maximize} \quad (\text{Objective 1}) + f \times (\text{Objective 2}).$$

Unfortunately, most people do not have an intuitive feel for an appropriate value for f. The parameter f is varied from 0 to infinity to produce a graph analogous to that in Figure 18.7. The one objective might be to minimize cost, while the other is to maximize the quality of service. As the weight f applied to the service quality objective (e.g., measured as number of clients whose complaints were settled with no delay) is increased from zero to infinity, the piecewise linear curve is traced out from the origin.

Parametric programming has little to say about the exact compromise struck between service and cost, i.e., the best value of f. We can argue, however, that whatever compromise is struck, it should lie somewhere on the curve dubbed the "efficient frontier." This curve has the feature that for a given cost the curve specifies the highest achievable

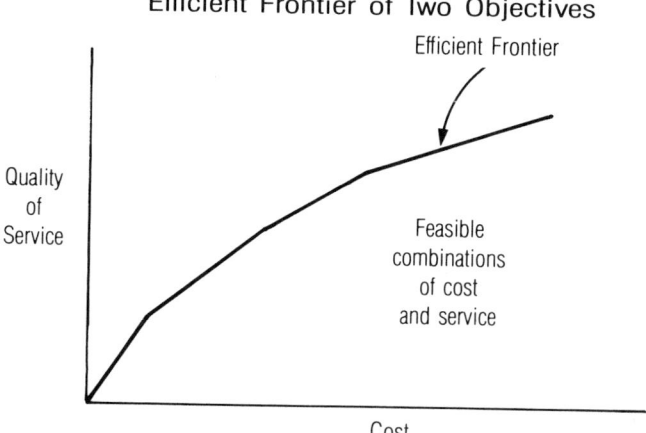

Figure 18.7

Efficient Frontier of Two Objectives

service level. Similarly, for a given service level the curve gives the lowest cost which can achieve this service.

Problems

1. For the example problem of page 306, draw the graphs of total profit and the value of variable C as the profit contribution of C varies from 0 to 100.

2. Add the constraint $C \leq b$ to the example problem used on page 306 and draw the graph of total profit and the dual price of the constraint $C \geq b$ as b is increased from 0 to 50.

3. In a parametric LP analysis it is possible for the optimal objective value to first increase and then decrease.

    (a) Is this possible with a right-hand side analysis? If yes, give an example.

    (b) Is this possible with a parametric objective coefficient analysis? If yes, give an example.

4. Suppose that you have an LP procedure which can do parametrics on an arbitrary constraint coefficient but not on the right-hand side or objective function row. Show that by appending appropriate constraints or variables that this capability nevertheless allows one to indirectly to parametric analysis on either right-hand side or the objective.

5. Suppose that variable y is zero in the optimal solution to a certain LP and has a reduced cost of 5. Now modify this LP by appending the constraint $y = 6$. What can you say about the dual price of this constraint in the optimal solution to the modified LP?

19

Methods for Solving Linear Programs

Methods

The graphical method of solution outlined in Chapter 1 is an acceptable means of solution if there are only two decision variables. Its use in higher dimensions (more decision variables) must await, however, further technologic advances in holography or other technology which will allow us to have three-dimensional or higher graphical systems.

The ideas of the graphical method have algebraic equivalents, however, which do in fact extend to an arbitrary number of variables. The algebraic method which has proven to be very successful is the Simplex method. It was developed by George Dantzig in approximately 1947 while he was working on Project Scoop for the Air Force. It is a tribute to the elegance and efficiency of the method that the essential steps of the Simplex method as originally described by Dantzig are still incorporated in almost every LP solution procedure used today.

Recently Khachian (1979) and Karmarkar (1985) proposed radically different algorithms for solving linear programs. The most notable feature of both algorithms is that their worst case performance is considerably better than that of the Simplex method, that is, in contrast to the Simplex method, there are no problems which require an extremely long time to solve with new algorithms. Unfortunately, with Khachian's algorithm it seems that essentially all problems require a long time to solve. It appears that Karmarkar's algorithm may be competitive with the Simplex method on certain very large problems with very few nonzero coefficients.

The Simplex Method

Most users of LP today get along quite nicely without knowing the steps of the Simplex method. Thus, the presentation here is mainly for the mathematically curious. You will discover, however, that the method is not difficult to comprehend. Further, understanding the Simplex method will help develop the skill of making correct formulations.

First let us review how we would solve the Astro/Cosmo problem graphically. Recall that the problem is:

$$\text{Maximize} \quad 20A + 30C$$
$$\begin{aligned}
\text{subject to} \quad A &\leq 60 \\
C &\leq 50 \\
A + 2C &\leq 120
\end{aligned} \qquad \begin{aligned} A &\geq 0 \\ C &\geq 0 \end{aligned}$$

The problem can be described graphically as in Figure 19.1. The feasible region is those combinations of values for Astro production (A) and Cosmo production (C) which are in the area bounded by the lines JK, KL, LM, MN, and NJ. All points on a particular dotted line $20A + 30C = Z$ generate the same profit, Z. We want to shift the dotted line upward and to the right as much as possible. From the graph it is obvious that the maximum shift occurs when the dotted line passes through the point M. Therefore the point M, which corresponds to $A = 60$, $C = 30$ is the optimum.

It is apparent from the graph that you need only consider corner points as candidates for the optimum. A possible solution procedure is to enumerate every corner point, evaluate the profit at each, and select the best. This is not a good method if there are many corner points; and there will be many if there are lots of constraints and/or variables.

A myopic approach may do better. Suppose we start at the point J with $A = C = 0$, and consider the two possible paths along the feasible boundary for moving away from J. By increasing C we move up towards point K. By increasing A we move horizontally towards point N. If we are myopic we note that we make \$30/unit increase in C versus

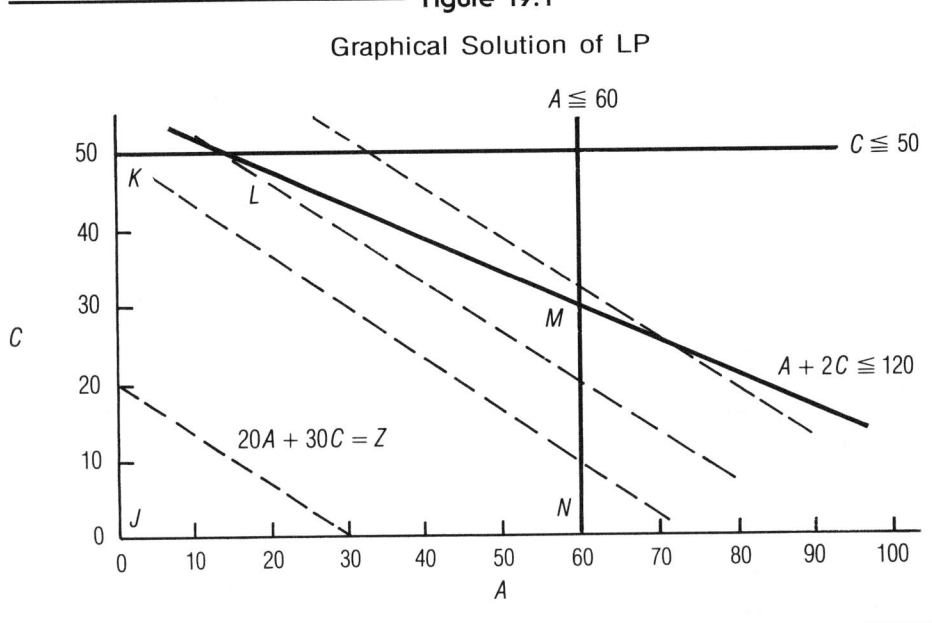

Figure 19.1

Graphical Solution of LP

only $20/unit increase in A. We might use this as justification for moving to point K which corresponds to $C = 50$, $A = 0$.

Once at K the dotted line can be shifted further to the right if we move to the point L. Once at L it is again obvious that profit can be improved by moving to M. Once at M, neither of the two paths out of M leads to an improvement and we stop.

The point N was not examined, so this method is more efficient than complete enumeration of all corner points. In retrospect it would have been wiser at the outset to move to point N rather than K from point J. The next step would have been to point M and the optimum would have been reached in only 2 instead of 3 steps. From the computer solution of this problem you can take solace in the fact that the computer also took the longer, 3-step path.

The Simplex method proceeds from an initial feasible solution which need not be optimal, through a sequence of better and better feasible solutions, until finally the optimum solution is encountered. This is exactly what the graphical method does. Similarly, the Simplex method looks only at "corner point" solutions; further it will generally consider only a very small fraction of all the corner points.

Equality Form, Slack and Surplus Variables

For internal computations the computer will convert every LP into one in which the objective is to maximize, and all constraints other than the nonnegativity constraints are equalities. This conversion is very easily executed by the following steps where necessary:

1. A "Minimize" objective is converted to a "Maximize" objective by multiplying the objective by -1. For example,

    Minimize $2x_1 - 2x_2$

    is equivalent to

    Maximize $-2x_1 + 2x_2$.

2. A "less than or equal to" constraint is converted to an equality constraint by adding a "slack" variable to the left-hand side. For example, if row i is:

    $$4x_1 + 5x_2 \leq 12,$$

    then it is equivalent to:

    $$4x_1 + 5x_2 + s_i = 12$$
    $$s_i \geq 0.$$

    The nonnegativity constraint on the slack variable s_i prevents $4x_1 + 5x_2$ from exceeding 12.

3. A "greater than or equal to" constraint is converted to an equality constraint by subtracting a "surplus" variable from the left-hand side. For example, if row k is

    $$6x_1 - 3x_2 \geq 9$$

then it is equivalent to

$$6x_1 - 3x_2 - s_k = 9$$
$$s_k \geq 0.$$

When the Astro/Cosmo problem is converted to equality form we obtain:

$$\begin{aligned}
\text{Maximize} \quad & 20A + 30C \\
\text{subject to} \quad & A \phantom{{}+{}} + s_2 \phantom{{}+ s_3 + s_4} = 60 \\
& \phantom{A + {}} C \phantom{{}+ s_2} + s_3 \phantom{{}+ s_4} = 50 \\
& A + 2C \phantom{{}+ s_2 + s_3} + s_4 = 120 \\
& A \geq 0 \\
& C \geq 0 \\
& s_2, s_3, s_4 \geq 0.
\end{aligned}$$

Corner Points, Basic Solutions, and Number of Nonzero Variables

For a formulation in equality form it is always true that in a corner point solution the number of nonzero variables will at most equal the number of constraints. Generally it will exactly equal the number of constraints. If it is less than the number of constraints, the solution is referred to as degenerate. For the time being we will disregard the possibility of degenerate solutions.

An alternate and more frequently used term for a corner point solution is basic solution. Some standard terminology typically used is:

1. *Technological constraints:* constraints of the LP other than the nonnegativity constraints.
2. *Basic solution:* a solution which satisfies the technological constraints but not necessarily the nonnegativity constraints and has the number of nonzero variables less than or equal to the number of technological constraints.
3. *Basic variable:* a variable that is nonzero in a basic solution.
4. *Basis:* the set of basic variables.
5. *Basic feasible solution:* a basic solution that also satisfies the nonnegativity constraints.
6. *Degenerate solution:* a feasible solution in which the number of nonzero variables is strictly less than the number of technological constraints.

The validity of the Simplex method is based upon the following two facts, stated without proof:

1. If there is an optimal solution, then there is a basic feasible optimal solution. For example, if there are 12 technological constraints and you have an optimal solution with 14 variables nonzero, you can find another optimal solution with at most 12 variables nonzero.

2. For any nondegenerate basic feasible solution which is not optimum there is an "adjacent" basic feasible solution (i.e., an adjacent corner point) which is strictly better.

Assuming that degeneracy does not rear its ugly head, then facts (1) and (2) suggest the following procedure for finding the LP optimum:

1. Find an initial basic feasible solution.
2. Try to find an adjacent basic feasible solution which is better. If none go to (5).
3. Move to the new basic feasible solution.
4. Go to (2).
5. We have found an optimal solution because any basic feasible solution which is not optimal must have a better solution which is adjacent to it.

Now we can specify the steps of the Simplex method in slightly more detail:

1. Find an initial basic feasible solution.
2. Find a variable, call it j, which is zero in the current solution which can be profitably increased. If none, go to (5).
3. Increase variable j while adjusting the values of the nonzero variables so as to maintain feasibility. The solution will temporarily be nonbasic because there will be one too many nonzero variables. However, as variable j is increased, one of the nonzero variables will be driven to zero (if there is a finite optimum). At this point we will have a new basic feasible solution.
4. Go to (2).
5. Stop. We have found an optimum solution.

Tableau Representation of the Equations

It is convenient to make one additional rearrangement before introducing the Simplex method. If we denote the profit by Z, then we can write

$$Z = 20A + 30C$$

Bringing all the variables to the left-hand side, the objective function appears just like any other constraint and the Astro/Cosmo problem appears as

$$
\begin{aligned}
Z - 20A - 30C & & & & &= 0 \\
A & & + s_2 & & &= 60 \\
& C & & + s_3 & &= 50 \\
A & - 2C & & & + s_4 &= 120
\end{aligned}
$$

It is implicit that we wish to Maximize Z and keep A, C, s_2, s_3, and s_4 nonnegative.

For display purposes these equations can be equally well described by the following tableau.

	Z	A	C	s_2	s_3	s_4	RHS
	1	-20	-30				
		1		1			60
			1		1		50
		1	2			1	120

That is, only the coefficients of the equations need be stored if we keep track of which row and which variable is associated with the coefficient. For computational purposes the above format or tableau will be used. In fact, only the information within the double lines need be stored.

Basic Variables

Because the number of basic variables will, barring degeneracy, be equal to the number of constraints, it is not surprising that each basic variable in a particular basic solution can be associated with exactly one constraint or equivalently one row of the tableau. The variable is said to be basic in that row. Intuitively, that row or constraint is used to solve for or compute the value of the variable basic in the row. To show this correspondence between basic variables and rows we will augment the tableau with a column called "Basis." For example, for our example, the initial tableau with basis is:

Basis	Z	A	C	s_2	s_3	s_4	RHS
Z	1	-20	-30				0
s_2		1		1			60
s_3			1		1		50
s_4		1	2			1	120

The value appearing under the "RHS" heading in a particular row will always be the value of the variable appearing under the "Basis" heading in that row. The initial basic feasible solution has $A = C = 0$, so $Z = 0$, $s_2 = 60$, $s_3 = 50$ and $s_4 = 120$. Thus, s_2, s_3 and s_4 constitute the basis.

Interpretation of Coefficients in the Tableau

The numbers in the columns of the tableau have the following interpretation:

(a) If the column is "RHS," then the number in a specific row of the column is the value of the variable which is basic in that row.

(b) If the column corresponds to a nonbasic variable, say, j, then the number in a specific row, say row i, is the rate at which the variable which is basic in row i will decrease as variable j is increased. For our example problem at the initial solution, increasing C by 1 unit means that Z will decrease by -30 units, i.e., it will increase by 30 dollars; similarly the slack in the labor supply, s_4, will decrease by 2 hours if C is increased by 1 unit.

(c) If the column corresponds to a basic variable, then the column will be all zero except for a 1 in the row in which the variable is basic.

At each step, the Simplex method will adjust the tableau so that the above three features are maintained.

We can now see how step (2) of the Simplex method is performed. Variable Z will always be basic in the first row. Thus, any variable which can be profitably increased will have a negative coefficient in the first row of the tableau. The tableau corresponds to an optimal solution if all the coefficients in the first row are nonnegative. If there are negative coefficients in the first row, the variable associated with the most negative is usually chosen to enter the basis.

Suppose we decide to increase C in our example. How much can we increase C before a basic variable is driven to 0? Considering column C of the initial tableau, we see that as C is increased

s_2 remains at 60

s_3 decreases 1 unit per unit increase of C,

s_4 decreases 2 units per unit increase of C.

Thus, $s_3 = 0$ when $s_3 = 50 - C = 0$ or when $C = 50$, and $s_4 = 0$ when $s_4 = 120 - 2C = 0$ or when $C = 120/2 = 60$. Therefore s_3 reaches 0 first as C is increased.

At the new basic feasible solution we will have $C = 50$; s_3 will have been forced to 0; Z must have increased from 0 to $30 \times 50 = 1,500$; and s_4 must have decreased from 120 to $120 - 2 \times 50 = 20$.

Updating the Tableau/Pivoting

We have seen essentially half of the Simplex method by way of example. It remains to be demonstrated how the tableau is updated. This can be done if we recall that the tableau is simply a shorthand way of representing a set of equations. Further, when we say that variable x_j is basic in row i, it will mean that:

(a) equation i has been used to solve for x_j and

(b) x_j has been substituted out of the other equations.

Updating the tableau corresponds to performing operations (a) and (b) for the entering variable. The row or equation which is used is the one in which the variable departing the basis has been basic. In the terminology of linear algebra or simultaneous linear equations this operation is called pivoting.

In the first iteration, for example, variable C enters and the variable s_3 departs the basic. Substep (a) is easy to perform. The relevant row in equation form is

$$C + s_3 = 50.$$

It is obvious that if $s_3 = 0$ then $C = 50$. Step (b) requires us to use this equation to eliminate C from all the other equation (rows). The objective function row is:

$$Z - 20A - 30C = 0.$$

Multiplying the previous row by 30 and adding it to this row gives the new objective function row:

$$\begin{array}{rl} Z - 20 - 30C & = 0 \\ 30C + 30s_3 & = 1{,}500 \\ \hline Z - 20 + 30s_3 & = 1{,}500. \end{array}$$

This makes sense; i.e., $C = 50$, $A = 0$ implies $Z = 30 \times 50 = 1{,}500$. The only other row containing C is the last row:

$$A + 2C + s_4 = 120.$$

The appropriate multiple in this case is -2, giving

$$\begin{array}{rl} A + 2C + s_4 & = 120 \\ -2C - 2s_3 & = -100 \\ \hline A -2s_3 + s_4 & = 20. \end{array}$$

The basic variable for this row is s_4 and it makes sense that the slack in the labor capacity is 20 if $C = 50$ and $A = 0$.

The entire tableau corresponding to this new basic feasible solution is:

Basis	Z	A	C	s_2	s_3	s_4	RHS
Z	1	-20	0		+30		1,500
s_2		1		1			60
C			1		1		50
s_4		1			-2	1	20

The TABLEAU and PIVOT commands of LINDO can be used alternately to show the successive steps and tableau leading to the optimum.

From the second tableau it is obvious that A should enter the solution. As A increases, Z will increase by \$20/unit while both s_2 and s_4 will decrease at the same rate as A increases. Variable s_4 will decrease to 0 after A has increased by 20 units. Therefore, s_4 is the departing variable. The new tableau is:

Basis	Z	A	C	s_2	s_3	s_4	RHS
Z	1				−10	20	1,900
s_2				1	2	−1	40
C			1		1		50
A		1			−2	1	20

In the third tableau variable s_3 should enter; *i.e.*, one should allow slack in the constraint $C \leq 70$. Each unit of increase in s_3 will increase profits by $10. The tableau contains sufficient information to explain why this happens. A 1 unit increase causes C to decrease by 1 unit. This costs us $30. However, A increases by 2 units, and this makes us $2 \times \$20 = \$40$ for a net of $10. Now we must determine which of s_2 or C reaches 0 first as s_3 increases. If s_2 is forced to zero this corresponds to $2s_3 = 50$ or $s_3 = 50/2 = 25$. If C is forced to zero this corresponds to $s_3 = 50$. Therefore s_2 reaches 0 first as s_3 increases, and so s_2 is the departing variable. The new tableau is:

Basis	Z	A	C	s_2	s_3	s_4	RHS
Z				5		15	2,100
s_3				.5	1	−.5	20
C			1	−.5		.5	30
A		1		1			60

There are no variables with negative, coefficients in the objective function row so there is no variable which can be profitably entered and this must be the optimal solution.

Other Difficulties

There are several minor difficulties with the Simplex method which our judiciously chosen example did not illustrate. A well-written LP code will handle these difficulties in matter-of-fact fashion. These difficulties are:

1. *An initial, basic feasible solution need not be obvious.* Thus, we must provide some way of getting a basic feasible solution if, in fact, one exists.

2. *Unboundedness.* The problem below has an unbounded solution:

   Maximize $3x$

   subject to $4x \geq 12$.

   There is nothing to prevent us from making x arbitrarily large and making an infinite profit. An LP code should clearly identify such desirable but unrealistic situations.

3. *Degeneracy.* If the number of nonzero variables in a basic feasible solution is less than the number of constraints, then the solution is said to be degenerate. In such a situation, the Simplex method need not find a strictly better solution at the next iteration. In fact, degeneracy is the major problem in solving large LPs. The Simplex method may iterate merrily alway without improving the objective function value.

The Revised Simplex Method and Coefficient Sparsity

An LP with 2000 rows and 5000 columns can be represented by a matrix with $2000 \times 5000 = 10{,}000{,}000$ coefficients. This is a lot of storage space. In a typical real LP, less than 2% of these coefficients will be nonzero. There is therefore a temptation to exploit this coefficient sparsity. Ideally, you would like to get by with storing only $0.02 \times 10{,}000{,}000 = 200{,}000$ coefficients, rather than 10,000,000. This exploitation can be very valuable in large problems where the coefficient density is less than 1%.

The Revised Simplex method has been developed to exploit this sparsity. It follows the same path to the optimum; however, it stores the results of the computations in a way which exploits this sparsity. Most commercial LP codes uses the Revised Simplex method. Consider an LP with 500 rows and 1000 columns. The standard simplex method would require a matrix with $500 \times 1000 = 500{,}000$ elements to do the computations. On a typical computer this would require a least 2,000,000 bytes of storage. This much storage may be expensive. Further, updating 500,000 elements at each pivot may be time consuming.

Fortunately, the real world is easier than the simple theory of the standard simplex method suggests. A typical real world LP has about four nonzero elements per column. Thus, a 500×1000 problem might have only 5000 nonzero elements out of the 500,000 possible. The revised simplex method with product form inverse exploits this sparsity so that the number of storage elements required is approximately twice the number of nonzeroes. The factor of 2 arises because we must store not only the nonzeroes but also the index of the row in which each occurs.

Many commercial packages use a variation of the product form inverse which is called the elimination form of inverse. The essential idea is still the same.

We will first summarize the features of the Revised Simplex Method with explicit inverse. The explicit inverse is conceptually simpler than the product form but it does not exploit sparsity nearly as well as the product form.

Let E be the matrix or updated tableau as it would appear under the standard simplex method at any given iteration. The key observation that makes the revised simplex method attractive is that only a small fraction of the elements of E are needed to select the pivot at each iteration. Specifically:

(a) We need the first or objective function row of E in order to choose the entering variable.

(b) We need the column of E corresponding to the entering variable so we can choose the pivot row. Similarly, we need the updated right-hand side.

Thus, to choose the pivot element at an iteration we need examine at most $1000 + 500 = 1500$ elements out of the 500,000 elements in E. This is an attractive reduction. The question of how to represent the effect of each pivot so that we need calculate only 1500 rather than 500,000 numbers at each pivot remains to be answered.

In general, suppose an LP has m rows and n columns. The revised simplex method with explicit inverse stores the original m by n LP matrix in sparse form and does not modify it from one pivot to the next. Rather, a smaller m by m matrix called B^{-1} is adjusted at each pivot.

If the original m by n LP matrix is denoted by T, then the updated matrix or tableau can be obtained by doing a matrix multiply of B^{-1} and T, i.e., $E = B^{-1}T$. In particular, if we want the first row of E, we multiply the first row of B^{-1} times T. Because T is stored in sparse form and each column contains about four nonzeroes, the total multiplications is about $4 \times n$, or 4000 for our 500×1000 example. Further, we don't have to "price out" every column at each iteration but rather let us say about 200 in order to find with an attractive reduced cost in the first row. Thus, the work might be more like 800 multiplications to find the entering variable in our 500×1000 example.

Once the entering variable has been selected, the updated column in E corresponding to this variable can be generated by premultiplying the corresponding column in T by B^{-1}. The number of multiplications involved is approximately $4 \times m$ or 2000 for our example.

How is B^{-1} stored and how is it updated at each pivot? Here is where the explicit form inverse and product form differ. The explicit form simply stores a full m by m matrix. Updating at each iteration is simple. Pivots are done exactly as in the standard simplex method except that the pivot operations are done on B^{-1} rather than on E. That is, the pivot row in B^{-1} is divided by the pivot element. Appropriate multiples of the pivot row are subtracted from the other rows in B^{-1}. Thus updating B^{-1} at a pivot requires about $m \times m$ multiplications and divisions. Mathematically, B^{-1} is the inverse of the matrix of (possibly permuted) columns of T corresponding to the basic variables.

Now let us compare the work required by the revised simplex method with explicit inverse and the standard simplex method for our example problem.

Operation	Standard	Revised with Explicit B^{-1}
(1) Select entering column	0 multiplications	800 multiplications
(2) Select pivot row	0 multiplications	2,000 multiplications
(3) Pivot	500,000 multiplications	250,000 multiplications
Total, One Iteration	500,000 multiplications	252,800 multiplications

Example of Revised Simplex Method with Explicit Inverse

We will illustrate the calculations under the revised simplex method with explicit inverse using the example that was used to illustrate the standard simplex method.

The original tableau, T, is

Row	Basis	A	C	S_2	S_3	S_4	RHS
(1)	Z	-20	-30				
(2)	S_2	1		1			60
(3)	S_3		1		1		50
(4)	S_4	1	2			1	120

The initial B^{-1} is the identity matrix:

1	0	0	0
0	1	0	0
0	0	1	0
0	0	0	1

Multiplying the first row of B^{-1} times T gives the original objective function row:

A	C	S_2	S_3	S_4
-20	-30	0	0	0

We select C to enter. Multiplying C's column and the original RHS by B^{-1} gives the relevant part of E:

Row	Basis	C	RHS
(1)	Z	-30	0
(2)	S_2	0	60
(3)	S_3	1	50
(4)	S_4	2	120

The minimum ratio of 50/1 and 120/2 is 50, so the pivot row is (3). Adding 30 times row (3) to row (1) and subtracting 2 times row (3) from row (4) gives the new B^{-1}:

1	0	30	0
0	1	0	0
0	0	1	0
0	0	-2	1

Multiplying the first row of B^{-1} times T gives the updated objective function row:

A	C	S_2	S_3	S_4
-20	0	0	30	0

So A should enter. Multiplying A's original column and the original RHS by B^{-1} gives the relevant part of E:

Row	Basis	C	RHS
(1)	Z	-20	1500
(2)	S_2	1	60
(3)	C	0	50
(4)	S_4	1	20

The minimum of $60/1$ and $20/1$ is 20, so the pivot row should be (4). Adding 20 times row (4) to row (1) and subtracting row (4) from row (2) gives the new B^{-1}:

1	0	-10	20
0	1	2	-1
0	0	1	0
0	0	-2	1

Multiplying the first row of B^{-1} times T gives the updated objective function row of E:

A	C	S_2	S_3	S_4
0	0	0	-10	20

So S_3 should enter. Multiplying S_3's original column and the original RHS by B^{-1} gives:

(1)	Z	-10	1900
(2)	S_2	2	40
(3)	C	0	50
(4)	A	-2	20

The minimum ratio of $40/2$ and $50/1$ is 20 so the pivot row is (2). Adding 5 times row (2) to row (1), subtracting $1/2$ times row (2) from row (3), adding row (2) to row (4) and finally dividing row (2) by 2 gives the new B^{-1}:

1	5	0	15
0	$1/2$	1	$-1/2$
0	$-1/2$	0	$1/2$
0	1	0	0

Multiplying the first row of B^{-1} gives the updated objective row of E:

A	C	S_2	S_3	S_4
0	0	5	0	15

All variables price out positive so we have an optimal solution. Multiplying B^{-1} times the original RHS gives:

Row	Basis	RHS
(1)	Z	2100
(2)	S_3	20
(3)	C	30
(4)	A	60

Thus, the optimal solution has $z = 2100$, $s_3 = 20$, $C = 30$, and $A = 60$. The dual prices are found in the first row of B^{-1}. Specifically, the dual prices of rows (2), (3), and (4) are 5, 0, and 15 respectively.

Revised Simplex Method with Product Form of Inverse

The Revised Simplex Method with product form inverse uses a substantially different method for storing and updating B^{-1}. For most practical LP's the density of B^{-1} under the explicit inverse method is approximately 50%, that is, about half the elements of B^{-1} are nonzero. Thus, the sparsity of the original data does not carry over to the explicit inverse. The product form inverse is able to retain much of the sparsity of the original data. This is true in particular for transportation or network LP problems.

The basic idea of the product form inverse is very simple, namely, instead of performing the pivot at each iteration, simply append the column that should have been pivoted to a list of the (updated) columns that should have been pivoted. This contains all the information about a sequence of pivots. One of these "should have been pivoted" columns in usually called an eta vector. The entire list of eta vectors is called the eta file. We must now show that this information can be stored compactly and that it can be efficiently exploited. We can efficiently generate a column from E by simply starting with the corresponding original column from T and then applying the list of "should have been pivoted" columns to it. Thus, we already see how to efficiently create the information needed to select the pivot row, given that we know which variable is to enter.

Now we must show how to generate the objective function row of E with the product form inverse representation. Here we recall how it was done with the explicit inverse: we simply multiplied the first row of B^{-1} times the original LP matrix. We will show how to construct the first row of B^{-1} from the eta file. The first row of E can then be reconstructed just as with the explicit inverse method.

For mathematical purposes it is convenient to think of each eta vector as being stored in the following fashion:

    (a) divide each element in the column, except the pivot element, by the negative of the pivot element,

    (b) replace the pivot element by its reciprocal,

    (c) if the pivot element is in row k, embed the column in the kth column position of an identity matrix.

For example, suppose that the column that should have been pivoted was

Row
(1) −10
(2) 2
(3) 1
(4) −2

and the pivot was to be in row 2. Think of this being stored in the eta file as the matrix:

1	10/2	0	0
0	1/2	0	0
0	−1/2	1	0
0	1	0	1

Call this an eta matrix.

The reason for thinking of it in this form is that a pivot in row 2 of the column corresponds to premultiplying by the above matrix. For example, observe that premultiplying by this matrix corresponds to:

(a) adding 5 times the pivot row to row (1), subtracting 1//2 of the pivot row from row (3), adding the pivot row to row (4) and

(b) dividing the pivot row by 2.

Call the eta matrix corresponding to the kth pivot, h_k. Recalling how B^{-1} was updated at each pivot under the explicit form, we can then write B^{-1} at pivot k as the matrix product:

$$B^{-1} = h_k \times h_{k-1} \times h_{k-2} \cdots \times h_1 \times I$$

where I is the identity matrix.

We can get the first row of B^{-1} by the following procedure. Take the first row of h_k and multiplying it times h_{k-1}. This gives a row vector as a result. This is multiplied times h_{k-2} etc. This process for getting the first row of B^{-1} may sound complicated but it requires only about twenty FORTRAN statements to describe.

Example of Revised Simplex Method with Product Form Inverse

We shall illustrate the method with the example used earlier.
The original LP matrix is:

Row	Basis	T A	C	S_2	S_3	S_4	RHS
(1)	Z	−20	−30				
(2)	S_2	1		1			60
(3)	S_3		1		1		50
(4)	S_4	1	2			1	120

The eta file is empty so the first row of B^{-1} or the pricing vector is (1 0 0 0). C prices out at -30 so it is chosen to enter. Because the eta file is empty, the entering column and RHS of E are the same as in T, thus

Row	Basis	C	RHS
(1)	Z	-30	0
(2)	S_2	0	60
(3)	S_3	1	50
(4)	S_4	2	120

The minimum ratio appears in row (3) so the pivot should be in row (3). Thus, we add the following eta vector to the eta file:

$$
\begin{array}{c}
h_1 \\
30 \\
0 \\
1 \\
-2 \\
\hline
3
\end{array}
$$

Pivot row

In practice only the nonzeroes are stored.

At the start of the second iteration, we must find the first row of B^{-1}. This is simply the first row of the eta matrix corresponding to h_1, i.e.,

$$1 \quad 0 \quad 3 \quad 0$$

Multiplying this row vector times T gives the first row of E:

A	C	S_2	S_3	S_4
-20	0	0	30	40

Thus, variable A should enter.

The updated column of E corresponding to A is obtained by doing the matrix multiplication

$$
\begin{pmatrix} 1 & 0 & 30 & 0 \\ 0 & 1 & 0 & 0 \\ 0 & 0 & 1 & 0 \\ 0 & 0 & -2 & 1 \end{pmatrix}
\times
\begin{pmatrix} -20 \\ 1 \\ 0 \\ 1 \end{pmatrix}
=
\begin{pmatrix} -20 \\ 1 \\ 0 \\ 1 \end{pmatrix}
$$

The relevant part of E is

Row	Basis	A	RHS
(1)	Z	-20	1500
(2)	S_2	1	60
(3)	C	0	50
(4)	S_4	1	20

The minimum ratio is in row (4) so the pivot is in row (4) and the new eta file is:

$$\begin{array}{cc} h_2 & h_1 \\ 20 & 30 \\ -1 & 0 \\ 0 & 1 \\ \dfrac{1}{4} & \dfrac{-2}{3} \\ \text{Pivot row} & \end{array}$$

The first row of B^{-1} is obtained by the matrix multiplication:

$$\begin{bmatrix} 1 & 0 & 0 & 20 \end{bmatrix} \times \begin{bmatrix} 1 & 0 & 30 & 0 \\ 0 & 1 & 0 & 0 \\ 0 & 0 & 1 & 0 \\ 0 & 0 & -2 & 1 \end{bmatrix} = \begin{bmatrix} 1 & 0 & -10 & 20 \end{bmatrix}$$

Multiplying this times T gives the first row of E:

$$\begin{array}{ccccc} A & C & S_2 & S_3 & S_4 \\ 0 & 0 & 0 & -10 & 20 \end{array}$$

Thus, S_3 should enter. The updated column of E corresponding S_3 is obtained by applying the eta file to S_3's column in T. The original column of S_3 was

$$\begin{array}{c} 0 \\ 0 \\ 1 \\ 0. \end{array}$$

Applying h_1 gives:

$$\begin{array}{c} 30 \\ 0 \\ 1 \\ -2. \end{array}$$

Applying h_2 gives:

$$\begin{array}{c} -10 \\ 2 \\ 1 \\ -2. \end{array}$$

Thus, the relevant part of E is:

Row	Basis	S_3	RHS
(1)	Z	−10	1900
(2)	S_2	2	40
(3)	C	1	50
(4)	A	−2	20

The minimum ratio occurs in row (2) so row (2) is the pivot row. The new eta file is:

	h_3	h_2	h_1
	5	20	30
	1/2	−1	0
	−1/2	0	1
Pivot row	1/2	1/4	−2/3

The new first row of B^{-1} is constructed as follows: The first row of the h_3 matrix is:

$$1 \quad 5 \quad 0 \quad 0.$$

Multiplying this times the h_2 matrix gives:

$$1 \quad 5 \quad 0 \quad 15.$$

Multiplying this times the h_1 matrix gives:

$$1 \quad 5 \quad 0 \quad 15.$$

Multiplying this times the T matrix gives the new first row of E:

A	C	S_2	S_3	S_4
0	0	5	0	15

There are no negative reduced costs so this corresponds to the optimal solution:

Row	Basis	RHS
(1)	Z	2100
(2)	S_3	20
(3)	C	30
(4)	A	60

Revised Simplex Method: Summary of Computational Performance

We will now give a slightly optimistic estimate of the work per iteration using the revised simplex method with product form inverse. We will make the following slightly optimistic assumptions which we will justify later.

(a) A problem with m rows has an eta file that contains m eta vectors on average.

(b) The density of nonzeroes in an eta vector is the same as the density of a column in the original LP matrix, e.g., four nonzeroes per column.

It is realistic to assume that only the nonzeroes in an eta vector are stored. In general, assume there are d nonzero elements per column in the original LP matrix.

Now the steps in performing one iteration can be described as follows:

	Step	Number of Multiplications and Divisions
(i)	Get first row of B^{-1} (Get dual prices).	$d \times m$
(ii)	Get first row of E (Price out).	$d \times n$ (less if not all columns are priced in each pass)
(iii)	Construct updated entering column	$d \times m$
(iv)	Select pivot row.	m
(v)	Do the pivot and update RHS	m
	Total work per iteration	$2(1 + d)m + dn.$

Compare this with approximately mn for the standard simplex method and m^2 for the revised simplex method with explicit inverse. For our example parameters with $m = 500$, $n = 1000$ and $d = 4$, the comparisons are approximately 9000 vs. 500,000 and 250,000.

Our analysis has been optimistic. Each iteration adds another eta vector. Thus, we might have more than m eta vectors in a problem requiring many iterations. We might realistically expect each eta vector added to be at least 50% dense. The key is that every few iterations, e.g., m, we may perform a process called reinversion. All the accumulated eta vectors are discarded. We then do at most m pivots to bring the current basis back into the solution. We can do these m pivots in any order. If the order is chosen wisely, then for reasonable problems the density of these at most m eta vectors will be about the same as for columns in the original LP matrix.

Let us illustrate reinversion for our example problem. The final basis consisted of the columns C, A, and s_3. The final eta file contained 10 nonzeroes. We discard this eta file and we decide to pivot A into row (2), then C into row (4), and finally, s_3 into row (3). The corresponding eta file is:

	h_3	h_2	h_1
	0	-30	-20
	0	0	1
	1	1	0
Pivot row	$\dfrac{0}{3}$	$\dfrac{2}{4}$	$\dfrac{1}{2}$

Note that h_3 corresponds to an identity matrix and thus has no effect. Therefore, it need not be stored. Thus, a judicious reinversion has reduced the eta file to two vectors from three and to six nonzeroes from ten, and regular inversion provides some justification for our earlier optimistic assumptions.

The motivation for the chosen order can perhaps be understood by considering the following permutation of the rows and columns in the basis.

Row	A	C	S_3
(2)	1		
(4)	1	2	
(3)	0	0	1
(1)	-20	-30	

The noticeable feature of this matrix is that it is lower triangular. Pivoting A into row (2) has no effect on columns C and S_3. Pivoting C into row (4) has no effect on column S_3. Thus, the density of each eta vector is exactly the same as the original column associated with that pivot.

The basic goal of a good reinversion routine is to find that triangular order if it exists. The revised simplex method with product form inverse tends to perform well on problems which have bases that can be permuted to this lower or almost lower triangular form. Basis matrices for Network LP's can always be permuted to this lower triangular form.

You can observe the row and column permutation which LINDO uses to get an (almost) triangular basis configuration by executing the INVERT followed by BPIC commands. The latter command prints a basis picture which shows the locations of the nonzeroes in the permuted basis.

Getting an Initial Basic Feasible Solution

Our examples for illustrating the Simplex method have had the property that the slack variables by themselves constituted a basic feasible solution. What do we do when this convenient property does not hold?

Consider the following problem:

$$\text{Maximize} \quad 2X_1 + 7X_2 + 5X_3$$
$$\text{subject to} \quad 2X_1 + X_2 + 4X_3 = 5$$
$$X_1 \quad\quad - 2X_3 \geqq 2$$

There is no obvious initial basic feasible solution. A simple trick allows us to still use the simplex method. The trick consists of:

1. Add artificial variables as needed so that an initial basic feasible solution is obvious,
2. Give the artificial variables relatively unattractive coefficients in the objective function so that if there is a solution with all the artificials zero, then this solution will be found.

We will discuss three ways of doing part (2) of the trick:

(a) Big M method,
(b) Phase I/Phase II method,
(c) Little Epsilon method or composite method.

The Big M method is easiest to explain so we will illustrate it first. Let M denote an arbitrarily large positive number. Our example with surplus and artificial variables added is:

$$\text{Maximize} \quad 2X_1 + 7X_2 + 5X_3 - MA_2 - MA_3$$
$$\text{subject to} \quad 2X_1 + X_2 + 4X_3 \quad\quad + A_2 \quad\quad = 5$$
$$X_1 \quad\quad - 2X_3 - S \quad\quad + A_3 = 2$$

An obvious initial solution is $A_2 = 5$, $A_3 = 2$.

Putting it in tableau form and making variables A_1 and A_3 basic gives:

Row	Basis	X_1	X_2	X_3	S	A_2	A_3	RHS
(1)	Z	$-2-3M$	$-7-M$	$-5-2M$	M			$-7M$
(2)	A_2	2	1	4		1		5
(3)	A_3	1		-2	-1		1	2

If a value is specified for M then the simplex method can be applied. There are two related difficulties, however, with the Big M method insofar as computer implementation is concerned:

(a) How do we know that we have chosen M sufficiently large? That is, if termination occurs with some of the artificial variables still greater than zero, is it because there is no feasible solution or is it because we chose M too small?

(b) If we choose M too large, then the true objective coefficients may be swamped or lost in the finite precision of computer arithmetic. The resulting "optimal" solution may be feasible but not optimal for the original objective because of roundoff error.

The Phase I/Phase II methods allows us to effectively use an $M = \infty$ without incurring any of the roundoff difficulties of (b). This is achieved by separating the optimization into two phases:

(I) Minimize the sum of the infeasibilities and thereby either obtain a truly feasible initial basic solution or demonstrate unambiguously that there is no feasible solution,

(II) Optimize the true objective function, starting with the basic feasible solution supplied by Phase I.

It is convenient to think of appending an additional Phase I objective row to the tableau as shown below:

Row	Basis	X_1	X_2	X_3	S	A_2	A_3	RHS
(1)	Z_{II}	-2	-7	-5				
(2)	A_2	2	1	4		1		5
(3)	A_3	1		-2	-1		1	2
(4)	Z_I	-3	-1	-2	1			-7

The bottom row corresponds to the Phase I objective: Minimize $A_1 + A_2$. The bottom row of the tableau was obtained by pivoting A_2 in (2) and A_3 in (3), i.e., eliminating A_2 and A_3 from row (4). Thus, the Phase I objective would select X_1 as the first variable to enter, just as the Big M method would if M were ∞. As soon as all the artificial variables are driven to zero, we switch to the Phase II objective.

A misgiving that you might have about the Phase I/Phase II method is that it pays no attention to the true objective during Phase I. Thus the first feasible solution may be far from optimal.

The Little Epsilon or Composite method combines the desirable features of both the Big M and the Phase I/Phase II methods. It uses a Phase I and a Phase II, but during Phase I it uses a composite or weighted combination of the Phase I and Phase II objectives, specifically, (Phase I objective) + ϵ × (Phase II objective) where ϵ is a suitably small number. The Big M and Little Epsilon methods produce the same sequence of pivots if $M = 1/\epsilon$.

A typical starting value for ϵ is 1. The value of ϵ is decreased towards 0 as needed until Phase I is complete. The hope is that when Phase I is complete the solution will also be close to optimal for the Phase II objective.

Let us illustrate the Little Epsilon method with the previous tableau. Starting with $\epsilon = 1$, variable X_2 prices out to -8 and it is chosen to enter. The departing variable is A_2 and the new tableau is:

Row	Basis	X_1	X_2	X_3	S	A_2	A_3	RHS
(1)	Z_{II}	12		23		7		35
(2)	X_2	2	1	4		1		5
(3)	A_3	1		-2	-1		1	2
(4)	Z_I	-1		2	1	1		-2

With $\epsilon = 1$ no variable is attractive to enter, thus, ϵ must be decreased if it is not yet zero. We arbitrarily reduce ϵ to 0.01 and now X_1 prices out to $-1 + 0.12 = -0.88$, so it enters. The departing variable is A_3 and the new tableau is

Row	Basis	X_1	X_2	X_3	S	A_2	A_3	RHS
(1)	Z_{II}			47	12	7	-12	11
(2)	X_2		1	8	2	1	-2	1
(3)	X_3	1		-2	-1		1	2
(4)	Z_I					1	1	

All artificial variables are at zero so Phase I is finished. All nonartificial variables price out unattractive in the Phase II objective so we are done. If the solution had not been optimal, we would have reset ϵ to 1 as Phase II began.

A number of other features of the Phase I/Phase II and Little Epsilon methods are important with regard to implementation. First notice that the coefficient of a nonbasic variable in the Phase I objective is always the sum of its coefficients in rows in which an artificial variable is basic. Thus, the Phase I objective need never be stored. Portions of it can be easily constructed as needed. This construction is particularly easy with the Revised Simplex method. The essential modification is that an additional pricing vector corresponding to the Phase I objective is constructed. This "construct-as-needed" feature is also very compatible with partial pricing strategies, i.e., strategies that at each iteration consider but a small subset of the set of all columns as possible entering variables. Also notice that because an artificial variable will never be considered as an entering variable, these columns need never be stored. In our example, columns A_2 and A_3 never played a role once the initial tableau was constructed; thus, they could have been deleted. The net effect of all this is that the Revised Simplex method needs almost no modification to find

Figure 19.2

Path of Naïve Interior-Path Method

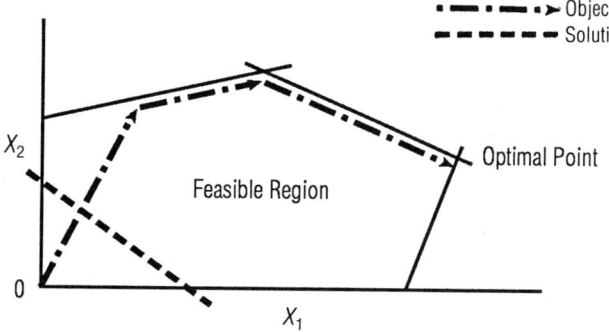

an initial feasible solution. No columns or rows need be added to the problem. The only modifications are:

(a) Initially, rows which would otherwise be infeasible are marked as having an artificial variable basic in them,

(b) During Phase I the construction of the pricing vector is modified so that the price vector is a weighted sum of the first row and the infeasible rows of B^{-1}.

Interior Path Methods for Solving LP's

Many people, after looking at a geometric view of how the simplex method follows a path around the exterior of the feasible region, have proposed an interior path method. Figure 19.2 illustrates this intuition.

Some people, after having proposed the use of a path through the interior, have realized that this approach is more easily proposed than implemented. The difficulty is that, unless chosen carefully, a path all the way through the interior will, as in the example in Figure 19.2, soon strike the exterior. Once on the exterior, the path very quickly follows a simplex-like path. Thus, we want to prevent the path from returning to the exterior until it reaches an optimum point. We will consider a problem of the following form:

$$\text{Minimize} \quad \sum_{j=1}^{n} c_j x_j$$

$$\text{subject to} \quad \sum_{j=1}^{n} a_{ij} x_j = b_i \quad \text{for } i = 1, m$$

$$x_j \geqq 0 \quad \text{for } j = 1, n$$

We would like to encourage paths that stay away from the boundary. The device we will use is to replace the inequality constraints $x \geqq 0$ by a "barrier" function that "repels" x if it gets close to 0.

Figure 19.3

The $-\ln(x)$ Barrier Function

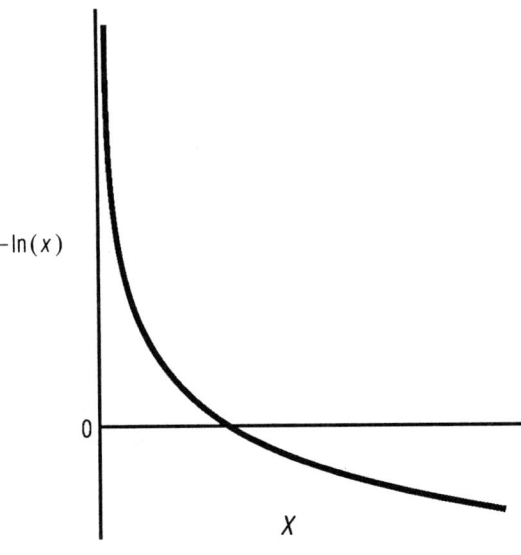

The "barrier" function we will use is the log barrier: $\ln(x)$. This function is illustrated in Figure 19.3. The key feature of the barrier function is that its cost approaches infinity as its argument approaches zero.

With the barrier function the problem becomes

$$\text{Minimize} \quad u_1 \sum_{j=1}^{n} c_j x_j - u_2 \sum_{j=1}^{n} \ln(x_j)$$

$$\text{subject to} \quad \sum_{j=1}^{n} a_{ij} x_j = b_i \quad \text{for } i = 1, m$$

The parameters u_1 and u_2 allow us to express how strongly we wish to minimize the objective and how strongly we would like to stay away from the boundary. For u_2 large and positive the barrier function will keep all x's > 0.

We can now describe in spirit how an interior path method works. If we hold u_1 fixed at some positive value and let u_2 approach zero, then the solution to the above problem will approach the boundary of the feasible region at a point at which $\sum_{j=1}^{n} c_j x_j$ is minimized.

Example

The Astro-Cosmo problem when written in equality form is:

Maximize $\quad 20A + 30C$

subject to
$$A \quad + s_2 \quad\quad\quad\quad = 60$$
$$\quad\quad C \quad\quad s_3 \quad\quad = 50$$
$$A + 2C \quad\quad\quad\quad s_4 = 120$$
$$A, C, s_2, s_3, s_4 \geq 0$$

In barrier function form the objective becomes:

Maximize $u_1(20A + 30C) + u_2[\ln(A) + \ln(C) + \ln(s_2) + \ln(s_3) + \ln(s_4)]$

This is a nonlinear program. We can solve it with a program such as GINO.

If we let $u_1 = 0$, then we get the point which in a sense is the center of the feasible region:

$$A = 23.3; \quad C = 16.4; \quad s_2 = 36.7; \quad s_3 = 33.6; \quad s_4 = 63.9.$$

If we let u_1 be some positive value and let u_2 approach zero, then the solution will approach:

$$A = 60; \quad C = 30; \quad s_2 = 0; \quad s_3 = 20; \quad s_4 = 0.$$

The complete path that is traced out as u_1 is increased and u_2 is decreased is shown in Figure 19.4.

Eliminating the Nonlinear Feature

As stated, for a given value of u_2 we must solve a nonlinear problem. Further, it appears

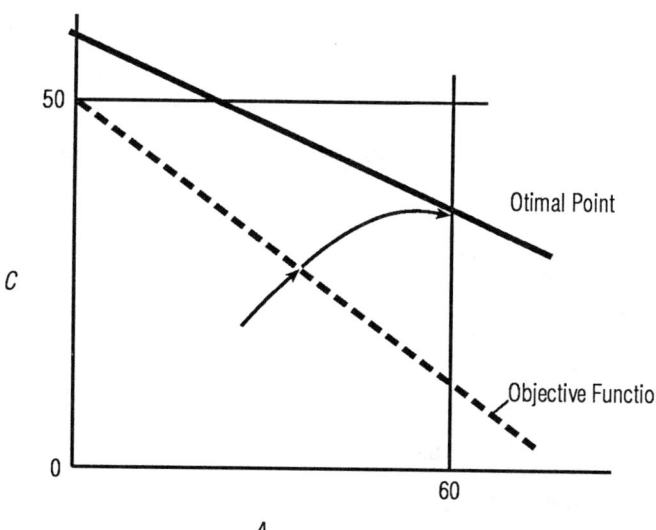

Figure 19.4

Continuous Path Version of an Interior Path Method

that we must solve infinitely many of these nonlinear problems as we let u_2 decrease to zero.

We will eliminate the nonlinear feature by using linear approximations. If we introduce Lagrange multiplier variables y_i for $i = 1, \ldots, m$, then the Lagrange mulitiplier problem is

$$\text{Minimize} \quad \sum_{j=1}^{m} c_j x_j - u_2 \sum_{j=1}^{n} \ln(x_j) + \sum_{i=1}^{m} y_i \left(\sum_{j=1}^{n} a_{ij} x_j - b_i \right).$$

The first order conditions are obtained by differentiating with respect to x_j and y_i to obtain:

for x_j:
$$c_j - u_2/x_j + \sum_{i=1}^{m} y_i a_{ij} = 0 \tag{19.1}$$

for y_i:
$$\sum_{j=1}^{n} a_{ij} x_j = b_i \tag{19.2}$$

Suppose that we have a solution, $\{\bar{x}_j\}$, that is feasible to the constraints (19.2). We want to find a new point $\{x_j\}$ that is better. Define the differences:

$$d_j = x_j - \bar{x}_j.$$

Dealing with the nonlinear terms u_2/x_j in 19.1 is a problem. A linear approximation based on a Taylor series first order approximation to $1/x_j$ at $\bar{x}_j$ is $1/\bar{x}_j - d_j/\bar{x}_j^2$. Thus, a linear approximation to the first order conditions is:

$$c_j - u_2/\bar{x}_j + u_2 d_j/\bar{x}_j^2 + \sum_{i=1}^{m} y_i a_{ij} = 0$$

and

$$\sum_j a_{ij} x_j = b_i \quad \text{or equivalently} \quad \sum_j a_{ij} d_j = 0.$$

So for $\bar{x}_j$ given we want to solve for the d_j's and y_j's in the system of equations:

For $j = 1, \ldots, n$
$$u_2 d_j/\bar{x}_j^2 + \sum_{i=1}^{m} a_{ij} y_j = u_2/\bar{x}_j - c_j \tag{19.3}$$

and for $i = 1, m$
$$\sum_{j=1}^{n} d_j a_{ij} = 0 \tag{19.4}$$

The general outline of the steps of an interior path method is then:

1. Obtain an initial solution that satisfies (19.1).

2. Based on the current point, solve the linearized first order conditions system (19.3) and (19.4).

Figure 19.5

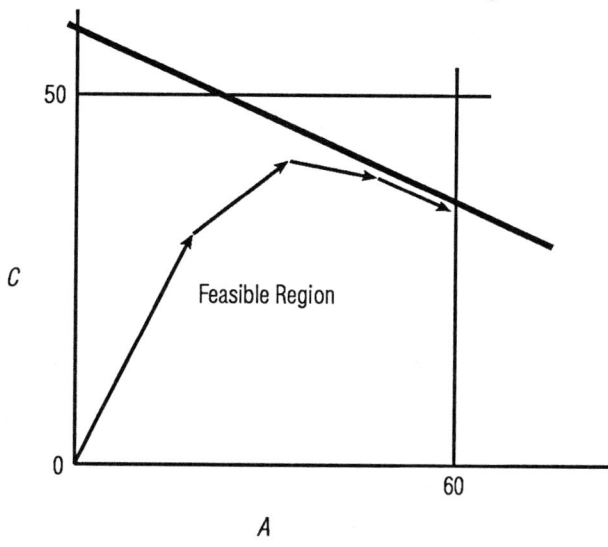

Path of Piecewise Linear Interior Path Algorithm

3. Using the d_j's obtained in step (2) as a direction, choose a stepsize to move to a new better solution if possible.
4. If a stopping criterion is satisfied, stop, else go to (2).

The Astro/Cosmo Problem Continued

Figure 19.5 shows the path followed by a "linearized and discretized" version of the interior path algorithm. For this particular version we held $u_1 = u_2 = 1$ for each iteration. The values of the variables at each iteration were:

Iteration	A	C	s_2	s_3	s_4	Objective
0	1	1	59	49	117	50
1	21.96	31.94	38.04	18.06	34.16	1397.4
2	34.16	41.15	25.84	8.85	3.54	1917.7
3	49.33	35.19	10.67	14.81	0.28	2042.4
4	59.91	30.01	0.09	19.99	0.06	2098.6

At iteration 4 it is apparent that s_2 and s_4 are going to zero and thus the solution should be $A = 60$, $C = 30$. At iteration 4 the three y variables, corresponding to the three dual prices, had values: 5.003, 0.006, and 14.998. Thus, they are close to the optimal dual prices of 5, 0, and 15.

Other Versions of Interior Path Algorithms

The interior path method we described is known as the primal affine method. The interior path method first popularized by Karmarkar (1985) required that the variables be scaled so that the constraint $\sum_{j=1}^{n} x_j = 1$ was satisfied. That approach has come to be known as the projective scaling approach.

One could also consider the dual of a problem and apply an interior path method to it. This has been the approach used by Marsten *et al.* (1989) in their successful implementation of an interior path algorithm.

The first suggestion of interior path methods of the kind described here is attributed to Dikin (1967).

Problems

1. The following tableau arose during the application of the standard Simplex method.

	x_1	x_2	x_3	x_4	x_5	x_6	RHS
Objective	12	0	−15	0	5	0	1400
	4	0	2	1	1	0	12
	−2	1	−2	0	0	0	18
	5	0	3	0	−1	1	15

(a) Which variable should enter?

(b) In which row should the pivot occur?

(c) Which variables are basic in the above tableau and what are their values?

(d) Which variable goes to zero (departs) if the pivot mentioned in step (b) above is performed?

(e) Perform the pivot mentioned in step (b).

(f) Is the resulting solution optimal?

2. Consider the following problem:

$$\text{Maximize } 4x_1 + 3x_2 - 9999a_1 - 9999a_2$$
$$\text{subject to } 2x_1 + 4x_2 + a_1 = 6$$
$$\phantom{\text{subject to }} 6x_1 + x_2 + a_2 = 7$$

(a) Can you identify an initial feasible solution without doing any arithmetic? What variables are nonzero at which values?

(b) Temporarily disregard the Simplex method rule for selecting entering variables and perform the two iterations necessary to bring these two variables into the solution.

(c) Now perform the regular simplex method to find the optimal solution.

3. Apply the simplex method to the following problem. In words, what can you say about the optimal solution?

$$\text{Maximize } 5x + 4y + 3z$$
$$\text{subject to } x - 2y \leq 5$$
$$\phantom{\text{subject to }} 3x + y - z \leq 3$$
$$\phantom{\text{subject to 3x }} + 7y + z \leq 8$$

APPENDIX

Summary of LINDO Help Commands

This appendix provides summary information about LINDO (Linear, INteractive, Discrete Optimizer), then lists LINDO commands by category, and follows with a list of detailed HELP commands organized by category. If you type simply "help", you will get the following information on your screen.

The LINDO program is licensed material with all rights reserved (Copyright © 1984, 1985, 1991 Lindo Systems). Copying except as authorized in license agreement is prohibited.

LINDO solves linear, integer, and quadratic programs entered in natural form. The following would be valid input:

```
MAX 2X + 3Y
ST
4X + 5Y < 9
7X + 6Y < 13
END
GO
```

To learn the available commands type "COMMANDS" and ↵ (Enter or Carriage Return). The commands will be listed on your screen by category as they are in the next section of this appendix. To get help for a particular command, type "HELP name" where "name" is the command name. For example, for more help on entering a formulation, type "HELP MAX".

To get out of a command which is prompting for input, type either "END" or simply a ↵. You will return to command mode. See specific commands for the effect, if any, on processing done by that command.

Maximum size of inputs are:

Input	Maximum Size
Nonzeroes	60,000
Columns	20,000
Rows	6,500
Integer Variables	14,900
Var/Row Name Characters	8

Larger versions are available.

LINDO Commands by Category

The LINDO commands listed below are divided into descriptive categories. You may get this same information on your screen by typing "help com" after the LINDO prompt (" : ").

1. *Information:*

   HELP   CAT   COM   LOCAL   TIME

2. *Input:*

   LEAV   MAX   MIN   RDBC   RETR   RMPS   TAKE

3. *Display:*

   BPIC   CPRI   LOOK   NONZ   PIC   RANGE   RPRI
   SHOC   SOLU   TABL

4. *File Output:*

   DIVE   RVRT   SAVE   SDBC   SMPS

5. *Solution:*

   GO   PIV

6. *Problem Editing:*

   ALT   APPC   DEL   EDIT   EXT   FREE   SLB
   SUB

7. *Quit:*

   QUIT

8. *Integer, Quadratic, and Parametric Programs:*

   BIP   GIN   INT   IPTOL   PARA   POSD   QCP
   TITAN

9. *Conversational Parameters:*

   BAT   PAGE   PAUS   TERS   VERB   WIDTH

10. *User Supplied Routines:*

    USER

11. *Miscellaneous:*

    BUG   DEBUG   INV   SET   STAT   TITL

Description of the Help Commands

HELP *command*

: help

> Type "HELP" to list general information about LINDO. To get help on a specific command, type "HELP command", where "command" refers to the specific command of interest.

The LINDO commands described in the remainder of this appendix are separated by subheads into the previously listed categories.

Information

CAT *command*

: help cat

> Lists the categories of commands and optionally the commands in selected categories.

COMMMAND *command*

: help com

> Lists all LINDO commands.

LOCAL *command*

: help local

> Gives information specific to your local version of this program.

TIME *command*

: help time

> Displays the cumulative CPU time for LINDO session.

Input

LEAVE *command*

: help leav

> Is the last command in a TAKE command file.

MAX/MIN *commands*

: help max *or*
: help min

> These commands are used to enter a new LP model consisting of an objective function that will be MAXimized or MINimized subject to the list of constraints.
> Enter "MAX" or "MIN" followed by the first row (objective function) in natural format. Then enter "SUBJECT TO" (abbreviated "ST") followed by all the other rows (constraints). Then enter "END" to return to command mode. You may then wish to give the "GO" command to begin optimization.
> Variable names may be from one to eight alphanumeric characters, and must begin with a letter. Coefficients may not be in exponential form, e.g., coefficients like .258E+29 are not allowed. The number of significant digits in

any coefficient is about 6.5 digits. The keywords ("MAX", "ST", "END"...) and the rows must all be separated by one or more blanks. Blanks may be included within a row, but may not be imbedded in variable names or coefficients. A carriage return is equivalent to a blank.

Following are two legitimate ways of entering the same problem:

1. MIN   2X+3Y   SUBJECT TO −5X − 2Z <= 10
   +10X − Y >5   END

2. MIN   2X + 3 Y
   ST   −5X − 2Z
   < 10
   10X − Y > +5
   END

Optionally, a constraint may be prefaced by a name, e.g.:

DEMAND) 10X − Y > 5

RDBC *command*

: help rdbc

Tries to get an initial solution to current formulation from previous solution stored in an SDBC file.

RETRIEVE *command*

: help retr

Fetches a model from disk. LINDO will prompt you for a specific file name or unit number. The model being retrieved must have been previously saved via the "SAVE" command.

RMPS *command*

: help rmps

Inputs a problem from a file in MPS format. See IBM MPSX manuals for details of this format.

TAKE *command*

: help take

Allows a series of commands to be taken from a file. The file contents should appear exactly as terminal input, e.g., the file cannot contain line numbers. The last command in the file should be: LEAVE.

Display

BPICTURE *command*

: help bpic

Prints logical picture of current basis using row order of the last invert/triangularization.

CPRI/RPRI *commands*

: help cpri   *or*

: help rpri

> Prints selected information about selected columns (CPRI) or rows (RPRI). The format for CPRI is:
>
> > CPRI print-list : conditional-expression
>
> for example,
>
> > CPRI N P : N = M%%X .AND. D > 0
>
> will print the name and primal value for every column with first character of the name = M, the fourth character = X, and with a dual activity greater than zero. If "print-list" is omitted, only the number of matches is printed. Symbols for column/row attributes are:
>
> > N = Name
> > P = Primal value (slack for rows)
> > D = Dual value (reduced cost for columns.)
> > R = RIM (objective coefficient for columns; RHS for rows)
> > U = Simple upper bound; L = Simple lower bound
> > T = Type ("C", "I", or "F"; "<", "=", or ">")
> > Z = Number of nonzeroes in a column or row.
> > % = Wild card character in names
>
> Other useful symbols allowed in the conditional expression are:
>
> | Arithmetic | Logical | Relational | Order |
> |---|---|---|---|
> | + − / * ^ | .AND. | > < = # | ( ) |
> | LOG( ) EXP( ) | .OR. | | |
> | ABS( ) | .NOT. | | |

LOOK *command*

: help look

> Use "LOOK" to examine all or part of the current model. Type "LOOK ALL" to look at all the model. Type "LOOK row1,row2" to look at rows row1 thru row2.
>
> All coefficients will be rounded off to five decimal places. There is a limit of nine digits printed in the integral part of a coefficient. Anything larger will be printed as *****.

NONZEROES *command*

: help nonz

> Prints an abbreviated solution report covering only the variables which are nonzero in the solution. *Note:* NONZ does not solve the problem so you must first use the GO command. The use of NONZ makes sense only if you have set the conversational style to TERSE.

PICTURE *command*

: help picture

> An abbreviated picture of the coefficients of the LP are printed in matrix form.

It is useful for debugging a formulation. The following letter code is used to represent numbers:

Z	.000000	THRU	.000001
Y	.000001	THRU	.000009
X	.000010	THRU	.000099
W	.000100	THRU	.000999
V	.001000	THRU	.009999
U	.010000	THRU	.099999
T	.100000	THRU	.999999
A	1.000001	THRU	10.000000
B	10.000001	THRU	100.000000
C	100.000001	THRU	1000.000000
D	1000.000001	THRU	10000.000000
E	10000.000001	THRU	100000.000000
F	100000.000001	THRU	1000000.000000
G		>	1000000

RANGE *command*

: help range

    Prints range report on RHS and OBJ coefficients.

SHOCOLUMN *command*

: help shoc

    Displays a specified column.

SOLUTION *command*

: help solu

    Prints solution report.

TABLEAU *command*

: help tabl

    The coefficients in the current Simplex Tableau are printed.

File Output

DIVERT *command*

: help dive

    You will be asked for a file. All subsequent hi-volume output, e.g., solution reports, will be diverted to this file until a RVRT (REVERT) command is given.

REVERT *command*

: help rvrt

    Causes all subsequent output to revert to the terminal. It undoes the effect of the DIVERT command.

APPENDIX: Summary of LINDO Help Commands **351**

SAVE *command*

: help save

Saves the current model in a file in condensed LINDO format. The model may be retrieved using "RETR."

SDBC *command*

: help sdbc

Save in data base format a column report. NAME, VALUE, REDUCED COST, VARIABLE TYPE and SUB are stored in (A8,2G13.6,A1,G13.6) format.

SMPS *command*

: help smps

Saves current problem to a file in MPS format. See IBM MPSX manuals for details.

Solution

GO *command*

: help go

Solves the current formulation. The formulation remains intact through the solution process. A positive integer typed after GO is interpreted as an upper limit on the number of iterations.

PIVOT *command*

: help piv

One pivot step of the Simplex Method is performed. If a variable name is typed after PIV, then that variable is entered into the solution. A row name may be given after the variable name.

Problem Editing

ALTER *command*

: help alter

Use "ALTER" to edit the current model. the format for the command is "ALTER row-id var-id". "row-id" is the ID of the row you want to edit and "var-id" is the name of the variable whose coefficient you want to change. LINDO will then prompt you for the new value. If you wish to change the RHS, direction, or name of a row, use a "var-id" of either "RHS", "DIR", or "NAME".

Notes: Valid directions for the objective are "MAX" or "MIN"; for all other rows use "<", "=", or "<". Do not try to delete a row with "ALTER". Use "DELETE" instead.

APPEND COLUMN *command*

: help appc

Name of new column or variable is entered after APPC. Follow this with the row/value pairs for the column. One pair per line; row and value separated by a space. End by entering a 0 for the row. A column name of RHS will cause the input to be interpreted as a new RHS.

DELETE *command*

: help del

Type "DELETE row-id" to delete the row "row-id" from the current model. You cannot delete the objective.

EDIT *command*

: help edit

Switches LINDO to full screen edit mode. Cursor keys can be used to navigate through your model. Other useful edit features include:

[Home]	Moves top start of model text
[End]	Moves to end of model text
[PgUp]/[PgDn]	Moves a pageful through the model text
[Ctrl]-[S]	Moves to start of current line
[Ctrl]-[E]	Moves to end of current line
[Ctrl]-[→]	Moves to end of current word
[Ctrl]-[←]	Moves to start of current word

EXTEND *command*

: help ext

Permits you to add constraint rows to a previously defined model. Enter new rows as you would for "MAX" or "MIN". Do not type the keywords "MAX", "MIN", or "SUBJECT TO". New rows will be appended to the end of the model. Indicate end of extensions by typing "END".

FREE *command*

: help free

Typing: FREE X causes X to be a free variable in the current formulation, i.e., its lower bound is minus infinity and its upper bound is plus infinity.

SLB *command*

: help slb

Enters or changes a simple lower bound for a variable. Form is:

SLB VARIABLE LB

where VARIABLE is a variable name and LB is a numeric value. For large problems, SLBs are more efficient for stating constraints like:

X > 10

SUB *command*

: help sub

Enters or changes a simple upper bound for a variable. Form is:

SUB SUBVARIABLE UB

where VARIABLE is a variable name and UB is a numeric value. For large problems, SUBs are more efficient for stating constraints like:

X < 10.

Quit

QUIT *command*

: help quit

Use to leave the LINDO package. Any unsaved formulation will be lost.

Integer, Quadratic, and Parametric Programs

BIP *command*

: help bip

Permits user to specify a bound on the worst IP solution, e.g., based on a known feasible solution, that will be considered in the branch and bound search for the IP optimum.

GIN *command*

: help gin

The GIN command identifies the variables which are to be integer in the model. The first form is "GIN n" where n is the number of these variables. LINDO requires that these variables appear first in the model. The second form is "GIN var-id" where "var-id" is the name of a variable. When the GO command is given the LP solution is printed first followed by each better IP solution as it is found.

INTEGER *command*

: help int

The integer command identifies the variables which are to be 0/1 in the model. The first form is "INTEGER n" where n is the number of these variables. LINDO requires that these variables appear first in the model. The second form is "INTEGER var-id" where "var-id" is the name of a variable. When the GO command is given the LP solution is printed first followed by each better IP solution as it is found.

IPTOL *command*

: help iptol

The form is "IPTOL F" where F is a nonnegative fraction. When searching for another IP solution, only solutions which are fraction F better than the best one found so far will be considered.

PARA *command*

: help para

Does parametric RHS analysis. You specify a row and a new value for its RHS. PARA varies the RHS of this row from its current value to the new value, displaying the optimal objective value at each basis change along the way. The problem must be optimized before calling PARA.

POSD *command*

: help posd

Checks if the submatrix of the constraints corresponding to the quadratic form in a QCP problem is positive definite.

QCP *command*

: help qcp

The QCP command helps solve linear complementarity problems, e.g., quadratic programming problems. Suppose we wish to:

```
MIN 3X*X + Y*Y - X*Y + .4Y
ST
1.2X + .9Y > 1.1
X + Y= 1
Y <.7
```

The problem must be converted to linear (complementary) form by preceding the real constraints with the first order conditions for the variables. This requires us to add a dual variable for each real constraint. We will use RT, ONE, and UL for our example. For QCP problems the first row (the objective in an LP) is used solely to specify the order of the variables corresponding to the constraint order. We enter our problem as follows:

```
MIN X + Y + RT + ONE + UL
ST
6X - Y - 1.2RT + ONE > 0.
- X + 2Y - .9RT + ONE + UL > -.4
1.2X + .9Y > 1.1
X + Y = 1
Y < .7
END
QCP
  ROW NO. OF FIRST REAL CONSTRAINT:
  4
G
```

TITAN *command*

: help titan

A powerful command for tightening up an LP/IP formulation. First it will try to tighten simple upper bounds. e.g., given:

```
2X +  Y < 12
-X + 2Y < 3
```

it will deduce the SUBS:

```
SUB X 6
SUB Y 4.5
```

Second, it will try to tighten coefficients of integer variables. If additionally we have:

$$30W - 3X + 2Y > 3$$

where W is 0/1, then it will tighten this to:

$$21W - 3X + 2Y > 3.$$

Conversational Parameters

BATCH *command*

: help bat

> Sets conversational mode to batch. If you are running the job in BATCH, it makes the output more readable and will stop the run at the first major error.

PAGE *command*

: help page

> Sets page or screen size in lines. For example, PAGE 24 will cause a pause before printing the 24th line of a report. Hitting a ↵ will cause the next batch of lines to be printed. PAGE 0 sets the size to infinity.

PAUSE *command*

: help paus

> Used in a TAKE file, it causes a pause until the next ↵ is typed at the terminal. Any text after PAUSE on the line is typed to the terminal.

TERSE *command*

: help ters

> Changes the conversational style to TERSE. For example, it does not automatically print the solution report at LP OPTIMUM. The user may browse thru the solution with commands like NONZ.

VERBOSE *command*

: help verb

> Converts the conversational style back to the default VERBOSE style.

WIDTH *command*

: help width

> Width N tells LINDO that your terminal is N characters wide. For example, WIDTH 132 indicates that your terminal uses line printer width paper.

User Supplied Routines

USER *command*

: help user

> Executes a user supplied subroutine called USER(IN), where IN = current input unit. The following subroutines are available to the user:

INIT
> Initialize storage at start of new problem

DEFROW(IDIR,RHSVAL,NUROIS,TOOBIG)
> Add a row where IDIR = −1 if less than (or max); 0 if equal to; 1 if greater than (or min). RHSVAL is the RHS value; NUROIS returned as the row identification; TOOBIG returned .TRUE. if too big.

APPCOL(NAME,NONZ,VAL,IRO,TOOBIG)
> Add column called NAME (in 8A1 format). Its coefficients are stored in the vector VAL with the row numbers in the vector IRO. NONZ is the number of nonzeroes. TOOBIG returned .TRUE. if problem too big.

GO
> Go solve current problem.

REPVAR(J,PRIMAL,DUAL)
> Return the value and reduced cost of variable J in PRIMAL and DUAL.

REPROW(I,PRIMAL,DUAL)
> Return the SLACK and DUAL price of row I in PRIMAL and DUAL.

SETSUB(J,UB)
> Set the SUB of variable J to UB.

Miscellaneous

BUG *command*

: help bug

> Bug reports or information requests should be sent to:
> LINDO SYSTEMS, INC.
> P.O. Box 148231
> Chicago, IL 60614
> Tel: 312-871-2524

DEBUG *command*

: help debug

> If a model has no feasible solution because of an error in a constraint coefficient or RHS, DEBUG will identify a smallest set of constraints which could contain an error. In VERBOSE mode, this set of constraints will be listed. It cannot be used for quadratic programs.

INVERT *command*

: help inv

> Inverts the current basis. Results tend to be a bit more accurate.

SET *command*

: help set

> Allows you to reset LINDO internal parameters. Form is:
> SET   PARAM-ID   NEW-VALUE

Accessible parameters are:

Parameter ID	Purpose
1	Final constraint tolerance
2	Initial constraint tolerance
3	Entering variable reduced cost tolerance
4	Fixing threshold for integer variables

STATS *command*

: help stat

Gives STATS (e.g., rows, columns) of current formulation.

TITLE *command*

: help TITL

Specify or display title of current model. To associate the phrase, "THIS IS PROBLEM XR-9" with the current model, you would type:

titl THIS IS PROBLEM XR-9

BIBLIOGRAPHY

Arnold, L., and D. Botkin. "Portfolios to Satisfy Damage Judgement: A Linear Programming Approach," *Interfaces*, Vol. 8, No. 2 (Feb. 1978).

Baker, E. K and M. L. Fisher (1981), "Computational Results for Very Large Air Crew Scheduling Problems," *Omega*, Vol.9, pp. 613–618.

Balas, E. (1979), "Disjunctive Programming," *Annals of Discrete Mathematics* Vol. 5, pp. 3–51.

Bessent, A., W. Bessent, J. Kennington, and B. Reagan (1982), "An Application of Mathematical Programming to Assess Productivity in the Houston Independent School District," *Management Science*, Vol. 28, no. 12, December, pp. 1355–1367.

Bland, R. G. and D. F. Shallcross (1989), "Large Traveling Salesman Problems Arising in X-ray Crystallography: A Preliminary Report on Computation," *O.R. Letters*, vol. 9, no. 3, pp. 125–128, (1989).

Bradley, G. H., G. G. Brown and G. W. Graves, "Design and Implementation of Large Scale Primal Transshipment Algorithms," *Management Science*, Vol. 24, 1977, pp. 1–34.

Bradley, S. P., A. C. Hax and T. L. Magnanti. *Applied Mathematical Programming*. Reading, Mass.: Addison-Wesley Publishing Company, (1977).

Braess, D. (1968), "Uber ein Paradoxon aus der Verkehrsplanung," *Unternehmensforschung*, Vol. 12, pp.258–268.

Brearley, A. L., G. Mitra, and H. P. Williams. "Analysis of Mathematical Programming Problems Prior to Applying the Simplex Algorithm," *Mathmatical Programming*, Vol. 8, (1975), pp. 54–83.

Brown, G. G. and D. S. Thomen (1980), "Automatic Identification of Generalized Upper Bounds in Large-Scale Optimization Models," *Management Science*, Vol. 26, No. 11, pp. 1166–1184.

Charnes, A., W. W. Cooper and E. Rhodes, "Measuring the Efficiency of Decision Making Units," *European Journal of Operational Research*, 2 (1978) 429–444.

Clarke, G. and J. W. Wright (1964), "Scheduling of Vehicles from a Central Depot to a Number of Delivery Points," *Operations Research*, Vol. 12, No. 4 (July–Aug.), pp. 568–581.

Cunningham, K., and L. Schrage. *LINGO Optimization Modeling Language*. LINDO Systems, Chicago, 1991.

Dantzig, G. B. *Linear Programming and Extensions*. Princeton: Princeton University Press, (1963).

Dantzig G. and B. Wolfe (1960), "Decomposition Principle for Linear Programs," *Operations Research*, Vol. 8, pp. 101–111.

Davis, L. S. and K. N. Johnson (1987), *Forest Management*, 3rd ed., McGraw-Hill Company.

DeWitt, C. W., L. Lasdon, A. Waren, D. Brenner and S. Melhem (1989), "OMEGA: An Improved Gasoline Blending System for Texaco," *Interfaces*, Vol. 19, No. 1 (Jan.–Feb.), pp. 85–101.

Dikin, I. I. (1967), "Iterative Solution of Problems of Linear and Quadratic Programming," *Soviet Mathematics Doklady*, vol. 8, pp. 674–675.

Dutton, R. G. Hinman and C. B. Millham. "The Optimal Location of Nuclear-Power Facilities in the Pacific Northwest," *Operations Research*, Vol. 22, No. 3 (May–June 1974), pp. 478–487.

Fields, C., J. F. Hourican and E. A. McGee. "Developing a Minimum Cost Feed Blending System for Intensive Use," Joint National TIMS/ORSA Meeting, New York, (1978).

Florian, M. "An Improved Linear Approximation Algorithm for the Network Equilibrium (Packet Switching) Problem," *Proceedings 1977 IEEE Conference Decision and Control*, (1977).

Gomory, R. E. (1958), "Outline of an Algorithm for Integer Solutions to Linear Programs," *Bulletin of the American Mathematical Society*, Vol. 64, pp. 275–278.

Grötschel, M., M. Jünger and G. Reinelt (1985), "Facets of the Linear Ordering Polytope," *Mathematical Programming*, Vol. 33, pp. 43–60.

Gunawardane, G., S. Hoff and L. Schrage (1981), "Identification of Special Structure Constraints in Linear Programs," *Mathematical Programming*, Vol. 21, pp. 90–97.

Hadley, G. *Linear Programming*. Addison-Wesley, (1962).

Hanson, W. and R. K. Martin (1990), "Optimal Bundle Pricing," *Management Science*. Vol. 36, No. 2 (February), pp. 155–174.

Jenkins, L. (1982), "Parametric Mixed Integer Programming: An Application to Solid Waste Management," *Management Science*, Vol. 28, No. 11 (Nov.), pp. 1270–1284.

Karmarkar, N. K. (1985), "A New Polynomial Time Algorithm for Linear Programming," *Combinatorica*, Vol. 4, pp. 373–395.

Khachian, L. G. (1979), "A Polynomial Algorithm in Linear Programming," *Soviet Mathematics Doklady*, Vol. 20, No. 1, pp. 191–194.

Kruskal, Jr., J. B. (1956), "On the Shortest Spanning Subtree of a Graph and the Traveling Salesman Problem," *Proc. Amer. Math. Soc.*, Vol. 7, pp. 48–50.

Lawler, E. L. (1963), "The Quadratic Assignment Problem," *Management Science*. Vol. 19, pp. 586–599.

Lawler, E. L., J. K. Lenstra, A. H. G. Rinnooy Kan and D. B. Shmoys (1985), "The Traveling Salesman Problem: A Guided Tour of Combinatorial Optimization," John Wiley & Sons.

Leontief, W. *The Structure of American Economy*, 1919–1931. New York: Oxford University Press, (1951).

Levy, F. K. "Portfolios to Satisfy Damage Judgements: A Simple Approach," *Interfaces*, Vol. 9, No. 1 (Nov. 1978), pp.106–107.

Lin S. and B. Kernighan (1973), "An Effective Heuristic Algorithm for the Traveling Salesman Problem," *Operations Research*, Vol. 21, pp. 498–516.

Madansky, A. (1962), "Methods of Solution of Linear Programs Under Uncertainty," *Operations Research*, Vol. 10, pp. 463–471.

Markowitz, H. M. *Portfolio Selection, Efficient Diversification of Investments.*" John Wiley & Sons, Inc., (1959).

Markowitz, H. and A. Perold (1981), "Portfolio Analysis with Scenarios and Factors," *Journal of Finance*, Vol. 36, pp. 871–877.

Marsten, R. E., M. P. Muller and C. L. Killion. "Crew Planning at Flying Tiger: A Successful Application of Integer Programming, *Management Science*. Vol. 25, No. 12 (Dec. 1979), pp. 1175–1183.

Marsten, R. E., M. J. Saltzman, D. F. Shanno, G. S. Pierce, and J. F. Ballintijn (1989), "Implementation of a Dual Affine Interior Point Algorithm for Linear Programming," *ORSA J. on Computing*, Vol. 1, No. 4, pp. 287–297.

Maschler, M., B. Peleg, and L. S. Shapley (1979), "Geometric Properties of the Kernel, Nucleolus, and Related Solution Concepts," *Math of O.R.*, Vol. 4, No. 4, (Nov.), pp. 303–338.

Miller, H. E., W. P. Pierskalla and G. J. Rath. "Nurse Scheduling using Mathematical Programming," *Operations Research*, Vol. 24, 1976, pp. 857–870.

Murchland, J. D. (1970), "Braess's Paradox of Traffic Flow," *Transportation Research*, Vol. 4, pp. 391–394.

Nauss, R. M. (1986), "True Interest Cost in Municipal Bond Bidding: An Integer Programming Approach, *Management Science*, Vol. 32, No. 7, pp. 870–877.

Nauss, R. M. and B. R. Keeler (1981), "Minimizing Net Interest Cost in Municipal Bond Bidding," *Management Science*, Vol. 27, No. 4 (April), pp. 365–376.

Nauss, R. M. and R. Markland (1981), "Theory and Application of an Optimization Procedure for Lock Box Location Analysis," *Management Science*, Vol. 27, No. 8 (August), pp. 855–865.

Neebe, A. W. (1987), "An Improved, Multiplier Adjustment Procedure for the Segregated Storage Problem," *J. Opl. Res. Soc.*, Vol. 38, No. 9, pp. 1–11.

Padberg, M. and G. Rinaldi (1987), "Optimization of a 532-City Symmetric Traveling Salesman Problem by Branch and Cut," *O. R. Letters*, Vol. 6, No. 1.

Perold, Andre F. (1984), "Large Scale Portfolio Optimization," *Management Science*, Vol. 30, pp. 1143–1160.

Plane, D. R. and T. E. Hendrick. "Mathematical Programming and the Location of Fire Companies for the Denver Fire Department," *Operations Research*, Vol. 25, No. 4 (July–August 1977), pp. 563–578.

Ross, G. T. and R. M. Soland (1975), "Modeling Facility Location Problems as Generalized Assignment Problems," *Management Sciene*, Vol. 24, pp. 345–357.

Rothstein, M. (1985), "OR and the Airline Overbooking Problem," *Operations Research*, Vol. 33, No. 2 (March–April), pp. 237–248.

Sankaran, J. (1989), *Bidding Systems for Certain Nonmarket Allocations of Indivisible Items*, Ph.D. dissertation, University of Chicago.

Schrage, L. and L. Wolsey (1985), "Sensitivity Analysis for Branch and Bound Integer Programming," *Operations Research*, Vol. 33, No. 5 (Sept., Oct.), pp. 1008–1023.

Sharpe, W. F. (1963), "A Simplified Model for Portfolio Analysis," *Management Science*, Vol. 9 (Jan.), pp. 277–293.

Srinivasan, V. "Linear Programming Computational Procedures for Ordinal Regression," *Journal of ACM*, Vol. 23, No. 3 (July 1976), pp. 475–487.

Stigler, G. (1963), "United States vs. Loew's, Inc.: A Note on Black Booking," *Supreme Court Review*, p. 152.

Stigler, G. J. "The Cost of Subsistence," *Journal of Farm Economics*, Vol. 27, No. 2 (May 1945), pp. 303–314.

Strevell, Michael and Philip Chong. "Gambling on Vacation," *Interfaces*, Vol. 15, No. 2, March–April 1985, pp. 63–67.

Thompson, R. G., F. D. Singleton, R. M. Thrall and B. A. Smith, "Comparative Site Evaluations for Locating a High-Energy Physics Lab in Texas," *Interfaces*, 16 (1986) 35–49.

Tomlin, J. and J. S. Welch (1985), "Integration of a Primal Simplex Algorithm with a paper on WHIZNET. Large Scale Mathematical Programming System," *ACM Trans. Math. Software*, Vol. 11, pp. 1–11.

Vickrey, William. "Counterspeculation, Auctions, and Competitive Sealed Tenders," *Journal of Finance*, March 1961, Vol. 16, No. 1, pp. 8–37.

Wall Street Journal, "UAL's United Alters Schedule, Cuts Costs, Boosts Flights in Face of Discount Fares," (19 June, 1978), p. 8.

Warner, D. M. "Scheduling Nursing Personnel According to Nursing Preference: A Mathematical Programming Approach," *Operations Research*, Vol. 24, No. 5, September–October 1976, pp. 842–856.

Weingartner, H. M. "Municipal Bond Coupon Schedules with Limitations on the Number of Coupons," *Management Science*, Vol. 19, No. 4 (Dec. 1972), pp. 369–378.

What's Best User Manual. LINDO Systems, Chicago, (1991).

INDEX

100% rule, 41

A

accounting constraint, 53
activity-on-arc, 99, 101
activity-on-arrow, 95
activity-on-node, 99, 100
advertising, 293
affine, 343
aggregation, 272
airline, 82, 130, 231, 273
ALTER, 19, 32
alternate optima, 292
analysis, 37
APPC, 32
approximation, 56, 272
arbitrage, 113
archeology, 239
assignment problem, 94, 231
auctions, 171
automobile, 253

B

backlogged, 276
banking, 250
barrier function, 339
basic solutions, 320
basis, 320
BATCH, 33
batch size constraints, 216
Bessent, A., 303
big M method, 336
bimatrix game, 186, 206
BIP, 32

Bland, R. G., 234
blending, 54, 133
BPIC, 336
BPICTURE, 32
Bradley, G., 91
Braess's paradox, 179
branch and bound, 28
Brearley, A., 277
Brown, G., 91
BUG, 33
bundling, 244

C

capacitated, 221
    multiple TSP, 238
    plant location, 219
cash flow matching, 119
CAT, 31
certainty equivalence, 154
chance constrained, 165
Charnes, A., 303
checkerboard, 254
Clarke, G., 238
coal, 133
column generation, 286
COM, 31
composite method, 336
computational difficulty, 215
concave function, 40
constant-sum game, 183
constrained least squares, 205
consumer surplus, 168, 244
convex function, 40
Cooldot, 76

Cooper, W., 303
core, 187
corner points, 320
costing out operation, 36
covering, 54, 73, 240
covering problems, 283
CPM, 55, 91, 95
CPRI, 32
crashing, 100
crew scheduling, 81
critical path, 98
currency exchange, 112
cutting stock, 54, 73, 76, 241, 285

D

dam system, 151
Dantzig, G., 317
data envelope analysis, 303
dates, 276
Davis, L. S., 106
DEBUG, 33
decision support systems, 271
decisionmaking under uncertainty, 151
decomposition, 272
definitional, 53
degeneracy, 11
degenerate solution, 320
DEL, 32
demand curve, 168, 202
diet problem, 134
Dikin, I. I., 344
disk storage, 251
distribution, 55, 91
DIVERT, 23, 25, 32
domino, 254
dormitory, 241
downside risk, 161, 192
dual, 43, 186, 229, 260, 263, 268, 344
dual degenerate, 15
dual price, 8, 35
duality, 99
dummy activity, 100
Dutton, R., 278
dynamic lotsizing, 220
dynamic production, 116

E

economic analysis, 35
economic equilibria, 167

EDIT, 19, 21, 32
efficient frontier, 313
efficient market, 200
electrical, 278
energy, 278
enginola problem, 3
equality form, 319
equilibrium, 168
errors, 56
eta matrix, 331
exams, 241
expected return, 191
expected value of perfect information, 160
explicit form inverse, 327
EXTEND, 32

F

facility layout, 240
factors model, 197
feasible solutions, 276
file, 25
file allocation, 240
financial models, 119
first order conditions, 193
fixed charge, 217
fleet mileage, 211
Florian, M., 177
Flying Tiger, 82
football, 252
forest planning, 106
FORTRAN, 284
fractional programming, 143
FREE, 32
fuel ferrying, 111

G

game theory, 56, 183
gasoline, 133
gasoline blending, 138
general cost curve, 221
generalized networks, 94
generator, 249
Geoffrion, A., 105
GIN, 28, 32
GINO, 341
GO, 19, 31
goal programming, 291, 296
goodness of fit, 258, 260
goodness of ordinal fit, 268

H

graphical analysis, 3
Graves, G., 91, 105
Graves, R. L., 171
grouping, 240

H

Hanson, W., 244
HELP, 31
Hinman, G., 278
hiring and firing, 116
hub, 231
hyperbolic programming, 143

I

income taxes, 126
index, 197
infeasible, 9
initial basic feasible solution, 336
input-output, 55, 239
INT, 27, 32
integer programming, 27, 215, 289
interior path methods, 339
INVERT, 33, 336
IPTOL, 32

J

Johnson, K. N., 106

K

Karmarkar, N., 317, 343
Karush, W., 192
Kennington, J., 303
Kernighan, B., 233
Khachian, L., 317
Killion, C. L., 82
Kuhn, H., 192

L

LaGrange, 192
landlord, 43
Lawler, E., 233
least absolute deviations, 256
least maximum (LMAX) deviation, 258
least squares, 203, 255
LEAVE, 31
Leontief, W., 227
lexico minimization, 298
LINDO, 7, 19
linear complementarity problem, 208
linear ordering problem, 239
linear regression, 255
linearity, 4
linearizing products, 241
LINGO, 273
Lin, S., 233
LOCAL, 31
lockbox location, 218
longest path, 94
LOOK, 19, 32
Lotus, 1-2-3, 273

M

Madansky, A., 196
mail, 87
mailing lists, 86
map, 241
market index, 197
marketing the model, 273
Markowitz, H., 191
Marsten, R., 82, 344
Martin, R. K., 244
mastermind, 251
matching, 240
material balance, 117
material requirements planning, 227
matrix generators, 284
MAX, 19, 31
measures of risk, 200
metals, 133
Millham, C. B., 278
milling in transit, 105
MIN, 19, 31
minimax strategy, 184
minimum spanning tree, 238
Mitra, G., 277
model formulation, 51
money pump, 113
MRP, 227
Muller, M. P., 82
multicommodity network flows, 106
multiperiod planning, 55, 115
multiple criteria, 291
multiple optimal solutions, 11
multi-objective problems, 313
Murchland, J. D., 179

N

National League, 234

INDEX

naturally integer, 227
negotiation, 183
network, 55
network LP, 91, 227
networks with gains, 94
nonlinear cost curves, 223
nonsimultaneity error, 59
nonsymmetric distributions, 162
NONZEROES, 32
nonzeroes, 282
nonconstant-sum game, 206
numerical considerations, 33
n-person game, 186

O

octane, 138
On-the-fly column generation, 285
optional stop TSP, 237
ordinal regression, 264

P

packing, 240, 253
Padberg, M., 233
PAGE, 33
paper, 241
PARA, 32
parametric analysis, 194, 305
pareto optimal, 292
partitioning, 240
path formulations, 105
pattern selection, 76
PAUSE, 33
peak power, 278
perfect information, 160
Perold, A., 196
PERT, 55, 91, 95
petroleum, 249
PICTURE, 32, 93
PIVOT, 31, 324
pivoting, 323
plant location, 217
portfolio, 191, 293
POSD, 32
prayer algorithm, 227
preemptive objectives, 291
price/production decisions, 202
primal degenerate, 15
printer, 25
printing, 241
prisoner's dilemma, 207

process selection, 66
producer-consumer surplus, 168
product form inverse, 326, 330
product mix, 1, 54, 63
projective scaling approach, 344

Q

QCP, 32
quadratic assignment problem, 240
quadratic programming, 191
quality, 133, 140

R

radio frequency assignment, 240
random elements, 55
random strategy, 184, 208
RANGE, 32
range, 37
RDBC, 31
Reagan, B., 303
reduced cost, 8, 35
reducing model size, 277
reduction by aggregation, 279
redundant constraints, 15
regression, 255
reinversion, 335
renter, 43
reports, 274
reservation price, 244
RETR, 23, 32
revised simplex method, 326
Rhodes, E., 303
Rinaldi, G., 233
risk aversion, 160
RMPS, 32
room scheduling, 280
Rose, P., 234
Rothstein, M., 273
routing, 73, 231
row generation, 290
row operation, 229
RPRI, 32
RVRT, 26, 32

S

salt, 154
Sankaran, J., 298
SAVE, 23, 32
scaling, 33
scenario, 196

scenario approach, 152, 196
schools, 303
SDBC, 32
sealed bid auctions, 249
segregated storage, 248
sensitivity analysis, 8, 42
separation of data and system structure, 273
sequencing, 231, 239
SET, 33
Sharpe, W., 197
Shallcross, D. F., 234
SHOCOLUMN, 32
shortest path, 94
signing off, 276
silo, 248
simplex method, 307, 317
slack, 319
SLB, 32
SMPS, 32
snake eyes, 13
snicker test, 275
soft constraints, 296
SOLUTION, 30, 32
SOS2, 224
sources-equals-uses constraints, 53, 106, 117
sparsity, 326
special ordered sets, 223
stable solution, 208
staff, 283
staff scheduling, 73
staffing, 54, 296
STAT, 33
statistical estimation, 56
steel, 135, 241
Stigler, G., 134
stochastic LP, 151
stochastic program, 152
strategy, 208
SUB, 32
superworker, 276
supply and demand, 167, 312
supply curve, 168
surplus variables, 319
symmetric distribution, 162

T

TABLEAU, 32, 324
tableau, 322
TAKE, 32
taxes, 122

technological constraints, 320
template, 54
template approach, 52
TERSE, 33
tetraethyl lead, 139
textile, 241
TIME, 31
TITAN, 32
TITLE, 32
tournaments, 239
tradeoff curves, 292
transaction costs, 198
transportation equilibria, 174
transshipment problems, 94
traveling salesman problem, 233
tree, 226
triangular basis, 336
Tucker, 192
two-person games, 183
two-person nonconstant-sum games, 206
two-dimensional cutting stock, 81

U

unbounded, 9
unboundedness, 326
undirected networks, 107
USER, 33
user's manual, 276
utility function, 292

V

validation, 272
vapor pressure, 138
variance, 161, 191
vehicle routing, 238, 276
VERBOSE, 33
verification, 272
volatility, 138

W

Wardrup's principle, 174
What's Best, 273
WIDTH, 33
wildcard, 24
Williams, H. P., 277
wine, 133, 149
Wright, J. W., 238

Z

Zzyzx, 219

LOADING & PRINTING INSTRUCTIONS

MacLINDO

Loading

You may run MacLINDO directly from a floppy drive by doubleclicking on the MacLINDO program icon that appears on your screen after inserting the distribution diskette.

To install MacLINDO on your hard disk you should first create a LINDO folder. This may be done by means of the following steps:

1. Select your hard disk by doubleclicking on its icon, which appears in the upper right corner of the desktop.
2. Select the "New Folder" command from the "File" menu.
3. The new folder will appear under the name "Empty Folder". Now type "LINDO" to rename the folder.

Next, you will want to copy MacLINDO into the new LINDO folder on your hard disk. You may do this by:

1. Inserting the MacLINDO disk into a floppy drive.
2. Select the MacLINDO program by clicking on its icon. Select all the other documents on the disk by shift-clicking on them.
3. Drag all the selected items into the LINDO folder on the hard disk.

MacLINDO may now be run from the hard disk by doubleclicking the MacLINDO program icon.

Printing

See "Printing" section on the next page.

LOADING & PRINTING INSTRUCTIONS

LINDO/PC

Loading

You may run LINDO/PC directly from your floppy drive by placing it in the "A" drive and typing the following commands in DOS:

A:	(*make "A" drive the default*)
LINDO	(*start up* LINDO)

To install LINDO/PC on your hard disk in a subdirectory called LINDO, give the following commands:

C:	(*make the hard disk the default*)
CD \	(*go to the root directory*)
MD LINDO	(*make a* LINDO *subdirectory*)
CD LINDO	(*make* LINDO *subdirectory the default*)
COPY A:*.*	(*copy the* LINDO *software from the floppy disk to the* LINDO *subdirectory*)

You may start up LINDO by typing:

C:	(*make the hard disk the default*)
CD \LINDO	(*go to* LINDO *subdirectory*)
LINDO	(*start up* LINDO)

Of course, if you are already in the LINDO subdirectory, you need only type LINDO.

Printing

To print output from LINDO/PC or MacLINDO, you should first send the output to a file. The file may then be read by a text editor and printed. For example, to create a report file called "MYREPORT" containing the formulation and solution, you would give the following commands in LINDO:

DIVERT MYREPORT	! OPEN OUTPUT FILE
LOOK ALL	! SEND FORMULATION TO THE FILE
GO	! SOLVE MODEL
YES	! ASK FOR RANGE ANALYSIS
RVRT	! CLOSE OUTPUT FILE

You may then start your text editor, open "MYREPORT", and print the file with the editor's print command. (Some editors do not require that you open a file in order to print it. Consult your editor's manual for its method of printing a file.)

Note: With LINDO/PC, if you wish to read a printout of the LINDO output without creating and saving a file, then give the command PRN rather than a file name after the DIVERT command. The LINDO output will be sent directly to your printer, rather than to your screen, and *will not be saved* as a file that you can print from your editor. (Also, while in LINDO/PC, you may print the current screen by holding down the shift key and pressing the PrintScreen key.)